EBENEZER ALLEN - STATESMAN, ENTREPRENEUR, AND SPY

by

Allen H. Mesch

I hope you enjoy reading about this unknown figure in Texas history.

A. H. Mesch

Published by Waldorf Publishing
2140 Hall Johnson Road
#102-345
Grapevine, Texas 76051
www.WaldorfPublishing.com

Ebenezer Allen – Statesman, Entrepreneur, and Spy

ISBN: 978-1-64764-920-3

Library of Congress Control Number: 2020930140

Copyright © 2020

All rights reserved. No part of this book may be reproduced or transmitted in any form or by any means whatsoever without express written permission from the author, except in the case of brief quotations embodied in critical articles and reviews. Please refer all pertinent questions to the publisher. All rights reserved. No part of this book may be reproduced or transmitted in any form or by any means, electronic or mechanical, including photocopying, recording, or by an information storage and retrieval system except by a reviewer who may quote brief passages in a review to be printed in a magazine or newspaper without permission in writing from the publisher.

Design by Baris Celik

Front Cover
Top row images (from left)
Sam Houston (Library of Congress), Anson Jones (Texas State Library and Archives Commission), John Tyler (Library of Congress), Andrew Jackson Donelson (Mathew Brady)
Middle row image
The Annexation of Texas to the Union (Donald M. Yena)
Bottom row images (from left)
Paul Bremond (Texas State Historical Association), Thomas House (Public Domain),
Gabriel Rains (Library of Congress), Ebenezer Allen, Jr. (Rosenberg Library)

© 2019 Allen H. Mesch. All rights reserved.

No part of this book may be reproduced or transmitted in any form or by any means, electronic or mechanical, including photocopying or recording, or by any information storage and retrieval system, without permission in writing from the author.

Other Books by Allen H. Mesch

The Analyst

Teacher of Civil War Generals -
Major General Charles Ferguson Smith,
Soldier and West Point Commandant

Your Affectionate Father, Charles F. Smith

Charles A. Marvin - "One Year, Six Months, and Eleven Days"

Preparing for Disunion - West Point Commandants
and the Training of Civil War Leaders

ISBN-13:
ISBN-10:

A RETROSPECT

Written on My Birthday, April 8, 1855, and addressed to my wife
by Ebenezer Allen
Now the dark leaden cloud, and the cold drifted snow,
And the ice-crested stream, and the white-mantled earth,
Just looked on by Spring, but inert to the glow
Of the queen of the year, scarce acknowledge her birth;
What time bright Arcturus,[1] with rose-tinted ray,
Is orient at twilight's last gleaming of day,
In the clime of the high-lands [sic], that part with their chain
The streams of St. Lawrence[2] from those of the main,
Near thy banks, Wesserrunset,[3] oh, many a year
Hath passed since the voice of thy wave met mine ear;
But my spirit goes back to the time when I heard,
First blent [sic] with that voice, the sweet notes of my Bird!
I had wandered alone from the place of my birth,
Where Sunapee's mountain[4] is gazed on with fear,
Left the shades of old Dartmouth,[5] whose time-honored worth
Is yet fresh to my thought as its name to my ear.
I had heard the deep roar of Niagara's flood --
I had stood where the fallen of Bridgewater[6] stood.
Fair Lewistown,[7] grateful the memories come
Of the scenes and the seasons while thou wert my home!
Return they, resplendent with gems of the past,
Set in tablets of love that forever will last!
Mementoes of pupils – (my twenty-fourth year
Saw me charged with that Institute on the frontier.)
Fair nymphs of the border! by distance refined,
How glow your bright forms on the page of my mind!
But my star led me eastward, o'er valley and plain,
Till I reached the bold streams and dark forests of Maine.
Succeeds day to day; the procession of time
Leaves the joys and regrets of mankind in its rear,
While the pyramid, piled by the sages, I climb,
Whose ermines[8] through ages yet dimly appear.

'Twas Spring. Eighteen hundred and thirty-one years
Had passed since the Crucified entered the spheres,
And my walks were on Somerset's[9] valleys and streams
The past brought its fruits, and the future its dreams;
Fair science her treasures, and study its lore,
And beauty its roses, and fancy its store;
But my spirit was sad, and I brooded alone
On the journey of life I had entered upon,
And I looked for the hope of fruition in vain,
To the realms of the air and the earth and the main;
For, engraven [sic] on tablets more lasting than stone,
I read – "Man shall never be happy alone!"
How thrilled then my pulses with raptures untold
When my Bird flew towards me on pinions of gold,
And entranced with her notes, as from bow'rs [bowers] of the blest,
I wooed her forever to dwell in my breast.
She came – and there sweetly we sojourned until
Seven times the broad path of the zodiac, trod
By worlds, their bright missions on high to fulfil [sic],
Saw the earth pass each sign round the throne of her God!
When, leaving fair Kennebec's[10] borders, we hied [sic]
Past the 'father of waters'[11] to waters more wide;
Nor staid until strange constellations looked down
From zones further south than the antarctic [sic] crown,
On our home by the shore of the far-spreading sea
That cradles the isles of the dark Caribbee[12] [sic].
O'er the prairie's green bosom, the ocean's wild wave,
Stars unseen before, guide, sparkle, and save.
Canopus,[13] the pilot of Argo, whose rays,
Refulgent and mystic like Sirius,[14] blaze,
As he looks from his dome in the deep southern sky,
Yet steers his famed bark through the billows on high!
Antarus [sic] is lurid with blood-tainted fire,
And Phaet returns with her branch to the ark![15]
So my Bird, while we traversed the lonely domain
On the trail which the Indian oft traversed of yore,

From thy waters, Red River,[16] to those of the main,
To found our new home on its murmuring shore,
While nightly we couched by the warbling stream,
Our repose oft disturbed by the panther's wild scream.
Or by day, through the forest our steeds rode and reined,
The dove of my ark hath ever remained.
How mighty the contrast! the regions of snow
And of streams stopped by frost in their gurgling flow,
Of the evergreen wild wood – the fierce *loup-cervie*,[17]
Of the ice-covered lake and the dark hemlock tree,
Were exchanged for oak-openings and boundless domains
Of tropical verdure,[18] soft airs, and green plains;
And the deer, from the shade of the wide-spreading tree,
As our horses – fleet, graceful, and joyous as he--
Bore us onward, gazed wondering and fearless upon
Our forms by his green covert hurrying on;
For his eyes met another of kindness and love,
Which said, "Do not fear!" 'Twas the voice of my dove,
And the rifle, impulsively raised, was depressed,
And hung at my saddle-bow [sic], charged, but at rest!
Years gather to years – the "Lone Star" no more
Looks down on the fields where its heroes repose; -
'Twas shorn of its brightness – so peerless of yore,
By the doom of its friends, not the sword of its foes!
Years gather to years – fields yellow with grain,
Or green with the corn and the vine and the cane,
Are seen where the wild horse and buffalo roamed,
And the arch spans the stream where the wide torrent foamed.
Fair gardens arise under art's fost'ring [sic] hand,
"And the voice of the turtle is heard in the land."[19]
Where was solitude once, now the mansion and dome,
And the temple of God mark [sic] the immigrant's home;
And the smoke-jetting steamer – the wind-wafted prore[20]
Daily come to our home on the murmuring shore.
Hearts joyous with mirth, and eyes beaming with love,
At the hearth or the altar, are round thee, my dove,

And wealth, far more valued than gold from the mine,
For jewels − so prized by Cornelia − are thine![21]

DEDICATION

To the people of Allen, Texas

PREFACE

The biography of Ebenezer Allen began at a meeting of the Allen Heritage Guild. I asked if the historical society had a pamphlet on the city of Allen, Texas' namesake, Mr. Ebenezer Allen. Unfortunately, they did not have any detailed information to give to visitors. I learned from Mr. Allen's biography in the *Handbook of Texas Online* that he emigrated to Texas from New England, helped draft the documents associated with Texas joining the United States, launched a railroad venture from Galveston to the Red River, and served in a Confederate engineering company during the Civil War.

This introduction piqued my interest, so I did some preliminary research on the Texas Historical Association website and in the Civil War records. I turned my preliminary findings into a post on my blog Salient Points (www.salient-points.blogspot.com).

The initial examination of Ebenezer Allen's life produced more questions than answers.

- Why did Allen leave Maine and come to Texas?
- How did this Yankee newcomer gain the attention of Texas leaders?
- What was his role in Texas' annexation to the United States?
- Why did Galveston residents refuse to fund the Galveston and Red River Railroad?
- How did he become involved in negotiations between the residents of the Peters' Colony and the empresarios?
- Did the Allen family own slaves?
- After working on annexation, what was his attitude about secession?
- What did he do in the Confederate Torpedo Bureau?
- Was his death in Richmond from natural causes or a homicide?
- What happened to his body?

These questions led me to begin my investigation into this mysterious Texan.

Regrettably, Mr. Allen did not leave a diary, journal, or letters to explain his actions. The 1900 Galveston Hurricane destroyed any remaining traces of Allen's personal life. Therefore, I used peripheral information to answer the many questions about him. The absence of his personal documents forced me to suggest reasons for some of Allen's decisions. In these cases, I used words such as "likely, probably, and possibly" to show conclusions I reached from these other sources.

I tried to present Ebenezer Allen's life without judgment and interpretation. Historians must refrain from examining the attitudes and beliefs of the nineteenth century through the lens of the twenty-first century.

The biography includes the full text of Allen's surviving letters and public communications to give readers an understanding of this complex statesman, entrepreneur, and spy.

Allen H. Mesch
Plano, Texas

TABLE OF CONTENTS

A Retrospect iv

Dedication viii

Preface ix

Childhood in Newport, New Hampshire 1
    David and Hannah Allen 1
    Young Ebenezer Allen 1
    Newport, New Hampshire 5
    Sarah Joseph Hale 7
    The Allens of Newport 8

Dartmouth College 9
    "A Small College" 9
    Curriculum 11
    Classmates 12

Teacher and Law Student 14
    Lewiston, New York 14
    Clerkship with Amasa Edes 16
    A Necessary Evil 16
    Studying the Law 17
    Lawyers from Newport 18

Marriage and Early Career 20
    Passing the Maine Bar 20
    Orono, Maine 21
    Sylvinia Morse 22
    James T. Leavitt 23
    Skowhegan, Maine 24
    The Panic of 1837 24
    The Lure of Texas 27

Gone to Texas 29
    Clarksville, Texas 30
    Six Hundred and Forty Acres 32

New Englanders in Texas	34
The Clarksville Academy	37
Law in Texas	38
Attorney at Law	39
Texas Freemasonry	42

The Long Journey to Annexation ... 47
Re-annexation	47
Early Annexation Efforts	48
Mirabeau B. Lamar's Presidency	51
Houston Renews Annexation Overtures	52
John Tyler's Expansionist Goals	53
International Negotiations	54
Tyler Reopens Annexation Talks	57

Allen's Role in Annexation ... 64
Sam Houston's Attorney General	64
President Anson Jones	65
Attorney General and Secretary of State	67
The Duff Green Misadventures	68
Tyler's Joint Resolution Efforts	69
Developments in Washington	72

Texas Considers Her Options ... 74
Donelson's Annexation Mission	74
Jones Calls for Annexation Convention	80

Immediate and Aggressive Protection ... 97
Texas at Peace with the World	97
Stockton and Sherman's Intrigue	97
"The Republic of Texas is No More"	110
Mr. Polk's War	112

State of Texas Service ... 115
Colonel Ebenezer Allen	115
The First Elected Attorney General	116
Duties of the Attorney General	118
Peters' Colony	121

Entrepreneur 125
    St. Joseph Island 125
    Transportation in Texas 126
    Galveston and Red River Railway Company 128
    Galveston's Attitudes about Railroad Development 133
    Other Railroad Ventures 137

The Houston and Texas Central Railroad 139
    Allen Transfers the Charter 139
    Paul Bremond Takes Control 141
    Building the Line 144
    The Pride of the Railroad 150
    Allen's Involvement in the Line 151

Texas Lawyer 160
    Partnership with William G. Hale 160
    Partnership with Sam Houston 161
    The Union Bank of Louisiana vs. Stafford 162
    Impeachment of Judge Watrous 164
    The Harmony Lodge No. 6 168
    Slavery in Galveston, Texas 169
    Allen's Slaves 170
    Salmon Portland Chase 171
    Financial Problems 171

Spiritualism 174
    Spiritualism 174
    News from the Northeast and Midwest 175
    Spiritualism Comes to Texas 178
    Yellow Fever Epidemics 181
    The Allens Interest in Spiritualism 182
    Paul Bremond and Moseley Baker 183
    Jean Lafitte 183
    Ada Stone 187
    Mrs. A. E. Force 194

Galveston and the Civil War 198
    Slavery and Secession 198

Secession Convention ... 199
Federal Blockade ... 201
Impact on Ebenezer Allen ... 202
Committees of Public Safety ... 203
The Civil War Comes to Galveston ... 204
Under Union Control ... 206
Galveston Recaptured ... 207

The Torpedo Bureau ... 209
General Gabriel Rains ... 209
Singer and Fretwell's Mine ... 211
Creuzbaur and the Sea King ... 213
Engineer Bureau ... 220
Was Allen a Spy? ... 222

Death ... 224
"The Clouds are Truly Dark Over Us" ... 224
Breakfast with "Friends" ... 225
"Sudden and Mysterious Death" ... 229
Hollywood Cemetery ... 232
Sylvania Allen Lawsuit ... 234
Heart Attack or Assassination? ... 235
The Allen Family After Ebenezer's Death ... 236
From Watering Station to Town ... 247

Appendix ... 252
The Annexation Process: 1836-1845 ... 252
Ordinance of Annexation ... 254
Joint Resolution for Annexing Texas to the United States ... 256
An Act to Establish the Galveston and Red River Railway Company ... 258
Allen's Broadside on the Act Relating to Lands in Peters' Colony ... 261
An Act Relating to Lands in Peters' Colony ... 266
Spiritualism in the Allen Family ... 274
The Ordinance of the Texas Convention ... 276
Texas Declaration of Causes ... 278
Act to Admit Texas to the Confederate States of America ... 283
Texas Ordinance of Secession ... 284
Ordinance to Ratify the Confederate Constitution ... 286

  Ebenezer Allen Will 287
  Josephine Allen vs. William R. Baker 289
  Ebenezer Allen Timeline 295

Acknowledgements 299

About the Author 301

Bibliography 303

Index 341

Endnotes 354

ILLUSTRATIONS

Childhood in Newport, New Hampshire
Ebenezer Allen Family Tree 2
Old Allen Homestead in Newport, New Hampshire 3

Dartmouth College
Dartmouth College in 1834 9

Teacher and Law Student
The Lewiston Academy 14

Marriage and Early Career
Annotated Map of Somerset and Penobscot Counties in Maine 22
Marriages 23
The Panic of 1837 25

Gone to Texas
Allen Homestead in Clarksville, Texas 30
Conditional Certificate Granting Ebenezer Allen
Six Hundred and Forty Acres of Land 32
Survey of Land Granted by Conditional Certificate to Ebenezer Allen 33
Certificate Granting Ebenezer Allen Six Hundred
and Forty Acres of Land 34
"Eben'r Allen – Attorney at Law" in Clarksville, Texas 39
Abia Dyer vs. William Dyer 40
District Court, Fall Term, 1843 40
William C. Young vs. Thomas J. Newbern 41

The Long Journey to Annexation
Map of The United States in 1819 47
Sam Houston 49
Mirabeau Lamar 51
John Tyler 57
Abel P. Upshur 58
James Pinckney Henderson 59
Isaac Van Zandt 60
James Knox Polk 62

Andrew Jackson Donelson	62

Allen's Role in Annexation
Appointments by the President	64
Law Notice Ebenezer Allen and Wm. S. Todd	65
Dr. Anson Jones	65

Texas Considers Her Options
A Proclamation	88
Ebenezer Allen to Andrew Jackson Donelson June 23, 1845 - page 1	92
Ebenezer Allen to Andrew Jackson Donelson June 23, 1845 - page 2	93

Immediate and Aggressive Protection
The Annexation of Texas to the Union	110
The Army of Occupation Camp at Corpus Christi	113

State of Texas Service
Election Results	117

Entrepreneur
St. Joseph Island	125
Memorial to the Texas State Legislature Requesting Railroad Charter	131

The Houston and Texas Central Railroad
Thomas William House	139
Paul Bremond	140
Map of the Houston & Texas Central Railroad	145
Houston & Texas Central Railway Advertisement	147
4-4-0 Train Engine Similar to Ebenezer Allen	150

Texas Lawyer
Allen & Hale, Attorneys at Law	160
Houston & Allen Counsellors and Attorneys at Law	161

Spiritualism
Spiritualism Séance	174

Galveston and the Civil War
Attack on the Federal Fleet at Galveston, January 1, 1863	207

The Torpedo Bureau
Gabriel J. Rains 209
Civil War Torpedo 212
Confederate Torpedoes 213
Map of the State of Texas by Robert Creuzbaur................................. 214
Alfred L. Rives 220

Death
Gem Saloon Announcement 225
The Masons' Hall in Richmond 228
Annotated Map of Richmond Virginia in 1863 229
Confederate Dead Named Allen Buried at Hollywood Cemetery 233
Edward Allen Substitute Volunteer Enlistment 237
The Summerland Libel Suit 240
Fred. Allen & Co.'s 242
Ebenezer Allen, Jr. 244
Notice About Cedar Point 246
Old Stone Dam – Cottonwood Creek 248
Allen Train Depot 249
Original Plan of the Town of Allen - February 10, 1876 250

Appendix
Ebenezer Allen's Will 288

About the Author
Allen Mesch at Allen Depot 301

CHILDHOOD IN NEWPORT, NEW HAMPSHIRE

David and Hannah Allen

David Allen moved to Newport, New Hampshire from Killingworth, Connecticut around 1800. Allen was the son of Gideon and Patience Allen and was born on May 13, 1777 in Killingworth. David's brother Samuel Allen also settled in Newport. Around 1803, David married Hannah Wilcox, the daughter of Uriah Wilcox. Hannah (Wilcox) Allen was born on July 12, 1780. The Allens lived on a large farm on Goshen Road in Newport. Mr. Allen ran an inn and tavern, which were popular stops when the Croydon Turnpike[22] was an important commercial road. David Allen was one of the town's wealthiest and influential residents. He paid $11.55 in taxes in 1802-1812.[23] Allen was also involved in local politics. He was a selectman[24] for eight years and a high sheriff for five years.[25] He served as justice of the peace in 1844 and represented Newport in the New Hampshire legislature in 1823 and 1826.[26] David Allen died on December 27, 1840 and his wife, Hannah, died on October 13, 1850.[27]

Young Ebenezer Allen

Ebenezer Allen, the first child of David and Hannah Allen, was born on April 8, 1804 in Newport. Other children joined the Allen family several years after Ebenezer. David Allen Jr. was born in 1806, Uriah Wilcox Allen in 1807, and Elvira Allen in 1809. The 1810 census lists nine people in the David Allen household. There were three males under ten: Ebenezer (6), David (4), and Uriah Wilcox (3); one white female under 10: Elvira (1); one white male 16-25, one white female 16-25, one white male 26-44: David Allen, one white female 26-44: Hannah; and one white female over 45.[28]

The Allen family continued to grow with the births of Nahum Wilcox Allen in 1812, Hannah Cordelia Allen in 1814, Roxanna Allen in 1817, Samuel Johnson Allen in 1819, Harriet Allen in 1821, Albert G Allen in 1823, and William Allen in 1825. By 1830, Ebenezer had four sisters and six brothers.[29]

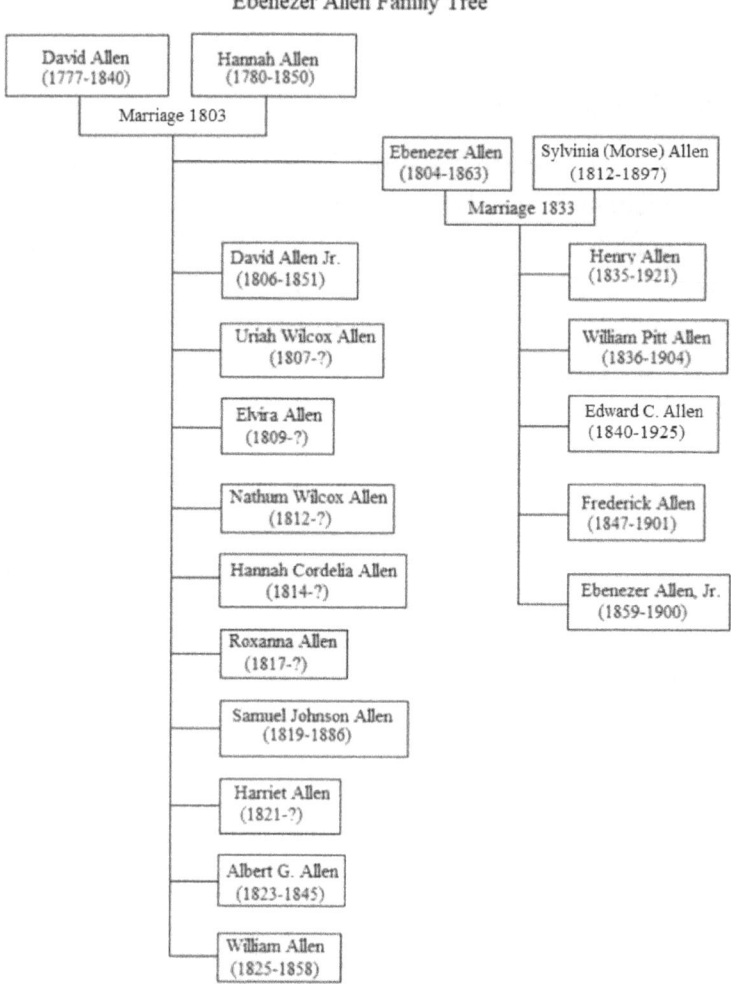

Ebenezer Allen Family Tree
(Judith M. Johnson, Johnson-Morrow Family Tree, Ancestry.com)

Old Allen Homestead in Newport, New Hampshire
(Judith M. Johnson, Johnson-Morrow Family Tree, Ancestry.com)

As the eldest child, Ebenezer had many responsibilities in the Allen farm and businesses. Farm parents expected their children to contribute to the family's productivity. Small children helped with simple, unskilled tasks. As the children grew and gained skills, their work became more difficult. Farm boys always had work because of the daily need for firewood and water. Boys cared for the livestock and guarded the animals in the pasture. The children assisted their parents in preparing the fields for planting and sowing the seeds in the furrows. At harvest, they helped gather the crops. Boys hunted and fished for recreation and to supply food for the family. Like other oldest sons, Ebenezer was "early made acquainted with labor."[30]

David and Hannah Allen believed in education and their children attended the "common schools"[31] in Newport. The Allens enrolled their children in the Newport Academy after the school opened on June 24, 1819. The citizens of Newport and neighboring towns organized the school to give their children a "more advanced education than was to be had at our common schools" and "to fit them for college." The residents hired a teacher for $400 and pledged to make up any deficiency in the salary not covered by student tuitions. The 1823 school directory contained the names of sixty-nine students: forty-eight boys and twenty-one girls. The town constructed a two-story building on the south side of Elm Street for the Academy.[32] The school had "ample rooms nicely fitted up." William Shedd (1819), Christopher Marsh (1820), and William Clark (1821-1823) were instructors at the Academy during Ebenezer's time at the school.[33] In 1822, a Town Warrant article asked for money to support the academy, but the citizens denied the request.[34] Amasa Edes,[35] a local lawyer, taught at the Academy in 1825 and served as a school trustee.[36]

After school and their chores, the Allen children may have played Copenhagen, button, hunt the slipper, blind man's bluff, and the gracehoop.[37]

Most of Ebenezer's brothers and sisters stayed in New England. David Allen, Jr. became a lawyer. Uriah W. Allen moved to Stonington, Connecticut, where he was a farmer. Uriah was married twice and had one son, Albert. Alvira Allen married Philo Fuller, a "manufacturer" from Newport. The Fullers had five children Eugene, Nelson, Allen, Ellen, and Edith. Nahum W. Allen went west as a teacher and became a clergyman. He had a daughter, Harriet.

Hannah Cordelia Allen married Gilbert Beach, a merchant in Perrysburg, Ohio.[38] Hannah and Gilbert had four children Anna, Mary, Edmund, and Eugene. Roxana Allen married J. Manning Hall, a businessman in Perrysburg, Ohio. The Halls had two children, Harriet and Frank. Harriet Allen married Dr. Thomas Sanborn.[39] Albert G. Allen joined his sisters, Harriet and Roxana in Perrysburg and was a merchant until his death in 1845. William Allen was a farmer in Newport and died in 1858.[40]

Ebenezer's brother, Samuel J. Allen became a doctor. He attended the Newport and Unity Academies. Samuel studied medicine in the office of Dr. J. L. Swett. He graduated from Castleton Medical College in 1843 and received an honorary degree from Dartmouth College in 1870. He opened his first practice in Hartford, Connecticut, but spent most of his life in Hartford, Vermont. He was a surgeon in the Union Army during the Civil War. On June 4, 1844, he married Mary J. Lyman. Their son Samuel Jr. was born on April 30, 1845 in Woodstock, Vermont. Samuel Jr. graduated from Dartmouth College and became a surgeon in the army. Samuel and Mary's son, Frederick, was born in 1848. Frederick graduated from Dartmouth College and studied religion at Andover Theological Seminary. Harry was born in 1857. Harry attended Norwich University.[41] Dr. Allen died on August 8, 1886.[42]

Ebenezer's brother, David Allen, Jr., spent his youth helping his father on the farm. He studied at the common school and the Newport Academy. After graduating, David moved to Johnstown, New York[43] where he taught school for several years. He decided to become a lawyer and studied the law under Edmund Burke[44] in Newport, and his brother Ebenezer, in Orono, Maine. David opened a law office in Perrysburg, Ohio. He returned to Newport to run the law office and practice of Mr. Burke while Burke was in Washington, DC. Burke served in the nation's capital as a member of Congress and Commissioner of Patents. David represented Newport in the state legislature in 1849 and 1850. He was also Superintendent of the School Committee and member of the Society for the Promotion of Temperance. David married Emeline B. Sanborne of Sanbornton, New Hampshire.[45] He continued to practice law until his death on September 1, 1851 in Newport.[46]

Newport, New Hampshire

The town of Newport, New Hampshire traces its roots to a charter granted in 1753 by Colonial Governor Benning Wentworth. The town's first name was Grenville in honor of George Grenville, Prime Minister of the United Kingdom and brother-in-law of William Pitt. Hostilities during the French and Indian War delayed settlement. In 1761, the government incorporated the town as Newport, named after Henry Newport,[47] a distinguished English soldier and statesman.

In 1766, eight families came from Killingworth, Connecticut[48] and founded the first permanent settlement in Newport.[49] The Connecticut River was the only route to the town until settlers cut a road through the wilderness to Charlestown in 1767. The following year, pioneers built the first gristmill. In 1781, citizens who were dissatisfied with their treatment by the state government, joined thirty-three other towns along the Connecticut River. They seceded from New Hampshire and joined Vermont. However, George Washington dissolved their union with Vermont and the towns rejoined New Hampshire in 1782.

New Hampshire incorporated the Croydon Turnpike on June 21, 1804. The thirty-five-mile road extended from or near the Branch Turnpike[50] to the Fourth Turnpike.[51] It passed through Plainfield, Enfield, New Grantham, Croydon, Newport, and Lempate.[52]

Newport became a prosperous community because of the excellent soil for farming and the abundant waterpower from the Sugar River and its South Branch to run mills. Colonel James D. Wolcott built the first cotton mill in 1813. Cabinet making thrived, and local craftsmen produced fine furniture.

Citizens in the neighboring communities recognized the Sugar River was important to industrial development. In 1820, mill owners from Claremont, Sunapee, and Newport created the Sunapee Dam Corporation. The corporation built a dam to regulate the Sugar River's flow, which allowed the mills to run even during drought conditions. The dam attracted more industry to the community and over 120 water wheels operated along the stream. By 1859, the population was 2,020 and Newport had three woolen mills, two tanneries, and a scythe manufacturer.

Residents and visitors described Newport's main village as a charming place. A beautiful meadow, several miles in length and one-half mile in width, divided the town into two nearly equal parts from north to south. The Croydon Branch of the Sugar River bordered the village on the north, the Goshen Branch flowed over the Granite Falls in the south, and the two rivers emptied into Sunapee Lake on the east side of the village.

The rivers flowed gracefully through the meadows beneath elm trees along the banks until they joined and ran into the Connecticut River. Gentle green hills bordered the town on the west. On the east, a slightly elevated plain extended back to the base of the Coit and East mountains. "On this plateau, beneath these mountains, overlooking such scenery, lying on either side of the river and extending up along its banks, [Newport] is one of the most pleasant villages in the state." The main street is nearly two miles long and lined on both sides by neat and attractive homes.[53]

In 1816, the Freemasons formed the Corinthian Lodge - No. 28 in Newport and held their first meeting on July 2. Neither Ebenezer nor his father were members of the lodge although "many other prominent citizens" were Freemasons. The lodge continued to grow until May 1833 when it closed and surrendered its charter.[54]

The Allens were members of the Congregational Church.[55] Congregationalists built a frame meetinghouse in Newport in 1791 and erected a brick church in 1823.[56]

Sarah Joseph Hale

Sarah Joseph Hale is Newport's most famous native. She was the daughter of Gordon Buell and Martha Whittlesey and was born in Newport in 1788. Sarah married scholar and attorney David Hale when she was twenty-five. They studied together and when he died in 1822, Sarah began her literary career. She published her first book *Northwood* in 1823. The novel was one of the first works written by a woman to be published in America. The success of the book led to her appointment as editor of the *Ladies Magazine* published in Boston. In 1841, she joined publisher, Louis Godey[57], as editor of *Godey's Ladies Book*.

In addition to her editing responsibilities, Mrs. Hale wrote thirty books and poems. She was a champion of women's rights. However, it was her children's poem, "Mary Had A Little Lamb" that made her world famous.

Thanks to Mrs. Hale's efforts, President Abraham Lincoln proclaimed a national Thanksgiving Day to be celebrated on the 26th, the final Thursday of November 1863. She championed elementary education for girls equal to that for boys and higher education for women. She was the first to advocate women as teachers in the public schools. With Matthew Vassar, she helped organize Vassar College.[58] She began the fight for property rights for married women. She fought for improvement in women's wages, reduction of child labor, and physical training for women. Her community service included advocating for public playgrounds, raising funds to finish Bunker Hill Monument, and fighting to preserve Mount Vernon as a national memorial.[59]

The Allens of Newport

David Allen's family were not the only Allen family in Newport. David's brother, Samuel Allen, lived on a farm next to David's on the north. Samuel was married to a "woman from Massachusetts." Samuel had three children: Mary, Marilla, and Almira. Mark Allen, who was not related to David or Samuel, came from Hopkinton, New Hampshire and lived on the East Mountain. Mark was married to Betsey Weber and had four children: Richard W., Seth Jewett, Elizabeth D., and Mark Washington.[60]

Among the other Allen families in Newport, citizens said Augusta Allen was a "popular singer" and M. W. Allen was a "leading bass singer."[61] Seth Allen's son, Benjamin Rush Allen, was a joiner, the town's leading tenor singer, and long-time leader of the South Choir. Villagers said Benjamin was an "extraordinary voice teacher" and taught music in New Hampshire and other states. Benjamin directed the Newport Cornet Band in their first public appearance in 1860. In October 1862, the eighteen-piece band enlisted for nine months service in the Union Army. The Army appointed the Newport musicians as a brigade band.[62]

DARTMOUTH COLLEGE

Like other young men in Newport, Ebenezer Allen went to Hanover, New Hampshire to attend Dartmouth College. He entered Dartmouth around 1822 and graduated in 1826 with a Bachelor of Arts degree. Newport town records list nearly fifty residents who obtained degrees from Dartmouth from the school's founding in 1769 to 1878. The graduates became clergymen, physicians, and lawyers. Allen was the only Newport resident and Dartmouth graduate to move to Texas.[63] Most stayed in New England, but a few went "west" to New York, Pennsylvania, and Ohio. Prentice Cheney practiced medicine in Cuba; Frank H. Carleton was a lawyer in Minneapolis; Charles Chaplin became an attorney in St. Louis; and Robert Hearth was a lawyer in Jefferson, North Carolina.[64]

Dartmouth College in 1834
(Library of Congress)

"A Small College"

Eleazar Wheelock,[65] a Congregational minister from Connecticut, founded Dartmouth on December 13, 1769. Before he established Dartmouth, Wheelock started Moor's Indian Charity School in 1755 to train Native Americans as Christian missionaries. Although the school was initially successful, Wheelock needed more funds to continue its operation. Two of Wheelock's friends traveled to England in 1766 to raise money from churches. The men used the funds obtained to create a trust to help Wheelock. The head of the trust fund was a Methodist named William Legge, Second Earl of Dartmouth.

The trust provided Wheelock with substantial financial support for the Charity School. However, Wheelock experienced problems recruiting Indians to the institution because the school was far from tribal territories. Wheelock decided to expand the school into a college and move it to Hanover, New Hampshire. The move from Connecticut followed a lengthy and sometimes frustrating effort to find resources and secure a charter. The Royal Governor of New Hampshire, John Wentworth, gave the land to build Dartmouth. Wentworth issued the college's charter on December 13, 1769. The grant created an institution "for the education and instruction of Youth of the Indian Tribes in this Land in reading, writing & all parts of Learning [sic] which shall appear necessary and expedient for civilizing & christianizing [sic] Children of Pagans as well as in all liberal Arts and Sciences and of English Youth and any others." The document included the reference to educating Native American youth, which allowed Dartmouth to gain access to the Charity School's remaining trust funds. Although the college was named for William Legge, the Earl of Dartmouth, he opposed the college's creation and refused to donate to the school. The college granted its first degrees in 1771.[66]

In 1819, Dartmouth College was involved in litigation with the state. New Hampshire tried to amend the college's royal charter in 1816 to make the school a public university. Another institution, called Dartmouth University, seized the college buildings and began operations in Hanover in 1817. Dartmouth College continued teaching classes in rented rooms nearby. Daniel Webster,[67] an alumnus of the class of 1801, presented the college's objection to amending the charter to the Supreme Court. The court decided the amendment of Dartmouth's charter was an "illegal impairment of a contract" by the state and reversed New Hampshire's takeover of the school. Webster concluded his summation with the famous words, "It is, Sir, as I have said, a small college. And yet there are those who love it."[68]

Curriculum

Ebenezer Allen's curriculum was probably like those published in 1811:

> *The immediate instruction and government of the students is with the president, who is also professor of civil and Ecclesiastical history, a professor of the Latin, Greek, Hebrew and Oriental Languages, a professor of Mathematics and Natural Philosophy, a professor of Divinity, and two tutors. The qualifications for admission into the Freshman class are, a good moral character, a good acquaintance with Virgil, Cicero's Select Orations, the Greek Testament, knowledge to translate English into Latin, and an acquaintance with the fundamental rules of Arithmetic. The members of the classes, in rotation, declaim [make a formal speech] before the officers in the chapel every Wednesday, at two o'clock, P. M.*

> *The Senior, Junior, and Sophomore classes, successively pronounce such orations and other compositions, written by themselves, as the president and professors shall direct, on the last Wednesday of November, the second Wednesday of March, and the third Wednesday of May. Tragedies, plays, and all irreligious expressions and sentiments are sacredly prohibited.*

> *The Languages, the Arts, and Sciences are studied in the following order: The Freshman Class study the Latin and Greek classics, Arithmetic, English Grammar and Rhetoric. The Sophomore Class study the Latin and Greek classics, Logic, Geography, Arithmetic, Geometry, Trigonometry, Algebra, Conic Sections, Surveying, Belles-lettres [light and elegant literature] and Criticism. The Junior Class study the Latin and Greek classics, Geometry, Natural and Moral Philoso-*

phy, and Astronomy. The Senior Class read Metaphysics, Theology, and Natural and Political Law. Chemistry was introduced at about this period. The study of the Hebrew and the other Oriental Languages, as also the French Language, is recommended to the students. Every week some part of the classes exhibits composition according to the direction of the authority. All the classes are publicly examined at stated periods; those who are found deficient lose their standing in the class. It is a fixed rule that the idle and vicious shall not receive the honors of college.

The punishments inflicted on offenders are admonition, suspension and expulsion. The President attends morning and evening prayers with the students in the chapel, and often delivers lecture to them on ecclesiastical history, on the doctrines of the Christian religion, or other important subjects. He hears the recitations of the Senior class; his fund of general science renders this an interesting part of collegiate life.[69]

Classmates

Thirty-six men graduated in Allen's class. Half of his class entered the ministry, eleven practiced law, two became teachers, two were physicians, one was a merchant, one was a professor, and the occupation of one was unknown. The following men were among those receiving degrees in 1826: Edward Parker Alden, Constantine Blodgett, Isaac Boyd, Samuel Augustus Chandler, Salmon Portland Chase, Horatio Gates Cilley, Rufus Claggett, William Claggett, Ansel Russell Clark, Francis Cogswell, William Elliott, Charles Milton Emerson, John S. Emerson, Allen Gannett, Edward Pratt Harris, Solyman Heath, Osgood Herrick, Isaac Hosford, Spofford Dodge Jewett, John Kendrick, Caleb Kimball, Moses Kimball, Henry Little, Cutting Marsh, George Punchard, Jeremiah Russell, Charles Shedd, Henry Shedd, Frederick Smith, James Wilson Ward, Thomas Broadhead Waterman, William Pickering Weeks, and James Wheelock Woodward. Most of these men stayed in the New England States.

Ebenezer's most famous classmate was Salmon Portland Chase who was governor of Ohio (1855-1859), U.S. Senator (1849-1855 and 1861), Secretary of the Treasury in the Lincoln Administration (1861-1864), and Chief Justice of the U.S. Supreme Court (1864-1873). Another graduate, John S. Emerson, became a successful missionary in the Hawaiian Islands.[70]

TEACHER AND LAW STUDENT

Lewiston, New York

After graduating from Dartmouth, Allen accepted a teaching position at Lewiston Academy in western New York.

The Lewiston Academy
(The Historical Association of Lewiston)

The Lewiston Academy was a large four-story building constructed in 1824-1825 by F. Stewart. Residents considered it as the pre-eminent private school in western New York. The Lewiston Masonic Lodge endowed the large library and excellent chemistry laboratories. The school featured a rooftop observatory. A building committee composed of Benjamin Barton, William Hotchkiss, David M. Smith, and Robert Fleming supervised the construction of the academy. Most of the teaching staff was from Dartmouth College. The 150 students came from Canada and western New York. In 1826, the State Legislature approved a petition from Lewiston residents to distribute fees from the Queenston-Lewiston ferry to help support the school. The Reverend David M. Smith, the first minister of the Lewiston Presbyterian Church, was an active fundraiser for the church and the Lewiston Academy. Reverend Smith was the school's first principal from 1826 to 1829.[71] The Academy prospered until the Canadian students withdrew during the 1837-1838 Mackenzie Rebellion,[72] and adverse local economic conditions reduced enrollment. The school closed in 1851 after the Lewiston suspension bridge was built, which ended ferry transportation and resulted in the loss of revenue for the endowment.[73]

Allen enjoyed his time in Lewiston and celebrated his experience in his 1855 poem to his wife:

> *Fair Lewistown, grateful the memories come*
> *Of the scenes and the seasons while thou wert my home!*
> *Return they, resplendent with gems of the past,*
> *Set in tablets of love that forever will last!*
> *Mementoes of pupils - (my twenty-fourth year*
> *Saw me charged with that Institute on the frontier).*[74]

In addition to visiting Niagara Falls and learning about western New York's experiences during the War of 1812, Allen heard about the area's many religious movements. This part of New York State became known as the "burned-over district."[75] Many in this frontier region thought direct communication with God or angels was possible. In the early nineteenth century, churches held religious revivals and "inspired" residents started different religious movements. The Latter-Day Saints, Millerites, and Jehovah's Witnesses trace their roots to this area. In addition to attracting followers to the new religions, people in the region investigated and supported social experimentation and radicalism. The Spiritualism movement began in western New York in the 1840s.[76]

The frontier communities of western New York held religious revival meetings. These gatherings allowed people to confess their sins, receive Christ's blessings, promise to be good, and perform good deeds in the future. The person confessed his sins publicly during the revival, and the remorseful sinner left the meeting as a "new" individual. It was an emotional and inspiring experience. The revival provided a release from the stress of the harsh frontier conditions. The meeting encouraged fellowship during the day's religious events and social interaction in the evenings. It presented an opportunity for young people to meet members of the opposite sex. The revival was an important "social-cultural-religious event" in rural America in the first half of the nineteenth century.[77]

Charles Grandison Finney[78] advanced the revival movement in the "burned-over district." Finney was ordained as a Presbyterian minister in 1824 and conducted revivals in New York and Pennsylvania. The charismatic Finney "saved" hundreds of converts in his 1830-1831 revival in Rochester, New York. The Rochester events became known as the "Great Revival" or Second Great Awakening."[79]

Among such religious fervor, the seeds might have been sowed for Allen to embrace his belief in Spiritualism.

Clerkship with Amasa Edes

After two years in Lewiston, Allen returned to Newport, New Hampshire in 1828 to begin studying law. Allen divided his time between his legal internship and working in his father's businesses. He was fortunate to learn under the guidance of Amasa Edes. Edes probably agreed to instruct his fellow Dartmouth alumni because of his relationship with David Allen. Edes knew Ebenezer Allen through business dealings with his father and as his teacher at the Newport Academy.[80]

A Necessary Evil

The English settlers who came to North America in the late seventeenth century disliked English law and considered the legal system to be "mired in precedent, antiquity, and corruption." In the colonies founded on religious principles, the "legal profession, with its special privileges and principles, its private, esoteric language, seemed out of place in a government that aimed to be both efficient and godly." The colonists were unfriendly and hostile towards the few professional lawyers who lived in their settlements. The "ancient English prejudice against lawyers secured new strength in America" and "distrust of lawyers became an institution."[81]

However, the increasing complexity of business and personal interactions made lawyers a necessary part of life. The young nation was "almost inevitably bound to rely on lawyers to perform a wide range of functions. Lawyers became the technicians of change as the country expanded economically and geographically." As a result, the number of American lawyers increased, and, despite the public's continued resentment of the legal profession, lawyers rose to levels of "political and social prominence."[82]

Studying the Law

The growth of the United States led to new states and more local, state, and federal laws. The new laws increased the demand for lawyers and led to the development of training programs. The apprenticeship programs provided legal instruction in the early days of the republic. The uninspiring and irregular system allowed prospective lawyers to pay to hang around an office, read law books, copy legal documents, and watch "real lawyers" at work. If the apprentice was lucky, the lawyer tried to teach him something. Under the "right" lawyer, the apprentice gained practical experience and received excellent instruction

The first formal legal apprenticeship or clerkship program began in New York in 1730. The clerkship involved serving a seven-year apprenticeship. The conditions changed in 1756 to include a four-year college degree, a five-year clerkship, and an examination. Later, the New York bar reduced the college education to two years.

The internship required extensive study. The mentoring lawyer "carefully selected" materials for the clerk to learn and tested the clerk to ensure the material was absorbed. The student assembled notes from his reading assignments into a "commonplace book." His mentor expected the clerk to memorize these notes. Regrettably, in most cases, the clerks were overworked and unable to study the law individually as expected. The mentoring attorney assigned his clerks tedious administrative tasks such as making handwritten copies of documents. While the apprentice was well trained in the operations of a law office, they were generally unprepared to analyze legal issues or provide legal guidance. There was no standardized list of required readings. The attorney composed the list based on his opinion of the law, which might have been very different from other attorneys. Lawyers described the clerkship program in 1745 as "severely flawed" administered by mentors who had "no manner of concern for their clerk's future welfare… [T]is a monstrous absurdity to suppose, that the law is to be learnt by a perpetual copying of precedents." This was the system in place when Allen began his clerkship with Amasa Edes. For the next several years, Allen learned under a rigorous clerkship program administered by this highly respected lawyer and teacher. The apprenticeship allowed Allen to gain practical experience and excellent legal knowledge.

Law students supplemented their apprenticeship assignments by reading Blackstone's *Commentaries*. Blackstone's *Commentaries* was the most popular textbook for independent study. The self-taught legal education of Andrew Jackson and Abraham Lincoln became part of the profession's lore. Lincoln wrote, "[T]he cheapest, quickest and best way [to become a lawyer was to] read Blackstone's *Commentaries* ..., get a license, and go to the practice and still keep reading."[83]

The goal of the clerkship and study of Blackstone's *Laws of England* was to become sufficiently knowledgeable of the law to pass the exam for admission to the bar. The difficulty and formality of the admission process depended on location and local custom. The rules were neither uniform nor stringent. Most states required a bar examination. The exam was described as "oral and normally casual." The lax requirements and weak standards for bar admission diminished the "perceived need for institutionalized legal education."[84]

During Allen's apprenticeship, advocates of "Jacksonian Democracy" attacked the legal profession and training. The movement championed equality for white men and promoted a "contempt for intellect" and disdain for the elite members of society such as lawyers. Attacks on lawyers increased and peaked in the 1830s. Many local bar associations became unpopular and collapsed after 1800. The apprenticeship prerequisite for admission to the bar became less necessary. In 1800, fourteen out of nineteen jurisdictions demanded an apprenticeship, however by 1860, only nine of thirty-nine jurisdictions required an internship.[85]

Lawyers from Newport

Ebenezer Allen was among several Newport residents who became attorneys. Many of these attorneys practiced law in other places: Daniel J. Atwood (Boston, Massachusetts); Horatio Buell (Glens

Falls, New York); William Breck (Rochester, New York); James Breck, Jr. (Chicago, Illinois); William F. Bascom (Orwell, Vermont); Tully Bascom (Ohio); Jonas Cutting (a judge of the supreme judicial court in Augusta, Maine); James Corbin (Santa Fe, Texas), Rufus Claggett (Brooklyn, New York), Charles H. Chapin (St. Louis, Missouri), William J. Forsaith (Boston, Massachusetts), Horatio Hale[86] (Philadelphia, Pennsylvania), William G. Hale[87] (New Orleans, Louisiana), Solomon Heath (Belfast, Maine), Elijah D. Hastings (St. Louis, Missouri), Henry H. Metcalf (Littleton, New Hampshire), David F. Huntoon (Grand Haven, Michigan), Erastus Newton (Lockport, New York), Ira B. Person (New York City, New York), Simeon Wheeler, Jr. (Portsmouth, Virginia), and Charles H. Woods (Minneapolis, Minnesota).[88]

MARRIAGE AND EARLY CAREER

Passing the Maine Bar

After completing his apprenticeship under Amasa Edes in Newport, Allen traveled to Orono, Maine around 1830 to gain admission to the State Bar. Probably, the region's bustling economy attracted him to the area. He might have sought association and/or advice from Dartmouth alumni who practiced law in the state. Several members from the 1826 graduating class were attorneys in Maine Jeremiah Russell opened a law office in Solon, Maine in 1830 and Solyman Heath was a lawyer in Belfast, Maine.[89]

In 1821, the Maine legislature passed regulations on the admission of attorneys. The first section provided: "That no person shall be admitted and allowed to be an Attorney of any Court in this State, unless he is a person of good moral character and is well affected towards the Government and Constitution of this State, nor until he shall have faithfully devoted seven years at least to the acquisition of scientific and legal attainment, whereof three years shall have been spent in professional studies with some Counsellors [sic] at law, and two of the three with such Counsellors in this State."

The candidate had to take and pledge to the oath stipulated in the Maine constitution and promise to conduct himself in a prescribed manner. The applicant would swear to the following conditions:

> *You solemnly swear, that you will do no falsehood, nor consent to the doing of any in court, and that if you know of an intention to commit any, you will give knowledge thereof to the justices of the court or some of them, that it may be prevented; you will not wittingly or willingly, promote or sue any false, groundless or unlawful suit, or give aid or consent to the same: that you will delay no man for lucre or malice, but will conduct yourself in the office of an attorney within the courts, according to the best of your knowledge and discretion and with all good fidelity, as well to the*

courts, as to your clients. So, help you God.

On February 2, 1822, the state legislature approved "An Act establishing the duties to be paid by Attorneys." Attorneys who wanted to practice in the Circuit Court or Court of Common Pleas had to pay twenty dollars to the county. If the lawyer was admitted to the Supreme Judicial Court, the fee increased to thirty dollars. The payments collected to practice in the Circuit Court or Court of Common Pleas were used to establish a law library.

An act approved on February 25, 1825, allowed "persons who had been approved to practice in the highest courts of other States, where the qualifications for admissions were equal to those needed in this State, to be admitted to practice [sic] in Maine."[90]

The only requirement Allen needed to satisfy was the two years of study with a Maine attorney, but this might have been waived because of his apprenticeship with Amasa Edes. Alternatively, he could have apprenticed with fellow Newport resident and Dartmouth graduate, Jonas Cutting[91] in Orono. Cutting was one of the lawyers in Orono prior to 1834.[92]

After the Maine Bar admitted Ebenezer, he offered his legal services in Orono.[93] His brother, David, studied under Ebenezer during the latter's time in Orono.[94]

Orono, Maine

Orono is in Penobscot County, Maine on the west side of the Penobscot River about three miles northeast of Bangor. The city of Orono was settled in 1774 and incorporated on March 12, 1806. Lumbering was Orono's main industry. In addition, the town's very productive mixture of clay and sand soil encouraged farming.[95]

Waterpower from the Penobscot and Stillwater Rivers provided the energy necessary to operate the town's mills. Local entrepreneurs built several mills along the rivers. The "Basin Mills" powered a variety of machines to manufacture wood products from trees harvested in the area. The mills on the Penobscot provided power to eight single saws, four gangs, two lathes,[96] two clapboards,[97] one shingle, two rotary saws, and a machine shop. The industries on the Stillwater

River contained twenty-two single saws, ten gangs, five rotary saws,[98] twelve lathes, three shingles, four clapboard mills, two planing-machines, one machine-shop, two gristmills, and a match-factory.

The village, at the mouth of the Stillwater River, was somewhat cluttered, which was typical of lumber towns. However, the houses were neat and attractive, and the streets were lined by many elms and maples.[99] The Congregationalists, Methodists, Universalists, and Catholics built churches in the town. The State College of Agriculture and Mechanic Arts was built about one mile from the village on the east bank of the Stillwater River.[100]

When Allen arrived in Orono, the town was about to begin the Great Land Speculation. The boom began in 1832-1833. It declined in 1834. It rose again, culminated in 1835, and burst in 1836. The population rose from less than 1,500 in 1830 to nearly six thousand in 1836.[101]

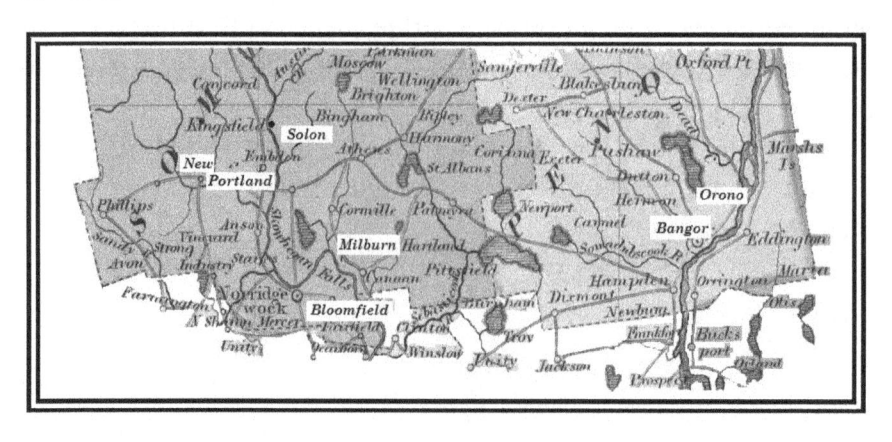

Annotated Map of Somerset and Penobscot Counties in Maine
(Based on a map of Maine from T. G. Bradford's *A Comprehensive Atlas Geographical, Historical and Commercial* (Boston), 1835)

Sylvinia Morse

Allen moved to Solon, Maine in 1832 and gained admission to the Somerset County bar in June 1834. He opened his practice that summer. His legal work often required him to travel to Skowhegan, the county seat of Somerset County. During one of his visits, Allen met Sylvinia Morse[102] from Bloomfield.[103] Bloomfield was on the south side of the Kennebec River opposite Skowhegan about fifteen or sixteen miles southeast of Solon. Sylvinia was the daughter of Andrew and Hannah (Brigham) Morse.[104] Mr. Morse was a significant property owner and prominent citizen in Bloomfield.[105]

In his 1855 poem to Sylvinia, Ebenezer recalls their time in Maine:

How thrilled then my pulses with raptures untold
When my Bird flew towards me on pinions of gold,
And entranced with her notes, as from bow'rs [bowers] of the blest,
I wooed her forever to dwell in my breast.[106]

Ebenezer married Sylvinia on March 23, 1833 in Bloomfield.[107] The June 5, 1833 edition of *The Advocate* announced the wedding of Mr. Ebenezer Allen of Solon to Miss Sylvinia Morse.[108]

Marriages
(E. F. Danforth, Hinckley, Me.: Good Will Publishing Co.)

James T. Leavitt

Allen continued in private practice until 1834 or 1835, when he joined James T. Leavitt's[109] law practice. Comparable to Allen, Leavitt was beginning his legal career after admission to the Somerset County bar on February 29, 1832.[110] Leavitt was born in Bangor and settled in

Skowhegan in 1834. He served as a Judge Advocate in the militia, was a member of the Maine Legislature, and County Attorney.[111] *The New England and New York Law Register for the Year 1835* lists Leavitt as an attorney and Justice of the Peace in New Portland, Maine[112] in Somerset County.[113] Allen and Leavitt had an office on Madison Street near the corner of Russell Street.[114] During their partnership, Leavitt met Sylvinia's older sister Hannah B. Morse. He married Hannah on September 3, 1837.[115] Mr. Leavitt was one of the best-known and most popular citizens in the community. His family lived in a two-story house on Leavitt Street in town.[116] During his life, he bought many pieces of property in the Skowhegan area.[117] He died on April 18, 1857.[118]

Skowhegan, Maine

Skowhegan was the county seat of Somerset County, Maine. The Abenaki Indians named the place Skowhegan which means "watching place [for fish]." The first permanent settlement in the area began in 1771, when a small group of pioneers from southern Massachusetts traveled by ship up the Kennebec River and walked over twenty-five miles on rough trails to establish a community. On February 5, 1823, the area separated from Canaan[119] and incorporated as the town of Milburn. However, inhabitants preferred the town's old name and re-named it Skowhegan in 1836.

Skowhegan was an agricultural community and farmers produced hay, potatoes, wheat, and wool. The citizens established numerous industries using the waterpower from Skowhegan Falls. Residents built mills on Skowhegan Island, which separates the Kennebec River into north and south channels. Skowhegan grew into a busy manufacturing town with lumber, paper, and woolen mills, and several factories.[120]

The Panic of 1837

Financial disaster hit the country as Ebenezer and Sylvinia were beginning their life together in Skowhegan. At this time, they had one child, three-year-old Henry. The Panic of 1837 altered their plans. The monetary event occurred after two years of economic expansion in the United States. During these two years, the prices of land, cotton, and slaves increased greatly. The silver trade with Mexico and China brought large amounts of silver into the United States and helped finance the strong economy. The additional revenue from land sales and tariffs on imports increased federal revenues. Through lucrative cotton exports and the marketing of state-backed bonds in British money markets, Great Britain made a sizeable capital investment in the United States economy. These bonds financed American transportation projects. British loans provided most of the capital for the United States to expand westward, improve infrastructure, expand industry, and grow the economy. However, the movement of funds into America caused a substantial drop in the Bank of England's monetary supplies. To restore reserves to a more appropriate level, the Bank decided to gradually increase interest rates from three to five percent and reduce loans. The Bank hoped these measures would cause money to move into the Bank and increase assets to their normal amount. The international banking community followed Britain's actions and increased lending rates and decreased loans. These actions added to the financial crisis.

The Panic of 1837
(Library of Congress)

The value of bonds dropped when New York banks raised interest rates and reduced lending. Great Britain's actions decreased the demand for cotton and lowered the amount of imports. The price of cotton fell by twenty-five percent in February and March of 1837. The price collapse harmed the American and especially the southern economies.

In 1832, President Andrew Jackson vetoed the bill to re-charter the Second Bank of the United States. As a result, state-chartered banks in the West and South lowered their lending standards, which reduced their holdings to unsafe levels. To restrain speculation in public lands, President Jackson issued an executive order, the Specie Circular of 1836. The circular stated the government would only accept gold and silver coins in payment for public lands. Unfortunately, the circular caused a collapse in real estate and commodity prices because most buyers could not obtain enough hard money or "specie" (gold or silver coins) to pay for the land. The Deposit and Distribution Act of 1836 distributed federal revenues among various local banks across the country. Many of these banks were in western regions. These two policies transferred hard currency from the nation's main commercial centers on the East Coast to western banks. The lower funds forced major banks and financial institutions on the East Coast to lower lending. The decrease in loans and the collapse of the real estate market led to the Panic of 1837.

Many Americans blamed domestic political conflicts for the panic. Some said President Jackson's refusal to renew the charter of the Second Bank caused the withdrawal of government funds from the bank. The public blamed newly elected president, Martin Van Buren,[121] for the disaster. Van Buren's political opponents criticized the president for refusing to intervene in the crisis. They thought the president should have provided emergency relief and increased spending on public infrastructure projects to reduce unemployment. His adversaries said his failure contributed to the hardship and duration of the depression which followed the panic. Jacksonian Democrats blamed the National Bank for "funding rampant speculation and introducing inflationary paper money."

The entire country suffered from the panic. Connecticut, New

Jersey, and Delaware reported the greatest damage in their commercial centers. The panic injured Vermont's business and credit systems. New Hampshire did not feel the effects of the panic as much as its neighbors. Conditions in the South, especially states in the Cotton Belt, were worse than in the East.[122]

Most historians believe a real estate bubble and erratic American banking policy caused the Panic of 1837. Most of the speculation occurred in western land, but northeastern forests were among the most overvalued holdings. "The speculation in Maine timber lands was the first in order, the most extravagant and irrational, and the most ruinous to those engaged in it." In Massachusetts, Nahant Bank and Boston's Oriental Bank were casualties of bad loans to gain investors. Their assets dropped to dangerous levels because their loans were concentrated in unimproved Maine land far from navigable waterways. An 1838 survey confirmed this property was grossly overvalued, and both banks failed.[123]

As a result, the Maine economy was badly hurt. The money supply was very limited between 1837 and 1840. Adding to the public's suffering, provisions were scarce and "ruled at prices beyond precedent."[124]

The Lure of Texas

Ebenezer Allen faced a critical decision. Should he stay in Maine until the economy recovered or move to a more favorable location? A combination of factors influenced his choice. First, the Panic of 1837 hurt the Maine economy. It undoubtedly became obvious that the Allen-Leavitt law firm could not support both partners. Second, after Texas won her independence from Mexico in 1836, the new nation offered countless prospects for talented men. The young country, like the United States decades earlier, needed lawyers to compose a new set of laws and help with personal and business transactions. This was a wonderful chance for attorneys to emigrate and begin a practice in the Republic of Texas. Third, the new nation offered an almost unlimited number of entrepreneurial opportunities which appealed to Allen's business instincts. Fourth, other New Englanders and Dartmouth graduates who had immigrated to the state could offer advice, introductions, and financial support. The prospects were greater in Texas than in Maine. Fifth, although Allen reached Texas on December 18, 1840 and his father, David Allen, died on December 27, 1840,[125] the family fortune might have passed to David Allen, Jr. rather than Ebenezer Allen, the oldest son and rightful heir. Other possible factors may have influenced Allen's choice: a lack of interest in managing the family businesses, a desire to strike out on his own, and an assortment of petty and serious disagreements with his father and other family members.

GONE TO TEXAS

An Invitation to Texas.
[By Mrs. Ebenezer Allen.]
From thy home in the north where the snow-spirit's wreath
Decks the height that looks over the valley beneath,
From thine islet, thy cottage, thy favorite bower
O, come to the land of the star and the flower!
To the clime of the ardent, the grateful, the free,
To the land of the prairie, wild - blossoming, come!
Where the hopes of the constant shall gather to thee,
And roses shall bloom 'round thy flowerd-decked [sic] home.
The star of thy fate where thou dwellest [sic] may wane,
And fade from the sphere it once brightened in vain;
Then come to the clime of the lone beaming star.
That illumines in peace and that dazzles in war.
Since the shock and the tempest of battle are gone,
And valley and plain shine in beauty secure,
No danger awaits thee in greenwood or lawn,
For the hearts of the brave guard the shrines of the pure.
Hath thy bosom oft thrilled with delight at the lay [adventure]
That told of our sires in the pride of their day,
With spirits of lightning each peril to dare,
That lowered o'er their country or threatened the fair?
And think ye their sons, who have won the domain
Of our homes and our hopes from such feelings have fled?
Nay! The flame ever springs from the dust of the slain
Where Milam hath fallen and Travis hath bled!
Then haste, lady, haste, for the soft breezes play
To waft the swift bark o'er the billows away,
Not to climes where the relics of cities are strown [sic],
And gray ruin points to the glory that's gone.
No! Not to the time honoured [sic] retreats of the east,
Where sighs the dim shade of imperial power,
But blithely where freedom anew spreads her feast,
And invites to the land of the star and the flower!
Mrs. Ebenezer (Sylvinia) Allen - Written in 1843.[126]

Clarksville, Texas

In 1840, the Allen family traveled from Maine to begin a new life in Clarksville, Texas. The early route to Texas was either on the Mississippi River or overland along the Old San Antonio Road from St. Louis.[127] They probably entered the Republic through the Red River gateway. The Red River flows across Texas from Palo Duro Canyon to Prairie Dog Town Fork and then forms the border with Oklahoma before cutting through the southwest corner of Arkansas and flowing south into Louisiana. The river runs through the state before joining the Atchafalaya River and connecting to the Mississippi River. The Allens likely traveled by riverboat from Skowhegan on the Kennebec River to the Casco Bay on the Maine coast. From Maine, they boarded a steamship for the trip to New Orleans. After they arrived in New Orleans, they traveled by riverboat north into Louisiana, Arkansas, and Texas. The Allen family apparently landed at Jonesborough or Pecan Point on the Red River. These river ports were the first Anglo-American settlements in Texas. Emigrants came to Jonesborough in 1815 and the town grew until 1841 when trading sites relocated upriver and many residents moved to Clarksville.[128]

In his poem to Sylvinia, Allen mentions passing "the father of waters to waters more wide." This suggests that the Allens traveled down the Mississippi to the Red River to reach Texas.

Allen Homestead in Clarksville, Texas
(Judith M. Johnson, Johnson-Morrow Family Tree, Ancestry.com)

According to court records, Allen arrived at Clarksville, Texas on December 18, 1840.[129] The Allens entered Clarksville only seven years after James Clark moved to the area in 1833 and laid out a townsite. When the authorities organized Red River County in 1835, they selected Clarksville as the county seat. The Republic of Texas Congress incorporated the town in 1837. Within a few years, Clarksville became an educational and agricultural center.[130]

County residents founded the Clarksville Female Academy[131] in 1840 on Pine Creek and later moved the institution to Clarksville in 1844. McKenzie College, four miles from Clarksville, opened in 1841. Charles DeMorse began publishing the *Clarksville Northern Standard* in 1842. The first issue appeared on August 20, 1842 and displayed the motto "Long May Our Banner Brave the Breeze - The Standard of the Free."[132] A post office opened in 1846 and semiweekly mail service began in 1848 between Clarksville and Natchitoches, Louisiana.

In the town's early days, itinerant preachers conducted religious services in a log schoolhouse. In 1833, religious leaders organized the First Presbyterian Church at Shiloh four miles northeast of Clarksville. The church moved to Clarksville in 1848. First Presbyterian is one of the oldest continuously functioning Protestant churches in the state. The Baptists and Methodists also built churches in the community.[133]

From the late 1830s until the Civil War, Clarksville was the most important trading center in northeast Texas. Steamboats brought goods from New Orleans on the Red River and unloaded them at Rowland's Landing, fifteen miles north of Clarksville. From the landing, wagons delivered the merchandise to Clarksville and other communities. The residents built a frame courthouse around 1840 after Clarksville became the government seat of Red River County. The courthouse became the center of the town and many businesses opened on and around the courthouse square. In the 1850s, entrepreneurs constructed steam-powered sawmills and cotton gins. By the start of the Civil War, Clarksville's population was nine hundred people.[134]

The McKenzie Institute opened in Clarksville, in 1839 as a private, co-educational, primary school. Under the direction of owner-President Reverend Dr. J. W. P. McKenzie the institute became a secondary school and then a college in 1848. In 1859, Dr. McKenzie donated the college to the East Texas Conference of the Methodist Episcopal Church, South. McKenzie College closed in 1868.[135]

Six Hundred and Forty Acres

On August 2, 1841, Allen appeared before the Board of Land Commissioners, applied for a conditional certificate, and received a "conditional grant of six hundred and forty acres of land."[136]

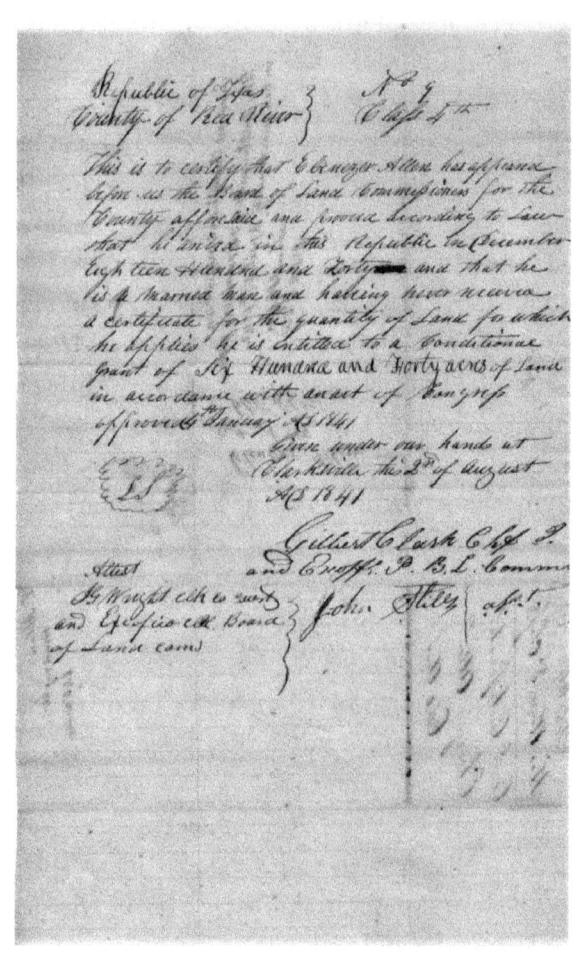

**Conditional Certificate Granting Ebenezer Allen Six Hundred and Forty Acres of Land
(The Texas General Land Office)**

The Texas Congress authorized "liberal" land laws in 1836. Under the constitution, the heads of families living in Texas on March 2, 1836, could apply for a square league (4,428 acres) and a labor (177.1 acres) of land. Single men over age seventeen could receive one-third of a league. No one was required to live on the land. To encourage settlement, Congress offered immigrants arriving between March 2, 1836 and October 1, 1837, a grant of 1,280 acres for heads of families and 640 acres for single men. Congress reduced the grant to 640 acres and 320 acres, respectively, to heads of family and single men arriving after October 1, 1837 and before January 1, 1842. However, after March 2, 1836, all new immigrants had to live in Texas for three years to receive a clear title.[137]

On April 2, 1842, Allen ordered a survey conducted on a tract of land on the South Bank of Sulfur Ford River in Red River County.[138]

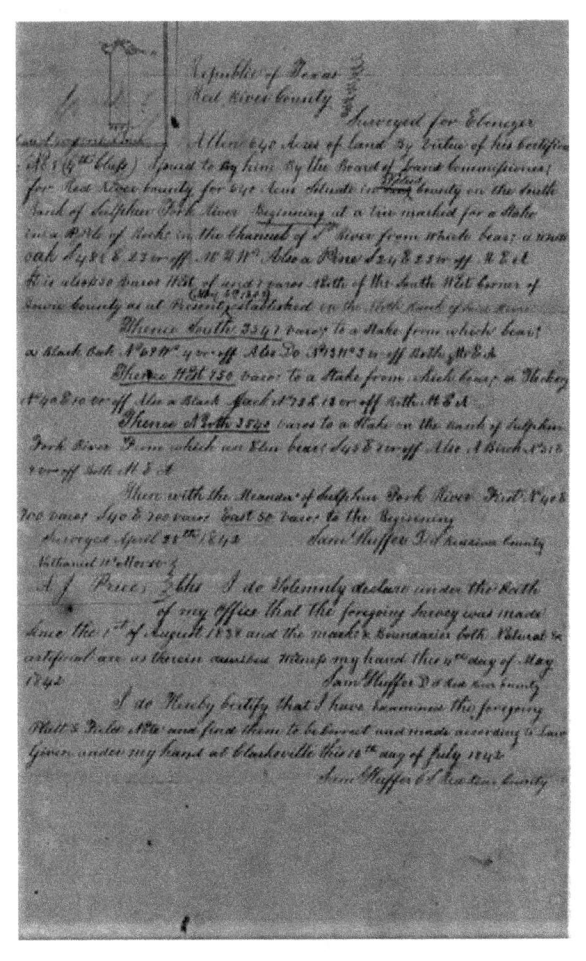

Survey of Land Granted by Conditional Certificate to Ebenezer Allen (The Texas General Land Office)

On August 5, 1844, the Board of Land Commissioners for Red River County awarded Allen six hundred and forty acres after he fulfilled the required three-year residency in the Republic of Texas and "performed all the duties demanded of him as a citizen."[139]

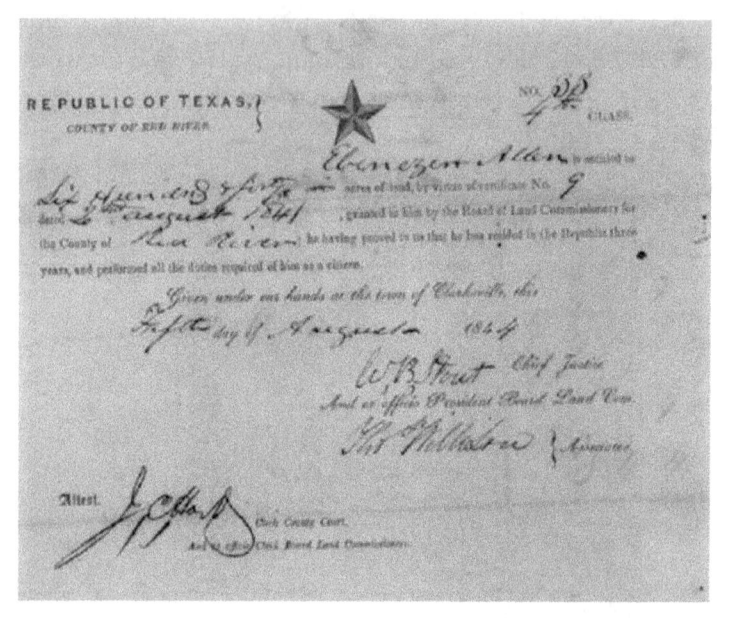

Certificate Granting Ebenezer Allen Six Hundred and Forty Acres of Land (The Texas General Land Office)

After beginning his residence, Allen had to gain admission to the Republic of Texas bar and find a way to support his family until he could begin to practice law.

New Englanders in Texas

Ebenezer Allen was one of many New Englanders who migrated to Texas. Eleazar Louis Ripley Wheelock moved his family to Texas in 1833. Wheelock was a "surveyor, land agent, lawyer, rancher, farmer, and soldier." During the Texas Revolution, Wheelock built a blockhouse and organized and commanded a company of Texas Rangers. Although Wheelock fought against the Indians, he was a steadfast "defender of Indian rights" and served as Indian commissioner under President Anson Jones[140] in the Republic of Texas.

Several New Hampshire and Vermont educators contributed to higher education in Texas. Rufus William Bailey was a Phi Beta Kappa graduate in Dartmouth's Class of 1813. He studied law under Daniel Webster and taught at Dartmouth and the Mary Baldwin Seminary in Virginia. He moved to Texas in 1854. The next year Bailey accepted the chair of languages at Austin College. In 1858, the college elected him as its third president. Bailey led the institution until 1862. James Huckins from New Hampshire was a charter trustee and enthusiastic fundraiser for Baylor University. Vermont's Chauncey Richardson was the first president of Rutersville College, which eventually merged with several other colleges to form Southwestern University in Georgetown. Tarleton State University in Stephenville is named for John Tarleton from White Mountain, Vermont.

Another Dartmouth alumnus, Edward Hopkins Cushing, taught in Texas schools in Galveston, Brazoria, and Columbia. He became a journalist and obtained control of the *Houston Telegraph* in 1856. Cushing was a staunch Southern Democrat and supported John C. Breckinridge in the 1860 presidential election. He publicized an alleged plot by abolitionists and blacks to overthrow slavery in Texas, which encouraged the state's secession movement. After Vermonter George Stanton Denison graduated from the University of Vermont in 1854, he went to San Antonio and taught in his uncle's private school. Denison supported the Union and left Texas in February 1861 when the state seceded. Samuel P. Chase, Abraham Lincoln's Secretary of the Treasury, appointed Denison as a special agent for the U.S. Treasury Department in New Orleans after federal troops captured the city in April 1862.

Hiram Chamberlain was a Vermonter who supported the Confederacy. In 1850, Chamberlain founded the First Presbyterian Church of Brownsville, the first Protestant church in the lower Rio Grande Valley. He was an ardent secessionist and served as a Confederate chaplain.

Ezekiel B. Turner came from Vermont to Texas in 1853 and was an outspoken Unionist during the secession crisis of 1860-1861. He was a member of the Union "Home Guard" and left Texas in 1862. When Union troops arrived in Austin in July 1865, Turner was one of the speakers who welcomed them to the capital. He served as Texas attorney general from 1867 to 1870 and later as a judge.

Several emigrants from New Hampshire and Vermont played significant roles in the entrepreneurial history of Texas. Jesse Obadiah Wheeler from Vermont brought steamboats in 1850 and railroads in 1861 to Victoria on the Guadalupe River and became the "wealthiest man in Victoria County."

Three Texas counties are named after immigrants from New England. Kendall County honors George Wilkins Kendall from New Hampshire. Kendall learned to be a printer in Burlington, Vermont and founded the New Orleans *Picayune*. He was America's first foreign war correspondent as a reporter in the Mexican War. Kendall was the original Texan to import Merino sheep, known for their fine wool, from Vermont. Wheeler County is named for Royal Tyler Wheeler, who was a member of the first State of Texas Supreme Court and served as chief justice until his death in 1864. Montague County is named for Daniel Montague who was born in Massachusetts and learned to be a surveyor and engineer in Vermont. He settled in Texas in 1837 and accumulated huge landholdings as a surveyor.

Thomas B. Chubb was a Vermont ship captain engaged in the coffee trade with South America. On one of his voyages, Chubb sailed eastward to Africa, captured 400 Africans in the Congo, shipped them to the West Indies, and sold them into slavery. He recruited free African Americans in the North to join his crew. When Chubb's ship docked at a southern port that allowed slavery, he claimed these sailors were slaves and sold them. From his base in Galveston, Chubb shipped arms to the Texans during the fight for independence from Mexico. His friendship with Sam Houston earned him an appointment as an admiral in the Texas Navy in 1836. During the Civil War, he was commander of a Confederate steamer called the *Royal Yacht* and was part of a militia that kept watch for Union ships from a tower on the Galveston Strand. When Union forces captured Galveston, they sentenced Chubb to death for engaging in the slave trade. Confederate President Jefferson Davis threatened to execute ten northern prisoners if the United States killed Chubb. The Union forces exchanged Chubb for a northerner in a southern prison.

West Point graduate, William Babcook Hazen from Vermont, fought Indians in Texas. Miles DeForest Andross, born in Bradford, Vermont, died defending the Alamo in 1836. New Hampshire brothers Henry and William Redfield fought for the Republic of Texas.

Cornelius van Ness, the son of a Vermont governor, served in the Fourth Republic of Texas Congress from 1839 to 1840 with another Vermonter, Daniel Pierce Coit. Philip Crosby Tucker, Jr., a Vermont lawyer and Confederate supporter, helped introduce the Scottish Rite of Freemasonry into Texas and worked to preserve the early history of Galveston. Timothy B. Phelps, from New Hampshire, was a teacher in Stephen F. Austin's[141] colony. Don Carlos Barrett, born in Norwich, was a Texas lawyer who worked to settle disagreements between Texas settlers and the Mexican government.[142]

The early emigrants from New England provided a foundation and defined a route for Allen to seek new opportunities in the young nation.

The Clarksville Academy

With Allen's academic credentials and prior teaching experience, he obtained a teaching position at the Clarksville Academy. The Academy opened in Clarksville in 1841 under the management of Reverend James Sampson. It was the first school of higher learning for both men and women in North Texas and, according to *The Northern Standard*, the school offered "high adventures of a useful, practical and polished education."

The coeducational school had separate classrooms for boys and girls and accepted students at elementary, high school, and college levels. The academic year was two sessions of five months each. In addition to such traditional subjects as grammar, history, math, Latin, and Greek, the school offered courses in French and Spanish. An announcement in *The Northern Standard* proclaimed, "No effort will be wanting, either on the part of Teachers or Trustees, to render this institution in all respects adapted to the wants and desires of this interesting section of our Republic, making it at once the nurse and the guardian of the sciences and the arts; the accomplishments and the virtues, which are inseparable from the very idea of an academic education." The Academy charged $10 tuition per session for reading and spelling classes, $15 for Arithmetic, Writing, Geography, and English Grammar lessons; and $20 for Moral and Natural Philosophy, Logic, History, Elements of Criticism, Mathematics, Latin, Greek, French and Spanish Languages. The paper reported Ebenezer Allen was one of the Academy's nine trustees, which included Dr. George Gordon and attorney B. H. Martin.[143],[144] Enrolment was only thirty-six by August 1846 and the school closed in 1847.[145]

Law in Texas

From 1821 to 1836, Mexican Texas was governed by Spanish law. During the Spanish rule, there were no formally trained judges or practicing lawyers in Texas. The only legal professional in the state was a self-taught notary in San Fernando. Administrators and citizens used Spanish law books to prepare legal documents and conduct civil trials to resolve disputes. In the 1820s and 1830s, several lawyers from the United States came to Texas with other Anglo-American colonists. They offered legal services to their fellow colonists and learned the principles of Spanish law. After the establishment of the Republic of Texas, the country kept some of the rules of Spanish law, especially those dealing with family property law.

In 1836, the Republic of Texas adopted the Anglo-American rules of criminal law governing jury trial. Those rules formed the basis of the Penal Code of 1856. The Republic based Texas civil law on rules adopted in 1840 founded on "the common law of England as the rule of decision." Common law included contracts, torts,[146] property claims,[147] legal status of citizens and rules governing corporations and partnerships, and legal doctrine according to the English concept of equity.[148] The government enacted many of those rules through formal legislation or codification.[149] Regulations specified by the legislature were subject to interpretation by the courts and expanded by court decisions. Court rulings and scholarly writings outlined other legal doctrines.[150]

Attorney at Law

Allen arrived in Texas when the Republic's legal system was still in its infancy, although its basis was well established on both Spanish and Anglo-American law.

EBEN'R ALLEN,
ATTORNEY AT LAW,
Clarksville. aug 20 tf

"Eben'r Allen – Attorney at Law" in Clarksville, Texas
(*The Northern Standard*)

Allen became a legal guardian to J. A. H. Hosack after the death of their mother in 1842 in Clarksville. Hosack wrote he knew Allen "well and intimately."[151] Hamilton Hosack was the son of famous actress Fannie Pritchard and Alexander Hosack. The couple also had a daughter. Following their mother's death, Allen was the children's guardian. He sent the boy to the McKenzie Institute[152] in Clarksville and placed the girl with Sterling Smith of Bowie County.[153]

Allen posted a legal notice in the June 23, 1843 issue in the matter of Abia Dyer vs. William Dyer. Abia Dyer, through her attorney Ebenezer Allen "charges [*that*] the said defendant with having left complainant with intention of abandonment and in fact did abandon, and hath ever since abandoned the complainant, without any just cause or reason."[154]

> **THE REPUBLIC OF TEXAS,**
> Red River County.
> In District Court,
> Spring Term, A. D., 1843.
>
> Abia Dyer,
> vs.   } Bill for Divorce.
> William Dyer,
>
> ORDERED by the Court, that publication be made in the Northern Standard six weeks, of the pendency of this suit, notifying the said defendant, William Dyer, to be and appear before the Honorable District Court, to be holden for the County aforesaid, at the Fall Term thereof, on the third Monday in September, and then and there, before the sixth day of said Term, to file his answer to said bill of complaint, or the matters and things therein set out and contained, will be taken "*pro confesso,*" and complainant allowed to proceed "*ex parte,*" to trial. The complainant's bill, as filed by her Attorney, Ebenezer Allen, Esq., charges the said defendant with having left complainant with intention of abandonment, and in fact did abandon, and hath ever since abandoned complainant, without any just cause or reason.
>
> Witness, W. H. Vining, Clerk of said Court
>
> {L.S.} Given under my hand and under the Seal of said Court, at my office in Clarksville, the 16th June, A. D., 1843.
>
> W. H. VINING, Clerk, District Court
>
> June 22, 1943. 40-6t

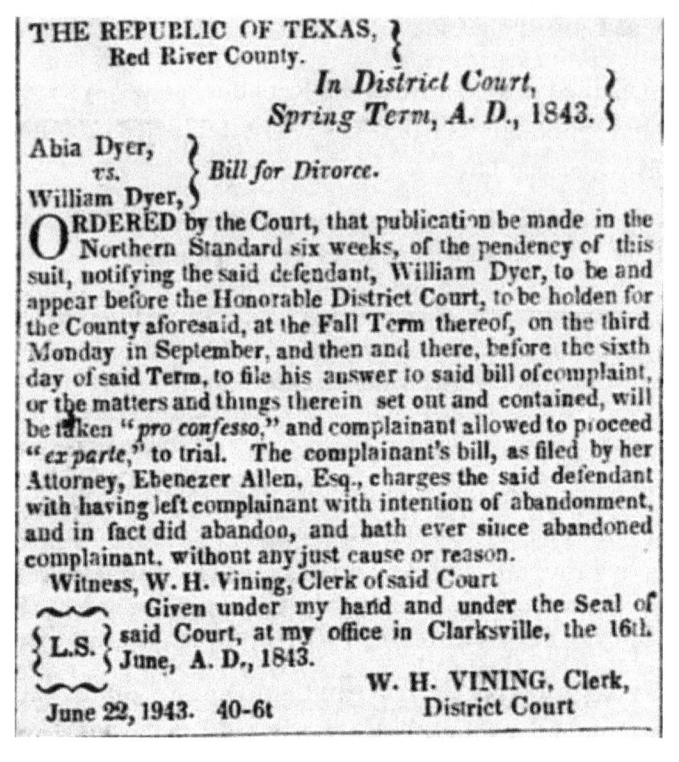

Abia Dyer vs. William Dyer
(*The Northern Standard*)

Allen helped sponsor lawyers like Hugh F. Young. Young was appointed Commissioner to take depositions in all the cases in the District Court.[155]

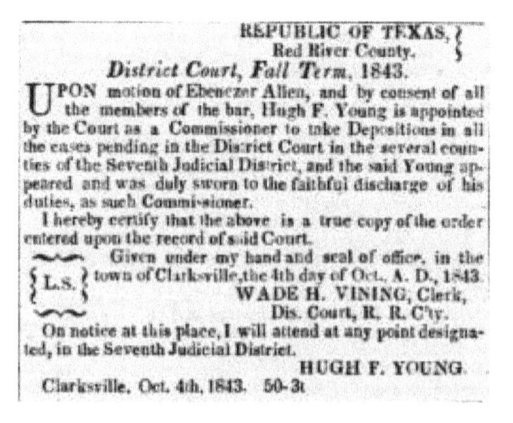

> **REPUBLIC OF TEXAS,**
> Red River County.
> District Court, Fall Term, 1843.
>
> UPON motion of Ebenezer Allen, and by consent of all the members of the bar, Hugh F. Young is appointed by the Court as a Commissioner to take Depositions in all the cases pending in the District Court in the several counties of the Seventh Judicial District, and the said Young appeared and was duly sworn to the faithful discharge of his duties, as such Commissioner.
>
> I hereby certify that the above is a true copy of the order entered upon the record of said Court.
>
> {L.S.} Given under my hand and seal of office, in the town of Clarksville, the 4th day of Oct., A. D., 1843.
>
> WADE H. VINING, Clerk, Dis. Court, R. R. C'ty.
>
> On notice at this place, I will attend at any point designated, in the Seventh Judicial District.
>
> HUGH F. YOUNG.
> Clarksville, Oct. 4th, 1843. 50-3t

District Court, Fall Term, 1843
(*The Northern Standard*)

Many of Allen's cases involved unpaid debts, as in the case of the $200 owned to the plaintiff for the sale of two "negroes."[156]

William C. Young vs. Thomas J. Newbern
(*The Northern Standard*)

Allen continued his solo practice in Clarksville until he formed a partnership with William Smith Todd[157] in 1844. Previously, Todd maintained an independent practice in Boston, Texas.[158] An advertisement in the March 13, 1845 issue of *The Northern Standard*, announced that on December 11, 1844, Allen had formed a partnership with William Smith Todd in Clarksville. Allen & Todd publicized their intention of practicing in the "Courts of 7th Judicial District, and in the Supreme Court of the Republic."[159] Numerous advertisements for

Allen and Todd's services appeared in *The Northern Standard* during Allen's time in Clarksville.[160] The partnership lasted until March 1, 1847 when Todd formed an association with Burrell P. Smith.[161]

Texas Freemasonry

Ebenezer Allen became a member of Friendship Lodge No. 16 in Clarksville on February 4, 1843. He served on the Committee for Communications in 1845 and was the District Deputy Grand Master in 1846. Membership in this important organization allowed Allen to gain access to the political elite in the new Republic of Texas. The lodge did not include him on the membership roll for 1852 and suspended him in 1853 for non-payment of dues.[162]

By 1820, the Freemason fraternity was well known throughout the United States. Stephen F. Austin and other Masons were among the first Americans to migrate to Texas in the 1820s. On February 11, 1828, Austin called a meeting of Masons at San Felipe de Austin. The group asked the York Grand Lodge of Mexico for a charter to form a lodge. The Mexicans refused to award a charter because government officials feared a Texas chapter would become a rallying point for the political philosophies of English-speaking and liberal Freemasons and promote schemes to gain independence. These concerns caused the Mexican government to outlaw Freemasonry in Texas on October 25, 1828. The following year, Austin arranged another gathering of Masons where the attendees, in an attempt to alleviate the fears of the Mexican government, decided it was "impolitic and imprudent, at this time, to form Masonic lodges in Texas."[163]

Six years later in March 1835, five Master Masons met "in a little grove of peach or laurel" trees in the town of Brazoria, near a place known as General John Austin's" to try to obtain a charter. They decided to petition Grand Master John H. Holland[164] of the Grand Lodge of Louisiana[165] for a dispensation[166] to establish a lodge in Texas. Dr. Anson Jones, who became Grand Master of the Texas Lodge and President of the Republic of Texas, was one of the five in attendance. The Grand Lodge of Louisiana issued and signed the charter that created Holland Lodge No. 1 in Brazoria on January 27, 1836. The Texas

Lodge appointed John M. Allen,[167] who was originally a member of Louisiana Lodge No. 32, to bring the document to Texas. Allen was in New Orleans recruiting volunteers for the Texas Army and did not reach Texas until before the Battle of San Jacinto on April 21, 1836.[168]

While the five Master Masons waited for a charter from the Grand Lodge of Louisiana, Texas began a war for independence from Mexico. Texas revolutionaries fired the first shots of the resurrection in October 1835 at Gonzales, Texas. Delegates gathered at Washington-on-the-Brazos and signed the Texas Declaration of Independence on March 2, 1836. The Mexican Army under General Antonio Lopez de Santa Anna crossed the Rio Grande, attacked and defeated the small garrison at the Alamo in San Antonio de Bexar. Freemasons James Bonham, James Bowie, David Crockett, Almaron Dickenson, and William Barrett Travis were among the nearly two hundred defenders who died at the Alamo.

The Holland Lodge struggled for several months until the Mexican army attacked Brazoria and destroyed the lodge's records and equipment. Subsequently, the members closed the lodge and scattered. After Texas won her independence, the Masons reopened the lodge in Houston in October 1837. After the revolution, the Grand Lodge of Louisiana issued charters to the Milam No. 40 at Nacogdoches and the McFarland No. 41 at San Augustine.

On December 20, 1837, Sam Houston, President of the Republic of Texas, led a Freemason convention meeting in Houston with representatives from the three lodges. The delegates were some of the most important men in the new republic Sam Houston, Anson Jones, Jeff Wright, and Thomas G. Western were from the Holland Lodge; Thomas J. Rusk, I. W. Burton, Charles S. Taylor, Adolphus Sterne, and K. H. Douglas represented the Milam Lodge; and G. H. Winchell spoke for the McFarland Lodge. The representatives decided to form a "Grand Lodge of the Republic of Texas." They elected Dr. Jones as the first Grand Master of Masons in Texas and selected other officers. The men agreed to hold the first meeting of the Grand Lodge "on the third Monday of April next."

The "Grand Lodge was opened in ample form" when the delegates met on April 16, 1838 in Houston. The Grand Lodge met again on May 11, 1838, installed the Grand Master and his officers, and selected this date as the official beginning of the Grand Lodge of Texas.[169]

Between 1838 and 1845, the Texas Grand Lodge issued charters to twenty-one more lodges, and membership increased from 73 to 357. The Austin No. 12 lodge was founded on November 7, 1839; Harmony No. 6 in Galveston on January 30, 1840; and Friendship No. 16 lodge in Clarksville on December 11, 1841.[170]

Masons played important roles in organizing the republic and state governments and served in prominent leadership positions in these administrations. Their presence introduced Freemasonry principles into the Texas constitutions of 1836 and 1845 and into the laws enacted, explained, and enforced under them.[171]

On March 1, 1836, a commission met in the town of Washington, Texas to form the new government. According to *The Journal of the Proceedings of the Convention*, Masons served on various committees of the conference. Four of the five delegates assigned to the committee to draft rules for the order and government of the convention were Masons. Twenty of the fifty-nine delegates who signed the Declaration of Independence, adopted on March 2, 1836, were Masons. Seven of the twenty-one members of the committee appointed to draft a constitution for the Republic were Masons.

Masonic leaders held important positions in the legislative, judicial, and executive branches of the government during the life of the Republic. All five vice presidents of the Republic, who presided over the deliberations of the Senate, were Masons. Seven of the nine speakers of the House of Representatives were Masons. Fifty-three Masons were members of the Congress of the Republic.

The Constitution of the Republic assigned the judicial powers of the government to the Supreme Court and other "inferior courts as the Congress might from time to time ordain and establish." The Constitution specified the Republic be divided into from three to eight judicial districts. The district judges of the several judicial districts and the Chief Justice of the Republic would compose the members of the Supreme Court. During the life of the Republic, eight of the fourteen judges who wrote opinions for the Supreme Court were Masons Chief

Justice Thomas J. Rusk[172] and Judges R. E. B. Baylor, John M. Hansford, Patrick C. Jack, John T. Mills, William B. Ochiltree, Richard A. Scurry, and A. B. Shelby.

Each of the four presidents of the Republic was a Mason. The following Masons served with David G. Burnet as provisional president of the ad interim government Lorenzo de Zavala, vice president; James Collinsworth, secretary of state; Thomas J. Rusk and M. B. Lamar, secretaries of war; and Warren Hall, adjutant general.

During President Sam Houston's first administration, his cabinet included the following Masons Mirabeau B. Lamar, vice president; Stephen F. Austin, secretary of state; Thomas J. Rusk, secretary of war; James Pinkney Henderson,[173] attorney general; and Robert Barr, postmaster general. President Mirabeau B. Lamar's cabinet continued the trend with the following Masons David G. Burnet, vice-president; Abner S. Lipscomb, secretary of state; Branch T. Archer, secretary of war; James Webb, attorney general; Robert Barr, postmaster general; and Thomas William Ward, commissioner of the general land office.

President Anson Jones included Masons in his cabinet Kenneth L. Anderson,[174] vice president; Ebenezer Allen, secretary of state and attorney general; William Gordon Cooke, secretary of war; and William Beck Ochiltree, secretary of the treasury.

On July 4, 1845, thirty-six of the sixty-one delegates to the convention to draft an ordinance accepting the terms of annexation to the United States and prepare a constitution for the state of Texas were Masons.

In addition to the Texas lodge members, approximately 1,100 Masons from other states lived in Texas. Although constituting only 1½ percent of the population, Masons held eighty percent of Texas' higher offices. All the Republics presidents, vice presidents, and secretaries of state were Masons. After annexation, Masons continued to be equally prominent in the state government. Between 1846 and 1861, five of the state's six governors were members of the fraternity. The Freemasons continued to grow, and by 1860, Texas had 226 active lodges and 9,000 members. During the Civil War, Masons composed from one-third to one-half of the Texans in military service. The Grand Lodge issued dispensations for thirty-two traveling military lodges opened within army units. The Grand Lodge experienced severe financial difficulties during the war, and many lodges were unable to pay their annual assessments. In 1861, Confederate authorities ordered the grand lodge's treasurer to sell all its United States government bonds and invest the money in Confederate bonds. After the Confederacy's defeat in 1865, the bonds were worthless, and the treasury of the Grand Lodge was empty.

Initially, the Texas Masonry's charitable and benevolent activities focused on education. The Grand Lodge created an education fund in 1847 and appointed a superintendent of education in 1848. Between 1850 and 1873, the Texas legislature chartered seventeen Masonic-sponsored schools. Texas Masons helped start more than 100 other unchartered schools. In addition, many of the early public schools initially held classes in lodge buildings.[175]

When Allen joined the Friendship Lodge No. 16 in Clarksville, he gained access to the most powerful men in the Republic. He only needed to present his qualifications and demonstrate his capability to become a member of the Texas aristocracy.

THE LONG JOURNEY TO ANNEXATION

The United States government became interested in obtaining Texas after the Louisiana Purchase in 1803. The possible addition was the subject of political and diplomatic discussions. Interest in annexation increased after Texas gained her independence from Mexico in 1836. From 1836 to 1845, the issue became an important subject of international concern.[176]

Re-annexation

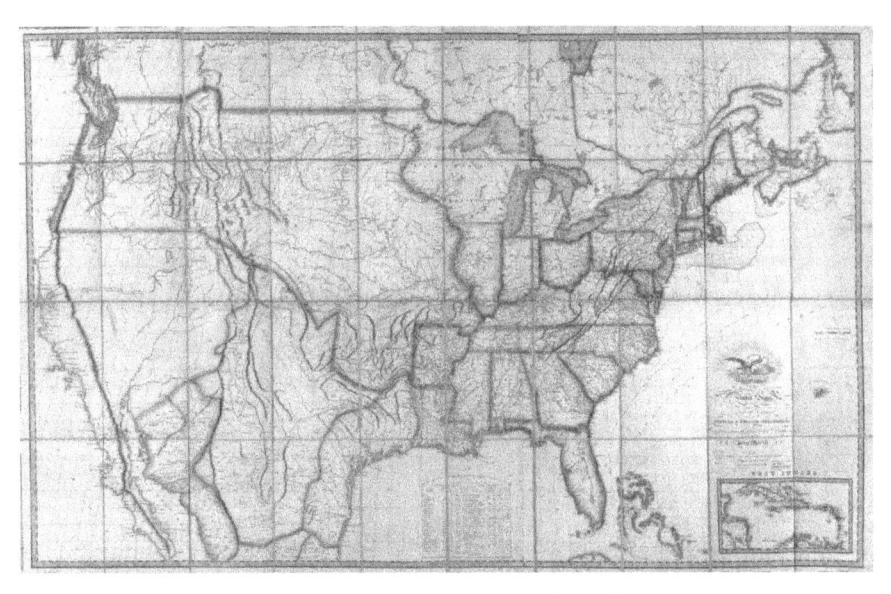

Map of The United States in 1819
(Library of Congress)

The question of Texas' annexation by the United States began in 1819, when the United States surrendered to Spain, "territories laying west and south" beyond the Sabine River in exchange for Florida. The language implied the United States extended west of the Sabine River and that territory was part of Louisiana. When the United States bought Louisiana, the Federal Government promised that its inhabitants would be "incorporated in the Union of the United States." If the land beyond the Sabine River was part of Louisiana, the United States had no right to surrender the territory in 1819. This understanding indicated "that Texas had formerly belonged to the United States" and "a part of the region covered by the name was easily overlooked." The term "re-annexation" became popular with annexation backers. These supporters reasoned that if Texas was reacquired, the United States would "only be recovering our own" and "ease the difficulty of acquiring a foreign state into the Union." This concept became a rallying cry and argument for Americans who supported adding Texas to the Union.[177]

Early Annexation Efforts

During the battle for Texas independence, commissioners from the rebelling Mexican territory traveled east to obtain supplies, money, and support. Americans watched events in the conflict and supported the Texans' struggle. America's enthusiastic response astonished and pleased the Texas emissaries. They believed the combination of support from the public, President Andrew Jackson, and the Democratic controlled U.S. Senate, would encourage the United States to provide military help to defeat the Mexicans. The Texas revolutionaries hoped that after the military victory, the United States would recognize Texas independence and quickly add Texas to the Union. Americans petitioned Congress for immediate diplomatic recognition of the independent Republic of Texas.

Most of the citizens of the Republic of Texas considered themselves to be Americans and believed the "United States was waiting to embrace them with open arms." In September of 1836, Texas voted overwhelmingly in favor of entering the Union. However, Texas president Sam Houston believed the adoption faced many obstacles. Despite the support for annexation in Texas, it seemed unreasonable to consider annexation when the United States and Houston's old friend Andrew Jackson refused to acknowledge the Republic's existence. The two governments were unable to negotiate a treaty for the next nine years. [Please see "The Annexation Process: 1836-1845" in the Appendix.]

While the government of the United States desired to acquire Texas, neither President Jackson nor the Senate wanted to risk going to war with Mexico to obtain the Republic. Jackson wrote to Stephen Austin: "The writer does not reflect that we have a treaty with Mexico, and our national faith is pledged to support it. The Texians before they took the step to declare themselves Independent, which has aroused and united all Mexico against them ought to have pondered well – it was a rash and premature act, our neutrality must be faithfully maintained."[178]

Sam Houston
(Library of Congress)

The Texans captured General Santa Anna at the battle of San Jacinto. One of the conditions for Santa Anna's release was his promise for Mexico to recognize Texas' independence. However, the Mexican government refused to honor Santa Anna's pledge. Citizens of the new Republic of Texas realized their country would never be secure and prosperous until Mexico accepted their status as an independent nation. The lack of international recognition and the possibility of a Mexican invasion discouraged the migration of white settlers and the importation of black slave labor into the Republic. American citizens who considered moving to Texas believed, "life and property were safer within the United States" than in the new Republic. This reluctance led to labor shortages, lower tax revenue, large national debt, and a smaller Texas militia.[179]

In 1837, President Houston sent commissioners, William Wharton,[180] Fairfax Catlett,[181] and Memucan Hunt,[182] to Washington to "seek recognition and explore the possibility of annexation."[183]

Wharton tried to persuade Congress to recognize Texas and begin annexation negotiations. He warned federal legislators the Republic was considering closer relations with Great Britain. Finally, in March 1837, the U.S. Senate passed an act recognizing the Republic of Texas. In one of President Jackson's last duties, he signed the legislation and appointed Alcée La Branche[184] as *charge d'affaires* to the new republic. However, the Texas commissioners failed to convince the Jackson administration and Congress to consider annexation.

Martin Van Buren replaced Jackson in the White House in March of 1837. Van Buren believed supporting Texas' annexation would destroy the Democratic Party. Commissioner William Wharton noted the "extreme rhetoric" from Southerners had offended the Northerners and convinced them not to add Texas to the Union. "The North must choose between the Union with Texas added – or no Union. Texas will be added and then forever farewell abolitionism and northern influence. Threats and denunciations like these will goad the North into a determined opposition and if Texas is annexed at all it will not be until after the question [of annexation] has convulsed this nation for several sessions."[185] When Texas formally proposed annexation to the Van Buren administration in August of 1837, the president refused to consider the application. The administration based the rejection on Constitutional principles and fear of war with Mexico. However, the real problem was the Northern States hostility to slavery. This opposition convinced Van Buren to reject the Texas request, and slavery became the chief obstacle to annexation.[186] Separate annexation resolutions presented in each House of Congress were either soundly defeated or postponed through filibuster. Before Houston left office at the end of 1838, he formally withdrew Texas' request. On January 23, 1839, the Texas Congress approved Houston's actions.

Diplomatic overtures to Britain and other European nations were unsuccessful. Britain refused to recognize Texas or sign a treaty of friendship or commerce.[187]

Mirabeau Lamar
(Library of Congress)

Mirabeau B. Lamar's Presidency

President Mirabeau Lamar began his term as Texas president with the country in a dangerous situation because the United States was the only nation to recognize her independence, the Republic had no commercial treaties, Mexico threatened to reconquer the Republic, Indians harassed Texas frontier settlements and travelers, the nation's treasury was empty, and the value of the Republic's currency had declined. Lamar tried to divert citizens' attention from these problems and have them focus on his dream of a great empire that reached the Pacific Ocean.[188]

After the 1838 election, Lamar ended further negotiations with the United States. Lamar promoted his vision of Texas as a future continental rival to the United States in size and power. Annexation was not part of Lamar's plans for the Republic. President Van Buren tried to avoid a conflict with Mexico and to negotiate a peace treaty between Texas and Mexico. Van Buren believed Mexico was so weak from continuous revolution that Texas could seize the best parts of her possessions north of the Rio Grande, including the Santa Fe trade, California seaports, and mineral resources. President Lamar tried to have Mexico recognize Texas as an independent nation and sign a peace treaty. When his efforts failed, Lamar formed a quasi-official alliance with the rebel government in Yucatán and leased them ships from the Texas Navy.[189]

At Lamar's suggestion, the Republic moved the capital to Austin, Texas and the government began operations there in October of 1839. Lamar's greatest achievement was his proposal to Congress to create an educational system endowed by public lands. Lamar's advocacy resulted in the passage of an act on January 26, 1839, which designated land for public schools and two universities. Lamar's efforts earned him the nickname the "Father of Texas Education."[190]

Although the United States and Texas ended annexation negotiations, both countries started to form "solid economic connections." Legal and illegal trade between the two nations grew significantly between 1838 and 1841. More importantly, many wealthy and prominent Americans loaned funds to finance the Texas government and speculated in Texas land. These investments demonstrated the large stake these men had in the future of Texas.

During Lamar's term, Texas established relations with France, Holland, and Belgium, and Great Britain recognized the Republic. The British remained frustrated by Texas' refusal to give up slavery, but the economic advantages of developing the cotton trade and the benefits from Texas smuggling were too attractive to resist.[191]

The Lamar administration ended with the Republic deep in debt, nearly bankrupt, and the president's popularity at its lowest point.[192]

Houston Renews Annexation Overtures

When Sam Houston regained the Texas presidency in late 1841, he inherited a bankrupt and defenseless country. Houston understood the dismal situation. The uneasy peace with Mexico discouraged immigration and the Republic's southern border was defenseless against invasion. The Republic's population was only 75,000. Joseph Eve,[193] the United States *chargé d'affaires* in Texas, predicted the young country would soon lose her independence.[194]

Houston sent James Reily[195] and Isaac van Zandt[196] to Washington to try to obtain a treaty of friendship with the United States. Houston instructed the envoys to investigate Congress' interest in reopening annexation talks or providing military aid.[197]

John Tyler's Expansionist Goals

Annexation was a dead issue when John Tyler entered the White House in 1841. Whig Party presidential nominee, William Henry Harrison,[198] defeated Van Buren in the 1840 election. When Harrison died shortly after his inauguration, Vice President John Tyler assumed the presidency. The Whig party expelled President Tyler in 1841 for repeatedly vetoing their domestic finance legislation. Without support from either party, President Tyler focused on foreign affairs to try to salvage his presidency. He allied with a southern states' rights faction that shared his interest in protecting and expanding slavery.[199] Tyler believed acquiring Texas could be the cornerstone for growing the country and annexation became the "primary objective of his administration."[200]

After the Tyler administration resolved other urgent diplomatic problems, the president made annexation his "top priority." Tyler provided the basis for Texas annexation when he announced his expansionist goal. He rationalized the new state would preserve the balance between state and national authority. He believed territorial growth would protect American institutions, including slavery, and avoid sectional conflict. Tyler's advisors told him obtaining Texas would guarantee him a second term in the White House. However, President Tyler postponed annexation negotiations to work with his Secretary of State Daniel Webster on other more demanding international issues.[201]

The situation changed in March of 1842 when Santa Anna ordered Mexican troops to invade Texas. The Mexicans captured Goliad, Refugio, and Victoria; sacked San Antonio; and withdrew across the border. Mexico warned Texas it was hopeless to continue the struggle to preserve its independence and threatened to make additional raids. Texas authorities learned the Mexicans were building two warships to capture Galveston and cut off Texas from the rest of the world.[202]

Texans were panicked and angry. Most people did not understand the impact bankruptcy had on the country and its military forces. They knew the government wanted them to volunteer to defend their country. However, they were reluctant to leave their farms unattended and their families unprotected from hostile Indians. In this dangerous situation, some settlers decided to leave Texas and return to the comparative safety of the United States.[203]

Despite the Mexican attack and Texas' financial problems, the United States refused to support the young republic. Worried Texas officials requested help from Great Britain. In July of 1842, Texas approved treaties with the British for commerce and navigation and agreed to end the slave trade. The Republic additionally authorized the British to mediate a peace treaty between Texas and Mexico.

In the fall of 1842, Mexican troops seized San Antonio, held the city for two days, and then withdrew across the Rio Grande. President Houston authorized a military response, which resulted in the Somervell Expedition[204] and the disastrous Mier Expedition.[205] Both operations failed, weakened the military, and lowered respect for the government.[206]

Near the end of 1842, President Houston decided an alliance with Britain was the only way to save Texas. In November of 1842, Houston appealed to Britain for immediate help in obtaining peace with Mexico. In 1843, he worked intensely to cut Texas' links with the United States and form new connections with Great Britain.[207]

International Negotiations

In February of 1843, Santa Anna released Judge James W. Robinson,[208] one of the prisoners-of-war captured in the September of 1842 Mexican raid on San Antonio. The Mexican dictator sent the judge home to Texas with a surprising and offensive proposal for Sam Houston. Santa Anna said if Texas agreed to accept Mexican sovereignty, Mexico would allow Texas to return to the Mexican union with control over her own internal affairs.[209]

Santa Anna's proposal was intended for Texas and British diplomats. He thought the offer might appeal to the British diplomats negotiating a peace treaty between Texas and Mexico. Santa Anna knew Britain wanted to extend her political and economic influence in Mexico and Texas. He also believed the idea of reuniting the two nations under Mexican rule would be attractive to the British. In addition, Santa Anna believed Texas was in a grave situation. If the Texans rejected his terms, Mexico could invade and conquer its former province.

Great Britain opposed annexation and even considered military intervention to stop the United States from acquiring Texas. The British government did not want to add Texas to their empire, but they hoped to prevent America's westward expansion, obtain commercial advantages from Texas trade, impede the U.S. tariff system, and eliminate slavery.[210]

The British enthusiastically endorsed Santa Anna's proposal. Great Britain's minister to Mexico, Richard Packenham,[211] advised his government that Texas was so weak that the peace negotiations were useless. Packenham concluded Texas was destined to return as a reconquered Mexican territory. The British thought the Mexican terms were a reasonable alternative to war. Britain's *chargé d'affaires* in Texas, Charles Elliot,[212] encouraged Houston to accept Santa Anna's conditions and promised Britain would negotiate terms that were "honorable and durable." In addition to the Mexican conditions, the British government also required Texas to abolish slavery.

President Houston replied to Mexico's terms. He sent his response in a confidential letter from Judge Robinson to Santa Anna. Houston was evasive about unification and quiet on abolition. Instead, the Texas president proposed an armistice during which the parties could discuss the terms.

In June of 1843, President Houston unilaterally declared a truce with Mexico, and the Mexicans agreed to the provisions in July. Later in the year, Houston sent George Hockley[213] and Samuel M. Williams[214] to represent Texas at the British-sponsored negotiations in Matamoros, Mexico. The discussions were a waste of time because Houston refused to return Texas to Mexican rule and Santa Anna continued his threats to raid and attack Texas.[215] None of the parties expected to accomplish much from the negotiations. Each country considered the talks as an opportunity to proclaim and promote their own goals. The British government needed to protect their investments in Mexico, cultivate Texas as a cotton supplier, and abolish slavery in the

Republic. Santa Anna's government needed to postpone any agreement until it suppressed the revolution in Yucatán and could threaten Texas with an invasion. President Houston's administration wanted to preserve Texas' independence and was prepared to align with Great Britain in order to protect the Republic's sovereignty. Houston even allowed or encouraged abolition efforts to begin in Galveston.

The United States declined to send representatives to the peace discussions. Earlier in 1843, the U.S. Senate rejected a commercial treaty with Texas because of instability along the Texas border. President Houston was frustrated with America's lack of interest and support and ordered the Texas *chargé d'affaires* in Washington, Isaac van Zandt, to stop trying to obtain American aid and end annexation discussions. In November of 1843, Houston angrily referred to the United States as an "enemy" and Great Britain as a "friend."[216]

The United States had other diplomatic issues to resolve in 1843. The Tyler administration sent executive agent Duff Green[217] to Europe to gather intelligence and organize talks with Great Britain about Oregon. Green worked with the American minister to France, Lewis Cass,[218] to defeat efforts by major European powers to end the maritime slave trade. Green heard rumors about British abolitionist schemes in Texas including providing funds to the Republic to free slaves and negotiating a peace treaty between the Republic and Mexico. In July 1843, Green told Secretary of State Abel Upshur[219] about a "loan plot" by American abolitionists and the British government to send money to Texas as compensation for the emancipation of its slaves. The U.S. government asked Minister Edward Everett[220] to verify the authenticity of these confidential reports about abolition activities in Texas. Everett's investigations determined the British were only "weakly" interested in ending slavery in Texas. This contradicted Secretary of State Upshur's belief that Great Britain was "manipulating" Texas. Green's report disturbed Tyler and he asked the U.S. minister to Mexico, Waddy Thompson,[221] to verify the rumors.

After the U.S. Senate ratified the Webster-Ashburton Treaty[222] in August of 1843, which settled border disputes with British North America, Tyler made the annexation of Texas his "top priority."[223] The administration authorized Thomas W. Gilmer[224] of Virginia to explain the benefits of acquiring Texas to the American voters. Gilmer said Texas' annexation would resolve the "North-South conflict"[225] and produce an "economic windfall" for business. His lobbying efforts avoided a national discussion of slavery, allowed the states to deal individually with bondage, and removed slavery from annexation considerations. Tyler contended annexation of Texas would increase domestic tranquility and improve national security while excluding slavery from annexation discussions.[226]

Tyler Reopens Annexation Talks

John Tyler
(Library of Congress)

As 1843 ended, U.S. Secretary of State Abel Upshur asked Isaac Van Zandt about the current state of affairs in the Republic of Texas. Upshur wanted to verify the rumors that Texas and England had reached an agreement on the emancipation of the slaves. The secretary also asked if Texas was earnestly considering an alliance with "America's distrusted old enemy", Great Britain. After Van Zandt confirmed the stories, Upshur told the *charge d'affaires* that he and President Tyler wanted to reopen annexation negotiations.[227]

Abel P. Upshur
(Library of Congress)

Upshur was more concerned about the disadvantages from an emancipated Texas than any benefits from annexation. He was afraid slaves would escape from the South to freedom in Texas and start a border war with the South. He was concerned Britain would develop Texas into a cotton empire and harm the U.S. economy. Upshur believed this would devastate Southern agriculture, damage Northern cotton shipments, and decrease markets for American goods. In his alarming scenario, he predicted bankrupt Southern planters would free their slaves and end the slavery-based Southern planter society. He also thought free blacks would travel to northern cities to find work and the additional workers would result in labor and racial conflicts, riots, and death. Although Upshur insisted Texas reopen talks, Van Zandt told Upshur Houston ordered him, "to drop the matter while Texas pursued an alliance with Britain."[228]

Van Zandt wrote to Texas Secretary of State Anson Jones about Upshur's annexation overture. Van Zandt supported annexation and continued informal discussions with Upshur while waiting for Jones' instructions. Secretary Jones told Van Zandt that Texas' options were either an alliance with Great Britain and peace or annexation by the United States and war. Van Zandt asked Jones to reconsider Texas' position and "pursue the golden opportunity for annexation" because the chance "might never come again."[229]

James Pinckney Henderson
(Library of Congress)

Around ninety percent of Texans supported annexation. Texans, especially those from the South, did not want to become part of the British Empire and strongly opposed the British demands to emancipate slaves. In response to public opinion, the Texas Senate demanded the Houston administration provide the details of his discussions with Great Britain.[230]

Although Houston doubted the U.S. Senate would pass an annexation treaty, he realized he needed to appease the Republic's annexation advocates. The president sent annexation campaigner James Pinckney Henderson, who had negotiated trade deals and diplomatic recognition with Britain and France, to join Van Zandt in Washington to represent Texas in the annexation treaty negotiations. Houston outlined Texas' terms for annexation protection against a Mexican attack, annexation as a state and not a territory, retention of slavery, and assumption of the Republic's debts. Houston authorized exchanging Texas' public lands to meet his demands.

Henderson's appointment indicated the Texas government was still open to annexation. The announcement provided Mexico with the perfect excuse to leave the British orchestrated negotiations and to threaten to invade Texas. In the U.S. Congress, Henderson's appointment indicated the Tyler administration was reopening annexation discussions.[231]

Isaac Van Zandt
(Texas State Library and Archives Commission)

President Tyler selected Mississippi Senator Robert J. Walker[232] to manage the political phase of annexation. Walker was a promoter of American territorial expansion and an "effective backroom politician." In February 1844, Walker began a public relations campaign to convince Americans to support adding Texas to the United States.[233] Upshur and Van Zandt continued to work on a draft treaty to admit Texas as a territory. On February 28, 1844, they joined President Tyler and other Washington officials on a cruise on the Potomac River aboard the USS *Princeton*. The Navy invited the dignitaries to watch a demonstration of a new naval cannon. The gun exploded and killed Secretary Upshur, the Secretary of the Navy, and six others. Many others were harmed, but Tyler and Van Zandt escaped injury.[234]

After Henderson arrived in Washington, the two Texans continued to work on the draft treaty and waited while the U.S. government recovered from the tragedy. At the end of March, President Tyler appointed John C. Calhoun[235] as the new secretary of state. Secretary Calhoun believed the acquisition of Texas was an opportunity to expand slavery and enlarge the plantation culture.

Calhoun accepted Van Zandt and Upshur's draft. However, the new secretary of state could not legally guarantee military protection. He only offered a vague promise to position ground and naval forces "near the frontier to meet any emergencies." Henderson and Van Zandt worried the time it took to receive instructions from Texas would allow the Senate enough time to debate and perhaps reject the treaty. Under the present situation and without authorization from the Houston administration, they boldly signed the annexation treaty on April 12, 1844 on behalf of the Republic of Texas.

When the news of Henderson and Van Zandt's decision reached Texas, Secretary of State Jones wrote the diplomats that he and President Houston felt "great mortification and disappointment" about their actions concerning the treaty. Jones and Houston believed an independent Texas under British protection was much better than becoming a U.S. territory under a government unwilling to guarantee protection. They decided to conceal their concern and wait for the U.S. Senate to confirm or reject the treaty.[236]

On April 22, 1844, President Tyler submitted the annexation treaty to the U.S. Senate for review and ratification. Tyler cautioned the senators that, with British support, Texas could become a dangerous competitor with the United States and jeopardize American prosperity. Annexation opponents claimed the probability of war with Mexico outweighed any benefits. Tyler tried to gain Southern support by explaining how Texas would add a huge new slave territory to the United States and increase the power of plantation owners. Secretary of State Calhoun declared Texas would be "acquired in one way or another." Calhoun said the South would not stand by and allow Texas to come under the domain of Great Britain. If the Senate rejected the treaty, Calhoun warned the Southern states would secede and join with Texas in a new confederacy.[237]

The Senate debate began in May. Senator Thomas Hart Benton[238] led the opposition forces. The Missouri senator was concerned about the Texas debt, high risk of war with Mexico, threat of disunion, and his dislike of empire-building. After heated debate, the Senate rejected the annexation treaty 35-16 on June 8, 1844.

**James Knox Polk
(Mathew B. Brady)**

The Democratic Party refused to nominate Tyler and selected James K. Polk[239] as their presidential candidate. The Democrats added a plank to their platform supporting Texas annexation to please the southern members and another plank backing acquisition of the Oregon country to please western voters.[240] After the Senate rejection, Tyler and Calhoun tried to explain to Sam Houston and Anson Jones what had happened and convince them this was only a temporary setback. Tyler appointed Andrew Jackson Donelson,[241] Andrew Jackson's nephew and former private secretary, as the new *chargé d'affaires* to Texas. In addition to his personal and political ties to President Houston, Donelson was "clever, intelligent, coolheaded, and sensible."[242]

**Andrew Jackson Donelson
(Mathew B. Brady)**

When Donelson reached Texas, he met an angry president Sam Houston. Houston was disgusted with the annexation negotiations and favored independence if Mexico recognized the Republic of Texas. Donelson assured Houston annexation was still being considered and was the major issue in the presidential campaign. Donelson also told Houston Congress had developed a new strategy. Congress was considering plans to annex Texas by joint resolution, rather than by treaty.[243] Under this approach, annexation could pass with a simple majority rather than by a two-thirds vote of the Senate. Donelson claimed Polk's election would assure passage.[244]

England and France had worked for months to arrange Mexican recognition of Texas. In the "Diplomatic Act"[245] of 1844, Great Britain and France guaranteed peace at the Rio Grande. The British promised to go to war to prevent U.S. annexation, if Mexico would acknowledge the independence of Texas. The British said the Senate debate revealed how divided America was on annexation. However, the prospects of secession and slave uprisings encouraged Mexican officials. In addition, Santa Anna believed that with the large British investment in Mexico, he could refuse the British and French terms. In the summer of 1844, Mexico ended negotiations with Texas and declared war.[246]

After the talks failed, Britain decided to end their involvement in future negotiations. The British recognized going to war with the United States would destroy the markets for British goods, encourage Americans to develop domestic manufacturing, and decrease British imports. In October 1844, the British government informed Mexico they were ending mediation efforts. Mexico and Texas had to settle diplomatic disputes without foreign assistance.[247]

ALLEN'S ROLE IN ANNEXATION

Since his arrival in Clarksville, Ebenezer Allen had developed a reputation as a talented attorney and gained the attention of the Republic's founding fathers. In the last months of Houston's presidency, he introduced a new player to the annexation negotiations.

Sam Houston's Attorney General

By the fall of 1844, the annexation of Texas appeared to be dying or dead. In November 1844, President Houston selected Allen to fill the opening created when Houston appointed Attorney General George Whitfield Terrell[248] as *chargé d'affaires* to Europe.[249] The election of Anson Jones, Houston's secretary of state, as president in September 1844 created a temporary vacancy. In December 1844, Houston asked Allen to serve additionally as secretary of state *ad interim*.[250]

> APPOINTMENTS BY THE PRESIDENT.
>
> Wm. B. Ochiltree, Secretary of the Treasury.
> Ebenezer Allen, Attorney-General.
> Moses Johnson, Treasurer.
> James B. Shaw, Comptroller—re-appointed.
> Charles Mason, Auditor—re-appointed.
> S. Z. Hoyle, President's Private Secretary.
> The Departments of State and War and Marine have not yet been filled. The Hon. E. Allen will act as Secretary of State *ad interim*; and M. C. Hamilton, Esq., as Secretary of War & Marine *ad interim*.

Appointments by the President
(*The Northern Standard*)

The Clarksville community was delighted to learn of Allen's appointment and *The Northern Standard* newspaper praised the governor's choice:

> *Our townsman, Ebenezer Allen Esq. has been appointed Attorney General of the Republic. There is*

> *perhaps not a man in the country, whose acquirements and capacity would do more credit to the station. He will leave many here who appreciate highly his talents, his virtues and his amiability of deportment.*[251]

The paper printed the following notice assuring Clarksville residents Allen's appointment would not interrupt Allen and Todd's legal services.[252]

LAW NOTICE.
The copartnership existing between the subscribers, will continue as heretofore. All papers and documents connected with causes now pending, have been placed in the hands of W. S. Todd, to whom our clients are referred. Mr. Allen expects to attend all the Courts in the District as usual.
EBENEZER ALLEN,
WM. S. TODD.
Clarksville, Nov. 27. 1844.   no 3 3t.

Law Notice Ebenezer Allen and Wm. S. Todd
(The Northern Standard)

Allen left Clarksville and traveled to Austin[253] to begin his new assignment. His service under President Houston lasted less than a month.

President Anson Jones

Dr. Anson Jones
(Texas State Library and Archives Commission)

During the First Congress of the Republic, Anson Jones became interested in public issues and increasingly critical of congressional policies. He was elected as a representative to the Second Congress because of his opposition to the Texas Railroad, Navigation, and Banking Company.[254] As chairman of the Committee on Foreign Relations, he recommended withdrawing Texas' proposal for annexation to the United States. He was also chairman of the Committee on Privileges and Elections and the Committee on Ways and Means. He helped formulate legislation to regulate medical practice, advocated a uniform system of education, and supported the creation of an endowment for a university. At the end of his congressional term in June 1838, President Houston appointed Jones minister to the United States and authorized him to withdraw the annexation proposal.

Jones managed foreign relations to create options for the Republic. Dr. Jones encouraged European countries to recognize and establish trade relations with Texas. He believed these actions would persuade the United States to annex Texas or to make the Republic strong enough to be autonomous.[255]

After Mirabeau B. Lamar was elected president in 1838, he recalled Jones after annexation negotiations were suspended. Jones was selected to finish William H. Wharton's[256] term in the Senate. Senator Jones disparaged the fiscal policies of the Lamar administration and the Texan Santa Fe expedition.[257] Jones was chairman of the Committees on Foreign Relations and the Judiciary and was president *pro tem*[258] of the Senate during the Fifth Congress. In the spring of 1841, he returned to his medical practice in Brazoria. He turned down an offer to be a candidate for the vice presidency in the 1841 election.

After Sam Houston was reelected to the presidency, he chose Jones as his secretary of state. Houston and Jones worked to obtain an annexation offer from the United States and to gain Mexican recognition of Texas' independence. They wanted to receive simultaneously the U.S. annexation proposal and the Mexican recognition of independence. After obtaining the U.S. and Mexican proposals, the Texas government could decide which alternative to accept.

In September 1844, Texans elected Dr. Jones president. He made no campaign speeches and refused to state his position on annexation. Jones remained silent even after James K. Polk's election as president of the United States on a platform of "reannexation of Texas," and President John Tyler's proposal of annexation by joint resolution.[259]

Attorney General and Secretary of State

After Dr. Jones's election, he consulted with friends and other Texas politicians to select officers for his cabinet. He chose the following men Vice President - Kenneth L. Anderson, Secretary of State - Ashbel Smith,[260] Secretary of War and Marine - George W. Hill,[261] Secretary of the Treasury - William Beck Ochiltree,[262] and Land Commissioner - Thomas W. Ward.[263] For the position of Attorney General, Jones selected a lawyer from Red River County - Ebenezer Allen. Jones' cabinet served from about December 1844 until February 1846.

Several years later, President Jones described his prior knowledge of Mr. Allen. Jones wrote, "... when I called him to that station I was almost a stranger to him personally, having never seen him but once or twice, and knew nothing of his opinions on this [annexation] or scarcely any other subject. I approved him because he had the character of possessing great ability and honesty."[264]

After Jones organized his cabinet, France and England demanded Texas send a representative to their courts "with full powers to conclude any arrangement that might be necessary for the safety of the country." The governments asked Jones to send Secretary of State Ashbel Smith, who was "known and highly appreciated." President Jones agreed to their request and appointed Smith to represent the Republic of Texas. Jones knew he would need a person who was comparable to Smith, with "the utmost firmness and caution," to successfully manage affairs in Smith's absence. Jones' cabinet recommended Ebenezer Allen to replace Smith. Allen was regarded as "a man of excellent sense, high character, and of the best disposition in this matter."[265] In addition to his position as attorney general, Allen was "charged with the duties of secretary of state *ad interim*."[266]

While Jones was non-committal about annexation, Secretary Allen was strongly in favor of independence. Two months before his appointment he wrote to William Kennedy, the British consul at Galveston, about his position:

> *You are well aware of the fact that I have from the beginning been decidedly opposed to the Annexation of Texas to the United States. It is my first object to*

defeat, if possible, the consummation of this most obnoxious measure, so decidedly hostile, as I conceive it to be, and fraught with such evil consequences to the ultimate prosperity and high destiny of this Country. If I am successful in the accomplishment of this great result, I shall consider it the proudest period of my life.[267]

The Duff Green Misadventures

President Tyler appointed Duff Green as the United States consul at Galveston in 1844. In addition to his consular duties, Tyler gave Green the added responsibility of communicating with Mexican officials about the possibility of obtaining Texas, New Mexico, and California for the United States. Green tried to persuade the Texas Congress to pass a bill creating the Texas Land Company and the Del Norte Company. Green proposed these companies, supported by a Texas army and Indians from the United States, occupy and claim the northern provinces of Mexico for Texas. Green offered President Jones stock in the proposed companies if he would back the plan. When Jones refused, Green allegedly threatened to start a revolution and overthrow the Jones administration. On December 30, 1844, Jones gave Green his passport and expelled him from Texas as a consular official. Fortunately, the incident had little impact on the existing relations between Texas and the United States.[268]

Washington, Dec. 30th, 1844

To his Excellency, Anson Jones, President, &c., &c.

The undersigned, officers of the Government, understand that Gen. Duff Green, United States Consul for the port of Galveston, has grossly insulted your Excellency, the President of this Republic, by threats that should you, as Executive, not sign and approve certain bills which he already had, or intended to introduce into Congress, he would call a convention of the people and revolutionize the country.

We accordingly respectfully demand that the Hon. Secretary of State be instructed for with [sic] to issue to the aforesaid Gen. Duff Green a passport out of the limits of the Republic, allowing him the time necessary to carry the same into effect.

Eben Allen, Att'y Gen. and Secretary of State ad interim.

M. C. Hamilton, Acting Secretary of War and Marine.

James B. Shaw, Acting Secretary of Treasury.

Charles Mason, Auditor.

James B. Shaw, Comptroller.

Moses Johnson, Treasurer.

Dan J. Toler, Bureau Gen. Post-Office.

Thomas Western, Superintendent of Indian Affairs.[269]

Tyler's Joint Resolution Efforts

After his confrontational presidency, the Whig Party decided not to nominate John Tyler and selected Henry Clay[270] as their presidential candidate in the 1844 U.S. election. The country chose Democrat James Knox Polk over Clay as the new president. In the final months of his administration, President Tyler continued his efforts to acquire

Texas. In his annual address to Congress on December 4, he declared that Polk's victory was a mandate for Texas annexation. Tyler recommended Congress employ a joint resolution procedure by which simple majorities in each House could ratify his suggested treaty. This method would avoid the constitutional requirement of a two-thirds majority in the Senate. By introducing the House of Representatives into the debate, Tyler advanced his acquisition agenda because the pro-annexation Democratic Party had nearly a two to one majority in the House.[271]

Problems increased when the Tyler administration resubmitted the same treaty, previously defeated by the Senate in June 1844, in a House-sponsored bill.[272] During their discussions about the treaty, representatives wondered if the Constitution allowed both houses of Congress to authorize the admission of Texas as a territory instead of a state. Even if the House approved annexation, the Senate would be required to ratify a treaty covering territorial boundaries, property affairs (including slave property), debts, and public lands. Northern Democrats in the House were uncomfortable about adding $10 million in Texas debt to U.S. liabilities. They hated the land speculators, who bought low-priced Texas bonds and now lobbied Congress to pass the House version of the annexation bill. The disagreements between northern and southern Democrats forced the House Democrats to turn over management of the treaty initiative to the southern Whigs.[273]

Whig party representatives from Tennessee and Georgia introduced new annexation legislation in the House on January 13, 1845. Their scheme was designed to strengthen the power of slaveholding states by admitting Texas as a slave state. Under the Whig legislation, Texas would retain all its public lands and its "bonded debt accrued since 1836." The proposal assigned the U.S. government with the responsibility for resolving the disputed Texas-Mexico boundary.[274]

Settling the border issue was important because moving the border from the Nueces River to the Rio Grande River would greatly increase the size of the new state. The Whig version also changed the options for creating new states out of the territory. The Tyler-Calhoun treaty permitted Texas to form four states from the annexed lands of which three would probably be slave states. The House plan allowed the State of Texas to form five slave states. With support from northern and southern Democrats and nearly half of the Southern Whigs, the House approved the revised Texas annexation treaty 120–98 on January 25, 1845.[275]

In early February 1845, the Senate began debate on the House version of the treaty. However, approval of the new agreement was unlikely because the pro-annexation senators did not have the necessary number of votes. Passing the treaty required all the Senate Democrats and at least three Whigs to vote for the proposal.[276]

As the discussion continued in the Senate, annexation supporters gained a surprising ally. Anti-annexation Senator Thomas Hart Benton of Missouri was the only Southern Democrat to vote against the Tyler-Texas measure in June 1844. Earlier, Benton proposed dividing Texas into two states – "slave-soil" and "free-soil" states. As support for annexation grew in Missouri, Benton removed his requirement for a free and a slave state in Texas. Benton recommended a panel of five bipartisan commissioners settle the border dispute between Texas and Mexico.[277]

President-elect Polk hoped the annexation of Texas would be completed before his inauguration on March 4, 1845, which was the day when the Congressional session ended. When Polk reached Washington, he found the Senate deadlocked over annexation legislation. Polk urged Senate Democrats to unite under a resolution including Benton's revisions. He asked supporters of the amended plans to pass the legislation and send it to him for his signature. In separate talks with the two factions, Polk gave each side the "impression he would administer their [respective] policy." Polk's political maneuvering convinced Northern Democratic senators to approve the senate-modified bill.[278]

On February 27, 1845, the Senate voted 27–25 to admit Texas. All twenty-four Democrats and three southern Whigs approved the measure. The next day, the Democrat-controlled House of Representatives passed the Senate version of the annexation bill.[279]

The joint resolution reached President Tyler three days before the end of his term. Tyler met with Secretary of State Calhoun, who advised him to take "immediate action" and call a cabinet meeting. His cabinet members backed the House version. Tyler directed Calhoun to discuss the situation with Polk, but the president-elect refused to "express any opinion or make any suggestion."[280] President Tyler signed the joint resolution on March 1, 1845.[281] [Please see "Joint Resolution for Annexing Texas to the United States" in the Appendix.]

Developments in Washington

During this critical period of Texan-American relations, Charles H. Raymond[282] kept Allen informed of developments in Washington. After Isaac Van Zandt resigned his post in the Houston administration, Secretary of State Anson Jones appointed Raymond to serve as *chargé d'affaires* to the United States. During the annexation debates in Congress, Raymond sent reports on the developments in Washington. His presence in the U.S. capital allowed him to inform Secretary of State Allen on the progress of annexation in the House and Senate.[283]

On January 27, 1845, Raymond wrote to Allen about the passage of the House resolution outlining the terms under which the Union would admit Texas. Mr. Raymond thought the Senate would pass the measure by a small majority. He enthusiastically declared, "The door will thus be opened for our admission into this great and glorious confederacy of states, and it will remain for Texas to say whether she will become a state of this Union, and upon what terms and conditions. If we but let the slavery compromise stand as the joint resolution leaves it, I am well satisfied that the Congress which convenes at this capital will agree [to] almost any terms we may name."[284]

Raymond's enthusiasm was misplaced, and he informed Allen on February 6 that the Senate committee on foreign relations had reported unfavorably on the House resolution on annexation. The committee recommended the "whole subject be laid on the table." He wrote, Senator Benton had withdrawn his annexation resolution and offered a substitute version. Raymond thought three-fifths of the Senate might approve the treaty with Benton's modifications.

On February 21, Raymond sent Allen a progress report on the annexation proceedings. He said the Democratic senators were "solid for the annexation resolution" thanks to efforts by Polk and other party leaders. Benton was finally "disposed to yield his views" to those supported by most of his party. Polk was anxious to have Congress pass the measure before it adjourned, and he was inaugurated. Raymond said in the *London Times* and *Harve Journal*, England made overtures to France to "unite with her with her in measures to prevent the annexation of Texas to the United States."[285]

By the end of February, Raymond was able to announce, "The door is at length opened for the admission of Texas into this Union." After Congress approved the joint resolution on March 1, 1845, Raymond sent Allen a copy.[286]

TEXAS CONSIDERS HER OPTIONS

Donelson's Annexation Mission

After helping James K. Polk win at the May 1844 Democratic National Convention, President John Tyler appointed Andrew Jackson Donelson to represent the United States in the Republic of Texas.[287] In December 1844, *chargé d'affaires* Donelson was concerned about the prospect of annexation. There were rumors the British had obtained Mexican recognition of Texas and proposed a liberal commercial treaty. Galveston residents believed if Mexico did not recognize Texas and the United States did not annex the nation, British *chargé d'affaires* Charles Elliot and his French colleague Alphonse de Saligny[288] would guarantee Texas' independence. Donelson was uncomfortable dealing with the sentiment and opinion of the Texans. Many Texas newspapers were angry about the terms offered by the United States. The chief government publication opposed annexation. The actions by the U.S. government had shifted Texas public opinion from annexation to independence and favorable commercial terms with the English.[289]

During the Congressional debates, Secretary Allen wrote to *chargé d'affaires* Donelson cautioning him about how Texas officials and citizens would respond to a "vague" treaty lacking a "definite, tangible, and eligible process" to achieve annexation:

> *Mr. Allen to Mr. Donelson*
>
> *President [Jones] directs me to acknowledge, meets his entire approbation; and was conceived in terms corresponding with the existing relations and the state and progress of the negotiations between the two governments, touching that subject. Should the present session of the Federal Congress pass by without fixing upon some definite, tangible, and eligible mode for carrying into effect the projected scheme for annexation, it is highly probably [sic] that the people*

and Government of Texas, yielding to the natural influence of disappointment, and to an irresistible [sic] reaction consequent upon procrastination; would feel compelled to consider their connexion [sic] with the measure dissolved.

The evidence required by Mr. Calhoun[290] touching the case before referred to will be furnished by this Department at its earliest possible convenience, and will, as I trust, be forwarded in season [time] for the necessary action of the Congress of the United States upon the subject, at the present session. In as much, however, as all the witnesses connsant of [agreed with] the necessary facts, reside some four hundred miles distant from our seat of Government, some time [sic] must necessarily elapse before the requisite testimony can be obtained and forwarded.

I am

Dear Sir

with sentiments of great esteem

Your obedient servant

E. Allen Attorney General of the Republic and Secty [Secretary] of State, ad interim[291]

After Congress ratified the joint resolution, Secretary of State Calhoun ordered *chargé d'affaires* Andrew Donelson to "proceed at once to Texas" and "urge speedy and prompt action." However, President-elect Polk suggested Donelson wait for further instructions before taking any actions.[292] After consulting with his cabinet, Polk instructed Secretary of State James Buchanan[293] to urge Donelson to use all his ability and energy to persuade Texas to accept the joint resolution "without qualifications."[294]

Donelson presented the United States proposal on March 31, 1845 to the Jones administration. On the evening he arrived, Donelson summarized the American proposition for then Secretary of State Ashbel Smith. Secretary Smith "seemed unprepared with views or opinions as to the course the President would adopt, and, if an inference had been drawn from the indefiniteness which marked his responses, it would have been most unfavorable."

The following day, Donelson introduced himself and the U.S. proposal to President Jones. Donelson was surprised to learn Secretary Smith had unexpectedly been given a leave of absence, and Attorney General Ebenezer Allen was serving in his place. He was more astonished when he discovered Allen also had a leave of absence. Donelson worried about "some settled scheme of delay, or of manoeuvre [sic] to promote the imputed project of a treaty with France and England." However, President Jones received him cordially and listened intently to his remarks. Previously, Jones favored convening Congress to decide to accept or reject the U.S. annexation proposal, but he now preferred to immediately hold a public election on the issue. If the voters approved annexation, Jones would call a convention to make the changes necessary for Texas' admission to the Union. Donelson was concerned about Jones' decision because the terms of the American proposal required the consent of the "existing government" in Texas and the approval of the U.S. Congress. Jones said, "the gravity of the subject required him not to act in haste: and that, although he had a decided opinion, he would dwell awhile on it, until he was aided by the advice of his cabinet."

Dr. Jones commented on his position on annexation in a memorandum written on February 19, 1850:

> *A party in the country have accused me of being opposed to annexation, basing the charge upon the assumed fact that the members of my Cabinet, and the other officers of the Government were opposed to it, and reflected my sentiments. As for the members of my*

> *Cabinet and the ministers sent abroad, there may have been some diversity of sentiment, individually, as was natural; and so far as the last class were concerned, I did not think it good policy to send a violent friend of annexation to Europe, any more than a violent friend of separate independence to the United States. When my Cabinet was first made up, the alternatives were not yet presented to the country; and I did not ask or know what their opinions would be upon an uncertain and unknown future event, any more than they themselves did, or that I knew what my own would be. The terms upon which annexation and independence would, severally, be offered, if offered at all, were unknown, and consequently no one [sic] could tell what opinion he would have upon a matter he knew nothing about, But after the offers were made, Mr. Allen, I believe, was the only member of my Cabinet who preferred independence over annexation ... * * * Col. William G. Cooke[295] I understood as having no very decided opinion either way * * * though both he and Mr. Allen were perfectly ready and willing to do all in their power in carrying out the will of the people.[296]*

After meeting with Jones, Donelson spoke to Ebenezer Allen and learned the secretary had a plan to prevent the Texas Congress from approving the American proposition. Allen argued that the matter was extra-constitutional,[297] and the executive branch could deal with it as well as the legislative. The *chargé* argued with Allen about the executive's power to act independently of Congress. Donelson indicated the joint resolution required the "assent of the existing government of Texas" before the annexation process could continue. Donelson believed the term "assent of the existing government" required approval from both the executive and the legislature. Donelson showed Allen a draft of a letter he had prepared for Jones' signature in response to the American joint resolution. He urged President Jones to assemble Congress as soon as possible and to work with the legislature "in whatever steps might be taken."[298] Eventually, Allen withdrew his objection and agreed to present the draft of Texas' reply to the American proposal to President Jones. However, Jones rejected the *chargé's* draft and said he wanted more time for reflection.[299]

In Tyler's last days at the White House, Donelson assured Allen the outgoing president would do all in his power to "guard the interests of Texas from injury." Tyler also confirmed that Mexican war threats could not persuade the United States to abandon annexation. Donelson said annexation was of a "mutual, equal, and vital benefit and safety to both Republics." He said Tyler expected Texas to "maintain her connection with the cause of annexation, so far at least as to consider it lost or abandoned, on account of the late action of the Senate."[300]

President Jones asked Allen to convince Donelson that Jones would not oppose or act negatively on annexation. However, Jones cautioned the result might depend on "causes" beyond his control because the "delay and apparent defeat" had decreased the "strength and ardor" for annexation in Texas.[301]

In a letter to Donelson on April 14, 1845, Allen acknowledged "the receipt of the note" of March 31 "transmitting the joint resolution recently adopted by the Congress." Donelson indicated the U.S. President thought the first and second sections of the resolution could serve as the basis of action." Allen responded:

> *The intimate acquaintance of Mr. Donelson with the institutions and organic law of this republic, renders it unnecessary for the undersigned to make known to him that the President [Anson Jones] is not clothed with the power either of accepting or rejecting the terms of the proposition presented by the note referred to. Under such circumstances, he is impelled by a sense of the high duties of his station, at so important a juncture, to call to his aid the assembled representatives of the people, and to avail himself of the benefit of their counsel and deliberations touching the important matters communicated by Mr. Donelson, to whom the*

undersigned has the honor of announcing, under the instructions of his Excellency, that he has determined at an early day to convene the Congress of the Republic, when he will lay before that honorable assembly, for its consideration and action, the note of the Hon. Mr. Donelson, and the joint resolution therewith transmitted.[302]

Two days later, Mr. Donelson replied to Allen's comments. Donelson said he expected Jones' response. He wrote: "The consummation of this important measure, changing, as it will, the organic law of the republic, necessarily requires the ratification and direction of the people, under such forms as the existing government may recommend."[303]

In an April 21, 1845 letter, Charles Elliot informed President Jones about the "successful progress of the preliminary treaty with Mexico." Elliot sent his "best regards to Mr. Allen."[304]

Donelson offered unsolicited advice on the "propriety of your [Jones] recommending to the people the election of delegates to a convention" in an April 29, 1845 letter. Donelson added "supposed" endorsements from "Mr. Allen and others of your friends have expressed a similar wish." This letter reveals how the United States government, through its agent Donelson, tried to orchestrate and influence the annexation process in Texas. Donelson wrote:

Feeling that you might have some embarrassment on the subject in consequence of the intimation to me through Mr. Allen, that it was necessary to convoke Congress in order to have an apportionment of the elective districts, I have taken the liberty to write this note; and to say to you that I trust you will not consider any declaration yet made to me as a reason for not adopting such suggestion, should it appear proper.

Donelson continued to lecture President Jones on the approval process:

The great object is to give effect to the public will

> *of Texas, and if this should be already sufficiently expressed to show that the proposals from the United States are satisfactory, all that remains is to resort to the earliest practicable [practical] mode of obtaining the requisite change in the Constitution and Government. For this purpose, the call you have made of Congress might be confined to that feature of the proposals which anticipate the consent of the existing Government of Texas; while at the same time, the Convention might be in session framing the new Constitution.*

The *chargé d'affaires* concluded his suggestions by apologizing for interfering in the process:

> *I feel a lively interest in your meeting the wish of the people of Texas; at the same time I am aware of the impropriety of my becoming to any extent the organ of these feelings. You will not, therefore, ascribe to me, in this communication, a departure from the line of conduct, which as a representative from the United States, should keep me from all interference with the independent judgment of the Government and people of Texas on the proposals for their admission into the Union.*[305]

Despite Donelson's desire not to interfere with the annexation process, the *chargé d'affaires* continued trying to manipulate the Republic's decisions.

Jones Calls for Annexation Convention

Compared with the thoughtful approach of government officials, the public thought the Jones administration was too cautious and too slow in response to the American government. Public support for annexation grew and animosity of Jones increased. He was burned in effigy, and threats were made to overthrow his government. However, Jones decided to remain silent until Charles Elliot returned from Mexico with the treaty of recognition.[306]

Citizens held enthusiastic annexation meetings throughout Texas.

County after county supported the terms offered by the United States and demanded prompt action by Congress or a convention. In a meeting at Brenham on April 11, 1845, participants voted unanimously for annexation. They recommended all the Texas counties elect representatives for a convention to ratify the U.S. joint resolution and form a state government. Secretary Allen advised Jones on the state's political situation and recommended calling a convention:

Galveston, 3d May 1845

Dear Sir, - I send you for inspection the enclosed note intended to be addressed to Mr. Donelson, if its contents should meet your approbation. It was prepared at his suggestion, and his reply will be, I think in all respects agreeable, or at least unobjectionable. General Houston [Sam Houston], who arrived in the "Bill" [Texas capital] this morning, says that the tone of the note corresponds with the course adopted during his administration: of its propriety, however, you can judge, and Mr. Eldridge will forward me a copy, which I can sign and transmit to Mr. Donelson.

Mr. Donelson has read to me his letter addressed to you on the subject of a convention, and requests me to express to you my sentiments on that subject. I have not, however, had time to examine the matter as fully as I could wish. There can be no doubt that a convention, framed upon a plan recommended by the Executive, would be as legal, satisfactory, and efficient as one formed upon a plan proposed by Congress.

If you think the measure a safe one, and not premature, I should be glad to see your proclamation issued recommending a convention to be assembled at as early a day as practicable, and presenting a basis whereby to regulate the election of deligates [sic].

I remain your friend and obedient servant,

Ebenezer Allen.

To His Excellency, Anson Jones.[307]

The following day, Allen warned "opponents of the Administration" were working to strengthen their "hostility to your administration." The secretary of state repeated his advice suggesting the President should call for a convention:

Galveston, 4th May 1845.

My Dear Sir, - From the signs now exhibited there can be but little doubt that the called session of Congress is intended to present a stormy scene. The opponents of the Administration do not intend to place it in your power to appear as the friend of that measure. They care not whether they place you in a false or true position, so that they can add strength and popularity to their determined hostility to your administration. Such is the conclusion to which I have been led by conversing with many, - some the pretended friends, others the fixed enemies, of your course; and of the latter I may say, of yourself. Between settled enmity and indifferent friends there is little to choose, except that the former generally take the lead, and the latter become tools. Unless I am greatly deceived, the members of Congress may be divided into two classes, viz.: the avowed, determined, irreconcilable foes to the Administration on the one hand, and inefficient, lukewarm, indifferent supporters, or rather apologists, on the other. The former will deal in denunciations, the later in regrets. Violence will be most likely to prevail, and what the result will be must depend upon the moder-

ation of the Opposition, rather than upon the moderation of pretended adherents. The facility with which those who ought to have sustained the Government, have not only yielded, but added to the unreasonable and factious excitement against it, - in many instances endeavoring, at least tacitly, to inflame the madness and increase the delusion of the masses, - shows how little justice is likely to be accorded to the Executive by the community under existing influences. Every mass meeting has been one of the Opposition.

Under such circumstances, it occurs most forcibly to my mind that the call of a convention, to be assembled under the advisory proclamation of the Executive, would not only neutralize and render harmless all the elements of opposition, and defeat the machinations of your enemies, but would even place you in such a position that they themselves, however loath, would be bound to sustain you, and to support your course and administration. Mr. Donelson is greatly in favor of such a call - so is Gov. Yell,[308] and the idea is universally satisfactory, so far as I can learn, and will be advocated by every paper in the country. Those who oppose it will be considered as opposed to annexation. I do not consider, however, that the measure of annexation is to be hastened or materially affected by the assembly of a convention. That body will be superior to Congress; it will deliberate upon the state of the Republic; it will submit the overture to the people; it will probably frame a new constitution, and by proper provisions fit it to become the organic law, whether annexation shall take place or not. I for one should be glad to see the Constitution renovated. I believe that a much better one than the present can be devised. Finally, I doubt not that the convention, thus assembled, would provide effectually against revolution, and take efficient mea-

sures for the continuance of the Government under the present Administration, until annexation shall be consummated, and the consequent changes follow in their course.

The plan for a convention might be, to have one delegate elected for each county, and one additional delegate for every two hundred voters - making the Convention judges of the qualifications of its members. The timely publication of your proclamation would prevent certain members of Congress from becoming members of the Convention, at which I, for one should rejoice.

It is because I confidently believe that the suggested course will place you at the head of the nation, by position and the concurrence of circumstances, as well as by election, that I have submitted to you my views recommending it. The armed, organized, and disciplined opposition to your Administration will thus be prostrated; and will be applauded and yourself sustained.

I beg you to accept these suggestions in the spirit which has produced the submission of them to your better judgment, from your obedient servant and friend,

Ebenezer Allen

To His Excellency, A. Jones.

P.S. - I think that Congress, when assembled, (in the absence of the call of a convention,) will assume conventional powers, and appeal to the people to sanction their usurpations and adopt their acts. A wise, but bold and decisive course by the Executive at this *crisis, in controlling the excitement, and turning the revolution, (for such it is,) to the permanent benefit of the nation, is what I desire to see successfully accomplished.*[309]

Jones did not need Allen's warnings because the president was aware of "the storm" and felt "its *blasts* all around me."[310]

Again, Mr. Donelson believed it was necessary to meddle in Texas affairs. He withdrew his advice about calling for a convention and urged Jones to wait for Congress to call the convention and thereby avoid the "score of discontent:"

GALVESTON, May 5th, 1845.

MY DEAR SIR,

I addressed you a private letter on the 29th ult. from Houston, in reference to the suggestion made by some of your friends, that it would be a judicious step for you to issue another proclamation, calling, on your own responsibility, a convention of the people for the purpose of hastening the decision of the annexation question. It was my object simply to assure you, if you – concurred in that suggestion, that the official declaration made to me need be no barrier to the execution of the suggestion. It is my duty, however, in the spirit of candor and friendship which dictated that letter, to say to you that I am not now so sure of the expediency of such a movement. Mixing, as I have done, pretty freely with the citizens of this place, I have perceived that there is much prejudice on the subject of the apportionment of the elective districts, and that there is a possibility of serious objection being made to any basis which the President alone, with the best intentions, might select. Under such circumstances, as you have called Congress, it would probably be the wiser course to await their action, and divide with them the responsibility of the plan which will be adopted. If you have not already issued this proclamation by the time you receive this, the doing so would gain only about a month in time – an object hardly sufficient to justify a risk on the score of discontent.

If you have acted, however, or are of the opinion that you had better call a convention in the course of June, as I stated before, let not any official declaration made to me be a barrier, one way or the other.

It is probable I may go to New Orleans with Gen. Houston, but I shall be at Washington a few days before the meeting of Congress; and in the mean time [sic] shall remain, with sentiments of great respect, your obedient servant,

A. J. DONELSON.

His Excellency, ANSON JONES, President of Texas.

P. S. – I have just discovered that I was under a wrong impression as to the contents of Mr. Allen's official note to me. Without referring to it, I had supposed, when I wrote you my private letter from that place, that he specified the propriety of calling Congress for the purpose of apportioning the representation to the Convention. But I see that it is not so. It was in verbal interviews that the idea was suggested, and hence it is said in my unofficial communications that this was a leading consideration in the call of Congress. But this is not material. What I said was only for your private consideration, and to show that I was sincerely anxious to see annexation accomplished in the most harmonious manner.

Yours, &c., A. J. D.

His Excellency, A. JONES, &c., &c [311]

Jones remarked, "Major Donelson's letter of 29th May *recommends* the call of a convention: this *revokes* that recommendation." Jones claimed Donelson's "correction" was based on influence from Sam Houston and his friends who "*denounced* it as revolutionary."[312]

On May 8, 1845, President Jones instructed Allen to issue a proclamation in which Jones recommended the citizens of Texas elect deputies for a convention to take "prompt and decisive action" on the United States Annexation proposal.[313]

Jones offered the people of Texas the alternative of peace and independence or annexation.[314] In the proclamation Jones recommended "to the citizens of Texas, that an election for 'Deputies' to a Convention be held in the different counties of the Republic on Wednesday the fourth day of June…" Jones suggested the number of deputies for each county could be delegated on the basis of the voters in the last election with each county having at least one deputy. Jones called for the deputies to meet on "The Fourth of July" next for "the purpose of considering the proposition for the annexation of Texas to the United States."[315]

A Proclamation
(Texas State Library and Archives Commission)

In early June, Allen informed Jones the public were unexcited about the prospects of peace with Mexico and believed the offer was "too late:"

New Washington,[316] 5th June 1845.

My Dear Sir, - I reached Houston on Sunday last, and soon after my arrival had a brief interview with Capt. Elliot, who was on his way to Washington

[Washington-on-the-Brazos] with the propositions from Mexico. I would have returned immediately with him to Washington, but he did not deem it necessary for me to do so, and I accordingly concluded to remain, thinking I might probably be as useful here as there. I was somewhat disappointed in ascertaining that his errand, although its import was understood in Houston, occasioned but little excitement there. The general impression, on learning the nature of the proposition whereof he was the bearer, was, "it is too late," accompanied in some instances with symptoms of regret. The election of delegates has come off since, and Swain[317] the anti-annexation delegate, has most probably been elected. The definite news or account of the election will, however, reach you in advance of this.

I am persuaded that some unaccredited and informal (perhaps self-constituted and unauthorized) agents, acting in pretended behalf of the United States, are endeavoring to take advantage of the crisis to hurry us into hostilities with Mexico. I hope that may be disappointed, and that in spite of their efforts we shall at least be able to preserve peace at present, if not the Republic.

The Bulletin, Picayune, and the Galveston News are exerting all their ingenuity, and concentrating all their bitterness in speculations and conjectures, and attacks upon the Texas President and Cabinet; but so far as my observation has been able to extend itself, as yet these attacks prove ineffectual. The Convention has been summoned, and the Administration is "rectus in curia."[318]

The Mexican propositions, as well as those from the United States, can safely and with all propriety now be laid before that body, and subsequently, with their approbation, submitted to the nation. Until the terms from Mexico shall have been definitely rejected, I cannot apprehend danger of attack from that quarter. In the mean time [sic] could any possible harm, disadvantage, or danger accrue from a proclaimed armistice, thereby securing temporary tranquility, until the important matters pending before the nation can be acted upon? Mr. Donelson passed in the steamboat today for Houston, but did not call here, leaving word, however, that he would be happy to see me at Houston to-morrow [sic]. Gen. Sherman[319] [Major General of the Texas Militia], who returned from Galveston, is going up to-morrow [sic] to see Mr. D. [Donelson], who, as Gen. S. [Sherman] says, approves of a military occupation forthwith of the territory west of the Nueces by Texas, but not [in his capacity] as Minister of the United States. I have only indirect news from Com. [Robert F.] Stockton,[320] who, in urging military operations on the part of Texas, seems to act through others, holding himself, in the mean time [sic], wisely aloof.

Under existing circumstances, I think that the policy of Texas should, for the present, be peaceful; and such a course, I trust, the nation will approve. Gen. [Sidney] Sherman has been strongly urged by the reckless agitators in this vicinity and at Galveston to call out the militia, and commence hostilities against Mexico, without regard to the approval or disapproval of the Executive. But I have no idea that he can be persuaded into so reckless a measure.

To secure peace, to submit all propositions affecting the interests of the nation to the calm consideration and decision of the people through their delegates, to restrain, if practicable, the current of events within the natural channel of causes and effects, until they shall produce their appropriate results in due time, is all that can be done by the Government. And then, whether the destiny of the nation shall be of weal or woe [good or bad], the Executive is free from censure.

I had come to the determination to proceed forwith [sic] to Washington with Major Donelson; but upon further reflection, have concluded to wait a few days longer, believing you would cause me to be informed if my presence were necessary.

With great respect, I remain your friend and obt. servant,

Eben. Allen

His Excellency, Anson Jones[321]

The representatives to the annexation convention met on July 4, 1845 to consider the joint annexation resolution from the United States Congress. Thomas Jefferson Rusk was elected president of the convention, and James H. Raymond was secretary. By a vote of fifty-five to one, the delegates approved the offer of annexation. Richard Bache of Galveston was the lone dissenter. Next, the convention prepared the Constitution of 1845 for the new state.[322]

President Jones informed President Polk "that the Deputies of the People of Texas assembled in Convention at the City of Austin on the 4th ... adopted on that day an ordinance expressing the acceptance and assent of the people to the proposals made by the government of the United States on the subject of the Annexation of Texas to the American Union."[323]

Jones called the Texas Congress to meet on June 16, 1845. He asked congress to choose between annexation or independence. The Texas Congress rejected the treaty with Mexico, approved the joint resolution of annexation, and passed motions censuring Jones.[324]

Allen sent Donelson a copy of the joint resolution adopted by both houses of the Congress of Texas on June 21 and approved by the President on June 23.

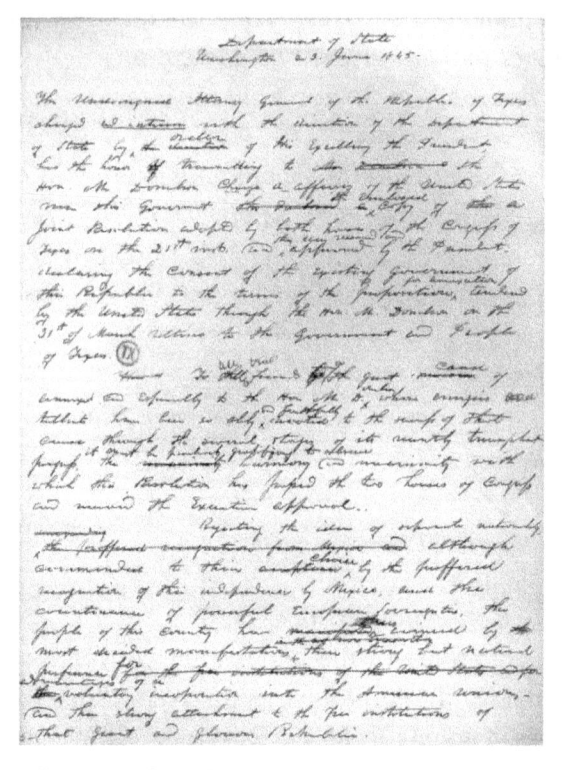

**Ebenezer Allen to Andrew Jackson Donelson June 23, 1845 - page 1
(Texas State Library and Archives Commission)**

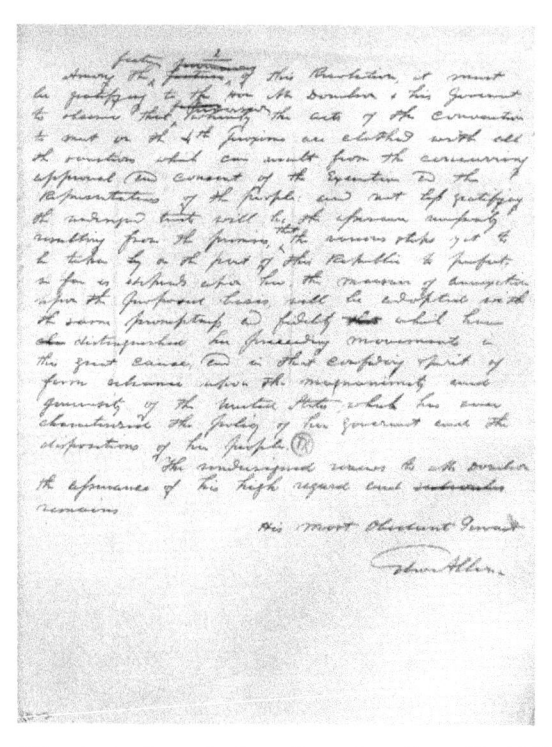

**Ebenezer Allen to Andrew Jackson Donelson June 23, 1845 - page 2
(Texas State Library and Archives Commission)**

Department of State

Washington 23. June 1845.

The undersigned Attorney General of the Republic of Texas charged ad interim with the direction of the Department of State by order of His Excellency the President, has the honor of transmitting to the Hon. Mr. Donelson Charge d Affaires of the United States this government the Enclosed copy of a Joint Resolution adopted by both houses of the Congress of Texas on the 21st inst. and this day received and approved by the President. Declaring the consent of the existing government of this Republic to the terms of the proposition for annexation, tendered by the United States through the Hon. Mr. Donelson on the 31st of March *ultimo to the Government and People of Texas.*

To all true friends of the great cause of annexation and especially to the Hon. Mr. Donelson, whose energies and talents have been so ably and faithfully devoted to the success of that process, it must be particularly gratifying to observe the harmony and unanimity with which the Resolution has passed thro [sic] the houses of Congress and received the Executive approval.

Rejecting the idea of separate nationality, although commanded to their choice by the proffered [offered] recognition of their independence by Mexico, and the countenance of powerful European sovereignties, the people of this country have thus evinced by most decided manifestations their strong but natural preference for the advantages of voluntary incorporation into the American union, and their strong attachment to the free institutions of that great and glorious Republic.

Among the features of this Resolution, it must be gratifying to the Hon. Mr. Donelson and his Government to observe that provision whereby the acts of the Convention to meet on the 4th proximo [the next month] are clothed with all the sanctions which can result from the concurring approval and consent of the Executive and the Representatives of the people. And not less gratifying the undersigned trusts will be the assurance expressly resulting from the proviso that the various steps yet to be taken on the part of the Republic to perfect [complete], so far as [it] expands upon her, the measure of annexation upon the proposed basis, will be adopted with the same promptness and fidelity which has distinguished her preceding movements in this great cause, and in that confiding spirit of firm reliance upon the magnanimity and generosity of the United States, which has ever characterized the policy of the Government and the disposition of the people.

The undersigned renews to Mr. Donelson the assurance of his high regard and remains

His most obedient servant

Ebenezer Allen[325]

In a letter of September 6, 1845, William D. Lee,[326] who was acting *chargé d'affaires* to the United States from Texas, wrote about the proceedings in Washington, DC. Under the assumption that Texas was now a member of the Union, the President refused to recognize Lee as a representative of a foreign government. The question of Texas statehood was relevant in President Polk's decision to send troops to Texas. Lee promised to send Allen news of Polk's decision on recognizing him.[327]

Lee sent Jones a status report on Polk's viewpoint on Texas' position on September 8, 1845. Lee explained why President Polk declined to accept him as a diplomatic agent. If the president recognized Lee, it would give "new weapons" to the "smothered Opposition" and acknowledge Texas as a "separate nationality" and "reanimate the Opposition." Lee sent copies of his correspondence with U.S. Secretary of State Buchanan to Secretary of State Allen.[328]

The new state constitution, prepared at the convention, was ratified by popular vote in October 1845 and accepted by the United States Congress on December 29, 1845, the date of Texas's legal entry into the Union.[329]

The Texas secretary of state posted the following letter on November 14:

Galveston, November 14th, 1845

My Dear Sir, - Since my arrival here the enclosed despatches [sic] have come to hand. That from Mr.

[William H.] Daingerfield [330] *I have replied to in a brief note, reiterating the instructions for his return, and that he bring along with him the archives of his legation, as well as those at London and Paris. It is most probable, however, that he will have received and acted upon Mr. [Ashbel] Smith's letter long before mine shall have reached him.*

Of the reasons assigned in Mr. [James] Buchanan's note for the detention of the despatch [sic] at the city of Washington you will judge. Perhaps, instead of complaining of the delay of that document, we should rather be thankful that Mr. Buchanan was so kind as to send it at all. Of course the letter addressed to Mr. [David S.] Kaufman[331] *as "agent of Texas, &c., &c.," by Mr. [William L.] Marcy,*[332] *requires no reply, and in common with other measures adopted by Mr. Polk and his Cabinet in relation to the Government of this Republic, demands no present comment.*

Since my arrival at Galveston, I have done all in my power to cause the collection of the revenue at Corpus Christi to be enforced. I am told that another secret agent from Mr. [Robert J.] Walker has arrived to-day. As to the object of his mission, I, as yet, know nothing.

Ebenezer Allen

His Excellency, Anson Jones[333]

IMMEDIATE AND AGGRESSIVE PROTECTION

The annexation procedure was further complicated by the threat of invasion by Mexico. As a new state, the United States was required to provide security from attacks by other countries and Indians. Did Texas ask for this protection or did the United States provide it to further its own territorial expansion goals?

Texas at Peace with the World

After Mexico recognized Texas as an independent nation, President Jones believed there was no need for U.S. protection. However, Donelson continued to try to manipulate Texas' actions. In association with the annexation process, groups in Texas and the United States formulated plans for the new state's defense. Many Texans were concerned Mexico might attack the new state, although outgoing President Anson Jones did not share these fears. He declared, "I have ever been an advocate of *peace*, and opposed to war as long as it could be avoided." When Jones assembled Congress in 1845 "to act upon the propositions of the United States, I [he] was enabled to announce to them the gratifying fact that *'Texas was at peace with all the world,'* Indians, and every body [sic] else; and it was the first time for ten years that this had been the case."[334]

Stockton and Sherman's Intrigue

Jones' position did not fit with Polk's plans to seize Mexican lands. Polk was interested in annexing Texas and provoking Mexico into war. To encourage a military response from Mexico, Polk ordered Commodore Robert F. Stockton to move his fleet to Galveston and stay there long enough to "make himself [sic] acquainted with the dispositions of the people of Texas toward the United States and Mexico." Stockton's taskforce arrived in May 1845, and the commodore sent an agent ashore to assess the residents' political attitude. When the agent reported that seven-eighths of the people favored annexation, Stockton sent an urgent message to Navy Secretary George

Bancroft warning the Mexicans were planning to "occupy valuable land on the Texan bank." Stockton believed President Jones "could not be trusted" and boldly decided to "take matters in his own hands."

Stockton contacted Major General Sidney Sherman, the Texas adjutant general, and Sherman raised a three-thousand-man army. Stockton made plans to "supply them in a private way with provisions & ammunition." Donelson was alarmed when he learned about Stockton's actions. He wrote to Secretary of State James Buchanan discarding Stockton's fears of a Mexican invasion. Despite Donelson's protests, Stockton continued his efforts to instigate hostilities between Texas and Mexico. President Jones could not stop General Sherman from openly promoting an attack by his forces, with the support of Stockton's fleet, on the Mexican town of Matamoros. Then Stockton revealed President Polk was interested in inciting hostilities.

The issue was resolved when Charles Eliot returned from Mexico City with an offer of recognition from the Mexican government provided Texas would never join any other country. The offer ended Texas' fears that Mexico might invade the state and allowed the people to choose between two options: accept recognition by Mexico or annexation to the United States.[335]

After Mexico recognized Texas as an independent nation, President Jones believed there was no need for U. S. protection. However, *chargé d'affaires* Donelson pressured Texas to ask for military intervention to guard against invasion by Mexico. President Jones wrote: "Texas never actually needed the protection" and the protection "was all a trick." Jones complained: "Major Donelson was always 'boring' me to ask for protection, protection, protection! (and conjuring up stories of Mexicans coming,) and I always laughed at him and the idea." Because Jones refused to cooperate with the American government's wishes and aspirations, Donelson sought more willing allies in the state. Donelson turned to Secretary of State Allen for support. The men met in Galveston in May 1845 and Donelson convinced Allen to write a letter asking for help.[336]

Jones believed that Donelson was once again interfering in the Republic's affairs. Jones recalled, "In 1845, when Major Donelson met Mr. E. Allen, the Secretary of State at Galveston, and over persuaded him to ask for protection, Mexico had ceased even her threats. The Preliminary Treaty had been negotiated, and Mexico had thereby acknowledged the independence of Texas..."[337]

In May 1845 Donelson sent the following letter to Jones:

Galveston, May 2, 1845.

Dear Sir, - I send you the correspondence with Gen. Almonte,[338] *and late [recent] accounts from Mexico, as the basis of the suggestion from Mr. Allen respecting the obligation of the United States to protect the western frontier of Texas in case of invasion.*

If you sanction the letter from Mr. Allen, I shall make it the basis of an immediate application to the President of the United States, who, I doubt not, will order the troops, as soon as Congress accepts the terms submitted by me, or leave a provisional power in my hands to convey the order as soon as the exigency arises.

I am very truly your obedient servant,

A. J. Donelson

His Excellency, A. Jones[339]

President Jones said the letter showed "that the protection ... was sought by the Government of the United States." However, Donelson attributed his letter to suggestions made by Secretary of State Allen. Jones "yielded a reluctant assent" blaming "the excitement at the time" and his "embarrassments."[340] He added, "Mr. Allen, too, had compromitted [compromised] me, actuated [motivated], no doubt, by the fact of my embarrassments."[341]

Jones finally yielded to Donelson's "encumbering us with help." The president notified the U.S. envoy "he might give us as much protection as he pleased." Therefore, as Jones recalled, "he brought down an army and a navy upon us, when there was a hostile foot ... in Texas; not to *protect* Texas, * * * but insure a *collision* with Mexico."[342]

In a February 1, 1849 memorandum, Jones wrote he refused to allow American military actions and said that if the United States wanted a war with Mexico, they should let their Congress decide.[343] Jones reiterated he "would not manufacture a war to please Mr. Polk." "The *advocate for peace* for ten years, I naturally turned with disgust and abhorrence from a proposition of Mr. Polk's through Com. S__n [*Commodore Stockton*], that I should manufacture a war for the United States:"

> *But I had no direct hand in bringing that war about. I made peace between Texas and Mexico and in good faith observed it. I resisted all importunities [requests] to manufacture a war for the United States.*[344]

President Jones' critics blamed him for manufacturing the Mexican War. Jones was anxious to prove his innocence of accusations and requested Ebenezer Allen to send a formal request to the *chargé d'affaires* asking the United States for financial help and military protection from a possible Mexican attack. Eventually, Donelson's persistence wore down Jones, and Allen wrote to Donelson reminding him Mexico still claimed Texas. The Mexican government threatened "belligerent measures" against Texas, England, and France to "maintain this claim." These warnings suggested Texas should expect a new Mexican invasion. Under these circumstances, Allen asked "for the United States to extend its protection to this republic:"

> *Mr. Allen to Mr. Donelson*
>
> DEPARTMENT OF STATE,
>
> *Washington, Texas, May 19, 1845.*
>
> *The undersigned, attorney general of the republic [sic] of Texas, charged ad interim with the direction of the Department of State, respectfully invites the atten-*

tion of the Hon. Mr. Donelson, minister chargé d'affaires of the United States near this government, to the following considerations respecting the interests of the two countries, whether viewed in the existing attitude of their mutual relations, or in that of their probable and prospective connections.

It cannot have escaped the notice of the Hon. Mr. Donelson that, from the tenor of the late communication of General Almonte to the President of the United States, when demanding his passports as minister plenipotentiary and envoy extraordinary of the government of Mexico, Texas is still claimed by the latter as one of its departments, and that belligerent measures are threatened to maintain this claim. Also, that from the newspaper accounts of the termination of all diplomatic intercourse with the American minister at Mexico, the same belligerent attitude is manifested by a circular alleged to have been addressed to the representatives of England and France at that court.

From the tone of these manifestations, a new invasion of the territory of Texas may reasonably be apprehended, if the proposals lately received from the United States, for the annexation of Texas to the federal Union, should be accepted by Texans; of which result the sure indications of the popular will exhibited from the various portions of the republic, present to the mind an assurance so strong as to challenge conviction, and leave scarcely a possible room for doubt.

For the reasons suggested, the undersigned deems it his duty respectfully to inquire of Mr. Donelson whether, under such circumstances, calculated to excite the reasonable apprehensions of the people of Texas, and especially to disturb the tranquillity of the settlements along her western frontiers, it would not be alike proper and consistent for the United States to extend its protection to this republic.

The people of Texas would regard the presence of the requisite force on their frontiers in no other light than as an act of justice and friendship properly accorded during the pendency of the measures in progress for annexation, and as an indication of the aid justly due them in the completion of the constitutional steps yet necessary to their admission into the Union.

The performance of the conditions required by the United States, of Texas, in acting upon the terms of the overture for annexation, necessarily subjects the people of this republic [sic] to very onerous expenses, the burden of which operates with for greater severity in consequence of the nonpayment [sic] of the sums due to this government from the United States, to claims arising in the cases of Snively[345] and the collectoral district of Red river [sic].

The undersigned cannot for a moment entertain the belief that the United States will require that Texas shall alone sustain those burdens, and especially, in the event of a renewal of the war by Mexico, that this republic [sic] will be expected to bear exclusively its burdens, since, in reality, such a war would be hastened and occasioned by the acts and aimed at the interests no less of the United States than of Texas.

To this subject, the undersigned has, by the direction of the President, solicited the attention of the Hon. Mr. Donelson; and, has been authorized by him to say, that, in case of the anticipated emergency, the passage of United States troops through the Texan territory, to its westerly frontier, will be welcomed and facilitated by the constituted authorities, as well as by the people of this country.

The undersigned renews to Mr. Donelson, the assurances of his distinguished consideration and regard, and remains his most obedient servant,

EBEN'R ALLEN[346]

Donelson answered Allen's May 19 letter with promises of United States security for Texas. Donelson had "not a doubt" that President Polk would provide "full protection against any invasion." The *chargé d'affaires* informed Allen that there was "a considerable force concentrated" on the U.S. – Texas border and the naval force in the Gulf of Mexico had been increased. Donelson wrote that if Texas joined the United States, the land and naval forces "can be readily brought to act in her defense:"

Mr. Donelson to Mr. Allen

LEGATION OF THE UNITED STATES

New Orleans, May 24, 1845.

The undersigned changé d'affaires of the United States, has had the honor to receive the note of the Hon. Mr. Allen, attorney general of the republic [sic] of Texas, charged ad interim, with the direction of the Department of State, dated the 19th instant, in which he states the considerations upon which he thinks it proper that Texas should receive the protection of the United States, if Mexico carries into effect her hostile declarations in consequence of the acceptance by Texas of the proposals submitted by the United States for her admission as one of the States of the Union.

In reply to this note, a copy of which has been forwarded to the Department of State at Washington city, the undersigned takes pleasure in saying that he has not a doubt the requisite instructions will be immediately issued by the President of the United States, securing to the western frontier of Texas full protection against any invasion that may be threatened or attempted by Mexico, under the circumstances anticipated. There is already a considerable force concentrated on the portion of the frontier of the United States adjacent to the territory of Texas, and also an increase in the naval force in the Gulf of Mexico. In the event of the renewal of the war against Texas, on account of her determination to adopt the terms of union, this force can be readily brought to act in her defense, and the undersigned doubts not it will be so ordered to act, if the exigency arises so reasonably anticipated by the Hon. Mr. Allen.

The undersigned admits the justice of the remarks made by the Hon. Mr. Allen, in relation to the burdens which will be thrown upon Texas by the steps which will be necessary to enable her to give the consent of the existing government to the proposals from the United States, and to consummate the requisite changes in her form of government.

Under nearly similar circumstances, the United States have borne the expenses incurred by their Territories when forming State governments, and the undersigned doubts not that the same liberality will be extended to Texas.

In respect to the claims arising in the cases of Snively[347] and the revenue district on Red river [sic], which were recommended for payment by the President to the last Congress of the United States, but for which no appropriation was made, the undersigned doubts not that the provision demanded by justice will be made by the next Congress. The Hon. Mr. Allen is aware of the circumstances which often prevent action on claims in time to bring them within the provisions of law, and secure their payment by the proper accounting officers, even when they have been favorably reported upon by the appropriate committees of Congress.

But concerning these claims and the extraordinary expenses to be incurred by Texas in an extra session of Congress and a convention, and also the other inconveniences to which she may be subjected by the acceptance of the proposals for her admission into the Union, the undersigned will address another communication to the Hon. Mr. Allen, by which he hopes to suggest a mode for settling them satisfactorily to Texas.

In the mean time [sic], he has the honor to renew to Mr. Allen assurances of the great regard with which he remains his obedient servant,

J. Donelson.

Hon. EBENEZER ALLEN, *Attorney General, &c. &c. &c.*[348]

On June 1, 1845, Donelson wrote President Jones about "the protection expected by you for Texas after she accepts the terms of union proposed to her." Donelson's letter included his reply to Allen's stipulation of protection as a condition for annexation. Jones said he asked for protection after a "rejection of annexation in 1844." However, his request was for "prospective and contingent protection, - not the aggressive protection sent." Jones referred to his June 4 "proclamation, which declared "Texas [was] at peace with Mexico."[349]

Various people tried to blame the Mexican War on Dr. Jones and, following statehood, he tried to answer these accusations. Jones wanted to distance himself from provoking the war and on February 2, 1850 he summarized his position in a memorandum:

> *In conclusion, therefore, of what I have to leave on record, (now,) in justice to myself and the integrity of history in regard to my own administration, and that of Mr. Polk, of two Governments now merged in one by our immediate instrumentality, I am bound to say, the war between the United States and Mexico grew directly out of annexation; that it was the "forgone conclusion" of Mr. Polk when he came into office, to have that war with Mexico; that, failing in his most cherished scheme of inducing me to take the responsibility of provoking and bringing it about, he blundered into it by other means, and was finally very glad to blunder out of it, as he did.*[350]

On February 17, 1852, former president Jones responded to Donelson's claim that the Texas president directed Allen to talk with Sam Houston about defeating annexation. Jones denied sending Ebenezer Allen to General Houston or others to convince them to join him in thwarting annexation.

Additionally, he challenged newspaper reports which misrepresented actions taken by his administration:

> *I have just seen a letter written by Gen. Duff Green of Washington city, to Mr. A. J. Donelson, editor of the "Union," and published in the "Southern Press," in which he states that Mr. Donelson told him, in 1845, that I had sent Mr. E. Allen, then Secretary of State, to visit Gen. S. Houston in order to induce him to join me in defeating annexation. I never sent Mr. Allen or anybody else to Gen. Houston while I was President, on this or any other errand, and never consulted him or asked his advice on any subject during the time; for I well knew, from the 8th of July, [sic] 1844, that he had "changed his front" on the subject of annexation,*

and did not wish ME to consummate it; but preferred breaking down my administration, which I took excellent care he should not have the pleasure of doing. I knew Gen. Houston too well to advise [sic] with him on any matter connected with my administering the government.[351]

Jones added to the above account in a February 23 memoranda entry. He repeated his denial of requesting Allen to convince General Houston or others to oppose that measure. In addition, Allen confirmed Houston's letter in the *National Intelligencer* was changed to be less disapproving of annexation:

Since writing the above, Col. Ward[352] *and Hon. E. Allen and lady arrived here from Austin, and spent the night at Barrington [Jones' home Barrington]. Mr. Allen states there is no truth in Gen. Duff Green's statement (or rather Mr. Donelson's,) as above, about him. That he did not go to Gen. Houston's house that year - nor was he ever, to his knowledge, "followed" anywhere "by the American Minister" - that I never requested him to use any influence with Gen. Houston, or any one [sic] else, in opposition to annexation, or in persuading any one to oppose that measure; that Gen. Houston wrote to his private secretary Wm. D. Miller, editor of the Washington newspaper, to urge upon him to use all his influence and power in opposing annexation; that he (Houston) approved every word which had appeared in his (Miller's) paper opposing it; promising to sustain him with all his means in so doing; requesting Mr. Miller to say the same for him to Mr. Allen, and get his co-operation in opposing the measure; and that he (Mr. Allen) saw said letters, in the handwriting of Gen. Houston, and read them at Mr. Miller's request, and at the request of General Houston at court, in Montgomery county, in the spring of 1845, and that Gen. Houston communicated the same sentiments to him verbally, and showed him a letter he had written to Major Donelson, condemnatory of annexation as proposed by the United States, and taking the most decided grounds against the measure, (which letter was also shown to me by Mr. Miller, but a copy refused, as per Gen. Houston's request and directions.) Mr. Allen also states that the letter published by Gen. Houston in the National Intelligencer, and purporting to be the letter read to him by Houston, is changed and altered in all its original features. (In this respect, my recollection corroborates Mr. Allen's statement - the original having been much more condemnatory of annexation than the published one.)*

Mr. Allen further states, that the despatch [sic] of Major Donelson of 31st March, [sic]1845, and shown to him next day, was not delivered to him until about two weeks afterward; and that Major Donelson made various alterations in the original paper after the 1st of April, resuming it for that purpose. (This last I also know to have been the case.)[353]

In response to Mr. Donelson's Communication, 31st March 1845.

1st. The matter has again to be acted on by Congress of the United States. The alternative adopted had not the sanction of the United States: in some respects it is the worst alternative. The Government of Texas has not the power to amend the Constitution, except in the manner pointed out therein. Texas (in the matter of Annexation) is passive, not active. She would equally advance the cause of "free Government" standing alone. She is in no danger from the "friends of a different system." Texas can sustain herself. * * * The Indian Policy of the United States should be extended over

*Texas in the event of annexation. Ask Mr. Donelson for the "guarantees." * * * Will the United States insist on the boundaries of the Rio Grande for Texas? Public debt of Mexico. Will the United States assume the ratable proportion of it, if Mexico should insist on it? * * * Will Mr. D [Donelson] stipulate that Texas shall absolutely be admitted if she accept [sic] the proposition for annexation? * * * The President cannot accept or reject the proposition. He will act in conformity with the public will. He must act with prudence and caution. Very grave considerations are involved. * * * He will hasten to convoke an extra session of Congress. * * * If Texas is so "necessary to the welfare, safety, and prosperity of the United States," they should give an equivalent for the boon. * * * Texas may well fear that, if the United States are close [tightfisted] when wooing, they will prove niggardly when married. Mr. D. [Donelson] thinks the terms are hard, but thinks they will be made more favorable hereafter. The President sees no hope of this.*

In Mr. Polk's Inaugural he expresses an apprehension that Texas may become a "dependency of some foreign nation." There is no danger of this.

Acceptance on the part of Texas involves a "Revolution" of a modified or particular kind. If matters are not prudently managed, this may prove disastrous to Texas; and if by any means annexation should fail on the part of the United States, our conditions would be worse than before.

April 2d, 1845.

[Endorsement. - The excitement at this time prevented the contemplated and proper response being

made by the State Department to Mr. Donelson - A. J. J[354]

"The Republic of Texas is No More"

In a January 19, 1846 letter, General J. P. Henderson wrote to President Jones about the conclusion of the annexation proceedings and anticipation of a future proclamation by Jones. Henderson discussed various candidates for "Supreme Bench" judgeships and suggested that "friend Allen would make an able Supreme Judge."[355]

According to President Jones, Charles Elliot told him he was perfectly satisfied "with the manner in which I had fulfilled all my promises to him, and with *my* whole conduct." Elliot suggested that the French Minister was "equally well satisfied."[356]

On February 19, 1846, in a ceremony in front of the Capitol, the Lone Star flag of the Republic of Texas was lowered, and the flag of the United States was raised. Anson Jones declared, "The final act in this great drama is now performed: Republic of Texas is no more."[357]

The Annexation of Texas to the Union
(painting by Donald M. Yena)

After Texas joined the Union, Jones retuned to Barrington, his plantation near Washington-on-the-Brazos.[358] During his retirement, Jones began writing *The Republic of Texas*. In this work, he explained the events during and after annexation.

Dr. Jones wrote in his memorandum book on February 1, 1849: "The annexation of Texas is an event the resulting consequences of which are too vast to be yet realized or calculated. Of this measure I was the Architect."[359] Jones' detractors and even his staunchest supporters would probably disagree with his claim.

After annexation, Jones hoped the Texas legislature would elect him to the United States Senate. However, the new government selected Samuel Houston and Thomas Jefferson Rusk. President Polk wrote enthusiastically to Donelson about Houston's appointment:

> *Nothing could give me more pleasure personally, and nothing I am sure would give a vast majority of our people more pleasure, than to see my Old friend Houston bring her constitution in his hand as one of Our Senators, [and] take his seat in the Senate of the United States next winter. Surely he will not, cannot, hesitate.*[360]

After leaving office, Jones was ignored and neglected by Texas' politicians for the next twelve years. This treatment increased his dislike of Houston and his political colleagues. His anger and disappointment did not prevent him from becoming a wealthy planter and building a large estate. After a disabling injury to his left arm in 1849, Jones became progressively more irritable and brooding. His dislike for Houston turned into hatred. Jones spent the next several years editing his *Republic of Texas*,[361] which included a brief autobiography, portions of his diaries, and annotated selections from his letters. However, his depression continued to worsen, and he committed suicide in Houston on January 9, 1858.[362]

Allen was unable to attend Anson Jones' funeral and sent his regrets to Colonel James Morgan:[363]

Galveston Jany [January] 11, 1858

Dear Col. [Morgan],

> *I thank you for your kind letter recd [received] this morning, and although the announcement of the melancholy end of our mutual friend Dr. Anson Jones, contained in it was read with deep sorrow both by my wife and myself; – yet I none the less thank you for its early communication.*
>
> *Were it not that the Court is in session and I cannot leave, I would come in person to Houston in order to be present and (if possible) of service, during the sad services that are to follow.*
>
> *My wife however will be there and say all that I could communicate by writing more at length. –*
>
> *Accept my kindest regards and believe me*
>
> *Your friend*
>
> *Eben. Allen*
>
> *Col. James Morgan*[364]

After Jones' death, his wife, Mary, arranged to have the D. Appleton Company of New York publish *The Republic of Texas* in 1859. Ashbel Smith and Ebenezer Allen helped her to get *The Republic of Texas* printed.[365]

Mr. Polk's War

On March 31, 1845, Mexican Minister to the United States, Juan Almonte, requested his passport and issued a proclamation that slandered America and indicated a state of war existed. Mexican President Herrera made it official when he issued a war proclamation on June 4, 1845.[366]

About the time Texans were approving annexation, Secretary of War William L. Marcy ordered General Zachary Taylor[367] to gather two thousand troops at Fort Jessup, Louisiana. Marcy instructed Taylor to have the Army of Observation ready to fulfill their duties to defend the new state. After the Texas Convention accepted annexation, Donelson urged Taylor to move his Army of Occupation to Corpus Christi. By July 31, 1845, Taylor's command was in camp at Corpus Christi. The army spent the rest of the fall and winter fighting boredom and each other, petitioning Congress, drinking, horse racing, and gambling.[368]

The Army of Occupation Camp at Corpus Christi
(Library of Congress)

On February 4, 1846, General Taylor received orders to move his camp down the Texas coast to Port Isabel. Taylor expected to march the first hundred miles south to the Arroyo Colorado without interference from Mexican troops. The land between the Colorado and Rio Grande was claimed by Texas and Mexico. Mexican soldiers on the south bank of the Arroyo Colorado warned the Americans crossing the river would be considered a hostile act. On March 20, four companies under the command of Captain Charles F. Smith marched into the water. The Mexican troops had left the area and Smith's men safely reached the other side. Taylor moved his army across the river and divided his force with some going to Port Isabel and the remainder proceeding to the Rio Grande. When the American army reached the Rio Grande, they were greeted by Mexican troops lining the bank in front of Matamoros.[369] Tensions increased when Taylor's quartermaster did not return from a horseback ride. Mexican troops attacked a small search party Taylor sent to find the quartermaster. After this incident, the Mexican commander moved 1,600 men across the river to challenge the Americans. Taylor sent sixty-three cavalrymen to intercept them and look for the quartermaster. The Mexicans attacked the cavalry, killed sixteen men, and captured the rest. On April 26, Taylor notified Washington that hostilities had "commenced." He also asked Texas to supply four regiments of volunteers. The *Washington Union* announced, "American blood has been shed on American soil."[370] Mr. Polk had his war and Texas volunteers would soon be fighting across the Rio Grande in Mexico.

In the space of about two months: Texas became part of the United States, Governor James P. Henderson replaced President Anson Jones, the Mexican War began, and Allen returned to his law practice. In six years, Allen went from new immigrant to Clarksville attorney to an important player in Texas joining the United States.

STATE OF TEXAS SERVICE

Following statehood in 1846, Ebenezer Allen returned to his home in Galveston. Over the next fifteen years, he practiced law, obtained a railroad charter, and served as attorney general for the State of Texas.[371]

Colonel Ebenezer Allen

Somehow, between 1846 and 1848, the Honorable Ebenezer Allen became Colonel Allen. The sarcastic references in the Dallas newspaper to men who became colonels suggests that the rank had nothing to do with Allen's military prowess. It appears that Albert Hamilton Latimer[372] was the source of the title as described in the following article from *The Dallas Daily Herald* of August 29, 1857:

> *The way our Misters are made Colonels is a caution. The Waco Convention*[373] *nominated Mr. H. R. Runnels for Governor, Mr. F. R. Lubbock for Lieut. Governor, Mr. F. M. White for Commissioner, and Mr. Guy M. Bryan for Congress. The race had hardly commenced before Mr. Runnels became a Col. So also Mr. White and Mr. Bryan - all good Colonels. We thought our Frank - Fervency and Zeal Frank - had escaped, but when he got to Dallas, Latimer at once, put him down as Col. Lubbock! Latimer, however, has a weakness for the militia. He believes in it, and don't believe in anybody out of it. This was the reason that Harvey H. Allen and Paul Bremond,*[374] *two very worthy railroad men, citizens of Houston, when they arrived at Dallas, became Col. Allen and Col. Bremond; and even our friend and next neighbor, E. W. Taylor,*[375] *who never got further in tactics than "Form in procession, light your torches and go ahead." After meeting the Herald*[376] *man last winter had the hardest sort of work to shut off that prefix. Latimer has made so many Col-*

onels, he ought to have some name himself. What shall we call him?[377]

The First Elected Attorney General

In June 1850, Ebenezer Allen and William S. Todd, Allen's former law partner in Clarksville, entered Texas politics. *The Northern Standard* reported Todd[378] was a candidate for Judge of the Eighth Judicial District and would address the people at various county seats in the district. Several lines below Todd's notice, Ebenezer Allen proclaimed his candidacy. "We are authorized to announce Ebenezer Allen Esq., as a candidate for Attorney General of the State." The same issue of the newspaper published the announcement of A. H. Evans,[379] Allen's opponent for the position. The *Standard* described Evans as an individual well fitted to the "arduous duties of Attorney General."[380] Several other men proclaimed their candidacy including A. J. Hamilton[381] and Judge George W. Paschal.[382] In July, Alexander H. Evans and A. M. Lewis entered the race. The state scheduled the election early in August.[383]

In August, Thomas F. McKinney[384] wrote to Samuel M. Williams[385] about Ebenezer Allen's prospects:

Austin Aug [August] 29 1850

Dear Sam [Samuel M. Williams]

In conversation with Judge Webb[386] yesterday he stated that he had no doubt but Allen was elected att Genl [attorney general] if the Rio Grande & Corpus Christi vote could be received here in time say 60 days from the time of holding the election but expressed some doubt whether it would reach here in time to be counted. I will write to Runnels[387] via N Orleans [New Orleans] on the subject & my object in writing this is that you may give to Allen the information if he has reached home so that he can take such steps as will insure their timely return or for such other purpose as you may think proper to use it. As yet for my life I can not [sic] tell the probable fate of the war [War] Bills now before the House but have a strong hope they will be defeated. With our best regards to Mrs. Williams & the Children.

[Your friend]

T. F. McKinney

I have handed Guy Austin's obligation. He kept it nearly a day & returned it without comment. I will keep him urged up until I get him to some point.

McK[388]

The election was held on August 3, 1850 and the results announced around August 16.[389]

> The election returns as far as heard from, indicate that Col. E. Allen has been elected Attorney General, by a majority of about one thousand.

Election Results
(Democratic Telegraph and Texas Register)

Allen won the election with 5,469 votes compared to Andrew J. Hamilton who received 4,081 votes. Allen and Hamilton received 47% of votes with Allen earning 27%. Of the state vote, Allen's support came from: Cameron (791 votes, 93% of county vote), Lamar (300 votes, 62% of county vote), Nacogdoches (408 votes, 84% of county vote), Red River (309 votes, 62% of county vote), Rusk (327 votes, 34% of county vote), and Webb (327 votes, 92% of county vote) counties. These six counties accounted for 45% of Allen's votes.[390] The election "passed off quietly in Galveston" with Allen winning 201 votes compared to 172 for Paschal, 10 for Yerger, 8 for Hamilton, and 7 for Lewis.[391] In Harris County, Hamilton received 134 votes, Allen 60, Paschal 32, Lewis 18, Evans 10, and Yerger 4.[392] Allen's salary as attorney general was $1,200 in 1850.[393]

Following his victory in the state election, Allen became "associated for practice in the Supreme Court of the State and the Federal Court at Galveston.[394]

Duties of the Attorney General

The Texas Attorney General was the chief legal and law enforcement officer in the Republic of Texas and performs the same duties for the State of Texas. The Republic of Texas authorized the Office of the Attorney General in 1836. The presidents and then governors appointed the attorneys general of the Republic of Texas and the first four attorneys general of the State of Texas.

The state constitution assigns the attorney general with the duties of defending the laws and constitution of Texas, representing the state in litigation, and approving public bond issues. To fulfill these responsibilities, the Office of the Attorney General serves as legal counsel to all boards and agencies of state government; issues legal opinions when requested by the governor, heads of state agencies, other officials, and commissions; and defends challenges to state laws and suits against both state agencies and individual state employees.[395]

The Texas legislature changed the state constitution in 1850 to allow voters to elect the comptroller, treasurer, attorney general, general land commissioner, district attorneys, supreme court justices, and district judges.[396] The 29th Amendment to Section 1 of the state constitution stipulated that the attorney general will "be elected by the qualified electors of the State"[397] and serve a two-year term.[398] Section 11 of the amendment states: "In case of any disability on the part of the President of the Republic of Texas to act as herein required, it shall be the duty of the Secretary of State of the Republic of Texas; and in case of disability on the part of the Secretary of State, then it shall be the duty of the Attorney-General of the Republic of Texas to perform the duties assigned to the President."[399]

Attorneys Generals in the Republic and State of Texas from 1836 to 1865[400]

Attorney General	Took Office	Left Office	Party
Of the Republic			
David Thomas and Peter W. Grayson	March 2, 1836	October 22, 1836	
J. Pinckney Henderson, Peter W. Grayson, John Birdsall, A.S. Thurston	1836	1838	
J. C. Watrous	December 1838	June 1, 1840	
Joseph Webb and F.A. Morris	1840	1841	
George W. Terrell, Ebenezer Allen	1841	1844	
Ebenezer Allen	1844	1846	
Of the State			
Volney Howard	February 21, 1846	May 7, 1846	Democrat
John W. Harris	May 7, 1846	October 31, 1849	Democrat
Henry Percy Brewster	October 31, 1849	January 15, 1850	Independent
Andrew Jackson Hamilton	January 15, 1850	August 5, 1850	Democrat
Ebenezer Allen[401]	August 5, 1850	August 2, 1852	Independent
Thomas J. Jennings	August 2, 1852	August 4, 1856	Independent
James Willie	August 4, 1856	August 2, 1858	Independent
Malcolm D. Graham	August 2, 1858	August 6, 1860	Democrat
George M. Flournoy	August 6, 1860	January 15, 1862	Democrat
Nathan G. Shelley	February 3, 1862	August 1, 1864	Unionist
Benjamin E. Tarver	August 1, 1864	December 11, 1865	Independent
William Alexander	December 11, 1865	August 9, 1866	Republican

Peters' Colony

Allen's term as attorney general was tarnished by disputes between entrepreneurs and colonists associated with the Peters' Colony.

The Peters' Colony was a North Texas impresario grant made in 1841 by the Republic of Texas to twenty American and English investors led by William S. Peters. Peters was an English musician and businessman who immigrated to the United States in 1827 and settled in Pennsylvania. Peters considered the colony primarily as a business venture, but he may also have imagined the colony offering new opportunities for the English industrial middle class. Half of the colony's investors were from England, and the other half from the United States. The colony headquarters was in Peters' son William's music store in Louisville, Kentucky. In June 1839, William S. Peters and Samuel Browning, Peters' son-in-law, left Louisville and traveled to Europe to obtain funding for the colony. Over the next few years, Peters searched for financing in England and France. In July 1841, William Peters returned from England with support from the London investors.

The Peters' Colony impresarios signed the first contract with the Republic of Texas in Austin on August 30, 1841. The contract defined the boundaries of the colony as beginning on the Red River at the mouth of Big Mineral Creek, running south for sixty miles, then west for twenty-two miles, north to the Red River and then east with the river to the point of origin. The terms of the contract required the impresarios to recruit 200 families from outside the Republic of Texas within three years. The Republic granted the colonists 320 acres for a single man and 640 acres for a family. Texas allowed the Peters' Colony investors to keep up to one-half of a colonist's grant as payment for services provided, land surveys, and title applications. The impresarios gave the colonists powder, shot, seed, and in some cases, built cabins for the settlers. The land agents also received ten sections[402] of premium land from the Republic for each 100 families.

There was not enough public land within the first boundary of the colony, and the land agents asked Texas officials to increase the size of the colony. On November 9, 1841, the Republic granted more land to the colony in a second contract. This contract extended the boundaries of the colony forty miles southward but increased the number of required colonists to 800. On November 20, a new group of investors formed the Texas Agricultural, Commercial, and Manufacturing Company in Louisville. Peters obtained seven new associates from Louisville to add to the funds previously obtained from the London investors. The new company sent its first group of immigrants to the Cross Timbers[403] area of Texas by steamboat in December 1841. However, difficulties in attracting and retaining colonists forced the company to ask the Republic for more time and land. Under the third contract, signed on July 26, 1842, the Republic gave the land company a six-month extension for the introduction of the first third of the colonists, and extended the boundary by ten miles on the west and twelve miles on the east. In return for these concessions, the Republic retained ownership of each alternate section of land.

On October 3, 1842, the English financiers transferred their interests to three new English investors and three new Americans: Daniel J. Carroll, Sherman Converse, and Charles Fenton Mercer. After a power struggle among the new investors, the winning stakeholder, Sherman Converse, obtained the rights from the Louisville group. The Republic of Texas granted Converse a fourth contract on January 20, 1843. The agreement gave the impresarios a five-year extension, to July 1, 1848, to satisfy the contract and added over ten million acres to the west of the colony. When Converse was unable to meet the Republic's terms, the Louisville group found other investors and reorganized as the Texas Emigration and Land Company on October 15, 1844. The company established its claim as the legitimate owners of the Peters Colony. However, continued confusion over ownership discouraged immigration to the colony. By July 1, 1844, only 197 families and 184 single men lived in the settlement. The company's efforts to attract settlers was further hindered by an order passed by the Republic of Texas Convention of 1845. The regulation demanded that all colony contracts be investigated to determine if they were unconstitutional. The company added to its problems in 1845 when they hired Englishman Henry O. Hedgcoxe as its agent. Hedgcoxe's foreign and bureaucratic behavior irritated the colonists and confirmed the commonly held belief the contractors were only land speculators. Moreover, the immigration of squatters into the settlement complicated the company's management of the colony.

The company's difficulties did not stop when the contract expired on July 1, 1848. The end of the agreement meant the land within the colony was now legally open for new settlers to apply for 640-acre grants from the State of Texas. Many of the early settlers objected to the company's claim of up to half of "their land" as specified in the first contract. The settlers demanded the legislature correct an "unjust situation." They protested with mass meetings, petitions, and at a May 21, 1849 convention in Dallas. In January 1850, the legislature tried to settle the dispute by passing a law to protect the colonists' claims. While the law was favorable to the settlers, the land company complained the legislation was harmful to their interests. The angry stockholders of the Texas Emigration and Land Company files a lawsuit to oppose the new legislation. A compromise was finally reached on February 10, 1852. The legislature passed an act that granted 1,700 sections of land in floating certificates[404] to the company. The state gave the colonists until July 1, 1852 to prove their claims, and the company 2½ years (January 1, 1855) from that date to use its certificates to acquire their own claims. The colonists were concerned about the possible sale of some claims, enraged with the legislature's generosity towards the land company, and decided to continue to fight for their land. [Please see "An Act Relating to Lands in Peter's Colony" in the Appendix.]

In May 1852, Hedgcoxe published an explanatory proclamation that stated the colonists had until August 4, 1852 to establish their claims with his office. The company's opponents considered the proclamation as arrogant and autocratic, and contributed to the colonist's misinterpretation of the compromise law.

The colonists were further incited when the attorney general, Ebenezer Allen, issued an opinion on June 3, 1852, which upheld the law. The Commissioner of the General Land Office, Stephen Crosby, asked Allen in his role as the State's legal officer, to review the compromise legislation. Most of Allen's evaluations were unfavorable to the colonists. He stated that land designated under past contracts between the State and various impresarios could not become part of the "vacant domain."[405] The attorney general concluded that the applicants were not entitled to the patents approved on February 10, 1852. He decided the colonists had "no right to appropriate" the "alternate sections reserved by the state." Allen determined the colonists were not entitled to "divide their claims" in order to "secure two surveys on one and the same certificate." [Please see "An Act Relating to Lands in Peters' Colony" in the Appendix.]

The *South-Western American* published "the opinion of Col. E. Allen ... upon the late law relating to lands in Peters' Colony." The paper reported that Allen's opinion was in response "to sundry questions propounded by the commissioner of the general land office." The paper concluded by encouraging all parties to reach a compromise as soon as possible. "There is land enough for all, and contests come to no good."[406]

At a mass meeting of colonists in Dallas on July 15, 1852, an investigating committee accused Hedgcoxe of fraud and corruption. The following day, about one hundred armed men from the Dallas meeting invaded Hedgcoxe's office in Collin County. The angry settlers seized Hedgcoxe's files and took them to the Dallas County Courthouse. The Englishman was ordered to leave the colony. Alarmed by the colonists' actions, the land company tried to satisfy the settlers. On February 7, 1853, the Texas legislature passed an amendment to the compromise law, which was satisfactory to both sides.[407] Disagreements between the settlers and investors led to ten legislative actions over nearly twenty years to finally settle the land titles. The colony that helped settle North Texas generated none or little profit to the investors and caused unhappy and angry settlers.[408]

Allen's term ended on August 2, 1852.

ENTREPRENEUR

In addition to practicing law, Allen and his law partner, William G. Hale, engaged in various entrepreneurial ventures. Allen's early experience working in his father's businesses nurtured his interest in commercial opportunities. The growing Texas economy heightened his pursuit of these money-making prospects.

St. Joseph Island

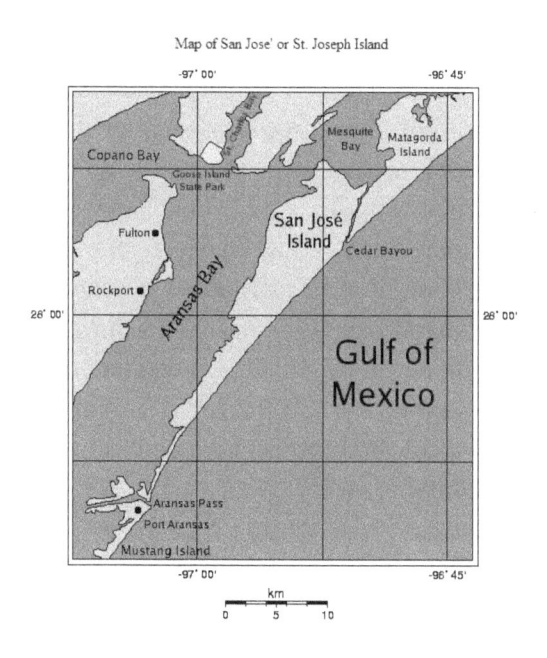

St. Joseph Island
(Kharker – Public Domain)

St. Joseph (San José) Island is a sand barrier island in Aransas County, Texas. The Cedar Bayou separates the island from Matagorda Island on the north and Aransas Pass splits the island from Mustang Island on the south. St. Joseph Island is about twenty-one miles long and five miles wide. It protects Aransas Bay and the mainland from the storms and tides of the Gulf of Mexico.

The French landed parties on the island in 1712 and 1718. José de Escandón explored St. Joseph, Padre, Mustang, and Matagorda Islands in 1766. United States troops under General Zachary Taylor's Army of Occupation arrived on St. Joseph Island on July 26, 1845. In preparation for a war with Mexico, Taylor established a depot on the island to supply his troops as they moved south. The military built several forts on the south end of the island.[409]

The island was "sparsely populated" until Taylor's troops arrived in 1845. After the war, the island's prominent residents were James B. Wells,[410] John Baker, and the "lawyers and land speculators" Ebenezer Allen and William Hale.[411] Allen and Hale are believed to have laid out the town of St. Joseph when they were residents in the late 1840s.[412] The inhabitants renamed the town Aransas and the place grew into a prosperous shipping port. Deep-draft ships used Aransas as a lightering port to unload part of their cargo onto smaller ships which allowed the larger ship to dock at shallow-water ports. Johnson and Johnson operated stagecoaches, wagons, and a boat ferry that connected the island with the mainland and brought passengers, goods, and mail to the town. Aransas continued to prosper as a seaport until the Civil War. The island changed hands several times during the war. During their final occupation of the island, Union soldiers removed livestock, destroyed every building, and left the town in ruins.[413] After the war, the town ceased to exist, and the island eventually became an exclusive hunting and fishing resort.[414]

According to Allen family records, Sylvinia Allen was a part-owner of a large tract of land near Aransas. Although Mrs. Allen's title was proven in 1872, there was an ongoing dispute over the ownership of this part of the tract. The parties finally settled the question in the 1890s.[415]

Transportation in Texas

Allen's most notable enterprise was in railroads.

Transportation was a major problem faced by early Texas settlers. As late as 1850, the lack of transportation limited settlements to the river bottoms[416] of East and South Texas and along the Gulf Coast. Steamboats traveled on the lower sections of the Rio Grande, Brazos, and Trinity Rivers. However, most Texas rivers were not deep enough for dependable navigation throughout the year. Texas had very few roads and the existing ones were in poor condition and impassable during rainy weather. Ox carts carrying three bales of cotton traveled only a few miles a day. Wagon shipping was expensive at a cost of twenty cents per ton-mile. Republic and state legislators studied many proposals to improve transportation. Entrepreneurs began various projects including improvement of rivers and construction of canals, plank roads, and railroads. Eventually, railroads became the most important mode of moving people and goods in the development of Texas and the state's economy grew with the increase in miles of track.

On December 16, 1836, the First Congress of the Republic of Texas chartered the Texas Rail Road [sic], Navigation, and Banking Company to construct railroads "from and to any such points...as selected." Many leading citizens helped incorporate the company and Stephen F. Austin and Sam Houston supported the charter. However, Texans were skeptical of the banking and monopoly terms in the charter. Concerned citizens, including Anson Jones and Houston newspaper editor Francis Moore, Jr., criticized these provisions. The charter and the company developed into major issues during the second congressional elections in 1837. The company struggled over the next two years and collapsed without trying to build a railroad.

Without a reliable transportation system, personal travel and shipment of goods to market became a serious obstacle to the state's growth. To encourage railroad development, the Republic of Texas granted charters for lines from Galveston Bay, Harrisburg,[417] and Houston to the Brazos Valley.[418] The Brazos and Galveston Railroad and the Harrisburg and Brazos Rail Road [sic] were part of several real estate promotion schemes. All three companies obtained contracts, but none of them built a railroad. The Harrisburg and Brazos chartered as the Harrisburg Rail Road [sic] and Trading Company, graded about two miles of line and tried to construct a railroad before it failed. Although unsuccessful, the Harrisburg project became the foundation for the first successful Texas railroad.

In early 1847, General Sidney Sherman, William M. Rice,[419] and John Grant Tod, Sr.[420] bought town lots and surrounding land from the founders of the Harrisburg Company and received financing from northern investors. Sherman obtained a charter for the Buffalo Bayou, Brazos, and Colorado Railway Company on February 11, 1850. Work on the railroad began in 1851 and the first locomotive, named for Sherman, arrived in late 1852. The first twenty-mile segment from Harrisburg and Stafford's Point[421] opened on September 7, 1853. The Buffalo Bayou, Brazos, and Colorado was the first railroad to operate in Texas, the second railroad west of the Mississippi River, and the oldest part of the Southern Pacific Railroad.[422]

Texas entrepreneurs were unable to obtain funding from the eastern United States and foreign investors. These financers were reluctant to invest in projects in a state on the American frontier. Therefore, Texas authorities offered incentives to develop Texas railroads. Three types of inducements were used: bonds, land grants, and loans. Between 1850 and 1876, bonds from cities and counties raised $2.4 million to help fund railroad construction. The State of Texas provided land grants and loans. Six of the railroads borrowed $1,816,500 from the Texas Special School Fund. The railroads repaid $4,172,965 in principal and interest. Only the Houston Tap and Brazoria defaulted, and the state recovered some of the debt when it foreclosed and sold the railroad.[423]

Galveston and Red River Railway Company

On February 3, 1848, Ebenezer Allen applied to the Texas legislature for approval to build the Galveston and Red River Railroad:

To the Honorable the Legislature of the State of Texas

The memorial of Ebenezer Allen of the City of Galveston respectfully shows, that he is an applicant to your Honorable Body for the right of organizing an association to be called the Galveston and Red River Railroad Company in accordance with the Bills herewith submitted.

In making this application, your memorialist is not activated by any motive of mere experiment or speculation; nor is it his object to obtain a franchise to be consummated without effort or perfected without regret on his part, accordingly as contingencies may eventuate. He seeks from your Honorable Body the honor to undertake an enterprise, the means for completion of which, are provided to be found here by gentlemen of unquestionable ability, including in the northern cities of our Union, and whose promise in this behalf, can with safety be relied on.

The importance of the measure and its incalculable influence on and among the value of our lands, developing the resources; promoting the prosperity and increasing the wealth of our State, if successfully consummated, can not [sic] be questioned. The proposed act gives no exclusive privileges in the nature of a monopoly or perpetuity. Under the provisions of the Constitution, it is at any time subject to be repealed by the State Legislature; and, should it be found for the interest of the community any similar improvement may be made to pass side by side with the one here sought. By the completion of the proposed enterprise, the community it is hoped and believed would be benefitted immensely more than the Company, which your memorialist seeks the honor to organize; and should your Honorable Body find no objectionable features in the proposed Act of Incorporation, and no cause to frown upon the enterprise thereby sought to be affected, he prays that the said Act may be passed by your Honorable Body and become a law.

And will ever pray to

Eben. Allen

City of Austin Feby. [February] 3, 1848[424]

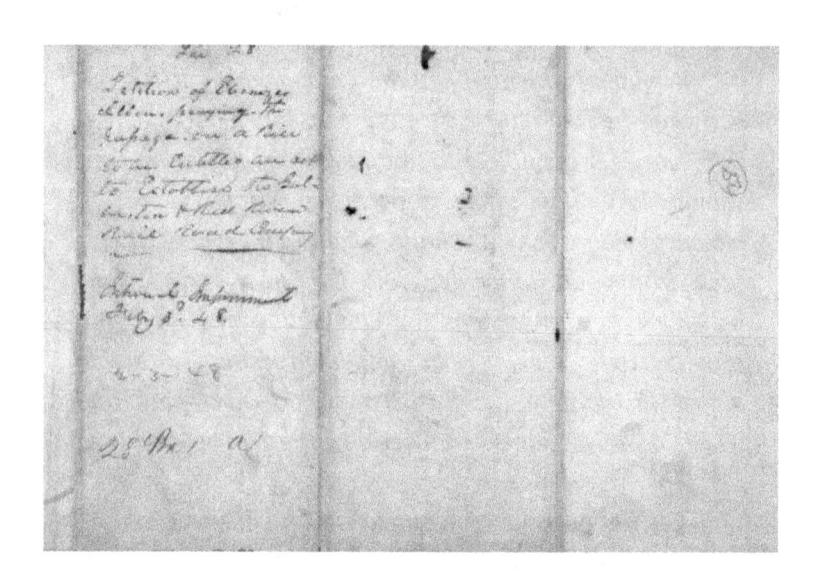

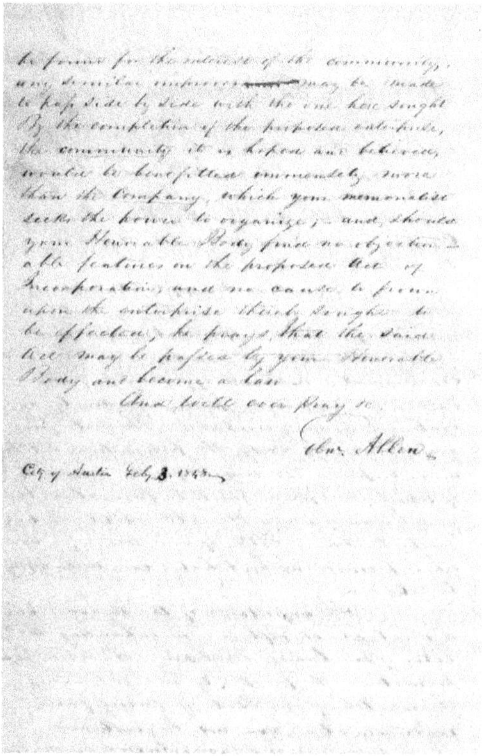

**Memorial to the Texas State Legislature Requesting Railroad Charter
(Judith M. Johnson, Johnson-Morrow Family Tree, Ancestry.com)**

The legislature approved Allen's application on March 11, 1848 and the Galveston and Red River Valley Railroad was born. The line planned to run "from some point on Galveston Bay to such point on the Red River between the eastern boundary line of Texas and Coffee's Station[425] as the said company may deem most expedient."[426] [Please see "An Act to Establish the Galveston and Red River Railroad" in the Appendix.]

The State specified two requirements when it granted the charter to Allen. The legislature expected: "That if the said company shall not commence its operations within two years from the first day of June, [sic] 1848, and shall not have completed at least one hundred miles of the said railway within five years thereafter, then, and in such case the rights, powers and privileges herein granted to the said company. for the construction of said railway shall cease and be determined [resolved]."[427]

After the railroad's incorporation, Allen faced the challenging task of raising funds to begin construction.

An article in the *Democratic Telegraph and Texas Register* described the undertaking in glorious terms:

> Red River and Galveston Rail Road [sic].
>
> *Messrs. Ebenezer Allen and A. J. Yates*[428] *have returned from their tour through the Eastern counties in search of means to construct the great rail road [sic] to connect Galveston with the Red River above the raft. This is a stupendous enterprise, and these gentlemen evince a zeal and energy commensurate with the undertaking. The distance is about 350 miles, and we understand there are scarcely 3,500 families now residing on the direct line of the route. Several flourishing villages however are situated near the proposed road. It is not a little remarkable that the inhabitants of the Trinity valley through which this rail road is to pass, have not yet raised means to remove the small raft above Porter's Bluff, and yet they talk about completing this great work as if it were entirely practicable. They [Allen and Yates] have held public meetings in most of the counties on the proposed route, [sic]and have subscribed [purchased or acquired] large quantities of land to form the basis of the capital for the project. We understand that more than thirty thousand acres have been subscribed in a few of the counties on the Upper Trinity, and the aggregate amount of subscriptions probably exceeds half a million acres. We doubt whether the people of any other section of the Union, would contribute more freely of their real estate, for such an object than the people of Eastern*

> *Texas have done. If they should succeed in obtaining a specio [species] capital sufficient to complete this rail road by mortgaging their wild lands, we may soon hope to see rail roads and canals traversing every section of the State, and the rivers, all rendered navigable from the Gulf to their mountain sources: for the people of Texas can furnish lands in any quantities to accomplish these objects. The only difficulty is in finding the capitalists who are willing to furnish the specie in lieu of the real estate.*[429]

Allen hoped that communities along the proposed route would realize the benefits of the line and help fund its construction.

The *South-Western American* reported the Houston City Council's enthusiastic reception:

> *The Galveston and Red River Railroad Company are now fully organized, by the appointment by E. Allen, Commissioner, of the following gentlemen as his associates: Messrs. Wm. M. Rice, W. J. Hutchins,*[430] *James H. Stevens, P. Bremond, J. W. House, James A. Thompson, Henry F. Fisher, W. A. Vandestyne, Harvey H. Allen, W. R. Baker, and J. W. Shrumph, Esq. They opened the books, and upward of seventy-five thousand dollars were subscribed at once. This amount will be daily increased. The City Council [of Houston] have voted $200,000 subscription almost unanimously – but six votes being cast against it. An election is called for Directors, which takes place on Monday, the 1st of November.*[431]

Other communities subscribed to the railroad. In December 1852, books of subscription opened in Robertson County and in one day $12,000 was subscribed.[432]

Galveston's Attitudes about Railroad Development

Unfortunately, the citizens of Galveston were uninterested in the railroad and focused their investments on port improvements.

At the "mass meeting" Railroad Convention held in October 1852 in Austin. Delegates from neighboring counties "had an equal voice with other gentlemen in attendance." The *South-Western American* reported:

> And if it will place the Attorney-General in any better light before the News, which has grown a little censorious towards that officer, we would premise that Col. Allen informed the Committee of Routes and Ways and Means, that he withdrew from the Galveston Committee, which reported the splendid scheme that was fulminated [criticized] by that body, and which has met pretty general reprobation.[433]

The newspaper comments indicate the public had become "a little censorious [severely critical] towards that office." His broadside on the Peter's Colony legislation was still fresh in people's minds. It is difficult to separate Allen's tarnished reputation from Galvestonians disinterest in financing railroads. Perhaps public opinion defeated any project Allen was associated with regardless of its merits.

Despite Galveston's excellent geographic advantages, the city's investors displayed few entrepreneurial qualities. Houston financiers organized and directed a series of railroad projects. By 1860, the city had become an important rail hub. Railroads from Houston reached north central Texas (The Houston and Texas Central), connected with the sugar producing region of Brazoria County south of the city (The Houston Tap and Brazoria), and stretched to the Louisiana border (The Texas and New Orleans). In addition, the Houston Tap and Brazoria linked with the Buffalo Bayou, Brazos, and Colorado Railway, which ran to Columbus in central Texas.

Galveston businessmen were only slightly interested in railroads. After Texas chartered the Galveston and Red River Railroad, Willard Richardson, editor and publisher of the *Galveston News*, praised Houston promoters. However, he believed the railroad should be mainly funded by the people who would gain the greatest benefits. Richardson wanted the landowners in the territory that the railroad would pass through to finance the line. Therefore, he did not encourage Galveston's citizens to support the company.[434] Hamilton Stuart, editor and publisher of the *Galveston Civilian*, was also cautious about the project's size and required resources:

> *The project, we think, is well worthy of the careful attention of our citizens ... The scheme is one of no insignificant magnitude. It will require time, energy, and means to carry it out; and these must be yielded liberally and boldly to secure success. On the other hand, economy and caution are equally necessary, and their neglect may defeat the measure after all the necessary means and appliances have been secured.*[435]

Based on Richardson and Stuart's advice, Galveston investors were unwilling to finance the railroad and rejected Allen's request to buy stock in the company. John B. Jones, a spokesman for the merchants, believed the investment was too uncertain because Texas' trade could not generate enough income to support even one railroad.

In October 1852, the railroad promoters in Houston challenged the Galveston business community to match their town's $200,000 subscription.[436] Richardson argued a matching investment did not make sense because the "immediate benefits would accrue to Houston:"

> *When the road is extended to Houston, we doubt not but that our citizens will endeavor to do their part by extending it still farther to Galveston ... We are willing the terminus should remain at Houston until the energies of the county may require it to be extended to this point. And we are all the more willing for this, because, as we have before said, our citizens admit their inability to build railroads at this time without taking the capital which is absorbed in business upon which they depend for support.*[437]

Galveston capitalists were content to allow Houstonians to build rail lines from their city to other parts of the state. Galvestonians were only interested in financing a line from Galveston to Austin. When the *La Grange Monument* appealed to Houstonians for investment in this Brazos valley railroad, Francis Moore, editor-publisher of the *Houston Telegraph and Texas Register*, cited Galveston's lack of interest:

> *If the railroad then is intended to be the main route from Austin to Galveston, the editor of the Monument should not complain of the citizens of Houston doing no more than the citizens of Galveston toward constructing the road. He surely cannot expect that the citizens of Houston will come forward and offer to furnish funds to complete the road, when as yet the citizens of Galveston have not subscribed to a single dollar stock in the railroad.*[438]

In the mid-1850s, Galvestonians reexamined their position on railroads. They continued to view the railroads as "subordinate to their city's advantages as a seaport." Richardson observed that the Houston and Texas Central Railroad would "enable the produce of the country to reach this place [Galveston] with almost as much cheapness and dispatch, as if the road had its terminus here; for the close connection that must be established and kept up between the steamers and the cars [trains], will prevent any material delay, beyond the few minutes required to transfer passengers and freight from one to another." Galvestonians only valued railroads as the mode to transport goods and people to Galveston steamboats.

Galveston continued to believe that shipping was critical and enough to ensure their city's economic prosperity. Richardson expressed the thoughts of other residents who considered railroads as the method to connect the rest of the state with barges from Galveston to docks at Houston.

> *We have always looked upon our navigation ... as affording to Galveston and the people of the country, nearly all the advantages of a railroad of the same extent. The great difficulty is that this navigation does not extend far enough and this deficiency can only be sup-*

plied by railroads. But for the purposes of transportation, this navigation ... answers nearly all the ends of a great railroad trunk, and we shall feel about the same interest in railroad connecting with it, and drawing trade from different parts of the country, as we should if those roads were the branches leading to this city.[439]

Galvestonians would not build their own railroads if waterborne transportation could connect the port with mainland rail systems. If Houston continued to allow barges from Galveston to dock at the city's wharves, Galveston would allow others to finance and build railroads. Galveston capitalists focused on harbor and wharf improvements based on the belief that the port would sustain future growth.

Richardson said Galveston businessmen were "capitalists without foresight, timid merchants who only sporadically invested in railroads and other internal improvements and who consistently expected others to carry the brunt of investment responsibility."

Richardson believed the business community thought "the great natural advantages of Galveston" could not "be counteracted by the rival interests and enterprise of other places." These advantages guaranteed the city's "future prosperity even in spite of ourselves." They concluded there was "no sense in investing their capital in railroad enterprises when the community's prosperity seemed ensured by its location on Galveston Bay." They assumed Galveston was "a natural staging point for all Texas commerce" and the railroads would be forced to connect with the city.[440]

Other Railroad Ventures

Allen continued to explore other railroad projects. The U.S. Congress considered a bill authorizing the Galveston and Red River Railroad Company to construct a railroad to California. The bill was referred to the Committee on Roads and Canals.[441]

Allen and his law partner William Hale were also involved in incorporating the Texas Western Railroad. In addition to Allen and Hale, eighteen other men helped create and establish the Texas Western Railroad Company.[442] Although the legislative act creating the railroad was titled the Vicksburg and El Paso Railroad Company, the body of the charter called the line the Texas Western. This difference in names was never questioned, and subsequent acts of the Texas legislature referred to the company as the "Vicksburg and El Paso Railroad Company or Texas Western Railroad Company." The company was one of several transcontinental routes chartered during the antebellum period and was projected to run from the eastern boundary line of Texas to El Paso. The charter was acquired for $600,000 in stock by the Atlantic and Pacific Railroad Company, which used it to bid for the right to construct the railroad authorized by the Mississippi and Pacific Act.[443] However, the eastern backers of the Atlantic and Pacific did not comply with the requirements of the latter act and the company was reorganized as the Texas Western in December 1854. The charter was subsequently reacquired by the Texas promoters of the line and was amended, and the name was changed to the Southern Pacific Railroad Company by the legislature over the governor's veto on August 16, 1856.[444]

The Buffalo Bayou, Brazos, and Colorado Railway was the first operating railroad in Texas. It completed its first segment of track between Harrisburg, Texas and Stafford's Point, Texas in 1853. The company established a western terminus at Alleyton, Texas prior to the Civil War. Jonathan F. Barrett was the railroad's first president and the company included some of the prominent men of the state General Sherman, Hugh McLeod, John G. Tod, John Angier, William Marsh Rice, Ebenezer Allen, William A. Van Alstyne, James H. Stevens, Benjamin A. Shepherd, and William J. Hutchins.[445]

THE HOUSTON AND TEXAS CENTRAL RAILROAD

Allen Transfers the Charter

Although Allen obtained the railroad company charter on March 11, 1848, the citizens of Galveston refused to invest in the new venture. Despite all of Allen's efforts, the Galveston and Red River Railroad was unable to raise enough capital to meet the construction deadlines required by the State, and he was in danger of losing the charter. Rather than give up the license, Allen approached board members and other entrepreneurs to take on the charter. After a series of meetings at Chappell Hill and Houston, Allen conveyed the grant to two Houston residents, Paul Bremond and Thomas William House.[446] Both men were current directors and staunch supporters of Texas railroads. The Texas legislature permitted Allen to transfer the charter to the Bremond-House group, and the legislature renewed the grant on February 14, 1852. In addition, the legislature approved changing the southern terminus from Galveston to Houston and extending the time to meet the state requirements.[447]

Thomas William House
(Public Domain)

Paul Bremond
(Texas State Historical Association)

On October 15, 1852, the *Telegraph & Texas Register* reported Ebenezer Allen had formed an association with several men to serve as commissioners to construct the Galveston and Red River Railroad. The newspaper listed the following men: Wm. Rice, W. J. Hutchins, J. H. Stephens, P. Bremond, T. W. House, J. A. Thompson, Henry F. Fisher,[448] W. W. van Alystyne,[449] Harvey H. Allen,[450] W. R. Baker,[451] and J. W. Schrimpf.[452] The newspaper announced the "Books are now open at the store of Bremond & Van Alystyne."[453]

Several weeks after the paper published the names of the new commissioners, the Houston City Council authorized the subscription of $200,000 for the Galveston and Red River Railroad.[454] In January 1853 the new owners had some success in raising funds. The citizens of Springfield, Texas subscribed $30,000 and the people of Corsicana pledged $20,000.[455] *The Leon Pioneer* announced "the books of subscription to the Galveston and Red River Railroad Company have been opened in Robertson County. The citizens raised $12,000 in one day, and subscriptions were rapidly increasing."[456]

Paul Bremond Takes Control

> *To serve the immense territory between the Trinity and the Brazos is the Mission of the great Corporation known as the Houston and Texas Central Railroad. — Donaldson in the Texas Almanac of 1868.*[457]

The Galveston and Red River Railroad was reorganized in Houston in May 1853. The following men were elected to serve as executives or directors: P. Bremond, President; Wm. R. Baker, Secretary; James H. Stevens; General Orville Clark, C. Ennis; Mark Healy; J. S. T. Stranahan; Col. E. Allen; W. J. Hutchins; Wm. Rice; and B. A. Shepherd. The subscribers were asked to pay the ten percent investment that each director had pledged. General Clark was confident that the road would be completed to the Brazos River[458] within one year[459] Based on Allen's pioneering efforts in obtaining the original charter and his stock ownership, he was included on the line's board of directors.

> *The company, we are informed are in the very highest spirits, Gen. [illegible] Clark subscribed for one hundred shares of one hundred dollars each, and the company are going on with the work in the most energetic manner possible. The stockholders are paying up their installments promptly, and the hope is confidently expressed that the road will be completed to the Brazos and the cars running on it during the next year. Governor Pain expressed himself highly pleased with the country between Houston and this city [Austin], respecting its adaptability to the cheap and speedy construction of a railroad, and we feel satisfied that if the citizens of Texas, who are so deeply interested in the construction of this road, will undertake it in the spirit they should, we may expect and calculate upon efficient aid from northern capitalists. We of the interior, however, cannot expect the citizens of Houston and northern capitalists to build the road to our doors, unless we aid to the extent of our ability; nor is it our in-*

terest that they should do so. Intelligent business men [sic] and shrewd capitalists express the confident belief, that when this road is completed from Houston to Austin, the stock will pay a handsome dividend – that it will be amongst the highest paying stock in America. This being the case, would not capitalists in the interior along the line of this road, be consulting their best interests, by at once taking stock, not only as a safe and profitable investment, but also to secure the benefits of the road at an early day?

We hope the President and Directors will immediately cause books of subscription to be opened to all the counties along the line of the road, that those who wish to do so may have an opportunity of taking stock. We are certain a large amount will be taken, and nothing would tend more to create an assurance in the public mind, that the road will be completed, that the enterprise has been undertaken in proper spirit, than the opening of books in the several counties interested, that the citizens thereof may become identified with, and actively engaged in the work. It is but right, also, that the citizen of the interior counties should have a voice in the location of the road, and this they cannot have until they become stockholders. The sooner our friends at Houston attend to this matter, the better for the success of the road. There are so many conflicting schemes, all having their advocates, visionary though many of them be, that the necessity is urgent for immediately concentrating public opinion on the most sensible and practicable project, and such we regard the Houston and Austin road. Nothing has exercised so destructive an influence upon the progress of railroad building in Texas as the multiplicity of roads proposed and of charters granted, for while public opinion is divided along these various plans, nothing can be done *towards the success of either. If books are at early day opened and stock taken in all the counties interested in this road, public opinion will at once settle down upon it as a road that is to be built, for we are satisfied that the amount of subscriptions will be such as to command public confidence in its success, not only at home, which is highly important, but also among capitalists abroad, which is, probably, equally important.*[460]

On September 1, 1856, the railroad still designated Galveston as its southern terminus. The legislature allowed the company to rename the line the Houston and Texas Central Railway Company on September 1, 1856.

Bremond took an active role in raising funds for the line. At a fall meeting in Washington County, Bremond said the object of his visit was "to procure stock in the Galveston and Red River Railroad." He asked the citizens "can conveniently subscribe." The chairman appointed a five-man committee to "take subscription of stock."[461]

A letter from Mr. S. W. Kellogg, of Wheelock, to the *Houston Morning Star*, stated that subscriptions in Robertson County had grown to $100,000.[462] In 1855, the railroad received $60,000 in purchases from New York and Boston investors.[463] The *Houston Telegraph* announced in May 1856 that forty-seven merchants in New York and Boston had subscribed for stock to the amount of $122,000 in the Galveston and Red River Railroad "commencing at Houston."[464]

Bremond appealed to Galvestonians to subscribe to the line. Unfortunately, he "did not carry away a heavy amount of the circulating medium" from the citizens.

The *New Orleans Crescent* stated on December 24, 1855, that the Galveston and Red River railroad was "progressing finely." Investors purchased nearly half a million dollars of stock, and the company had spent $205,032.29 for construction. One hundred and fifty-four miles of the route was surveyed, and a large tract of country was explored.[465]

Building the Line

On December 23, 1852, Bremond announced that the Galveston and Red River Railroad was accepting proposals to grade 18 ¾ miles of track. The applications had to be received by January 1, 1853, at the office of Bremond and Van Alstyne.[466]

Bremond and House broke ground for the Galveston and Red River Railroad at Houston on January 1, 1853. The same month Bremond received news from Col. Allen and Judge Baldwin that arrangements had been made with contractors to complete the line from Houston to the Red River.[467]

In January 1853, *The Houston Telegraph* reported that "the enterprising Commissioners" of the Galveston and Red River Railroad planned to begin work on the first section of the road about four miles from Houston on January 31. The commissioners hoped to continue the work "without intermission" until the line reached the Brazos River. The *Telegraph* stated, "about one million dollars have been subscribed in Texas for the construction of this road."[468]

Development of the road continued with the announcement in October 1853 about signing "a contract with General Orville Clark for the construction of a 'first class' Railroad."[469]

In April 1855, the company laid two miles of track in Houston.[470] The railroad planned to start grading the next twenty-five miles on January 1, 1856. They hoped to have fifty miles in "running order" by February 1.[471] Bremond received good news when he learned that "part of the iron, locomotives, cars, &c. were shipped from New York." The shipment would allow the first section of twenty-five miles to be completed by January 20, 1856.[472] *The Opelousas Patriot* reported on the "progress and present condition of the Galveston and Red River Railroad:"

> *1. The grade is nearly completed from Houston to a mile beyond Cypress Creek; 2. About 30,000 ties are now on the ground, and the contractors have ordered 10,000 more from Maine; 3. Construction of the bridges and culverts are underway and will be finished soon; 4. Half of the necessary rails have either arrived*

or on the way; 5. One locomotive of 19 ½ tons weight with tender called the Ebenezer [Allen], four cars, and equipment necessary for the first twenty-five miles are either here or on the way; 6. The road has been surveyed and levelled to the Brazos timber across the Navasota River passing near Boone and the town of Springfield.[473]

The pace of construction was slow, but the contractors completed extensive grading of the roadbed by the end of 1855. The company started laying track in early 1856, and the rails extended twenty-five miles to Cypress City on July 26, 1856.[474] By the end of 1856, the city of Houston had completed a seven-mile line to connect the Buffalo Bayou, Brazos and Colorado Railroad and the Houston and Texas Central Railway.[475]

Map of the Houston & Texas Central Railroad
(Library of Congress)

The Houston Tap Road Company loaned their iron to the Galveston and Red River Railroad to allow them to complete their twenty miles within the time required. Only five or six miles of iron remained to be laid. "It is, therefore, probable that the energy and perseverance of this company will even yet triumph over all the many difficulties they have had to encounter:"[476]

> *We understand that the company intend to extend the main trunk of the road, agreeable to the provisions of the charter, about one hundred or one hundred and twenty miles, in a northerly direction, with a view of ultimately connecting it with the great Pacific road, which will, in all probability, extend through Texas on or near the parallel of degrees.[477] Indeed it would be impossible to induce northern capitalists to invest funds for the construction of this road, unless it were to be connected with the great road that is to connect the Pacific with the Atlantic. The branch extending from Houston, or the navigable waters of Galveston Bay, will enable the contractors to transport all the materials required for the Pacific road directly from the port of Galveston to the main road on the parallel of 32 degrees, and the distance from Houston, to the main trunk of the Pacific in a direct line, will scarcely exceed 130 miles. There is not a single large river on the whole route, and the surface ascends so gradually from the coast to the parallel of 32 degrees, that the expense of grading will scarcely exceed $1,000 per mile.[478]*

The five-foot-six-inch gauge railroad extended northward twenty-five miles and reached Cypress[479] on July 26, 1856. The company completed laying thirty-five miles to Hockley on May 11, 1857; forty-eight miles to Hempstead in 1858;[480] and had seventy-five miles in operation by October 1, 1859. The railroad stopped construction in 1860 in anticipation of the impending Civil War. By the start of the war, the railroad reached eighty-one-miles from Houston to Millican.[481]

**Houston and Texas Central Railroad
Distance from Houston**[482]

Station	Distance from Houston, miles
Houston	
Gum Island	12
Cypress City	25
Hockley	35
Burton	42
Hempstead	48
Rock Island	52
Courtney/Retreat	59
Navasota	70
Millican	80

Although most of the Texas railroads escaped the damage and destruction by Union forces in other parts of the Confederacy, all were in poor condition when the war ended in 1865. Four years of constant use without materials and labor to make repairs damaged Texas tracks and trains.[483]

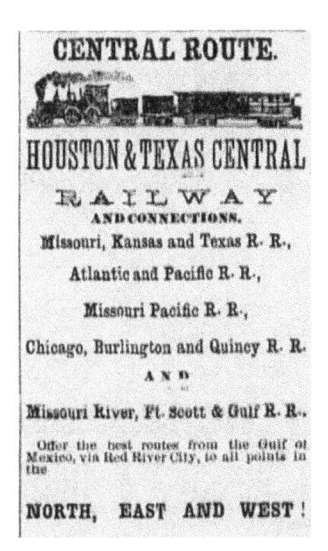

Houston & Texas Central Railway Advertisement
(The Dallas Daily Herald)

After the Civil War, the company resumed construction from Millican. The Houston & Texas Central Railway completed the road 100 miles to Bryan in 1867; 130 miles to Calvert in 1868; 210 miles to Corsicana in 1871; 296 miles to McKinney in 1872; and reached its terminus at Denison on January 1, 1873.[484] At Denison, the Houston and Texas Central Railroad connected with the Missouri, Kansas, and Texas Railroad. This junction linked Texas with St. Louis, Missouri and the rest of the United States.[485]

The Houston and Texas Central Railroad had a fleet of seven engines. Two engines weighed eighteen tons each and had the power to draw twenty-four loaded cars, four engines weighed twenty-two tons each and had the ability to draw thirty-two loaded cars, and one engine weighed twenty-four tons with capacity to draw thirty-eight loaded cars. Each locomotive had a sixty-pound bell and a steam whistle.[486] The fleet continued to grow as the line advanced to Millican.

Houston and Texas Central Locomotives[487]

Name	Number	Type	Date	Builder	Weight	Cylinders	Driver Dam
Ebenezer Allen		4x4x0	1/1856	Norris	20	12"x20"	60"
Paul Bremond		4x4x0	7/1856	Norris	28		
A. Groesbeck	3	4x4x0	10/1858	Norris			
W. J. Hutchins		4x4x0	10/1859				
W. M. Rice	5	4x4x0	10/1859	Norris			
Cornelis Ennis		4x4x0	5/1860				

A representative of "many English stockholders," questioned the basic assumption that railroad construction "requires more skill than is possessed by slaves." He believed this was a mistake, because "the chief work is mere labor, and the same science and skill to direct, with same close attention to the faithful and proper execution, are as necessary in the case of white labor as in that of slaves." In cases where both have been used, slave labor was found to be "decidedly preferable because more reliable and constant, equally skillful, less troublesome to control and manage, and much less expensive." Based on the facts the representative used to support his argument, he believed railway directors should prefer slave labor. He warned railroad investors that the difficulty with Texas railroads would be in obtaining the funds to purchase slaves.[488]

According to the *Vicksburg Daily Whig* of December 2, 1856: "About three hundred negroes are now at work on the Houston and Texas Central Railroad. The contractors have advertised for five hundred."[489]

The railroad had progressed almost entirely due to the efforts of the citizens of Houston.[490] The success of the Buffalo Bayou, Brazos and Colorado Railroad and the Houston and Texas Central Railway encouraged construction of additional railroads. Houston became the center of railroad construction and operations. By the end of 1861, Texas had nine railroad companies with about 470 miles of track. Five of the railroads were around Houston and eight of the lines ran from either a seaport or a river port.[491]

The railroads revolutionized transportation in the Lone Star State. In 1854 a thirty-five-mile trip by stagecoach from Houston to Hockley[492] over rainy roads took nearly 1½ days and required an overnight stop. In May 1857, the same trip aboard the Houston and Texas Central Railroad took only one hour and forty minutes. In December 1857, the railroads transported all the shipments from Galveston even though the water level in the Brazos River was high enough to allow waterborne deliveries.

The Pride of the Railroad

In January 1856, the *Galveston Weekly News* reported that one of the new locomotives for the Houston and Texas Central Railroad was in Houston. The company named its first engine *Ebenezer Allen* in honor of the man who obtained the original charter. "The *Ebenezer Allen* has arrived, [sic] and constitutes the chief attraction in our city at present." The paper said that the engine will "go whistling over" the mile of road now in operation.[493]

**4-4-0 Train Engine Similar to *Ebenezer Allen*
(Wikipedia)**

The *Athens Post* announced that the engine on the Galveston, Houston and Red River railroad "was put in motion" on February 22, 1856:

About 4 o'clock P. M. amidst the huzzas and cheers of an enthusiastic multitude assembled to wit-

ness the starting of the iron horse, he was brought forward from his [the engine's] temporary' resting place and placed on the road, seemingly in fine travelling order. After exhibiting some signs of restiveness, he set out steadily on his western journey - the first of his species that ever left the junction of White Oak and Buffalo Bayou. Quite a large number of our citizens availed themselves of the privilege of taking the first ride on the locomotive, which continued to make short excursions back and forth the distance of some half mile during the afternoon, much to the gratification of those present.[494]

On March 5, 1856, *The Weekly Telegraph* was exuberant about the *Ebenezer Allen*:

The whistle of the noble locomotive, the Ebenezer Allen, is continually sounding in the ears of our citizens. To see her start on a trip up the road under a full head of steam, is a "thing of beauty," and will be a "joy forever" to every inhabitant of Texas.[495]

In addition to being the first engine on the Houston and Texas Central line, the *Ebenezer Allen* was involved in the first train wreck in Texas. On June 9, 1856, a fence rail was placed "carelessly or maliciously" across the rails of "Paul Bremond's" railroad. An investigation failed to determine if the fence rail had been deliberately placed there. The site was about twenty-five miles from Galveston in an area where some landowners had strongly objected to the railway's route.

The *Ebenezer Allen* engine, the "pride of the railroad," leaped from the track and three cars were thrown off the embankment. Amazingly, neither the engine nor any of the seventy-five passengers were seriously injured. Its engineer reported the locomotive was "tearing up the track" at twenty miles per hour when the accident occurred.[496]

Allen's Involvement in the Line

Allen remained active in the railroad venture as a member of the line's board of directors and commissioners. In November 1852, the Board of Commissioners designated Allen as an agent with instructions to "proceed to the Eastern cities and obtain aid and materials to construct the road to its terminus."[497]

Not all the stockholders were satisfied with the management of the company and planned to complain at the May 1858 board election. At this meeting, the unhappy investors learned they held more than fifty percent of the stock and were prepared to take control of the railroad. These shareholders discovered "the board and their friends" had recently obtained an additional $350,000 of stock. The opposition stockholders considered this purchase as a "high-handed seizure of power" and left the meeting. Without the absent investors, the remaining stockholders reelected the old board of directors. E. H. Cushing, editor of *The Weekly Telegraph*, believed that the subscriptions were legally correct, but "morally wrong and not in good faith with their stockholders."[498]

On May 6, President Paul Bremond responded to the stockholders' complaints. Bremond said the charge of fraud was an "unqualified falsehood." "Not a dollar of 'illegal' or improper stock was taken or issued." He said the dissenting stockholders' grievances were designed to "affect the reputation of a majority of the late Directory and to prejudice the shareholders against them, in order to control the election for their own mercenary purposes."

Colonel Allen addressed the complaints in a letter to *The Weekly Telegraph* published on May 12, 1858. Allen addressed the rights of existing stockholders to buy additional shares and to cast votes for every share of stock they owned:

> *Amongst the legitimate and proper inducements held out to persons possessing the ability to become subscribers, were presented, not only the chances of a profitable investment and the consciousness of having subserved [useful or instrumental in promoting] the common weal [well-being], but also the acquisition of a power by each individual shareholder, to protect, in a degree, his interest, whether present, or prospective,*

> *in the common stock, and developing prosperity of the company, by exercising the right of a vote secured by the charter for every share he might own, at all meetings.*[499]

An editorial in the *Dallas Herald* accused Allen of "covert speculations" in relation to the Houston and Texas Central Railroad. Allen was forced to respond to these charges:

> *I have been, for nearly twenty years, a citizen of Texas; for a portion of which time I have occupied positions calculated to elicit scrutiny and reproof, had I acted unworthy. I am not aware, however that any stigma or reproach rests upon my name. I have expended thousands of dollars, and devoted the choicest years of my life to the development of this great enterprise, "without numeration. Not a dollar have I, ever received from speculation connected with it, or attempted to do so." I had hoped that my efforts might be partially appreciated, so far, at least, as to protect me from assaults of the kind to which I am now called to reply. I find it otherwise. I find myself the object of wholesale abuse, simply because I would not plead guilty to unfounded denunciations of fraud and wrong, and consent to be kicked out of the board, in order to make way for calumniators [make false and malicious statements about; slander].*[500]

Allen was elected to the Board of Directors on June 3, 1858 for the following year. He joined a distinguished group that included W. A. Rice, Harvey W. Allen, W. A. Van Alstyne, and Paul Bremond.[501]

On June 15, an editorial in the *Dallas Weekly Herald* reported the stockholders in the interior of the State, were "far from being satisfied with the late issue of $350,000 of additional stock."

> *Notwithstanding Mr. Allen's specious pleading, every unprejudiced mind will regard the whole proceeding in issuing that stock, as an unblushing swin-*

> dle, and shameless outrage on the rights of bona fide stockholders. Mr. Allen modestly contends that this road cannot progress under any other Directory than the present managers. He seems to think that the present Board monopolizes all the railroad talent in the country. We tell Mr. Allen and his associates, that the last particle of confidence outside of the particular circle of the Board's favored friends, is now lost in the management of the road. The Stockholders now believe from the late action of the Board, that they are driven to the necessity of retaining the management and direction by foul means, in order to cover up and keep from exposure a system of speculation and unfair dealing heretofore practiced.[502]

An editorial in the *Dallas Weekly Herald* of July 10, 1858 discussed accusations made against Allen in the May 22, 1858 edition of the paper:

> *Ebenezer Allen, Esq.*
>
> *The lofty ire and classic indignation of the gentleman whose name heads this article is aroused by the following paragraph which appeared in the Herald of the 22nd of May, elicited by a communication which Mr. Allen had volunteered to the Galveston News, justifying the doings of the Board of Directors of the Houston and Texas Central Railway in the matter of $350,000 stock subscriptions.*
>
> *Ebenezer Allen, Esq., one of the Directors of the Houston and Texas Central Railroad, and one of the subscribers to the $350,000 stock, taken to control the late election of Directors, attempts a justification of the doings of the Board in the Galveston News. Notwithstanding Mr. Allen's specious pleadings, every unprejudiced mind will regard the whole proceeding in issuing*

that stock, as an unblushing swindle, and a shameless outrage on the rights of the bona fide stockholders. Mr. Allen modestly contends that this road cannot progress under any other Directory than the present managers. He seems to think that the present board monopolizes all the railroad talent in the country. We tell Mr. Allen and his associates that the last particle of confidence, outside of the particular circle of the Board's favored friends, is now lost in the management of the road. The stockholders now believe, from the last action of the Board, that they are driven to the necessity of retaining the management and direction by foul means, in order to cover up and keep from exposure a system of speculation and unfair dealing heretofore practiced. If the proceedings have all been open and honest, why do they thus persistently shun investigation?

Mr. Allen, (beg his pardon) Col. Allen, seizes upon this little paragraph with the most impetuous avidity [eagerness or greediness], and with the stereotyped airs of an injured man, and the affected holiness of a persecuted martyr, proceeds to vindicate his character against imaginary charges, and improves the occasion to indulge in a strain of stately and elegant abuse of the editor of this paper. The magnificent contempt and heroic indignation which Ebenezer Allen, Railroad Director (nominal [exists in name only],) manifests for the unfortunate editor of this paper is absolutely excruciating.

The reader will at once see that what was said in the paragraph above, was intended for the Board of Directors – the managing, controlling members of the Board – the active operators-not the nominal attaches; but Col. Allen takes it all to himself – he is charged with "swindling and covert speculation &c;" he is ac-

cused of "a system of speculation and unfair dealings, &c., &c." And thereupon Col. Allen, with the instinct of a lawyer, proceeds to make protest of his fair character, and brilliant public services, hinting with pathetic effect to the "positions" he has occupied "calculated to elicit scrutiny and reproof had he acted unworthy," and not failing to recite his immense exertions and expenditure of time and money, in projecting and forwarding this great work – the Railroad. From a vague hint contained in this manifesto, we congratulate ourself [sic] in the distance that intervenes between Dallas and the indignant Director. But this heroic demonstration of Col. Allen, this morbid sensitiveness to imaginary insult, we assure him is a profligate waste of the raw material. We beg to assure him that in those desperate charges to which he refers, Col. Ebenezer Allen never entered our mind - never. We had known him for "the twenty years he has been a citizen of Texas" from the day he landed in the Republic, [sic] and accepted the hospitality of our father's roof. We know nothing in his antecedents to warrant a charge of swindling &c. We regarded him as a quiet, clever, harmless, amiable gentleman, hardly "rough and ready" enough for this latitude, - the very character to be made the tool and dupe of designing men.

If Mr. Allen commits a wrong, we will have the charity to believe that his childish nature was led into it. In speaking of the Directory of the Houston and Texas Central Road, the name of Ebenezer Allen never occurs to us, although we see it printed as Director in all the annual reports. It appears there merely as a compliment to the early interest he took in the road, as we are informed by one of his colleagues, and to gratify a pardonable vanity, we presume – Just as he has been immortalized by naming one of the locomotives

> *"Ebenezer Allen."* It is one of the fatalities of purblind [impaired or defective vision] human nature to cherish the most absurd delusions, and thus was a man whose connection with the Directory of this road is merely nominal, whose name was placed there as a matter of convenience, and who is a complete cipher[someone who is not important] in its management, laying the flattering unction [anointing] to his soul, that he is the head and front-the life and spirit-the ruling genius and embodiment of the enterprise.
>
> *Col. Allen will certainly receive this magnanimous explanation as a meade [amende] honorable [a public or open apology].*[503]

In July 1858, Paul Bremond resigned as a director of the Houston and Texas Central Railway Company. Bremond planned to join other capitalists to obtain a contract for the construction of the next thirty-two miles of road. The terms of the contract were quite favorable for the company. The agreement was anticipated to help complete the work as fast as possible.[504]

In August 1858, *The Times-Picayune* reported:

> *The Houston and Texas Central Road is pushing ahead bravely. It is now in good running order to Hempstead, fifty miles. The next thirty-five miles is recognized as the worst part of the road. A contract, however, has been recently entered into with Paul Bremond, Esq., late President of the company, for himself and others, to complete thirty-two and a half miles, ready for the cars, within the time required by law, at $24,000 per mile, $100,000, I believe, payable in cash, and the balance in the construction bonds of the company, secured upon the land bonus, to be received from the State.*

> *It is astonishing that capitalists have not more eagerly invested in railroads in this State, considering the extraordinary bonuses and loans granted in almost every instance.*[505]

Bremond's efforts had a significant impact on groups obtaining charters and building Texas railroads. By the time he left the Houston and Texas Central in 1858, the State of Texas had granted forty-four charters of which twenty-seven were still active.[506]

Dr. S. O. Young in his *Thumb-Nail History of Houston* wrote:

> *He [Bremond] accomplished something that was never accomplished before and has never been attempted since. He built fifty miles of railroad on very little cash and a great deal of faith. He had absolute confidence in himself and inspired others with his own faith and confidence. He was the first railroad builder to water the stock of his road but his method was different from that of his successors for he used faith, faith and more faith and that was all. Mr. Bremond's first care when the road got on its feet was to fulfill his promise to his men and their claims were the first he settled. No man ever trusted Paul Bremond whether willingly or unwillingly, who ever lost a cent by doing so.*[507]

Although Bremond left the company in July 1858, Allen remained a director until July 9, 1859. At this time, Allen owned three hundred shares. He arranged for William R. Baker[508] to hold 150 shares in trust and sold 150 shares to Baker. The transaction reduced Allen's ownership of the railroad to one-twentieth (150/3000). When Allen sold these shares, his rights dropped below the ten percent required to be a member of the line's board. The contract with Baker ended his involvement with the railroad. [Please see Josephine Allen vs. William R. Baker in the Appendix.]

By 1859, Allen's reputation had been tarnished, and his prominence greatly reduced. He was simply on the "wrong side" of too many issues. His association with Anson Jones, publication of the Peters' Colony proclamation, failure to finance the railroad he chartered, support of Judge Watrous, and his declining financial position sullied his image. Was his characterization in the Dallas paper as a "quiet, clever, harmless, amiable gentleman" a true description?

He could only wait until some event or venture would allow him to restore his status as a former district attorney and secretary of state.

TEXAS LAWYER

Partnership with William G. Hale

From Texas statehood to the Civil War, Allen provided legal and advisory services to clients throughout the state. Although Allen was busy with government service and entrepreneurial activities, he continued to practice law with William G. Hale. Allen and Hale dealt with property and land deeds, surveys, claims, grants, applications, acquisitions, and sales. They also paid state and county taxes for their patrons. The partnership lasted about fifteen years. The New Hampshire natives practiced law from their offices on twenty-second street in Galveston and other locations in the state.[509]

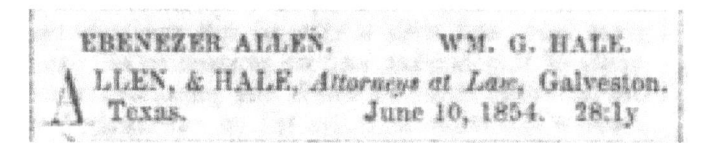

Allen & Hale, Attorneys at Law
(*The Texas State Times*)

Hale was an attorney for the Peters Colony and handled much of the litigation in Cameron County. Some of his clients were former customers of Judge John C. Watrous. This connection resulted in allegations Hale was special counsel for the same land speculators with whom Watrous was involved.[510]

The following receipt is typical of the tax payments the firm made for their clients:

> Rec'd Galveston 11th Dec. 1847 from William G. Hale agent for Charles Rowland Thirty Cents in full for State & County Taxes on lot no. 209 in Section Map on Galveston Island for the year 1846. (Eighteen hundred & forty six [sic])
>
> L. P. Lundberg
>
> By P. Shippy[511]

Mr. C. T. Stewart "made arrangements" with Ovid F. Johnson and William G. Hale to handle "debts to collect or business relative to lands to transact" in Texas.[512]

Allen was honored at a reception organized by the French consul to Texas, Mr. Guilbeau. The public celebration was held on June 7, 1847.[513]

Allen and Hale were among the thirty-one law firms in Galveston County in 1851. The list included Judges Megginson, Watrous, and Wheeler; George W. Paschal who was a member of American Legal Association; and retired attorney James Love.[514]

In 1852, Allen was admitted as one of "attorneys and counsellors" of the U.S. Supreme Court.[515]

Partnership with Sam Houston

Allen formed an additional legal partnership with Sam Houston on March 9, 1848.[516] *The Daily Union* reported that Houston and Allen "will practice in the State and Federal Courts."[517]

Houston & Allen Counsellors and Attorneys at Law
(*The Washington Union*)

In 1849, Allen was a member of the defense team in the trial of George A. Davis for the murder of E. W. Banton in Walker county. The *Huntsville Banner* reported that the trial was "of a highly interesting character." The lawyers for the defense included Sam Houston, J. M. Maxcy, A. P. Wiley, Ebenezer Allen, and H. N. Potter. The jury returned a verdict of "guilty of murder in the second degree" and decided the punishment would be three years' imprisonment in the penitentiary:[518]

Galveston 2 July 1851

My Dear Sir,

Business which cannot be postponed prevents me from having the pleasure of meeting you at Houston and I accordingly take this method of renewing to you the invitation which was expressed to you at Huntsville, that you will visit us at Galveston with Mrs. Houston and your children, if they are with you. I hope you will not return without coming to this place, for should you do so, I should almost despair of ever receiving a visit from you and your family. You will find a carriage at the boat on its arrival to bring you to my house.

I need not to say that my wife urges the request, nor that we wish to be remembered alike by yourself and your amiable wife with sentiments of friendship.

Yours ever,

Eben Allen

Gen. Sam Houston[519]

Ebenezer Allen is mentioned in a letter dated January 2, 1853 from Sam Houston to his wife.[520]

The Union Bank of Louisiana vs. Stafford

The case of the Union Bank of Louisiana vs. Stafford was one of the more interesting lawsuits handled by Allen and Hale.

The Union Bank of Louisiana filed a bill in the District Court of the United States for Texas for the "seizure and sale of certain negro [sic] slaves which had been mortgaged to them by Mr. and Mrs. J. S. Stafford in Louisiana and afterwards removed to Texas." The bank's complaint describes the events surrounding the mortgage obtained by the Staffords from the bank on June 6, 1837. The mortgage was a one-year loan of $45,000. The Staffords used 102 slaves and their future children as collateral to secure the loan. When the mortgage was due, the Staffords refused to pay and refused to sell the slaves to repay the loan. The defendants claimed the loan agreement was invalid because Mrs. Stafford was a minor when the mortgage was granted. The parties finally reached a compromise. The bank accepted Mr. J. S. Stafford's notes to cover about twenty thousand dollars of their debt, and Mr. and Mrs. Stafford obtained a new mortgage on the same property for $30,000. The mortgage was for the period of March 1, 1844 through 1851. The interest and principal were scheduled to be paid annually.

This mortgage document was completed on May 22, 1841. The agreement outlined the terms of the original loan obtained in 1837. Both parties acknowledged the conditions of the loan of $45,000 by the bank to the Staffords "for the purpose of assisting them in their pecuniary matters and for the particular purpose of paying debts due by the wife." In the new mortgage, Mrs. Stafford, who was now of legal age, was "anxious to do away with any vice, defect, or informality which might vitiate or impair the earlier mortgage." She "approves, ratifies, and confirms it to the amount and extent of $30,000, so that the two instruments shall be considered as one mortgage." Isaac Thomas also became a party to this mortgage as administrator of Michah P. Flint's estate. Thomas said Stafford mortgaged some of these negroes to Flint on June 9, 1836. Stafford made the mortgage to obtain approvals and $100,000. The mortgage to Thomas and Flint was signed on April 22, 1837 for "the same purpose," and Stafford agreed to pay back both mortgages with priority given to the Union Bank's mortgage.

However, the Staffords violated the terms of the loans. They kept the slaves from the date of the mortgage until February 1845, when they "fraudulently removed" the slaves to Texas. The lawsuit claimed they moved the slaves to avoid paying the debts that pledged the slaves as collateral. Stafford also threatened to move the slaves to Mexico, if necessary, to prevent them from being seized to satisfy his debts. To stop the removal of the slaves, the court appointed a receiver who recovered some of the slaves. The lawsuit claimed that the seizure was achieved "with much difficulty and at great expense."

Mrs. Stafford admitted having the two mortgages, bringing the slaves to Texas, and keeping them until the court reached a decision on the case.[521]

Ebenezer Allen became involved in the case in 1845. In December, Allen received a letter from the Union Bank stating, "no compromise whatsoever can be made with J. S. Stafford who ran off the slaves mortgaged to this Bank." The bank continued by protesting:

> *The object of J. S. Stafford in repeating through different channels his offer for a compromise, though sufficiently informed that the two banks will not enter into any arrangement with him, can be only to gain him. Whatever Mr. Stafford may say as to the validity of our title to the plantation purchases, our Bank prefers to run the risk, which our attorneys assures us does not exist shall rather than receive slaves in Texas even for the full amount of our claim.*
>
> *I do not think that the Bank would consent to stop proceedings against J. S. Stafford whenever and wherever they may be had, unless to the amount of 20 to 25000 [dollars] to be delivered without any condition as to the land now owned by our Bank, will not part with the claim without receiving for it its full value in cash or undoubted securities.*[522]

This back and forth continued until District Judge C. Watrous settled the matter temporarily in favor of the Staffords.

The proceedings progressed all the way to the United States Supreme Court in 1851. The court overturned the decision of the District Court of the United States for the District of Texas and entered a "decree in favor of the complaints," the Union Bank of Louisiana.

Impeachment of Judge Watrous

John C. Watrous came to Texas in 1837 and formed associations with several land companies as partner, stockholder, and legal adviser.

In 1838, he was appointed the attorney general of Texas but resigned in 1840 because of conflicts between his "private professional engagements and public duties." Watrous was an attorney for the Peters' Colony from 1841 to 1846. The colony was managed by the Texas Land and Emigration Company. After annexation, he was appointed a United States district judge on May 29, 1846. Watrous actively campaigned for the judicial post. He obtained the appointment because of his friendship with President James K. Polk. This position vested the district judge with the same authority as a U.S. Circuit Court judge. The only way to challenge his decisions was to present the complaint to the U. S. Supreme Court. Watrous presided over a large proportion of the important Texas land cases.

Judge Watrous had just begun his duties when he became involved in the "most serious difficulties." Congressman Evans from Texas said, the Judge "fell under suspicion, and it became the settled opinion of a large majority of the people, of Texas that he was engaged in fraudulent cases." No member of the Texas Congressional delegation defended him.

Watrous was severely criticized by state legislators because some members of the government objected to a number of his decisions and his personal connections with land speculators. He was accused of attempting to authorize forged land certificates. The Texas legislature passed a resolution in 1848 asking the judge to resign. Impeachment proceedings against him began in the United States House of Representatives in January 1851 with the presentation of three petitions. Watrous was charged with violating Texas statutes by dealing in fraudulent land certificates, misusing his judicial influence, and holding sessions of court improperly.

The charges against Watrous were extensive and his impeachment seemed likely. In 1848, Judge Watrous was a witness in a grand jury where he was presiding. He claimed he had no interest in the New York Land Company, which dealt in fraudulent land certificates, and named witnesses who would swear to his statement. However, evidence from the company records in New York showed that he was involved in the company. His indorsement was on a thousand headright certificates.[523] A former Commissioner of the Texas Land Office testified that the certificates were not only fraudulent but were actual forgeries.

Watrous was additionally charged with awarding $10,000 to Mr. Martin, who the judge placed in charge of the sale by the United States of the condemned schooner *Star*. Mr. Martin refused to refund the money, and the Federal Treasury was forced to replace the funds. It was suspected Watrous had received some of the money.

Authorities learned Watrous had granted a mortgage to Martin for lands on Galveston Island as payment for the money the judge owed to Martin. Watrous defrauded Martin because the mortgage document did not specify the land or amount of the loans. With the judge's legal knowledge, the legislature believed he should have known the document claiming to be a mortgage was worthless. This fake mortgage was prepared about the time Martin was awarded $10,000 to sell the schooner. It was believed the unspecified money mentioned in the mortgage was part of the $10,000.[524]

The U. S. Congress investigated the charges against the District of Texas judge: "As the complaints of oppression and corruption against the judge have been urged in the Legislature of Texas and the Congress of the United States, since 1848, the people seem to think it is time that Congress act finally upon the matter. The impeachment of a judge is fortunately a rare event, and as this one is destined to excite the attention of the whole country, we have taken pains to examine into the history of the case and the character of the complaints."[525]

In 1848, the Texas legislature examined the complaints against Judge Watrous. After an almost unanimous decision, the Texas congress approved the following preamble and resolutions:

> *Whereas, it is believed that John C. Watrous, Judge of the United States District Court for the District of Texas, has, while seeking that important position, given legal opinions in causes and questions to be litigated hereafter, in which the interests, of individuals and of the State are immensely involved, whereby it is believed he has disqualified the Court in which he presides from trying such questions and causes, there-*

> *by rendering it necessary to transfer an indefinite and unknown number of suits hereafter to be commenced, to courts out of the State for trial; and whereas it is also believed that the said John C. Watrous has, while in office, aided and assisted certain individuals, if not directly interested himself, in an attempt to fasten upon this State one of the most stupendous frauds ever practised [sic] upon any country or any people, the effect of which would be to rob Texas of millions of acres of her public domain, her only hope or resource for the payment of her public debt; and whereas his conduct in court and elsewhere, in derogation of his duty as a judge, has been marked by such prejudice and injustice towards the rights of the State, and divers of its citizens, as to show that he does not deserve the high position he occupies.*[526]

After many investigations and a vote of 111 yes and 91 no votes, the House refused to impeach Judge Watrous and ultimately dropped the case in December 1858.[527]

Allen and Hale were drawn into the scandal by virtue of their association with Watrous. Allen defended Watrous and said that the charge "of misconduct, or anything imputing the want of perfect integrity and propriety on the part of Judge Watrous … will be found, upon investigation, to manifestly most unjust and without justification."[528] District Attorney Allen said he held Watrous in "high opinion of the integrity, distinguished legal acumen, ability and learning of Judge Watrous … has ever remained unimpaired and unchanged."[529] Allen's opinion changed several days after his July 8 declaration. Allen switched his support and joined with others in testifying that Watrous was "directly or indirectly" concerned in purchasing and locating fraudulent land certificates, knowing them to be such.[530]

> Despite the criticism, William Hale defended Watrous:

Galveston, May 30th, 1851

Having acted, for some time, as District Attorney of the United States, for this District, at the request of Geo. W. Brown, Esq., while he held that office; and having also been employed as counsel in several of the cases mentioned in the charges preferred against Judge Watrous, in the House of Representatives, I am able, from personal knowledge, to state that there is no foundation in fact for the charges, either in the general official conduct of Judge Watrous, or in his action in the causes to which I have referred.

W. G. Hale[531]

In March 1857, "friends of Judge Watrous zealously urged his impeachment at Washington, in order to give him a chance of vindicating his name from the numerous charges against his judicial integrity."[532]

Complaints were presented to succeeding Congresses. Senator Sam Houston accused Watrous on February 3, 1859 of a "crime that is monstrous to contemplate."[533] Andrew J. Hamilton prosecuted the impeachment until Congress adjourned on March 3, 1861. Watrous had no duties during the Civil War when the district courts in Texas were under the Confederate government. He returned to his seat at the end of the Civil War and presided over the court until 1869 when he was stricken with paralysis and forced to resign. He moved to Baltimore, Maryland where he practiced law until his death in June 1874.[534]

The Harmony Lodge No. 6

The Masonic Harmony Lodge No. 6, A. F. & A.M. began when Galveston's population was less than five hundred people. In 1838, several Master Masons[535] living in Galveston presented a petition for dispensation to form a new lodge to Grand Master Anson Jones. Jones granted a dispensation, but health epidemics in the city delayed formation of the lodge. The following year a new grand master issued a second dispensation to establish the Galveston lodge.[536]

Ebenezer Allen's membership in the Clarksville Lodge assured him of a favorable reception at the Harmony Lodge. Allen was able to use his credentials to contact brothers in the Galveston Lodge and connect with the city's business and political elite. Allen became friends with Samuel Williams who is considered as the "father of the lodge."[537]

Although Allen was not an officer of the lodge, he took part in programs it sponsored such as the event mentioned in the *Civilian and Gazette* of July 26, 1847:

> *St. John's Day was celebrated, in Galveston, by Harmony Lodge, in a very handsome and appropriate manner. A chaste and eloquent address was delivered by Hon. Ebenezer Allen at Ryland chapel and a bountiful dinner supplied at the City Hall where great harmony and decorum prevailed. It may be worthy of remark that this Lodge never admits any intoxicating drinks at its festivities — a circumstance worthy both of praise and imitation.*[538]

Slavery in Galveston, Texas

Slaves were an important "property" of the state's wealthiest and most powerful citizens. By 1850, the slave population in Texas had increased to 58,161, and in 1860 there were 182,566 slaves which composed thirty percent of the state's population. In 1860, almost twenty-five percent of all white families in Texas owned at least one slave. Texas ranked tenth in total slave population and ninth in percentage of slave population in the United States.[539]

Most of the slaves lived on plantations in the low-lying farmlands of East Texas. Slavery was unusual along the Texas-Mexico border and in the Texas Hill County of Central Texas. The German families who immigrated to Texas and settled in the Hill Country were opposed to slavery.[540]

In 1860, there were fifty-one Texas planters who owned one hundred or more slaves. The largest slave owners were: D. G. Mills (313 slaves), Abner Jackson (285), J. D. Waters (216), H. Bass (172), A. C. Horton (167), John J. Hayden (150), Reese Hughes (147), John H. Crisp (146), William A. Kennedy (144), Jas. E. Hopkins (141), and John Mathews (140).[541] These fifty-one owners only accounted for 1.1% of the Texas slave population.

The average value of a slave was $400 in 1850 but had doubled to $800 by 1860.[542]

The number of slaves in Galveston grew from six in 1838 to 528 in 1845 including two planters who owned more than fifty slaves.[543] Galveston's population grew after the Texas Revolution. In 1847, Galveston had 4,458 people and 283 slaves. In the first Federal census in 1850, the number of Galveston residents had declined to 4,177, but the number of slaves increased to 678. Over the following decade, the city grew to 7,307 residents including 1,178 slaves.[544]

Allen's Slaves

Galveston tax records show that Allen acquired his first slave, a twenty-six-year old male, in 1848.[545] The 1850 records list four slaves with a combined value of $1,000.[546] The worth of Allen's four slaves increased to $1,200 in 1851. They ranged in age from a black male (26 years-old), a black female (15), a black female (40), and a black female child (2). In 1852, their value had increased to $2,250.[547] The 1858 tax rolls indicated that Allen owned one slave valued at $400.[548]

As a northerner and Spiritualist, Allen was most likely an abolitionist.[549] Although many Spiritualists opposed slavery, their religion focused on the liberation of all humanity, especially white women. "White spiritualists often discussed slavery and race in complex ways, but they ultimately affirmed their status as white Americans."[550] As a New Hampshire resident, Allen was raised in a state that outlawed slavery. In 1783, New Hampshire began a "gradual abolition of slavery."[551] As new Texans, the Allens tried to fit into plantation society in south Texas. The Allens had little use for field slaves and their slaves served as "house slaves"[552] or were leased to other citizens. Based on the ages of the Allen's slaves, they might have been part of a family: a forty-year-old mother and her three children or a forty-year-old mother and her son's family (twenty-six-year-old male, fifteen-year-old wife, and their four-year-old child.)

Salmon Portland Chase

Salmon Portland Chase was a Senator from Ohio (1849–1855) and later a Justice of the U.S. Supreme Court. He was an ardent abolitionist and known as the "fugitive slave lawyer" because he defended so many escaped slaves in court. On the afternoon of January 9, 1853 in Washington, Allen gave Chase an in-depth description of life and politics in Texas. The former Dartmouth classmates talked about the role of slavery in the Texas economy. Although they had different views on the subject, they respected each other's position.[553]

Financial Problems

The financial difficulties which began when Allen tried to raise funds for the Galveston and Red River Railroad continued to plague him. These problems increased after Allen completed his term as Texas attorney general as revealed in this letter to Samuel May Williams:

> *Galveston April 10, 1854*
>
> *My Dear Sir –*
>
> *I regret very much that combination of circumstances, involving my interest in the operations at Houston, and requiring again a brief visit to that place compels me to leave today without a personal interview with you, which I have for some weeks past desired. The arrival of Judge Baldwin from NY [New York] and his departure for Houston today makes it necessary for me to accompany him.*
>
> *The subject on which I desired to confer with you, is the $2000 note executed by myself & Martin. When*

the money was at first obtained, I had no interest in it. Mr. Martin received the money and loaned [it] to Judge Megginson[554] [Illegible] out of it 500. — Since then he has from time to time advanced to me divers [several, many, or numerous] sums of money and has received the transfer of the notes (amounting originally to $1500.) — executed by Mr. McKinney & yourself for the fee in the case of the Republic against Borden Collector.[555] Those notes he informed me some time ago, he left with you in order that they might, when agreeable to you be allowed in part payment of sd [said] loan of $2000 —

Now, owing to various disappointments I find that I shall in all probability be compelled to sell my house & lots in order to pay debts. It is to me extremely mortifying to find myself in such a position, especially as I know that my property, if cash could be raised on it, is worth thousands — (I honestly believe many thousands) of dollars more than enough to pay all I owe. But to me no Condition is more intollerable [sic] than that of being unable to comply promptly with my obligations. —

I wish then to make such an arrangement as will enable me to pay what I now owe, and to this end, I am under the necessity of requesting that you will aid me to the extent of the notes referred to, and as to the balance, I will make an arrangement with Mr. Martin either to pay the remainder out of the receipts for the sale of my lots — including also the $100 you loaned me, or in some other satisfactory manner to discharge such balance. — When I speak of an arrangement with Mr. Martin, I mean that if I am found indebted to him to the amount of said balance, I will thus discharge it. I presume that he does not consider me holden [sic] to *him for the $500 he loaned to Megginson.*

Mr. League[556] has offered to purchase my property – but whether he wants it or not, I have no doubt that I can find a purchaser at a tolerably fair price.

I trust that my proposition will be acceptable to you; and my existing necessities are my apology for making it.

Your Friend

Ebenezer

Col. Saml [Samuel] Williams[557]

Allen's financial situation prevented him from meeting subscription requirements and forced him to sell some of his Houston and Texas Central Railway Stock and property in Galveston. The decline in Allen's wealth is shown in his annual tax statements from 1850 to 1860. In 1850, Allen's assets amounted to $5,020. He owned four slaves and thirty-three properties. His worth dropped to $ 1,107 in 1858 and between $ 337 to $ 572 in 1860. This situation forced Allen to move to Cameron County in 1858[558] where his law partner, William G. Hale, handled most of the litigation.[559] When he was elected attorney general, 791 voters in Cameron County (93% of county vote) chose Ebenezer Allen. [Please see Allen's Involvement in the Line.]

SPIRITUALISM

Spiritualism

Spiritualism is the religious belief that the living can communicate with the dead. Spiritualists believe the spirits of the dead have the ability and the desire to connect with the living. They consider the afterlife or "spirit world" as a dynamic place where spirits continue to evolve. Spiritualists consider spirits to be more advanced than humans. These principles led believers to think that spirits can give useful knowledge about past events, moral and ethical issues, and the nature of God.

Spiritualism Séance
(Library of Congress)

The appeal of Spiritualism and other alternative theologies grew because of four factors: disappointment about the lack of progress in social and moral reforms, disruption in values accompanying industrialization, failure of mainstream religions to help members cope with changes in American life, and the belief that the influence of spiritual values and religious institutions was declining in American society. People disenchanted with current religions experimented with new spiritual ideas and practices and joined others in an assortment of cultural, social, moral, and scientific (or pseudo-scientific) reform movements. They hoped to find more satisfying forms of religious belief and expression and to introduce a new faithfulness in American life. The search for answers and guidance became a major subject of nineteenth century society. Those who converted to Spiritualism often disapproved of the status quo, were receptive to new and progressive philosophies, and came from liberal religions. Converts were also committed to one or more causes such as temperance, women's rights, abolitionism, communitarianism, phrenology, and mesmerism. Their desire for order and spiritual fulfillment led them to seek interactions with spirits and to create a new religion based on this communication.[560]

Interest in this spiritual connection increased significantly in the Northeast and Midwest during the 1840s and 1850s. This "need" to talk and learn from deceased relatives, friends, and historic figures caused the development of "innovative and experimental new movements in religion, social reform, and science." From this desire to explore the afterlife, spiritualism emerged as "one of the most peculiar, fascinating, and colorful 'isms.'" Spiritualists designated the principle of communication with departed spirits as the foundation for a "distinct and thoroughly spirit-centered system of religious belief and practice." Spiritualist ideology also believed in "the direct agency and immediate presence of bright ministering spirits – that would provide an alternative to traditional Protestantism."[561]

Spiritualism first appeared in the 1840s in the "Burned-over District"[562] of upstate New York. The emergence of Spiritualism followed other religious movements such as Millerism and Mormonism which appeared during the Second Great Awakening.[563] Many people thought that conditions in this part of New York State allowed direct communication with God or angels. The movement gained national recognition in 1848. On March 31, 1848, Kate and Margaret Fox, from Hydesville, New York, said a spirit communicated with them by making rapping noises. The physical evidence appealed to practical Americans, and the Fox sisters became a sensation.[564]

News from the Northeast and Midwest

Articles about spiritualist occurrences in the East were reported in Texas newspapers. It was only a matter of time before the phenomenon reached Texas:

> *Prometheus Outdone.–The spiritualists of the town of Ellsworth, Maine, have lately been "going it" at a most extraordinary rate. A young widow living in that village, being much interested in the subject, attended many circles, and shortly received a communication from her deceased husband, stating that he desired a "spiritual heir," and pointing out the medium through which the heir also might be expected. The medium was a good-looking young fellow, and the deceased husband's demand was preemptory, so the young widow submitted, with a degree of faith that would quite astonish an unbeliever. The result was a fine boy, and nobody has expressed a doubt that he is actually the "spiritual" offspring of the deceased, the event being regarded as a new proof of the wonders and realities of spiritualism.*[565]

The Galveston Standard said an educated woman had become a maniac because of the cursed influence of so called "spiritualism:"

> *Spiritualism – Another Victim – One of the most highly educated ladies at Ballston Spa, has just become a raving maniac, and is destined, we fear to end her days in a mad house. She has been for some months what is termed a "medium," and though possessing more brains and more finished education than any, or all of the other "mediums" at Ballston Spa combined, yet her Intellect has been the first to give way, and she has become a maniac through the cursed influence of so called "spiritualism." – She is continually raving about "spirits," alleging that "evil spirits" have seized hold of her and entreating her parents to cease believing "spiritualism," &c., &c. We understand from those: who have visited her, that it is a most pitiable*

sight to witness her insane ravings.[566]

The Texas press seemed concerned about the growth in spiritualism. *The Weekly Telegraph* reprinted an article from the *Victoria Advocate* that warned "Spiritualism seems to be gaining ground in Texas." The *Advocate* cited several papers "which have recently advocated its [Spiritualists] claims." They identified the *Houston Telegraph*, the *Lockhart Watchman*, the *Lavaca Herald* and the *Goliad Express* as "falling victim to the ideology."[567]

The *Spiritual Register* presented data on the number of believers:

Progress of Spiritualism

The Spiritual Register has recently published some statistics, wherein the total number of Spiritualists' in the United States is estimated at 1,294,000, and in the whole world at 1,940,000. Maine is credited with 40,000; New Hampshire with 20,000; Vermont 25,00 [25,000]; Massachusetts 100,000; Rhode Island 5,000; Connecticut 20,000; and New York 350,000. – The 'Register' give[s] the-names of 349 public speakers, and 238 professional mediums. The literature of the profession comprises 500 books and pamphlets, six weeklies, three semi-weeklies, and four monthlies. These figures are not, probably, exaggerated, and that Spiritualism prevails to an almost incredible extent in this country is beyond all question. Among the other monstrosities which have grown out of this superstition, is the spiritual wife system,[568] *a greater "abomination than Mormonism." We are glad to perceive that it is not in the "barbarous and uneducated South" that this, or any other demoralising [sic] humbug prevails.*[569]

Underlining the reports of Spiritualist occurrences was an effort to point out the foolishness of "Yankeedom." This was especially satisfying with the smug attitude and superiority shown by Northerners who fell prey to spiritualism and "a thousand other isms:"

The "universal Yankee nation" has for years set itself up as the model par excellence of modern civilization. Morally, mentally, and physically, they held themselves as superior to all other people, and in all that constitutes genuine humanity and refinement, they were perfect. They were the pattern from which the rest of the world were to copy. Strange to say, however, all the world and the rest of mankind could not see with Yankee eyes. The people of the Southern States and Europe, who claimed to be blessed with a few gleams of enlightenment, could not appreciate the beauties and attractions, socialism, and a thousand and one other isms which possessed such fascinating charms for Yankeedom. Yankee fanaticism could not brook such stupidity in the South; and when their free-soilism and abolitionism caused us to cut loose from them, they undertook to enlighten and civilize us at the sword's point.[570]

Spiritualism Comes to Texas

It was not long before Spiritualists discovered the fertile and unburned land of Texas.

In February 1848, the *Texas True Evangelist* became the first entry in the Lone Star State. The *Evangelist* was established "for the sturdy defence [sic] of spiritualism..."[571]

J. C. Morgan advertised spiritualist books in the April 26, 1855 edition of *The Indianola Bulletin*.[572]

Texas papers contained notices of speeches by leading proponents such as Mrs. Francis E. Hyer who would be lecturing on Spiritualism in Western Texas[573] and Thomas Gales Foster in Houston:

Lecture on Spiritualism.— A course of Lectures are advertised in another column, to be given by Thomas Gales Foster, Esq., a gentleman who seems to be well and favorably known by older citizens of Houston, on

> *the subject of Modern Spiritualism. Mr. Foster has the reputation of being a polished and eloquent [speaker], and from the warm and emphatic endorsements of some of his old friends here, we have no doubt that even the skeptical, with whom we class ourselves, will be well repaid for listening to his address. He speaks in what Spiritualists call the trance state.*
>
> *Mr. Foster is the editor of a spiritual paper, of which some twenty or more are now published in the United States.*[574]

The March 11, 1857 edition of the *Weekly Telegraph* in Houston was "sorry to see Spiritualism gaining ground in Grimes county."[575] A week later the *Telegraph* announced that Mr. A. I. Ambler was delivering a course of Spiritual Lectures in Houston. "He is highly spoken of by the adherents of this new philosophy."[576] Philosophical disagreements and/or irrational behavior were often attributed to being "under the influence of spiritualism."[577]

Texas newspapers advertised bookstores where readers could obtain spiritualist literature. *The Weekly Telegraph* announced that the Forsgard & Burke bookstore "have laid upon our table Dr. Gordan's *Three fold [sic] test of Modern Spiritualism*," a book worth reading by Spiritualists as it attacks them, and by others because it furnishes them with arguments. It is a well written and well printed book from the press of Scribner, New York."[578]

Texas papers reported on developments in the Spiritualism movement, but the press included both serious and humorous attacks on Spiritualists:

> ### *DOESTICKS GOES TO A SPIRITUAL PICNIC*
>
> *I have been receiving new light on the subject of Spiritualism within the last week, [sic] and am prepared now to believe any new developments. Months ago I heard mysterious communications tapped out on the dining-table with invisible knuckles, and terrible*

> *warnings conveyed by the poker and fire shovel. I became accustomed to that sort of thing, and rather enjoyed a conversation with my bed room [sic] furniture. I've passed many agreeable hour [sic] in talking with my writing desk – enjoyed many a pleasant dialogue with my wash stand; had many a dipute [dispute] with my boot-jack, many a dispute with my dressing-bureau, and - have argued with my bedstead and rocking chair by the hour together.*
>
> *Skeptically,*
>
> *Q. K. PHILANDER Doesticks, P. B.*[579]

Another article in the *Weekly Telegraph*, suggested that Galveston was a fertile ground for the movement.

> *The much talked of and more laughed at subject of spiritualism has just taken a novel direction in the town of Hume, N.Y. A Victor Mix, a "leading spiritualist" is now "setting" upon a dozen eggs for the purpose of hatching them himself. The spirit of some departed old hen has directed him to do this, and he piously performs the Gone Before's wish. His chickens have been "assured" by the spirits, and all are promised at $5 each to believers. Mr. Mix comes off his nest once a day for food, water, &c., and bears his "confinement" very well. We don't eggsactly understand who is the father of the eggs, but it is evidently a mixed up [sic] affair.*[580]

The *Civilian and Gazette Weekly* scolded Galvestonians in March 1859:

> *Oh yes, gentlemen, walk this way. Galveston is the place. Any gentleman having a genius for Astrology, Animal Magnetism, Biology, Clairvoyance, Demonology, Exhibiting [sic] a monkey, Fortune Telling, Geo-*

mancy, Homitetic, Ichtbyomacy, Jew Harp playing, Juggling, Kantism, Latrociny, Magic, Necromancy, Odontology, Organ Grinding, Phrenology, Quackery, Ranting, Spiritualism, Saponification, Table-Tipping, Thimblerig, Ultraism in general, Vagrancy, Vagabonding, Wrangling, Wheedling, Xenodocy, Yelling, Zany playing. &c., &c. &c. will find Galveston a most eligible location. Money is plentiful and the class who are proverbial for soon parting with it numerous. The maxim that the pleasure is as great of being cheated as to cheat is universally accepted. People love to [be] humbugged and are willing to pay liberally for the privilege. Anything new, or anything old, with a high sounding [sic] name, a little machinery, and a good deal of pretention, will pay. Walk this way gentlemen. Here is your road to fortune.

P. S. – We continue to print bills for, advertise, and puff all such enterprises on the usual terms. We have a large assortment of new type, and a book of Barnum's "first rate notices," suitable to all cases.[581]

Yellow Fever Epidemics

Fatalities from the annual summer outbreak of Yellow Fever in Galveston increased the community's interest in the afterlife and communicating with a departed loved one. There were two constants in Galveston, the arrival and departures of ships that made the island the capital of Texas' trade and commerce and the summer "sickly season." Each summer, Galvestonians faced the prospect of a horrible death from Yellow Fever. Between 1839 and 1867, nine major epidemics ravaged the island and killed more than two thousand people.

Death from Yellow Fever terrified everyone. The disease progressed ruthlessly from an initial condition of debility, fever, and pains in the extremities and thighs; to a stage of vomiting blood clots (called the black vomit); to jaundice; and finally, death. The doctors did not understand how Yellow Fever was transmitted. To prevent future outbreaks, physicians and town leaders supported improved sanitation and the quarantine of incoming ships. Neither of these measures prevented epidemics from occurring.

During a Yellow Fever epidemic in Galveston in 1853, approximately sixty percent of the 5,000 residents became sick and 523 died. In 1858, 175 people died from Yellow Fever in Houston. During Galveston's last Yellow Fever epidemic in 1867, thousands were ill, and 725 residents died.[582]

Allen played an important role in Galveston's response to Yellow Fever as a member of a committee to draft resolutions concerning the best method of preventing the introduction of yellow fever into the city.[583]

The Allens Interest in Spiritualism

The conditions that led to the rise of Spiritualism in Western New York combined with the fear of death from Yellow Fever made Galveston an excellent location for the introduction and growth of the religion. Several factors may have led to Ebenezer and Sylvinia Allens interest in Spiritualism in the early 1850s. The Allens were not immune to the national interest in Spiritualism. Allen's business associate, Paul Bremond, organized a Spiritualism group in Houston. Allen was also exposed to alternate religious beliefs during his time in Lewiston, New York. The Allens might have been attracted to spiritualism by the deaths of Allen's mother, Hannah, on October 13, 1850 and brother, David, on September 1, 1851.[584] National interest in the subject increased after the 1848 events in Western New York and might have added to their curiosity.[585]

A book published in 1870, *Modern American Spiritualism: A Twenty Years' Record of the Communion Between Earth and the World of Spirits*, by Emma Hardinge Britten, mentions Ebenezer Allen of Galveston, Texas. A chapter of the book is devoted to Spiritualism in Texas and contains quotes from an article Allen sent to the *Spiritual Telegraph*, a publication of the American Spiritualist Society. The piece describes a seemingly miraculous healing of the slave of a Galveston resident performed by a local, well-known medium.[586]

Paul Bremond and Moseley Baker

Paul Bremond was a spiritualist and organized a Houston society for the study of spiritualism. He believed the spirit of Moseley Baker,[587] a soldier in the Texas Revolution, directed Bremond to build another railroad. He obtained a charter in 1875 for the Houston, East and West Texas Railway to run from Houston to Shreveport through the East Texas piney woods. Though the Houston and Texas Central and most railroads were standard gauge (four-foot-eight-inches), Bremond decided to build a narrow gauge (three-foot) road. Bremond thought the narrow-gauge line would be more economical to build and run. Construction began in 1876 and progressed slowly. The line reached Livingston in 1879, Lufkin in 1882, and Nacogdoches in 1883. Because local funds and the state land grant did not supply enough capital, Bremond mortgaged the railroad to obtain loans from eastern bankers. The road continued to build north and east to the Sabine River and eventually linked with the Houston and Shreveport Railroad in January 1886. Unfortunately, Bremond died on May 8, 1885 before the line was completed.[588]

Jean Lafitte

In November 1853, Allen wrote to esteemed naturalist Dr. Gideon Lincecum[589] requesting his help in evaluating a paranormal occurrence:

> *{Private and strictly Confidential.}*
>
> *Galveston Nov 10th 1853*
>
> *My Dear Sir*
>
> *On the morning of my departure from Long Point[590] so interested and absorbed have I become in your con-*

versation and the various topics we were discussing, that I entirely forgot my bill, until it occurred to my recollection while on my way to Brenham in company with Mr. Campbell,[591] *by whom I returned, I fear, too small a compensation. The circumstances annoyed me the more, on account of the pleasure I had enjoyed during my brief stay with you arising from a similarity of tastes and much valuable information which I received from you relating to a variety of subjects not easy to investigate and for which I must always continue your debter [sic]; for, in the wealth of accumulated research and the treasures of experimental science I feel comparatively poor and insolvent.*

I presume my letter will come to you as I myself did, - an unexpected visitor; but the truth is that certain events have transpired since my return, which render me anxious to consult you, and I hope it will not annoy you to comply with the request I am about to make, and to favor me with a communication in reply, at your earliest convenience, for as I expect to be called away from home again in a short time, I am anxious to get your letter before I go.

On Saturday evening the 5th instant I attended a sitting at Ms. Bradbury's[592] *in this city, where she and another medium, Ms. McGuire*[593] *whose husband is a dentist residing in Galveston, being present, the usual experiment was made by laying our hands on the table, which soon began to move very powerfully. On asking "who was present"! - the reply by the alphabet was, "Lafitte."*[594] *He went on to tell us that there was a large treasure buried in the back yard of Dr. McGuire's house, - that the money was stolen from him by some of the men in his employ and concealed in that place - (probably while he occupied this island). He direct-*

ed us to search for it and said we could obtain it and he wished us to do so. Said it would take a man two days and (as I understood) part of another to dig it out. Directed in what shares it should be divided among us. Said it was six feet below the surface; also that he would show the spot by causing the table to march to it and stand over it. On Wednesday last (9th inst) the ladies, my wife being present, tried the experiment at Dr. McGuire's. The table (a small four legged one of the ordinary form) immediately after moving, commenced a regular walk, moving a side at a time and moving forward through the back door and along the walk upon the ground about 15 or 20 feet then turned at right angles, to the right and advanced through the grass and shrubbery to a small figtree [sic], which it went around and stopped on the other side of it some 5 minutes. It then started again very suddenly and advanced about 6 or 8 feet further and remained stationary under a large figtree [sic]. Upon inquiry, it said "the table stood directly over the money." A letter was received by Mrs. McGuire from a daughter I think in Tennessee; stating that the séance spirit had appeared there and told the same story. The letter was dated a short time back and described the spot pointed out by the table with great accuracy. On the evening of the 10th inst I went to Ms. McGuires [sic] at her request, who shew [sic] me the places where the table stopped, and I struck my walking stick into the ground making a small hole at each place. The statement was confirmed by what purported to by other spirits.

Now, I have given you these particulars, in order to request that you will examine this matter by means of your clairvoyant[595] daughter, Mrs. Campbell, and write me the results of your investigation. I asked the influence, if it was willing that I should write you and have the requested investigation made through your daughter; and the reply was that it "wished me to do so." It stated that the spirits could communicate as well through a clairvoyant, as, by means of a medium through the table; - that they were only different moves of like manifestations. -

Will you have the kindness to test the information thus received by mesmerism [hypnotism]? The coincidence, (if it should occur) would be both strange and interesting. I must acknowledge however a total lack of belief on my part in these statements; for belief is a conclusion and how can we reason but from what we know? Still I have right to dis-believe [sic], for this is also an act of the same faculties.

There can be no harm, under the circumstances in having just enough faith, which is not an offspring of reason to try the experiment.

If the account you obtain should correspond with what we have been informed from these singular sources, I will see that the trial is effectually made to obtain the supposed treasure; and further will see that you are amply benefited by a portion of the same. Please be as particular as possible – inquire how much there is etc. etc., if the subject should discover anything.

I am anxious for the letter you were so kind as to promise me on the geology and mineral resources of the County; and I hope that you will believe me when I [Illegible] you that, aside from mystic lore and the interesting developments of nature's mysterious laws, I shall hope to have opportunities to cultivate your acquaintance and evince the sincere regard and esteem with which I am

> *Your friend and Obedient Servant*
>
> *Ebenezer Allen*
>
> P.S. *Dr. McGuire has a large sign on the fence in front of his house with his name and profession "Dentist" printed upon it. I name all the particulars so as to help your Daughter find the place.*
>
> *Dr. Gideon Lincecum*[596]

There is no additional information on whether Mrs. Campbell confirmed the incident or if the treasure was discovered or ever existed.

Ada Stone

While Allen was an interested student, he remained skeptical and sought more evidence before reaching a conclusion. Allen continued to investigate Spiritualism and on July 24, 1854 he wrote to *The Spiritual Telegraph*:

> *Editor of the Telegraph:*
>
> *Not having access to your paper, and being unable to recollect your address or learn it from any one on board this boat, the jarring motion of which so affects my handwriting as to render it unnatural and, I fear, almost illegible, I labor under great disadvantages in arranging the facts which I am about to communicate, and which, I trust, will not prove barren of interest to the multitude of your intelligent readers.*
>
> *It is not, I presume, generally known that the subject of Spiritualism has either attracted the attention or excited the investigation of a portion of the citizens of Galveston (Texas), the place of my residence. Such,*

however, is the case, and the circumstances I am about to relate constitute a part of the fruits or results that have there been produced.

I may hereafter, if desired, give fuller details of the development and manifestations wrought by Spirit-influence in our distant and humble island; but it must suffice at present merely to mention some of the occurrences of the last few weeks, and those as connected with a single medium, partially, but in a degree, I believe, wonderful and astonishing, developed about the first of the present month, and still, I trust, progressing rapidly to a more elevated and perfect development as a poetic medium.

The subject of these remarks is a young girl whose name is Ada, only fourteen years of age, the adopted daughter of Mrs. Stone, whose husband is a highly respectable dentist of our city. Ada until quite recently has been known only as a quiet and affectionate child - a docile, modest, and amiable school-girl, attractive only by the sweetness of her disposition, the simplicity of her character, and a sedate, retiring deportment - in complexion, a rather pale brunette, with an exuberance of dark hair, rather large, deep-set eyes of a peculiarly soft, dreamy, and somewhat melancholy expression. She has not attained her growth, [sic] and retains all the naivete [sic] of childhood.

About the middle of June [1853] last several gentlemen and ladies of Galveston formed a circle and met twice a week at the house of her mother - she and her husband being members - for improvement in spiritual knowledge and intercourse. Ada was always present, but not until after several sittings was it intimated or suspected that she was or would be a medium. The me-

dium relied on was a gentleman (Mr. G.), who, being seized with illness soon after our organization, was unable to attend, and consequently the members met almost hopeless of success. After continuing around the table, however, for nearly two hours, faint and feeble raps were at length heard, which in the course of another half hour became very loud, frequent, and distinct. The alphabet was called for, and some seven or eight of the most distinguished musicians who ever lived announced their names, among whom were Mozart, Handel, Hayden, Paganini, Beethoven, Von Weber, etc.

They would not communicate or converse with any member of the circle but Ada; refused to answer any other; stated that their object was to aid in her development as a medium; directed that the circle should continue its sittings; and informed us that she was to become an extraordinary medium. All questions had to be put by and answered to her, with a few exceptions, and after a few sittings the physical manifestations became very astonishing.

About the first of July I was compelled to be absent from the city on business, and did not return until Saturday evening, the 15th inst. On entering my door my wife informed me that Ada had become developed as a poetess, [sic] and proceeded at once to exhibit [a] piece of her poetic composition, all written during my absence, upon reading which I was not only greatly astonished, but deeply affected.

I called at her residence the next morning, and after reading all the pieces she had then written - amounting to fifteen in number - I requested her to describe to me the mental and physical condition in which she wrote such charming poetry. She complied, and from her description it seems that she continue [sic] in her normal condition. She does not pass into a state of trance, but at some time during almost every day she feels strongly impelled, as by some resistless agency, to write. She takes her pen; the piece - be it poetry or prose - is vividly impressed on her mind, and her hand glides with great celerity [swiftness or speed], and without the action of her own will, over the paper, and in the course of a very few minutes, quicker than it could be copied by the most ready penman, the piece is completed.

She is delighted, but in no degree vain or elated with her talent; claims no merit of authorship; believes herself an instrument in the hands of some superior and beneficent intelligence for the accomplishment of a great work, which, by the way, has been repeatedly promised by the mysterious source from which she derives her inspiration, and God grant that she may never be other than the pure, humble, and unsophisticated being she now is.

I send you a number of her pieces, copied under the disadvantages mentioned, amid the confusion of a crowded steam boat [sic] and the jarring of discordant machinery. Her first effort was a prose composition, written on the 5th instant, as a school exercise. On the next day she warn [was] again impressed, and after two lines were written, she remarked to her mother, who warn [was] sitting by her side: "Oh, ma! it is going to be poetry!"

I have marked the copy of this piece thus (first piece), that you may distinguish it. It seems addressed to her, contain[s] excellent advice intended for her observance, and, like several others, manifests a ten-

der interest, an affectionate regard, a deep and pure friendship felt toward her by her heavenly guardians. This feeling on the part of her immortal friends has often been exhibited, and in divers [different or several] way. Her mother, who is a good writing medium, read to me a beautiful poem written with her own hand, evidently by the guardian intelligence of Ada, filled with directions touching her course toward her daughter, two lines of which, as nearly as I can recollect, were as follows:

"Thou hast one duty here below - To watch and guard thy child."

Just before I left my house on the 16th instant to go to the steamer on my present journey, Ada called with her mother, and read to me the short but sweet piece, written by her only a few minutes before my departure, and which I have copied and marked - in order that you may identify it - thus (sixteenth piece). She was desirous of furnishing me with some evidence of her talent before I left, and the result was the production of those beautiful lines.

I inclose [sic] also a brief note addressed by Ada to my wife (about the 7th inst., but undated), and an original poem entitled "The Anthem of the Sea," written, on the 13th instant, within the space of five minutes. The poem shows her handwriting, rapidly executed under Spirit-influence - all her pieces being in a similar hand - while the note exhibit, her ordinary handwriting. Thus you will be able to compare her chirography [handwriting or penmanship] under both conditions, and I think, upon close inspection, a great similarity between the two hands may be discovered.

Ada had written sixteen different poems at the time of my leaving Galveston, on the 18th of July inst. The first original poetry Ada ever wrote, the copy of which is marked (first piece), as aforesaid, was written on the 6th inst.; all the others between the 6th and 16th, making sixteen original pieces in ten days. I feel that any remarks or comments from me on the merits of these productions would be utterly useless. They speak for themselves, and have received from critical and competent judges, in New Orleans and elsewhere, to whom they have been submitted, the need [a deserved share or reward] of approval, commendation, and praise. All, of nice poetic taste and cultivated intellect to whom they have been submitted - and 1 have submitted them to none other - have expressed an enthusiastic surprise, delight, and admiration that a child - a young school-girl of fourteen - should display such cultivated taste, brilliancy or imagination, purity of diction, and maturity of poetic genius as the poems evince. I presume that ere [before] this day the number of her pieces has been more than doubled, and their character elevated and improved. May we not anticipate the accomplishment of something great through such a medium - the realization of the prophetic assurance announced in her behalf by the bright but invisible intelligence, which surround, guard, and inspire her? How superior to the graces of the drawing-room are those immortal graces, woven in the wreath yet to adorn thy brow, sweet Ada! daughter of the muses and beloved of angel-hearts! If thou canst but hold thee unsubdued by surrounding temptations, and ever pure as thy "Childhood's Prayer!"

It is a little remarkable that every poem is in a different measure from all the others - no two being in the same meter or measure.

Ada Note to Mrs. A.

My Kind Friend:

It was with mingled feelings of pleasure and almost surprise that I received the more than welcome note from yourself. To your many kind inquiries I am happy to give each a satisfactory answer. I do most surely feel as if I were surrounded by pure and heavenly Spirits. Oh! I do hope that it is not imagination on my part; indeed I am most certain it is not. Mamma bids me say she has not heard the whispers or the Angels again, but she prays that she may again hear those exquisite words buoying up the heart - "I will! I will!" If I am inspired to-day [sic] (and I do most sincerely hope I will be), I shall certainly hasten to show it (the piece) to you, and receive your comments, for it is very pleasing to myself to see you so enraptured (as it were). Do pardon all faults and in the expectation of seeing you very soon, I will close.

I am yours, most truly, Ada.

I may be mistaken as to the importance of the matters here communicated, but not as to the facts. Of the latter I am an eye-and-ear-witness - a member of the circle in which Ada was developed. I have exaggerated in nothing, but on the contrary, have related only a few of the leading facts leaving the rest, and all the circumstances connected with the history of Spiritual Manifestations in Galveston and elsewhere in Texas untold. Physical manifestations produced by Spirit - influence a series of wonderful examples not surpassed in "modern instances" I could relate; but these compare not, in my view, either in vitality or importance, with the intellectual development - one instance of which I have here recorded - the remainder rest untold.

Yours truly,

E. A.

Note by the Editor: - Our correspondent refers to Judge Harvey Baldwin of Syracuse, Henry Sheldon, of this city, and other distinguished gentlemen here and elsewhere, who will vouch for his character and the fidelity of his statements. E A. [Ebenezer Allen] will please except our thanks for these interesting contributions to the Telegraph. We shall expect to hear from him again soon, and as often as the nature of the developments or his own inclination may prompt him to write. We send the paper to the parties named by our correspondent.[597]

Mrs. A. E. Force

By 1856, Allen had become a regular and valued correspondent of *The Spiritual Telegraph*:

Spiritualism in Texas

Galveston, July 2, 1856

Gentlemen: Some five months ago, a letter from Mr. Henry Force of Madison, Orange County, Texas, appeared in the Telegraph giving an account of the singular apparition of a black hand in presence of several respectable gentlemen and ladies, while the medium, Mrs. A. E. Force, anticipating a communication from the spirit-world, sat waiting at the table in the attitude of writing ... In that portion of Texas where Mr. Force resides, Spiritualism was of spontaneous growth. Mrs.

Force was unexpectedly acted upon by mysterious powers, and she became, at what precise date I am not informed, a medium of superior capacities.

A gentleman living about two miles from her dwelling, had a favorite servant who was suffering under a severe rheumatic attack. He was in great pain and unable to rise from his bed. One dark, stormy night in January last, she was roused from her slumber, under the influence of a strong impression that she must get up immediately and go to her neighbor's. She waked [sic] her husband, who at first tried to dissuade her, but in vain. The impression was imperative and could not be resisted, and he consented to accompany her. Travelling over a prairie through deep mud, and facing a violent wind, with the rain falling in torrents, they reached the house of their neighbor an hour or more past midnight. At her request, she was conducted to the room of the negro [sic]. She found him in great agony, and immediately commenced making passes over him. She continued her manipulations at intervals as directed by her impressions, and before morning the servant was restored to health. So complete, indeed, was the cure that, at an early hour, he went to work as usual, and continued his labor without any relapse or inconvenience.

Other examples might be related but for want of space. Her mediumship is not restricted to the department of healing, and I send you some communications recently written by her hand.

Under the date of June 7, is the following addressed to J. H. C.:

"Dear Mortal Friends, - We will to-night, [sic]

speak of the conditions of other worlds. We may not tell anything altogether new, but all good spirits can add their testimony. Your system of worlds is progressing and becoming more refined.

The atmosphere, also, is becoming more suitable to the spiritual progress of your race.

When earth's inhabitants shall have progressed still further, they will have more perfect organizations - more love and wisdom. Then, new inventions, or rather, new applications of the agencies under their control, will be discovered by them. Then steam power will be dispensed with, and in its stead you will use electricity. Good night, dear friends.

Question: (By one of the circle) Spirits say the earth is receding from the sun. What is the cause?

Answer: The attractions are growing weaker in that direction and stronger in the opposite.

Q: Can spirits suppress crime? If so, how long before they will do it?

A: They do so now, in many instances. We think, probably in ten years it will be quite common; but mediumship is not properly established yet, so as to admit of dependence on communications. Evil spirits will communicate, as well as good, and mortals cannot always be guarded on that point; but, as a general rule, judge the spirits by what they write. Good night.

Many other communications of an interesting nature are furnished by Mr. Ebenezer Allen, proving the general coincidence of spiritual teachings everywhere, and the growth and progress of the cause in this section of the country.[598]

The interest in spiritualism continued with Ebenezer's son, William Pitt Allen.[599]

GALVESTON AND THE CIVIL WAR

Slavery and Secession

The perceived threats to the Southern economy and society made slavery the major political issue in America. The problem can be traced to the compromises made by the founding fathers to form a confederation of states. The measures created a political battlefield between federal governance and the right of the states to govern themselves. Both northern and southern states invoked "states' rights" when federal regulations conflicted with state laws or desires. Slavery and the power of the slaveholding states evolved into an issue in which secession became the only solution.

In the 1850s, many Texans believed that slavery was essential to the importance and growth of the state's economy. Slavery grew rapidly in Texas after annexation, and by 1860 slaves accounted for thirty percent of the population. Transportation limitations forced plantations to concentrate along the river valleys of eastern Texas and in the coastal counties below Houston and Galveston. Only the cotton grown in these locations could easily reach the market. In other settled parts of Texas, slavery was nonexistent, and the economy depended on livestock, corn, and wheat. By 1860, inadequate transportation divided Texas into a region dependent on slavery and another independent on slavery.[600]

Population and economic demographics influenced attitudes about secession. Most residents in the slaveholding areas came to Texas from the plantation society of the lower South. In areas where cotton was not grown, the settlers came from many different places in the country. Texas communities on the frontier were settled by non-slaveholders from the upper South and Germany. The farmers in north-central Texas were wheat growers from the upper South. In the southwest and along the Rio Grande River, the Mexican, German, and British American residents were opposed to slavery. Settlers from the upper South, who lived in cotton-growing, slaveholding areas, adopted the lower South culture and generally supported secession. Immigrants from the plantation society of the lower south preferred leaving the Union instead of abandoning slavery.

Political affiliations also influenced opinions on slavery and secession. Democrats defended the right of individuals to own slaves regardless of the impact on the Union. Whigs and other opposition groups were unwilling to divide the Union to maintain slavery. Germans, who did not own slaves, supported secession in Comal County out of loyalty to the Democratic Party. Whig slaveholders in Galveston and Harrison counties opposed secession.

Public anxiety and fear increased support for secession. Texans were afraid that Lincoln and the Republican Party would abolish slavery. White Texans were concerned abolition would be the first step toward racial equality with black Texans.[601]

Secession Convention

By October 1860, it was obvious the country would select Abraham Lincoln as the new president. In anticipation of the expected Republican victory, Texans began serious discussions on secession. After Lincoln's election in November, South Carolina seceded in December and ignited a chain reaction that resulted in five other states leaving the Union. Other slaveholding states governed by wealthy slave owners followed South Carolina's example. The threat of the abolition of slavery and emancipation of slaves terrified the slaveholders. Their financial wealth was based on the value of their slaves and the land the slaves worked. Their land would be worthless without slave labor to grow and harvest the cotton. Thus, with a single blow, abolition would deprive prominent Southern planters of their valuable assets in slaves and land and change their status from rich to poor. For wealthy Texas landowners, the decision was straightforward. The hard-earned statehood was discarded in favor of aligning Texas' fortunes with a new confederation.

The departure of additional slaveholding states increased the interest in secession in Texas. However, only the governor could call a special session of the legislature to consider the question, and only the legislature could meet in a convention to discuss and vote on the issue. Governor Houston refused to act and hoped over time enthusiasm for secession would decline. Several prominent Texans including Oran M. Roberts,[602] chief justice of the Texas Supreme Court, and John S. Ford[603] realized Houston needed to be forced to call the special session. In early December 1860, Roberts and Ford published announcements in Texas newspapers asking counties to hold citizen meetings on January 8, 1861 to elect delegates for a convention on secession. They proposed county judges to supervise the elections, and for the elected delegates to hold a convention on January 28 to discuss secession. When it became obvious that Texans were determined to hold a convention, Governor Houston decided to convene a special session of the legislature in mid-January to consider the meeting. He hoped legislators would declare the convention illegal. Instead, congressmen approved the convention, allowed the representatives to use the House chambers for the event, and adjourned.

The convention delegates were elected by a voice vote at meetings throughout the state. Unionists either refused to attend the meetings they believed were illegal or were discouraged from appearing. Not surprising, the elected delegates favored secession. Slaveholders constituted seventy percent of the delegates and nearly all of them originally came from slaveholding states.[604]

The convention began on Monday afternoon, January 28, 1861. The delegates selected O. M. Roberts as presiding officer. Roberts told the representatives they were acting as the special agents of the people: "All political power is inherent in the people. That power, I assert, you now represent." The following day, John A. Wharton[605] asked for a vote on whether Texas should secede. He moved "that without determining now the manner in which this result should be effected [sic], it is the deliberate sense of this Convention that the state of Texas should separately secede." George M. Flournoy[606] seconded the motion and the delegates voted for secession: 152 to 6. Over the next two days, the members drafted a formal ordinance of secession and requested a popular referendum to allow citizens to vote on secession. On February 1, the delegates approved the ordinance of secession: 166 to 8. [Please see The Ordinance of the Texas Convention in the Appendix.]

The delegates sent seven representatives to Montgomery, Alabama to meet with envoys from other states to organize the Confederate States of America. The convention representatives formed a committee on public safety. The committee authorized the seizure of all federal property in Texas including the arsenal at San Antonio.[607]

In the state referendum on February 23, 1861, Texans approved secession by a vote of 44,317 to 13,020. The delegates to the secession convention reconvened on March 5, declared Texas independent, authorized additional steps for Texas to join the Confederacy, and reorganized the state's government. The members demanded all the current officeholders swear a loyalty oath to the Confederate States of America. Sam Houston refused to take the oath and claimed the convention's actions, after it adjourned in February, were illegal. In response, the convention delegates declared the office of governor vacant and instructed Lieutenant Governor Edward Clark[608] to assume the office.[609] In the space of about two months, the delegates removed Texas from the United States of America, joined the Confederate States of America, and ended Sam Houston's political career. [Please see Texas Declaration of Causes, Act to Admit Texas to the Confederate States of America, Texas Ordinance of Secession, and Ordinance to Ratify the Confederate Constitution in the Appendix.]

The Confederate attack on Fort Sumter put a match to the powder keg of the Civil War. President Jefferson Davis' approval of the assault of the Union fort in Charleston Harbor damaged chances for a negotiated settlement to the South's grievances. When President Abraham Lincoln responded by calling for 75,000 volunteers to put down the rebellion, he ended any hope for peace.

Federal Blockade

On April 19, 1861, President Lincoln issued the "Proclamation of Blockade against Southern Ports." The order authorized "a competent force ... to prevent entrance and exit of vessels from the ports." The proclamation closed 3,500 miles of Confederate coastline to shipping. To enforce the order, the Federal Department of the Navy stationed its ships offshore at all critical ports. The Navy added new ports to the list as other states joined the Confederacy. The blockade had several important goals: to restrict the import of manufactured goods, (especially military material) into the Confederacy, to cut off the export of cotton, and to implement General-in-Chief Winfield Scott's "Anaconda Plan." This proclamation had significant consequences on Galveston and tested both the military authorities and citizens.[610]

General Scott's Anaconda Plan extended and refined the blockade. Scott's war strategy had two important elements: First, all ports in the seceding states would be strongly blockaded and second, a Union army of around 80,000 men would move down the Mississippi River to cut the Confederacy in half. Scott said a small amphibious force would advance rapidly down the river and capture Confederate positions along the route. A larger army would follow the advance troops and secure the victories. The Union troops would continue down the river and seize the forts below New Orleans. When they fell, the river would be in federal hands from its source to its mouth and cut the Confederacy in two.[611]

The federal blockade of Galveston began on July 2, 1861 with the arrival of the USS *South Carolina*. The Union steamer seized several small sailing ships that tried to run the blockade. Confederate artillery officer, John C. Moore, said the ship's arrival "threw the people of the city into a temporary state of violent convulsions." Citizens rushed to the tops of buildings and upper story windows to observe the Union threat and worry about "the terrible consequences they expected soon to follow." Fortunately for the residents, the blockading ships stayed outside the harbor.[612]

Despite the patriotic fervor for the Southern cause, many people recognized that Galveston would be difficult to guard against an expected Union attack. The Confederate military thought the city was indefensible, and the governor suggested burning the city rather than allowing it to fall into Union hands. Faced with destruction, abandonment, and/or occupation, many Galvestonians left the island for Houston and other inland cities and did not return until 1865.[613] Soon, those who stayed felt the sting of Union occupation.

Impact on Ebenezer Allen

Texas' secession and the outbreak of war added to Allen's financial problems. Allen's fortunes were tied to commerce with Northern businesses and access to the commercial center in New York City. Secession severed these connections and reduced Allen's income. Entrepreneurial projects in Texas lost financial support from eastern investors. Secession disrupted the extensive commercial dealings with merchants in England and New York. Because Galveston was the most important port in Texas and a strategic target, the Union blockade and potential military attacks would disrupt the peace necessary to conduct business and legal transactions.

Many of Allen's associates in the railroad and legal community supported secession. After Sam Houston was removed from office, Allen lost an important friend and benefactor. These situations forced Allen to either support the Confederacy or relocate to a Union state. Since coming to Galveston, the Allens tried to adapt to the Southern slaveholding society. Although Ebenezer and Sylvinia were Yankees in the truest sense of the word, their financial future was bound to Texas' prosperity.

Allen was a member of the Committee of Public Protection and participated in its initial meetings. Allen seconded the nomination of E. Malone as chairman of a commission to raise funds for the defense of the city. The group's membership increased from five to thirteen, and Allen was added as an additional associate. The board was charged with acting "for the ways and means and as an advisory body to the Commandant of Galveston."[614]

Committees of Public Safety

Representatives at the first meeting of the Secession Convention in February 1861 appointed fifteen members to a Committee of Public Safety and named John C. Robertson[615] chairman. The representatives authorized the commission to implement the secession program and overcome opposition by Texas Unionists. The group appointed Benjamin McCulloch, Henry McCulloch, and John S. Ford colonels and ordered the men to raise an army to suppress the Unionists and protect the citizens until the Confederate Army was able to defend the state.

The agency confiscated all federal commercial and military property in Texas. They seized the U.S. Army arsenal at San Antonio and forced about 3,000 federal troops to leave Texas. The capture of the San Antonio arsenal, expulsion of federal troops, and attendance at the secession conference in Montgomery made the secession referendum appear as an afterthought.[616]

To maintain law and order, the convention formed Committees of Public Safety throughout the state. The local committees organized armed forces to restrain Unionists opposed to secession. The militia seized federal property, defended the Texas frontier and coastline, and provided "general protection." In late February, the committee appointed three Galvestonians to lead the "public safety" efforts in their city. Sidney Sherman organized the city's defenses, John S. "Rip" Ford captured arms and equipment held by the federal authorities, and Ebenezer B. Nichols managed finances for Galveston's war effort.[617] James Pope Cole, chief justice for the county commissioners' court, chaired the Galveston committee.[618]

Allen's son, William Pitt Allen, described his father's involvement in the Civil War:

> *My father took an active part in the Confederate cause from the commencement of the agitation antecedent to hostilities until his decease in 1863. He, as much as Sam Houston and some other statesmen of the Republic of Texas, favored the resumption of the independence of Texas. He was a member of the "committee of safety" in Galveston, charged to preserve order in the city pending the change of government in the latter months of 1860 and the early part of 1861.*[619]

The Civil War Comes to Galveston

In 1860, Galveston was the largest city in Texas and the state's major seaport. The city's population was 7,207 including about 1,200 slaves. Forty percent of the non-slave population was born outside the United States. In 1860, 194,000 bales of cotton, seventy-five percent of the total shipped from Texas ports, moved across the island's docks. The editor of the *Galveston News* estimated that Galveston's commerce was growing at the amazing rate of fifty percent annually.

Initially, Galvestonians opposed secession because of the city's reliance on international and domestic trade. However, secession became popular after Lincoln's election.[620] Galvestonians were confident that Texas would secede, and the *Galveston Weekly News* published an extra with a black-bordered "Epitaph of the Union."[621] The city celebrated South Carolina's departure from the Union, and several of its leading citizens played an important part in the secession convention. In the statewide vote on secession on February 23, 1861, Galvestonians supported leaving the Union by a margin of 765 to 33.[622]

Governor Houston refused to sign an oath of allegiance to the Confederacy and resigned on March 16, 1861. He delivered a farewell speech in Galveston to a crowd of hostile Confederate supporters. He doubted that after "the sacrifice of countless millions in treasure, and hundreds of thousands of precious lives" the South would win their independence.[623]

The harsh realities of war overwhelmed the city. Father Louis C. M. Chambodut wrote to the Archbishop of New Orleans:

> *... the misery is very great. Many families are reduced to beg or starve. There is no work for laborers, money is scarce and provisions are at the highest prices. The exodus from Galveston is great every day and if the city is taken very few persons will be found in it except the soldiers.*

Another resident said the soldiers were "not as well trained as animals of the brute creation in Europe" that behaved like a "mercenary" army.

The *Galveston Civilian* moved to Houston. Merchants engaged in profiteering. Crimes by soldiers and civilians increased anxieties. From the summer of 1861 to the spring of 1862, the city settled into "a waiting game" that became "a monotonous routine."[624]

The federal blockade was not very effective, and shipping continued nearly at pre-blockade levels. Blockade-runners transported cotton to Havana and other ports and returned with military supplies and consumer goods. However, on October 4, 1862, conditions in Galveston changed from bad to worse.

Under Union Control

Captain Henry Eagle, commander of the USS *Santee*, was outraged by this illegal trade and demanded the surrender of Galveston on May 17, 1862. As a result, Brigadier General Paul O. Hébert,[625] the Confederate military commander for the District of Texas, realized that Galveston's defenses were not prepared to protect the city from a sustained attack, and ordered the evacuation of civilians, livestock, supplies, and cannon. Captain Eagle was unable to carry out his threat because his crew was sick with scurvy.[626]

After blockading the harbor for fourteen months, the Union Navy finally decided to occupy Galveston. On October 4, 1862, Commander William B. Renshaw, in charge of the Union ships guarding Galveston Bay, sent United States Revenue Cutter *Harriet Lane* into the harbor under a flag of truce. The officers on the Union ship demanded Galveston's surrender and allowed the military authorities one-hour to consider the ultimatum. The Confederate commander, Colonel Joseph J. Cook,[627] refused to travel to the Union ship or send an officer to receive the communication. Renshaw considered Cook's actions as a rejection of his demands, and the *Harriet Lane* returned to the fleet. Then Renshaw ordered four Union steamers, with a mortar boat in tow, to enter the harbor and move to the area where the *Harriet Lane* had anchored. In response, the single Confederate artillery cannon at Fort Point[628] fired several shots at the Union ships. The federal ships returned fire, disabled the gun, and fired at other targets in the city.

Two Confederate guns at Fort Bankhead[629] also fired at the flotilla but did not cause any damage and the Union Navy ignored them. Colonel Cook sent a boat with two Confederate officers to the USS *Westfield* to meet with Renshaw. Renshaw demanded the unconditional surrender of Galveston or he would begin bombarding the town again. Cook rejected Renshaw's terms and warned the Union commander he would be guilty of destroying the town and killing women, children, and immigrants.

Renshaw was unyielding, decided to resume the shelling, and prepared to tow the mortar boat into position. Faced with a destructive Union attack on the city, one of the Confederate officers on Renshaw's ship asked if he could talk with Colonel Cook again. The officer negotiated a four-day truce with Renshaw to evacuate the women, children, and foreigners from the city. Cook approved the truce. If Renshaw would not move troops closer to Galveston, Cook would not permit his men to come below the city.

During the truce, soldiers, and civilians abandoned the island and moved to the mainland. Union ships now held the harbor. However, it took until December 25 for the 264 men of Colonel I. S. Burrell's Forty-Second Massachusetts Infantry to arrive, occupy Kuhn's Wharf,[630] and patrol the town. This was the start of the year-long Union occupation of Texas' largest port.[631]

The capture of Galveston "produced a profound and painful sensation" among the people. Galvestonians were humiliated and indignant after some Texas newspapers blamed the residents "for the surrender of the city to a few ferryboats."[632]

Galveston Recaptured

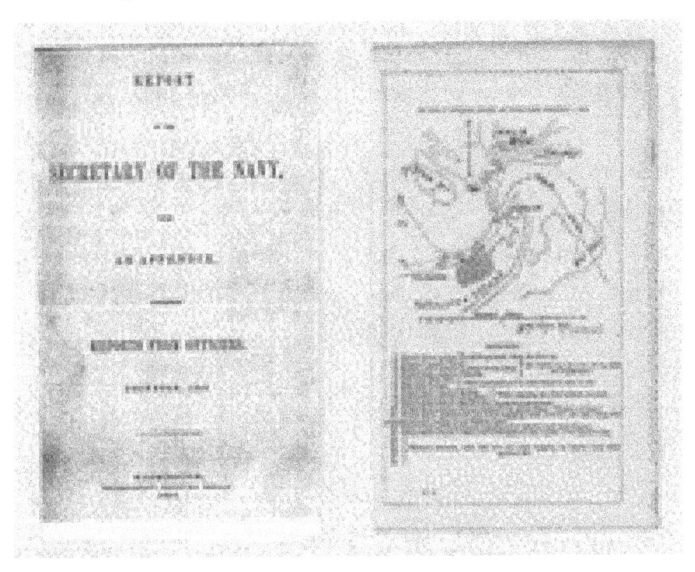

Attack on the Federal Fleet at Galveston, January 1, 1863
(Library of Congress)

After Major General John Bankhead Magruder[633] replaced Hébert in November 1862, the new district commander formed a plan to recapture Galveston. Magruder devised a joint naval and land attack on the federal forces. For the naval attack, he placed artillery and dismounted cavalry commanded by Colonel Thomas Green[634] aboard two river steamers. The *Bayou City* and the *Neptune* were led by Captain Leon Smith.[635] Magruder assembled infantry and cavalry, directed by Brigadier General William R. Scurry[636] for the land portion of the attack. Confederate artillery composed of twenty light and heavy cannons supported the assault. Under the plan, the Confederates would cross the railroad bridge onto the island and capture the federal forces at Kuhn's Wharf. Union Commander Renshaw had six ships with twenty-nine heavy artillery pieces to repulse the attack.

The Confederates entered Galveston on New Year's night, January 1, 1863, and opened fire before dawn. Colonel Cook's forces could not capture the wharf because the ladders supplied to his men were too short. Shells from Union naval guns helped repulse the assault. Two Confederate "cottonclads" attacked the rear of the Union squadron. The USS *Harriet Lane* sank the CSS *Neptune* when it tried to ram the Union ship, but soldiers and sailors from the CSS *Bayou City* boarded and captured the federal vessel. Renshaw's flagship, the USS *Westfield*, ran aground, and the commander died trying to blow up his ship rather than surrender it. The other Union ships ignored Confederate surrender demands, sailed out to sea, and forced the federal infantry in town to surrender. The port stayed under Confederate control for the rest of the war.[637]

Galveston provided between 1,000 and 1,500 men for the Confederate Army. Volunteer aid societies sewed bandages, uniforms, and flags. The societies supplied cartridge cases and other provisions. A local fair raised over $2,000 for uniforms, accoutrements, and support of widowed women and orphaned children.[638]

THE TORPEDO BUREAU

Torpedoes were used in warfare long before the Civil War. The Dutch placed underwater obstacles around 1588 to defend Antwerp against Spanish ships. The American military used an underwater device to blow up a British schooner in the Revolutionary War. Robert Fulton developed a submarine device during the Napoleonic Wars. The inventor of the steamboat named the underwater explosive weapon a "torpedo" after the torpedo fish that paralyzes its prey with an electrical shock. Advances in naval technology increased the interest in creating underwater ordnance. The Union blockade of Southern ports convinced the Confederate Navy to develop weapons to protect these ports and destroy the Union ships.[639]

General Gabriel Rains

Gabriel J. Rains
(Library of Congress)

Gabriel Rains was the genius behind the research, improvement, and implementation of mines and torpedoes. Rains graduated from the United States Military Academy in 1827. He served as an infantry commander in the Indian Territory. During the Florida War against the Seminole Indians (1839-1842), Captain Rains developed a mine using an explosive shell, with a friction primer, which was buried in the ground. The device was intended to alert his force of approaching

Indians.

When the Civil War began, Jefferson Davis recommended Rains be appointed a brigadier general. Rains led a brigade during the Virginia Peninsula Campaign (March – July 1862). During the Confederate withdrawal, Rains planted several subterranean shells along their route to Williamsburg, Virginia. He placed additional shells as the Confederate forces retreated towards Richmond. Union cavalry detonated the shells in Yorktown, Virginia and several men were killed. General George B. McClellan, commander of the Army of the Potomac, denounced the torpedoes as "murderous and barbarous" and "threatened to use Confederate prisoners to remove them." Confederate Commander Joseph E. Johnston of the Army of Northern Virginia deplored the practice. Brigadier General Rains defended the explosive devices because their use deterred and demoralized advancing Union troops. The Confederate Secretary of War, George W. Randolph, opposed the use of subterranean shells "merely to destroy life," but said the devices could be employed to protect defensive works and defend armies from enemy forces. Randolph permitted Rains to use the weapon to defend rivers and harbors from attacks and blockades. When General Robert E. Lee replaced Johnston in June 1862, he ordered Rains to use "submarine defenses" to protect the James and Appomattox Rivers.

Rains was selected to direct production of various explosive devices including land mines, naval mines, and "coal torpedoes." Over the next three months, General Rains developed and placed "submarine mortar batteries" in the James River. The bureau was officially authorized on October 25, 1862 as the Army Torpedo Bureau. The unit was responsible for guarding ports along the southern coast and defending Confederate forts on inland waters. At the same time the Confederate Congress sanctioned formation of the Naval Submarine Battery Service and the Secret Service Corps.[640] Since it was impossible to precisely define the areas of responsibility of the three agencies, the services cooperated with each other in joint operations. There were no restrictions on the Secret Service Corps, and it became the *de facto* senior organization.[641]

Singer and Fretwell's Mine

About the time the Confederate Congress authorized the Torpedo Bureau, events on the Texas Coast advanced the development of submarine weapons. During the Union attack on Galveston in the fall of 1862, federal ships patrolled and blockaded other points along the Texas coastline. The Union warships discovered a "backwater, mosquito-infested village" called La Vaca (Lavaca), which was about two days' sail south of Galveston. La Vaca's population peaked during the Civil War when the village became a center of military activity. Confederate authorities located a large arsenal and small-arms factory in the town. To protect the installations, the Confederate authorities garrisoned troops in La Vaca.[642]

In the fall of 1862, Captain Daniel Shea's[643] company of Texas Light Artillery defended the village. The poorly equipped home guard was mainly composed of middle-aged men who were unfit for active field duty. The war reached La Vaca in late October 1862 when a small Union fleet steamed into Matagorda Bay. On October 31 and November 1, federal gunboats fired more than 250 rounds onto La Vaca's streets and homes. Shea's two waterfront artillery batteries returned fire on the federal gunboats and forced them to withdraw.

The artillery bombardment enraged the town's residents and their home guard defenders. Private Edgar C. Singer was one of the men operating the guns. The Ohio gunsmith promised it would be the last time a Northern fleet slipped unnoticed into a Southern harbor. Singer was a nephew of Isaac Merritt Singer, the inventor of the first commercially successful sewing machine. Edgar Singer worked on his uncle's sewing machine design and received a patent for "improvements." Soon after the Union attack, Singer began experimenting with a device to protect the town from future attacks. He detonated small charges of gunpowder in a water-filled barrel. The test results convinced him that he could develop an underwater explosive device to destroy Union ships. However, he needed men and money to refine his ideas and conduct small-scale, backyard tests to turn his plans into an effective Confederate weapon.

Singer obtained help from fellow brothers in the Harmony Masonic Lodge. His first recruit was Dr. John Fretwell. Forty-seven-year old Fretwell was the lodge leader and a private in Captain Shea's artillery company. The men refined the concept into a device they called a "mine." They presented their new weapon to Captain Shea. Singer and Fretwell chose an old, partially beached hulk as the target for the demonstration. They placed the mine beside the wreck and detonated it. The mine exploded and blew the vessel to pieces. Shea was amazed and immediately sent the two inventors to General John Magruder in Houston.[644]

Singer and Fretwell arrived in Houston in 1862 to meet with Magruder. However, the general was busy organizing forces to recapture Galveston and postponed the meeting until Confederate troops regained control of the island. Magruder finally met with Singer and Fretwell in 1863 and gave them twenty-five pounds of gunpowder to demonstrate their device in Buffalo Bayou in Houston. The inventors submerged their mine in the bayou and floated an old wide-bottom boat above the mine. When the boat struck the mine, "she was blown into kindling wood."

Civil War Torpedo
(Author's Photograph)

Confederate engineers evaluated the mine and recommended its adoption "as a powerful accessory to our limited means." With the approval of the Confederate military, Singer began to construct the explosive devices in his small workshop. The water mine or torpedo he created consisted of a cylinder-shaped, watertight metal canister of gunpowder with four spring-loaded detonating rods. When a passing vessel triggered the mine by contacting one of its rods, the spring-driven rod slammed into the end of the metal canister and detonated two internal percussion caps. The entire device was chained to a small anchor and submerged about three feet below the water, with its four-pronged detonating triggers in an upright position.

Confederate Torpedoes
(Library of Congress)

In early February 1863, most of Singer's group traveled to Richmond to demonstrate the new mine to the War Department. The following month the Confederate Congress approved an act "to provide and organize engineer troops." Secretary of War James Seddon authorized Singer to form a company of no more than twenty-five men for a special torpedo service attached to the Bureau of Engineers. The company would report directly to the commander of the district where they were working. Captain Singer organized a unit called "Singer's Submarine Corps."[645]

Creuzbaur and the *Sea King*

Singer and Fretwell were not the first inventors to propose weapons for the Southern war effort. In 1861, Robert Creuzbaur,[646] a surveyor and drafter who worked with the General Land Office of Texas as a mapmaker, designed a gunboat to destroy Union ships.

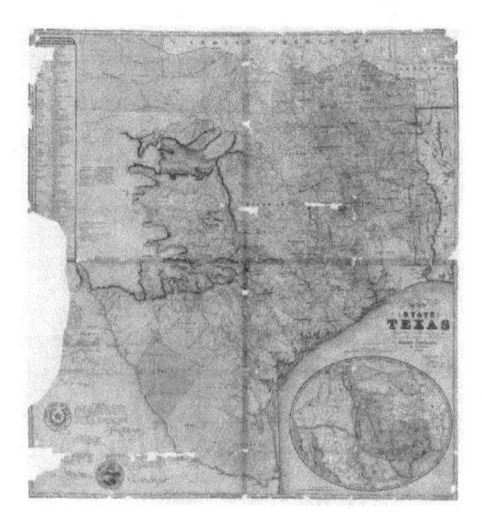

Map of the State of Texas by Robert Creuzbaur
(Texas General Land Office)

In November 1861, Creuzbaur submitted a plan to the Texas government. The officials were impressed, and recommended construction of an iron-plated gunboat called the *Sea King* for service in the Confederate Navy. Creuzbaur's gunboat was made of wood and iron with propellers at the stern powered by a hot-air engine.[647] The hot air engine produced enough energy to propel the ship at a rate of eighteen miles an hour. In addition to guns on the deck, he proposed equipping the *Sea King* with a "submarine cannon." The gun would be located below the waterline and would demolish the wooden hulls of the Union fleet.

Creuzbaur needed to obtain approval from Texas authorities before he could present his invention to the Confederate Government in Richmond. Governor Francis R. Lubbock[648] appointed a "commission of three scientific gentlemen:" William Van Rosenberg, James Brown, and Dr. J. M. Steiner, to examine the plans. The Texas legislature also formed their own boards to investigate the proposal. These committees concluded Creuzbaur's ship could potentially "destroy in a short time the whole naval power of our enemies."

On November 25, 1861, the Texas House approved the construction of an effective marine force and appropriated $500 for Robert Creuzbaur to present his plan to the Confederate War Department in Richmond. An article in the December 17, 1861 issue of the Richmond Dispatch quoted a report from the *Texas State Gazette*: "The invention of Mr. Creuzbaur, which is secret as yet, and for the bringing of which to the notice of the Confederate Government $500 has been appropriated, has been fully examined by a commission of three scientific gentlemen appointed by the Governor, who reported in its favour [sic], and express the opinion that a single vessel properly constructed will be sufficient to clear any port of a blockading fleet."[649]

In December 1861, Creuzbaur conducted demonstrations for Commander Matthew F. Maury aboard the CSS *Teaser*[650] on the James River. In 1862, the Confederate States Navy appointed Creuzbaur a ship or sailing master[651] and assigned him to the Richmond station. He resigned his position on September 1, 1862 and engaged Ebenezer Allen to act as his agent in negotiations with the Confederate government. Creuzbaur and Allen were both private citizens. Around this time, the South had won another victory at Second Bull Run and the Antietam Campaign was about to begin.

William Pitt Allen described his father's involvement with the torpedo bureau:

> *After the blockade of Southern seafronts was established, he strove to destroy it by promoting the torpedo service and was so employed until his death. He was not connected to the Confederate army in any capacity, but served as a volunteer for a few weeks in the defense of Richmond, Virginia, during the Gettysburg campaign.*[652]

On September 26, 1862, Allen presented Creuzbaur's designs for the *Sea King* to the Confederate Congress in Richmond:

C/

Confidential

Richmond, Sept. 26, 1862

To the Honorable Chairman and Members of the Committee on National Affairs of the Senate,

Gentlemen,

In view of the near adjournment of the present session of Congress and of the vast importance, as he humbly conceives, of the plans and means invented by Robert Creuzbaur for the destruction of the enemy's fleets now infesting our waters and laying under heavy and ruinous contributions the inhabitants and property of our river valleys and sea coasts, the undersigned, who is the specially authorized representative of Mr. Creuzbaur, would respectfully invite the attention of the committee to a few points proposed to be attained by the plans and appliances referred to. He can now do so only very briefly, referring however, as he begs to do, to the drawings and specifications, which he will be glad to exhibit to the committee, for the details.

The vessels which Mr. Creuzbaur proposes to build with the sanction and aid of Congress, are to be shot-proof [sic], to have superior speed and facilities of steering and maneuvering, and to be provided with destructive appliances for destroying with ease and certainty the enemy's ships.

As will be seen from the drawings and specifications, the form, material and construction of the proposed vessels secures the fulfillment of the first condition - the use of wood, cotton and iron, with the arched walls, to make them impenetrable to shot and shell. The form and power of the engine will give them the requisite speed to overtake the enemy and bring him to battle, while the novel expedient of the propeller working within the body of the vessel and entirely submerged, will give the desired facilities for steering and maneuvering, and enable the ship without danger from shot or shell of the enemy to evade or foil any onset from his rams. But the most important of all is, undoubtedly, the destructive appliances of the torpedo or floating battery and submarine cannon, which will enable the vessel to reach the enemy in his most vulnerable parts, under water. Until now, torpedoes have remained useless in naval warfare from the fact that no plan had been devised by which they could be made to sheer away from the vessel using them and come into contact with the adversary. As Comdr. Maury reports, after full experiment upon Mr. Creuzbaur's invention to obviate this apparently insuperable difficulty, made from on board the "Teaser" in James River, all the conditions claimed for it are fulfilled. There can be no more certain destructive agent employed for the contemplated purpose than these torpedoes made and used upon the plan of Mr. Creuzbaur. With their use from on board a shot-proof vessel of superior speed, the fleets of the enemy must inevitably be sunk or destroyed, whether they be large or small, iron-clad [sic] or wooden. So also, great effectiveness may be justly claimed for submarine cannon in contact with or near the enemy's ships. The experiments made by order of the Navy committee of the House and under the superintendence of Comdr. Maury, sufficiently demonstrate this. The tests were such as to show that at the distance of several feet, the effect of the submarine shot was such as to penetrate through the timbers of ordinary ships of war; and if it be remembered that in the use of shell under water it would only be necessary that they penetrate a sufficient depth to adhere until exploded, it is manifest that the destructive capacity of this means of attack give it a place second only in importance to that of the torpedo. With the use of both however, as is designed, there can exist no misgiving as to their value. One thing at least is certain, to drive the enemy from our rivers and coasts, we must put in use superior means and devices to his own. It will be worse than vain for us to hope for success in this all important particular in the old fashioned [sic] modes. We have not the means and facilities for building a navy mightier than his. We must rely upon the genius of our country for other means to attain the same end. This the undersigned is confident will be found in the plans and inventions of Mr. Creuzbaur, who is not only a man of genius and science but eminently a practical man. He comes before the Congress with the endorsement of the Legislature of Texas, the State of his residence, which appropriated money for the purpose of bringing his plans to the notice of the Confederate Government and by the favorable reports of Comdr. Maury upon them, all which it is hoped may incline the Committee to regard them with favor and induce the Congress to give them practical effect.

Very Respectfully,

The Committee's Ob't Serv't,

Ebenr. Allen[653]

Although the tests met the required "conditions" of the Confederate Congress, Creuzbaur did not receive a patent for the *Sea King* or funding to conduct more research and tests.[654] Unfortunately, Confederate naval officers reported, "that it is inexpedient to build such vessels at the present time, when the whole available force and materials at the command of the Department should be applied to the construction of vessels of acknowledged efficiency." The officers further stated, "That nothing has been done to prove the alleged claim to the speed, invulnerability, and efficiency of the vessel, in either or all of which we have no confidence." On October 13, 1862 President Davis returned the bill to Congress without his approval.⁶⁵⁵

The interest shown by Confederate officers and engineers in destructive below-surface weapons encouraged other inventors to develop new weapons for the war effort and propose naval devices to the Confederate authorities. The Confederate Navy decided to focus their efforts on a competing project, the *H. L. Hunley*. The *Hunley* demonstrated the advantages and the dangers of undersea warfare.

Horace L. Hunley financed the construction of the *Hunley* at Mobile, Alabama. She was launched in July 1863, nine months after Allen presented Creuzbaur's plans to the Senate Committee. In a demonstration for the Confederate navy, the *Hunley* successfully attacked a coal flatboat in Mobile Bay. The inventors shipped her by rail on August 12, 1863 to Charleston, South Carolina. The Confederate military confiscated the submarine from its private builders and owners shortly after its arrival and turned it over to the Confederate Army. The *Hunley* sank on August 29, 1863 during a test run, killing five members of her crew. The navy recovered the *Hunley*. She sank again on October 15, 1863 killing all eight of her crew. Once again, the navy raised the *Hunley* and returned her to service.

On February 17, 1864, the *Hunley* attacked and sank the USS *Housatonic*, which had been on Union blockade-duty in Charleston's outer harbor. Her triumph was short-lived, and she and her eight-man crew were lost returning to base. The *Hunley* sank three times and lost twenty-one crewmembers during her short career.⁶⁵⁶

According to Confederate patent records, Allen helped Creuzbaur obtain patent 197 on August 31, 1863 for a torpedo.⁶⁵⁷ Creuzbaur also received patents for a wood soled shoe (patent 167 on May 1, 1863), wooden sole shoe (patent 195 on August 28, 1863), and half-wooden shoe (patent 196 on August 28, 1863).⁶⁵⁸

In the fall of 1863, Creuzbaur was highly recommended to Major General Magruder with plans to use his invention of a "floating torpedo" to destroy the enemy's ships. Subsequently the Confederate authorities assigned him to Magruder's command in Houston on September 27, 1863. Creuzbaur's appointment was "for Special Service in constructing torpedoes and other infernal machines."⁶⁵⁹ He served the rest of the war as a captain in the engineer service. Creuzbaur's "enlistment" temporally ended Allen's representation. Creuzbaur surrendered at Austin, Texas on July 26, 1865 and the Union authorities paroled him. He was a locomotive inventor in Austin, Texas in 1880. He moved to Brooklyn, New York with his two daughters where he worked as a mechanical engineer in 1910.[660]

Engineer Bureau

Alfred L. Rives
(Library of Congress)

The Confederate Engineer Bureau was included as an "authorized division" of the General Staff and recognized as part of the Confederate States Army on March 6, 1861. The one-hundred-man Corps of Engineers was commanded by a colonel. The Corps was assigned "all the duties of sappers, miners, and pontoniers" and "overseeing and aiding laborers" in constructing fortifications.[661]

The initial success of the torpedoes convinced the Confederate War Department to authorize the formation of engineer companies to build devices to destroy enemy property. Secretary of War Seddon ordered Colonel Alfred L. Rives, head of the bureau, to form two engineering companies and assign them to the Trans-Mississippi Department and the Department of the West:

Engineer Bureau, August 20, 1863.

Lieut. Gen. E. Kirby Smith,[662] *Comdg. Trans-Miss. Dept.:*

General: I have the honor to send you the following list of men, who, by the wish of the honorable Secretary of War, are to be employed in your department on the special service of destroying the enemy's property by torpedoes and similar inventions, viz: John Kirk, Charles Littlepage, John Silure, Robert Creuzbaur, E. Allen, W. D. Miller,[663] *and C. Williams.*

These men should each be enlisted in and form part of an engineer company, but will, nevertheless, be employed, so far as possible, in the service specified above, and, when the public interests in your judgment require it, details of additional men may be made, either from the engineer troops or from the line, to aid them in their particular duties. Their compensation will be 50 per cent [sic] of the property destroyed by their new inventions, and all the arms and munitions captured by them by the use of torpedoes or of similar devices. Beyond this, they will be entitled to such other reward as Congress may hereafter provide.

Your obedient servant,

A. L. Rives

Lieutenant-Colonel and Acting Chief of Bureau.

[Indorsement]

Approved:

J. A. Seddon,

Secretary of War.

A similar letter to the above was written and sent to General Joseph E. Johnston, commanding Department of the West, with the following names: E. C. Singer, J. D. Braman, R. W. Dunn, B. A. Whitney, D. Bradbury, James Jones, C. E. Tracy, J. R. Fretwell, and L. C. Hirschburger (also approved by Secretary of War).[664]

The group assigned to General Johnson was essentially the same team Singer assembled to build their first torpedo. Allen and Creuzbaur were assigned to General E. Kirby Smith commanding the Trans-Mississippi Department. The department, formed on May 26, 1862, included Missouri, Arkansas, Texas, Indian Territory (now Oklahoma), Confederate Arizona (which included parts of New Mexico), and the part of Louisiana west of the Mississippi River. The department had headquarters at Shreveport, Louisiana, and Marshall, Texas.[665]

Confederate authorities gave the group the necessary ammunition and material for manufacturing the devices and transportation for both the men and the machines. Their inventions were protected by patents. As described in Secretary Seldon's letters to Rives, compensation for their efforts was fifty percent of the value of all enemy vessels of war and other federal property they were able to destroy.

Was Allen a Spy?

A rather vague Confederate chain of command placed the Confederate Secret Service as the *de facto* head of "Military operations and officially sanctioned Secret Service activities." The units included foreign and domestic agents, the Signal Corps, Torpedo Bureau, Submarine Battery Service Bureau, Bureau of Special and Secret Service, and Secret Service operations in Canada and the Maritimes. The Secret Service also oversaw "Sanctioned destructionists, privateers, and licensed operators, which included the bounty law, special and detached service, the coal torpedo, and active measures operations."

Allen could claim to be a "spy" through his connections with the torpedo bureau and the bounty law service as a member of the Engineering Bureau assigned to General Kirby Smith's Trans-Mississippi Department. Colonel Allen was a civilian during the Civil War. Allen continued to represent Creuzbaur through August 1863. He was placed in the Engineering Bureau charged with using "torpedoes or of similar devices" to destroy enemy property. His son described his wartime experience working to destroy the blockade of Southern ports "by promoting the torpedo service." Allen's interest in developing St. Joseph Island, immediately south of Galveston Island, also encouraged him to work on a project to protect the Texas Gulf Coast Islands.

DEATH

"The Clouds are Truly Dark Over Us"

Confederate fortunes turned sharply in 1863. On January 1, Lincoln signed the Emancipation Proclamation freeing slaves in Confederate held areas. The Confederacy suffered losses in the Battle of Stone's River at Murfreesboro, Tennessee on December 31, 1862 - January 2, 1863.[666] Wartime inflation reduced the buying power of the Confederate dollar to twenty cents. In February, the U.S. Senate passed the Conscription Act, which increased the size of the Union military. In Charleston, a half-pound loaf of bread cost $25 and flour sold for $65 a barrel. On March 13, an explosion at the Confederate Ordinance Laboratory at Brown's Island near Richmond killed sixty-nine workers including sixty-two women. Bread riots broke out in Richmond in March and April.[667] Confederate officials realized the economy was near the breaking point. The cost of feeding a family increased from $6.65 in 1861 to $68.25 in 1863. On May 3, General Lee was victorious at the Battle of Chancellorsville (April 30–May 6, 1863) but suffered a great loss when Stonewall Jackson died on May 10 after being wounded by his own men.[668] On June 20, Lincoln announced West Virginia as the thirty-fifth state in the Union. Within several days in early July, U. S. Grant captured Vicksburg, Mississippi,[669] George Meade defeated Lee's forces at Gettysburg, Pennsylvania,[670] and Confederate troops surrendered Port Hudson, Louisiana.[671] On July 15, President Jefferson Davis wrote to one of his generals: "The clouds are truly dark over us." An equally dejected Robert E. Lee offered his resignation in August, but Davis refused the request. A glimmer of hope appeared after General Braxton Bragg's Confederate forces defeated General William Rosecrans' Union army at Chickamauga[672] on September 18-20, 1863. The *H. L. Hunley* sank on August 30. The ship was raised and sank again on October 15.[673]

Breakfast with "Friends"

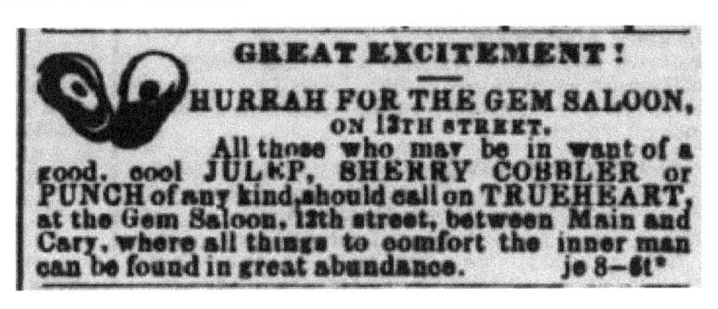

GREAT EXCITEMENT!
HURRAH FOR THE GEM SALOON,
ON 13TH STREET.
All those who may be in want of a good, cool JULEP, SHERRY COBBLER or PUNCH of any kind should call on TRUEHEART, at the Gem Saloon, 12th street, between Main and Cary, where all things to comfort the inner man can be found in great abundance. je 8—6t*

Gem Saloon Announcement
(Richmond Dispatch)

On October 15, 1863, Ebenezer Allen met some associates for a late breakfast at the Gem Saloon under the Linwood House in Richmond, Virginia. Allen remained at the table after "his friends" left the saloon. Sometime later, a waiter checked on Allen and discovered he was dead.

The following day *The Richmond Examiner* reported Colonel Allen's "mysterious death:"

"Sudden and Mysterious Death"

Yesterday, about the hour of noon, a gentleman named Colonel Allen, (and concerning whom nothing more is known up to last night,) entered the Gem Saloon under the Linwood House with some friends, and partook of breakfast in their company. Wine was called for and passed around, and the company left, the gentleman named retaining his seat at the table. In a short time, one of the servants notified Mr. Gough, one of the proprietors, that the gentleman had turned blue and that he must be dying. An investigation revealed that he was really dead, and Dr. Slack, a physician who happened to be in the house, pronounced death the result of disease of the heart. Acting Coroner Sanxay was notified and reviewed the body but did not deem an inquest necessary. The body was removed by an undertaker to the corner of Franklin and 18th Street,

> *where friends of the deceased can apply today for further information. The deceased was apparently about 40 years of age, dressed well in citizens' clothes, and had the appearance of a speculator.*[674]

The Examiner obtained additional information about Colonel Allen and published his obituary on October 17:

> *Colonel EBENEZER ALLEN, late of Texas, died suddenly of disease of the heart, in this city, on Thursday, 15th instant, aged about 55 years.*[675] *This is but another painful instance of the Biblical truth, "In the midst of life we are in death." But a few short moments before the fatal shaft had winged its way to his heart and laid low in death all that was mortal, Colonel Allen was in the full vigor of health and spirits and seated with a few friends at the breakfast table.*
>
> *He was born in the state of Maine.*[676] *Like the gifted and noble [Illegible], in early life he left the rock-bound shores of his native home to seek one in the far away South. When but a youth he commenced the study of law as a profession, and soon his energy and genius placed him with an honored brow and promising future at the bar. The rising glory and greatness of Texas stirred his youthful attraction and early in life he became one of her adopted sons. His being Secretary of State under the Republic, and Attorney General of the State of Texas, are instances of the high esteem in which he was held by his fellow citizens and as a mark of the chief properties of his talents and character. He was a man of comprehensive reading and literary research, and was much distinguished for his profound judgment as a jurist.*
>
> *When hostilities were commenced upon the South by the United States, he instantly gave up all legal pur-*

suits and became identified heart and soul, voice and purse, in the coming struggle. He gave the bent of his mind and the expenditure of his means mainly to the invention of that terrible instrument of death, the torpedo, in which enterprise he was engaged up to the hour of his untimely death.

Much might be said in honor of the lamented Allen, but the future historian of Texas and of this Revolution will do ample justice to his name. His many friends will truly mourn his untimely loss.

His remains are in the keeping of the Masonic Lodge 10, between Eighteenth and Nineteenth streets of this city - From thence they will be taken to Hollywood Cemetery on Sunday morning at 10 o'clock.[677]

The *Galveston Daily News* eventually reported his death in early December:

We regret to note the death of Colonel Ebenezer Allen of Galveston, of appoplexy [sic], in a restaurant in Richmond on the 20th ult. He was buried by the Masonic Fraternity, much respect being paid to his remains.[678]

The obituary in the Galveston paper is disrespectful. The date of his death is incorrect. Most notable is the absence of a biography highlighting his contributions to Texas. The lateness and brevity of the announcement adds suspicion about Allen's standing in the community.

**The Masons' Hall in Richmond
(Wikipedia)**

The mystery surrounding Allen's death continued with his burial at Hollywood Cemetery. There was no newspaper account of his funeral. There is no tombstone marking his grave and no record of his interment.

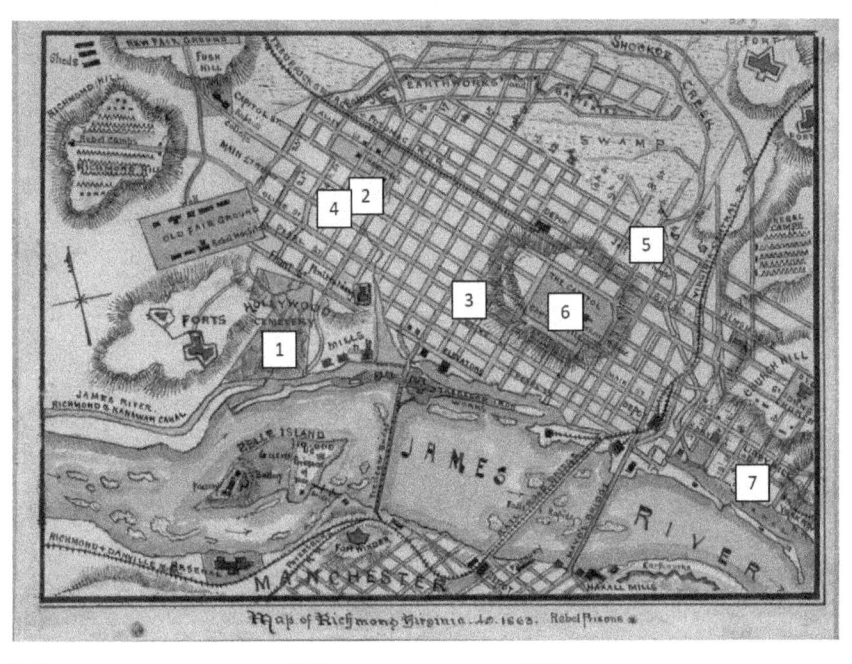

1	Hollywood Cemetery	2	Funeral Home	3	Gem Saloon
4	Masonic Lodge	5	Jeff Davis House	6	The Capitol	7	Libby Prison

Annotated Map of Richmond Virginia in 1863
(Library of Congress)

"Sudden and Mysterious Death"

The circumstances of Allen's death are perplexing. The heading on the October 16 newspaper suggested something was out of order. The article in *The Richmond Examiner* provides details in naming locations (Gem Saloon, Linwood House, undertaker at corner of Franklin and 18th Street); people (Mr. Gough, Dr. Slack, Acting Coroner Sanxay); and "turning blue before dying."

Allen's death raises many questions demanding further examination.

Allen's breakfast "friends" remain unknown. Who were these people and why did they leave Allen alone at the table? Were Allen's breakfast companions friends or foes? If they were friends, why did they not contact the police, Confederate authorities, *The Richmond*

Examiner, and/or the Masonic lodge? Even after Allen's death was reported in the *Examiner*, no one came forward to say what happened. The men who joined Allen at the Gem Saloon simply disappeared. If the breakfast companions were friends, they would have contacted the Masonic Lodge and arranged to be at the burial. It seems possible the mysterious men were not close to Allen and may have considered him a stranger or an enemy. They could have been Union or Confederate spies or business competitors. They might have left the city and not learned of Allen's death until after the funeral. The evidence suggests they were people who did not know about the death or did not want to be associated with his demise. The identities of Allen's breakfast companions remain a mystery as does their role, if any, in Allen's death.

Was Dr. Slack's presence in the saloon to pronounce Allen dead a coincidence or planned? Dr. Slack was from Georgia and conveniently happened to be in Richmond. His quick conclusion that Allen's "death [was] the result of disease of the heart" probably convinced Mr. Sanxay not to order an autopsy. Because Dr. Slack concluded the death was from natural causes, the local police or Confederate officials did not investigate the fatality.

Despite the mysterious circumstances, Acting Coroner and Alderman Sanxay decided not to perform an autopsy. Was Sanxay even capable of performing an autopsy? This was not the first mysterious death Coroner Sanxay decided was unnecessary for a post-mortem. On September 10, 1862, Sanxay declined to investigate the death of a child who was given "some potation of a detrimental nature" to keep the infant quiet.[679] According to the 1863 Directory of Richmond City Officials, the coroner was St. George Peachy. Richard D. Sanxay is listed as an alderman for Jefferson Ward from 1861 to 1865.[680] Richard S. Sanxay was a member of Masonic Lodge 10.[681]

Was Allen's death from natural causes, "a disease of the heart," or by homicide committed by his breakfast companions? The only "published" clue from the body was the servant's observation that Allen's face and hands had "turned blue." This medical condition is called *cyanosis* and is "usually due to a lack of oxygen in the blood." Cyanosis may develop suddenly with shortness of breath and other symptoms or appear gradually from long-term heart or lung problems with the

presence of less severe symptoms. The following medical difficulties can cause cyanosis:
- ☐ Problems with the lungs – A blood clot in the arteries of the lungs known as a pulmonary embolism, drowning or near-drowning, high altitude, viral infection in the smallest air passages in the lungs of young children known as bronchiolitis, long-term lung problems, which become more severe including chronic obstructive pulmonary disease (COPD), asthma, and interstitial lung disease, or severe pneumonia.
- ☐ Problems with the airways leading to the lungs – Breath-holding, choking on something stuck in the airways, difficulty breathing due to swelling around the vocal cords and a "barking" cough known as croup which is common in infants and children, or inflammation of the epiglottitis tissue that covers the windpipe.
- ☐ Problems with the heart - Congenital heart defects, heart failure because the heart is unable to pump oxygen-rich blood to the rest of the body causing the heart to stop known as cardiac arrest.
- ☐ Other problems - Drug overdose (narcotics, benzodiazepines, sedatives), exposure to cold air or water, a long-lasting seizure, or toxins such as cyanide.[682]

Some of these causes can be ruled out because of Allen's age and the circumstances surrounding his death. If the cause was natural, it was likely due to a pulmonary embolism, choking, or cardiac arrest. Since Allen was having a "late breakfast," choking may be the reason for the heart attack.

How does Allen's age at death compare with his male relatives? Allen certainly lived longer than the average life expectancy in 1863 of from thirty-seven to forty years.[683] The Allen family's medical history suggests his death from natural causes was not unusual. Ebenezer Allen's death at fifty-nine years of age is like the longevity of his father, male siblings, and sons. David Allen (father) died at sixty-three, David Allen, Jr. (brother born in 1805) died at thirty-three, Dr. Samuel J. Allen (brother born in 1819) died at sixty-five, William Pitt Allen (son born in 1836) died at sixty-eight,[684] M. Henry Allen (son born in

1835) possibly died at seventy-nine, and Frederick Allen (son born in 1849) died at fifty-two. The average age at death of Allen's male relatives is sixty compared with Ebenezer's death at fifty-nine. Without knowing the causes of these deaths, it is impossible to reach the conclusion Allen's death was related to family genetics.

If Allen was murdered, his dinner guests might have poisoned him. The possible toxins are strychnine, cyanide, and arsenic. Cyanide kills people quickly and generally painlessly. During the Civil War, both the Union and Confederate governments used cyanide. Spies used cyanide capsules to kill themselves quickly if caught. Cyanide produces unconsciousness, followed by convulsions, the inability to absorb oxygen, and death. Strychnine causes uncontrollable muscle spasms, frothing at the mouth, dramatic increases in reflexes, and eventual death from asphyxiation when the muscles become too tensed and erratic to permit breathing. Women used arsenic to create a "white-as-snow, composed face." Arsenic is tasteless, colorless, and odorless. A few grains could and did kill many men.[685] The symptoms of arsenic poisoning include the odor of garlic, abdominal pain, and myocardial depression.[686] If Allen was poisoned, Union or Confederate spies did it. Richmond, like Washington, was full of enemy spies and agents.

Hollywood Cemetery

The circumstances of Allen's "sudden and mysterious death" continued after his burial by the Masons. The lodge announced plans to inter Colonel Allen at Hollywood Cemetery[687] in Richmond on Sunday morning, October 18. There is no further information about his funeral or gravesite. His body seems to have disappeared. There is no tombstone marking his grave and no record of his interment at the Cemetery.

There is only one E. Allen listed in the cemetery's burial records for 1863. The other E. Allen in the burial roll was in 1864.[688] The record of "Confederate Dead" at Hollywood Cemetery contains a directory of twenty-nine burials of soldiers named Allen. However, the records contain only two men identified as E. Allen who were buried after Ebenezer's death on October 15, 1863. On October 22, 1863, an "E. Allen" was interred in section T, plot 555 without a marker.[689] Allen was listed as a member of Company G in the Forty-fourth North Carolina Regiment.[690] The other "E. Allen" was buried in section V, plot 400 on October 7, 1864, without a marker.[691] Allen was listed as a member of Company A in the twenty-third South Carolina Regiment.[692]

Confederate Dead Named Allen Buried at Hollywood Cemetery
(Register of the Confederate dead, interred in Hollywood Cemetery, Richmond, VA: Hollywood Memorial Association of Richmond, VA annotated by author)

The roster of Company G in the Forty-fourth North Carolina Regiment lists Edmund or Edward Allen as a private who enlisted on March 22, 1862, and was mortally wounded at Bristoe Station on November 26, 1863.[693] The date of death does not match the date of burial. There are twelve E. Allens listed in the Soldiers and Sailors Database, but none of them is a member of the Forty-fourth North Carolina Regiment. The roll of the Twenty-third South Carolina includes "E. Allen" who was a private in Company A of the infantry regiment.[694] The exclusion of Ebenezer Allen's name from the "Confederate Dead" is not surprising because Allen was a civilian working in the Engineer Bureau.

The absence of a record or headstone does not imply any wrongdoing. Many records were lost or destroyed during the last days of the Civil War.

Sylvania Allen Lawsuit

In 1873, Ebenezer's widow filed a lawsuit against William R. Baker. The complaint was about repayment of obligations to Ebenezer Allen. Mrs. Allen protested that the settlement was in Confederate money. [Please see Josephine Allen vs. William R. Baker in the Appendix.] This would have been an interesting historical document relating to Mrs. Allen's financial situation except for one phrase.

In her legal action, Mrs. Allen complained that "the several payments set up by Baker were made in Confederate money at a time when it was dangerous to refuse it, her husband being a Union man[695] and a fugitive from the state: that Baker took advantage of her situation and forced the Confederate money upon her against her will, and that the same was illegal and wholly worthless." This was an amazing statement. Taken at face value, it appears that sometime in 1863, Ebenezer Allen changed allegiances and began to work for or support the Federals. This public declaration is more significant than a private statement, especially when Mrs. Allen said Allen was a fugitive from the state. This declaration contradicts other information about Allen's Civil War service and areas under Union control in the fall of 1863. Sylvinia's statement seems like a rather weak effort to recover more money from William Baker's arrangements with Ebenezer Allen.

Heart Attack or Assassination?

The following table summarizes the evidence supporting either a natural death (heart attack) or a homicide (assassination).

Analysis of the Evidence

	Heart Attack	Assassination
Appearance at death – "gentleman had turned blue"	Choking while eating breakfast leading to heart attack	Cyanide poisoning
Dr. Slack's examination	Dr. Slack concludes "death the result of disease of the heart"	No autopsy performed of "mysterious" death
Age at death – Allen was 59 years old	Average age of male relatives at death was 60 years	Do not know causes of relatives' death May be a coincidence
"company left … the gentleman."	Allen was alive when they left the table Allen was dead and breakfast companions did not want to become involved	Companions left the scene of the crime after murdering Allen
Follow-up by breakfast companions after death and newspaper obituary	Left Richmond after breakfast	Escape capture by Confederate officials
Gravesite identification and record of internment	Loss or destruction of records Vandalism of cemetery after Union forces seized Richmond	Secretly buried in unmarked grave No marker or record of internment
Newspaper report of funeral and internment	Paper had already published an obituary Masons learned Allen was not an active member of Galveston Lodge	Masons learned something unfavorable about Allen

Sylvinia Allen's lawsuit	Sylvinia claims Allen was a "Union man" and was unable to pass through Confederate-held territory Son said Allen "strove to destroy" the Union blockade Allen appointed to the Engineer Bureau on August 20, 1863 Allen represented Creuzbaur until at least September 27, 1863	The Mississippi River was under Federal control making it difficult for a "Confederate man" to travel from Richmond to Galveston Mrs. Allen made the claim to obtain repayment in Union currency rather than nearly worthless Confederate money
Forgotten Texas official as evidenced in Galveston newspaper announcement	Allen was viewed unfavorably by Galvestonians because of his failure to raise funds from local investors for the railroad, support for Judge Watrous, and broadside favoring investors instead of colonists in the Peters' Colony	Confederate officials and Galvestonians obtained some new, unfavorable information about Allen

In the author's opinion, Allen's death was caused by choking on food. Of course, another researcher might interpret the data differently and make a case for his murder. It is doubtful historians will ever discover exactly what happened to Allen. His very public life contrasts with the secrecy of his death.

The Allen Family After Ebenezer's Death[696]

The surname Allen is the twenty-seventh most common last name in the United States.[697] Ebenezer and Sylvinia Allen had five children: Henry, William Pitt, Edward C., Frederick, and Ebenezer, Jr. In 1850, the Ebenezer Allen family resided in Galveston's 2nd Ward. Henry was 16, William P. 14, and Frederick 3.[698] By 1860, one-year-old Ebenezer Allen, Jr. had joined the family. The 1860 census reports that Henry 25,[699] William P. 23,[700] Edward C. 20,[701] and Frederick 12[702] were living with their parents in the 2nd Ward of Galveston, Texas. The 1860 census lists 25-year-old Henry as a brickmaker and 23-year-old William P. as a law student.[703]

When the Civil War began in 1861, Henry was 26, William 25, Edward 21, Frederick 14, and Ebenezer Jr. 2. Patriotic eagerness resulted in the enlistment of the three older boys. Records from the United States Civil War Soldiers Index records Henry as a private in the Texas Twenty-sixth Regiment (Debray's Regiment),[704] William as a private in the Eighteenth Texas Cavalry Regiment (Darnell's Regiment),[705] and Edward as a private in a Union regiment from Maine.[706] The service records do not provide any direct link to Ebenezer and Sylvinia Allen.

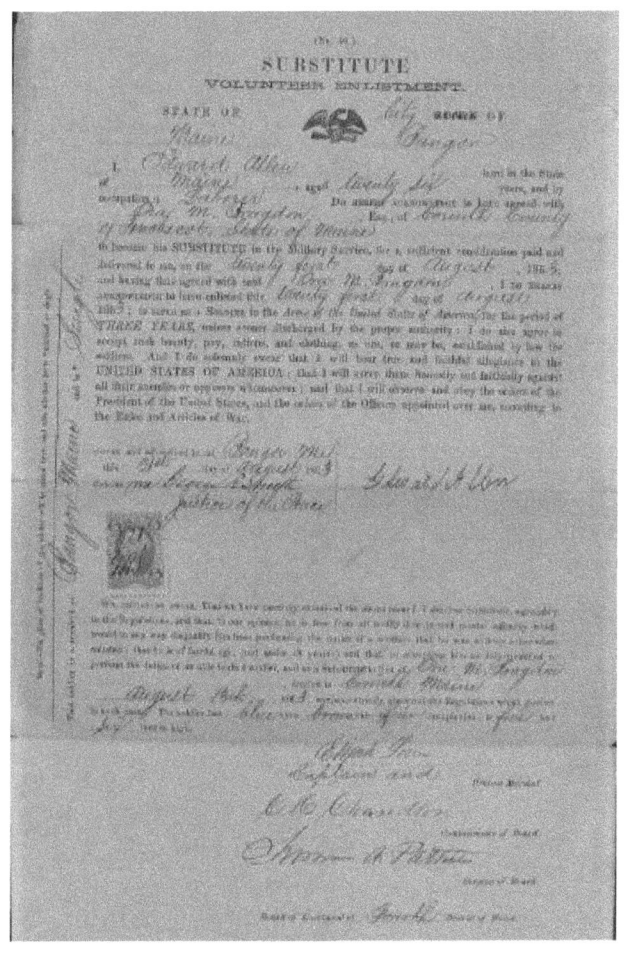

**Edward Allen Substitute Volunteer Enlistment
(Maine, Civil War Enlistment Papers, 1862-1865)[707]**

Ebenezer Allen wrote his will on June 4, 1862 in Richmond, Virginia. He awarded his "dear wife" Sylvinia Josephine Allen all his "property and estate both real and personal wherever situated or found." Ebenezer also appointed her as executive of his will and testament. If Sylvinia was unable to act as executrix, he designated his son, William Pitt Allen, to serve as executor. [Please see Ebenezer Allen Will in the Appendix.][708]

Following Ebenezer's death in 1863, Sylvinia, Frederick, and Ebenezer, Jr. remained in Galveston throughout the rest of the Civil War. After the war, the family scattered to different parts of the country. Edward remained in Maine, William Pitt settled in California, and Henry had businesses in Galveston and Houston, Texas. Frederick lived in Galveston until his death in 1901.[709] Sylvinia and Ebenezer, Jr. stayed in Galveston until 1866.[710] In 1870, Sylvinia and Ebenezer, Jr. lived in Skowhegan, Somerset County, Maine with Sylvinia's sister Hannah B. Leavitt and her family.[711]

The *Galveston City Directory* for 1866-1867 identifies Henry Allen as owner of a music store.[712] There are no listings for Henry, William, Edward, Frederick, Ebenezer Jr., and Sylvinia in the *Galveston City Directory* for 1868-1871.[713] *The Galveston Daily News* of June 2, 1871, reported Henry Allen had received three awards (diplomas) for musical instruments at the Texas State Fair.[714] The 1880 census places Henry Allen in Houston, Texas with his wife, Laura A. Allen, two sons, and three daughters. Henry worked as a piano agent.[715] Henry was a supporter of the *Houston Telegraph* and was one of the people in Houston responsible for the paper's resurrection.[716] Henry died on July 23, 1921:

> *Henry Allen, aged 87 died at his home in Los Angeles, Cal., early Sunday morning. Funeral services will be held in Los Angeles on Tuesday. Mr. Allen was a prominent business man [sic] in Galveston and Houston for a number of years. Besides his wife. Mr. Allen is survived by two sons, F. W. and Henry P. Allen of Houston; Mrs. J. W. Gordon, Miss Ettie A. Allen of Houston:*

> *Mrs. Lida B. Davis of Port Arthur; Mrs. Henry Butler and Mrs. Laura K. Holmstrom of Fort Worth, Texas. Mr. Allen was a veteran of the civil war.*[717]

After living in Galveston in 1860, William Pitt Allen resided in Florida, New Orleans, and Robinson County, Texas.[718] Census records show William married Mary B. Allen in 1886.[719] Eventually, he settled in California.[720] In the early 1890s, William moved to Summerland, California and joined other Spiritualists in the new town. In 1885, Spiritualist Henry Lafayette Williams purchased the land which became Summerland. He decided to sell lots in his new town and persuaded fellow Spiritualists to settle in the area. Lots of 60 feet by 25 feet sold for $25 each. In 1889, the early settlers named the town Summerland, the name of the Spiritualists' heaven. California Great Registers reveal William Pitt Allen was living in Summerland, Santa Barbara, California in 1892 and 1896.[721] William was an active member of the Spiritualist community.

In April 1893, President Grover Cleveland appointed W. P. Allen as postmaster for the newly established office at Gorda, Montgomery County, California. Evidently, not all citizens were pleased with this appointment and caused "great dissatisfaction" among Summerland residents.[722]

William was involved in a lawsuit filed by Summerland founder, H. L. Williams. Williams accused Allen of libel in The People vs. W. P. Allen litigation. The jury trial on January 18, 1894 found Allen not guilty. According to the *San Francisco Call*, "This verdict effectually stops further action on the part H. L. Williams to disturb his neighbors."[723]

> **THE SUMMERLAND LIBEL SUIT.**
>
> **A Jury Quickly Finds a Verdict for the Defendant.**
>
> SANTA BARBARA, Jan. 18.—J. W. Taggart, assistant district attorney, closed the argument for the prosecution this morning in the case of The People vs. W. P. Allen, otherwise known as the Summerland libel suit of H. L. Williams against W. P. Allen. It was a case of great interest to spiritualists all over the coast. At 4:07 o'clock this afternoon Judge Cope finished giving his instructions to the jury, which then retired and returned with a verdict of not guilty in just thirteen minutes. This verdict effectually stops further action on the part of H. L. Williams to disturb his neighbors, being the test case of a series of similar suits.

The Summerland Libel Suit
(San Francisco Call)

The Spiritualist Society of Summerland celebrated the fiftieth anniversary of modern Spiritualism at an "extensive basket picnic" gathering at Liberty Hall. At the meeting, W. P. Allen was elected secretary of the society for 1898.[724]

At the Populist[725] caucus held on Wednesday night August 16, 1898 in Summerland, W. P. Allen and J. W. Darling were elected as delegates to the county party convention.[726]

William Pitt died from consumption on April 6, 1904 in Santa Barbara. He was buried in the Bell family plot in Island Cemetery in Santa Barbara.[727]

In 1850, ten-year-old Edward C. Allen was living in Bloomfield, Maine with his maternal grandfather, Andrew Morse, and grandmother, Hannah Morse.[728] There is conflicting information about Edward. Marriage records say Edward married Lillian D. Ham on May 7, 1890 in Portland, Maine.[729] Maine statistics reveal Edward married Mary S. Bennett on May 15, 1858.[730] In 1880, Edward lived in Windham, Cumberland County, Maine with Mary and seven children.[731] The confusion may be due to a second marriage (Mary and Edward in 1858 and Lillian and Edward in 1890). The December 16, 1887 issue of the *Bangor Daily Whig and Courier* reports an Edward B. Allen was awarded a patent for a "burnishing machine."[732] The following year, the paper attributed a patent for a "heel nailing machine" to Edward B. Allen.[733] Edward died on March 23, 1925.[734]

In 1850 and 1860, Frederick Allen lived with his parents and siblings in Galveston, Texas.[735] Frederick was too young to join the Confederate Army. In 1868-1869, the *Galveston City Directory* lists an F. Allen as an engraver with Prince & Barnum.[736] In 1870, Fred was an engraver with the watchmakers and jewelers, F. Allen & Co.[737] Fred was thirty-two-years-old in 1880 and was married to Lizzie Allen.[738] *Morrison & Fourmy's General Directory of the City of Galveston* for 1886-1887 and 1890-1891 stated Frederick Allen was a bookkeeper.[739]

Tax records indicate Fred and Lizzie were living in Galveston in 1886, 1891, and 1894.[740]

An ad in the 1895 *Galveston Daily News* announced a sale "at greatly reduced prices" by the Fred Allen & Co's.[741]

Fred. Allen & Co.'s
(The Galveston Daily News)

The June 1900 census records said Fred, Lizzie, and their niece lived in their "long-time home" at 902 Post Office Street known as E Avenue in Galveston.[742]

The Fred Allen Company, a jewelry store, was located at the corner of Market and Tremont. The store and surrounding buildings suffered severe damage during the storm but were not destroyed like the areas closer to the beachfront. The *Galveston City Directory of 1900/1901*, published after the catastrophe, indicates the business and residence of Fred Allen were still used by the family.[743]

Fred's name does not appear on the register of the known dead from the Galveston hurricane.[744] However, the list is far from comprehensive and only a few hundred names appear on the roll. It is estimated 8,000 people perished as a direct result of the flood, and many more in the following days from injury and illness. It is unknown whether Fred Allen died as a result of the huge storm and subsequent tidal wave, but he passed away on May 9, 1901 and was buried at Lakeview Cemetery in Galveston. Fred and Lizzie Allen had no children.[745]

According to *Morrison & Fourmy's General Directory of the City of Galveston: 1901-1902*, Fred's widow, Lizzie, continued to operate Fred Allen & Co.[746]

Ebenezer, Jr. and Sylvinia returned to Galveston around 1872. The *Galveston City Directory* for 1875-1876 listed E. Allen as a clerk for the Southern Cotton Press and lived in room 21 between avenues N and N ½.[747] In 1877, Ebenezer worked as a pressman (operator of cotton press) and lived with his mother at the corner of Avenue S and 35th.[748] *Heller's Galveston Directory, 1878-1879* reported Mrs. Josephine Allen and Mr. Ebenezer Allen, a cotton press, lived at 35th and S ½ and F. Allen, an engraver, resided between 19th and 20th streets.[749]

**Ebenezer Allen, Jr.
(Rosenberg Library)**

Ebenezer lived with Sylvinia at Avenue S and 35th from 1877 to 1887.[750] Ebenezer married Cora Estelle Baldwin on May 3, 1882. The Allens lived with Ebenezer's mother until 1892.[751] In 1890, the Allens lived in the 7th Ward of Galveston.[752] Ebenezer and his wife Cora operated the Sea Side [sic] dairy in 1884 and 1885.[753] Ebenezer is described as a dairyman in the Galveston city directories from 1898 to 1900.[754] Ebenezer sent *The Galveston Daily News* "a specimen of some remarkedly fine Irish potatoes" which he raised on his vegetable farm at Hitchcock.[755]

There is some confusion over the photograph on the right. It is often identified as Ebenezer Allen when in fact it is his son Ebenezer Allen, Jr. The photograph was taken by Justus Zahn. The picture was made using cabinet card photography. Photographs were produced from 1860-1880 using this media. Zahn was born in 1847 in Marburg, Germany. At age 22, he travelled to America for the first time to visit his maternal grandfather in Hoboken, New Jersey. Zahn returned to

Germany briefly to fight in the Franco-Prussian War but later relocated to Chicago and established a photography business. He eventually moved to St. Louis and then to Belleville, Illinois where he met and married Elise Kreppelt. In the late 1880s, the Zahns moved to Galveston, Texas. For the picture to be of Ebenezer Allen, Sr., it would have to be taken before Allen's death in 1863. Zahn visited America in 1869 making it impossible for the photograph to be the senior Ebenezer Allen.[756]

Ebenezer and Cora died on September 8, 1900 in the Great Hurricane and Flood of 1900. Their home was a few blocks from the beach on the Gulf of Mexico. It was the first area destroyed by the tremendous hurricane winds and the rising water. Debris from this side of the island piled up further inland and protected some of the downtown from flooding as badly as it would have otherwise.[757]

Ebenezer Allen, Jr. is listed among the dead on the Rosenberg Library list, but his wife is not.[758] A report prepared in November by the Scottish Rite Masons of Texas includes Ebenezer Allen and his wife as victims. Their names never appear again in any city directory or census record.[759] There is no listing for Ebenezer and Cora in the 1900-1901 city directories.[760]

Sylvinia lived in Galveston during the Civil War. In 1866, she issued a notice in *The Galveston Daily News* warning potential buyers not to purchase the tract of land known as the "Cedar Point" tract in Chambers County claimed by Mrs. Sam Houston. Mrs. Allen said she had an unsatisfied claim on the property from a contract with the late Sam Houston.[761]

Ebenezer, Jr. and Sylvinia traveled to Maine and lived with her sister Hannah (Morse) Leavitt in 1870. Sylvinia and Ebenezer returned to Galveston in 1872. They lived at the corner of Church and 30th streets in 1872.[762]

> **NOTICE—All persons are hereby warned** not to purchase the tract of land known as the "Cedar Point" tract, in Chambers county, claimed by Mrs. Sam Houston, as I have an unsatisfied claim upon the same by contract with Gen. Houston before his death.
> JOSEPHINE ALLEN,
> aug1-tw3t   Executrix Eb. Allen.

Notice About Cedar Point
(The Galveston Daily News)

After they returned, Sylvinia filed several lawsuits to obtain funds from Ebenezer Allen's real estate and railroad holdings. In 1872 she brought a lawsuit against W. R. Baker-Harris regarding payment of Houston and Central Texas stock in Confederate currency. On October 28, 1872, the Supreme Court of Texas reversed an earlier lower court decision and found in favor of the defendant.[763]

In October 1873, the Texas Supreme Court stated:

> *... contracts based upon payment in Confederate money, or tainted with Confederate money considerations, would not be enforced by the Texas courts." The court also held, (and no reason appeared for changing the ruling) that those who had voluntarily executed their contracts of that character, would be left precisely where they have placed themselves.*

The judgment was affirmed.[764]

The *Galveston City Directory, 1875-1876* lists Mrs. Josephine Allen living on route 21 between avenues N and N ½.[765] Around 1877 Josephine (Sylvinia) and Ebenezer moved to the intersection of 35th and S ½ streets.[766]

Sylvinia was a plaintiff in the lawsuit Meyer vs. Andrews et al. On September 1873, Mrs. Allen had reached an agreement with Mr. Andrews to convey a one-sixth interest which the estate of Ebenezer Allen owned in two leagues on Clear Creek in Galveston County to William Pitt Allen. Andrews signed the agreement on December 11, 1873. In 1888, Sylvinia sued Andrews for failure to comply with the agreement. Unfortunately, the claim was made twelve years and two months after Andrews signed the obligation. The Supreme Court of Texas denied the claim on March 23, 1888 because it was made more than ten years after the commitment.[767]

From 1877 to 1878, Josephine and Ebenezer were living at 35th and avenue S ½.[768] In 1891 and 1892, Josephine stayed with Ebenezer at 1913 W. Ave. S ½.[769] She resided in the home of L. C. Hershberger, the US local inspector of steam engines, from 1893 to 1895.[770] From 1896 until her death, Sylvinia lived at 3412 Broadway in Galveston.[771]

Records at the Lakewood Cemetery in Galveston place Sylvinia Allen's death on September 7, 1897.[772]

From Watering Station to Town

> *Though the man for whom the town [of Allen] is named never lived here, Ebenezer Allen is an important ... character in the story of Texas and is, therefore, an important figure to the city as well.*[773]

Allen's charter for the Galveston and Red River Railroad was instrumental in founding the Town of Allen. After Paul Bremond and Thomas William House took over the line, they obtained financing, started construction, and renamed the line the Houston and Texas Central Railroad. The railway reached Millican, Texas in 1860.

Construction on the Houston and Texas Central Railroad resumed after the war. The railway began northward expansion in 1867 and the line reached Corsicana four years later. Dallas residents paid the Houston and Texas Central $8,200 to change construction plans, move the tracks eight miles, and cross the Trinity River at John Neely Bryan's[774] old homestead. The railroad completed the tracks to Dallas in 1872. The citizens of McKinney gave the railroad $20,000 to connect the line to the government center of Collin County.[775] The tracks reached Denison in 1873 and the line connected with the Missouri, Kansas and Texas Railroad to form the first all-rail route from Texas to St. Louis and the East.[776]

Steam provided the power to operate the train engines. Heat from wood and coal-fired boilers converted water into high-pressure steam. The steam from the boiler entered a cylinder and forced a piston to move forward and then backward in a reciprocating motion. This movement turned the train's wheels and moved the engine. The Houston and Texas Central's steam engines needed to add water every seven to ten miles to continue to produce steam. The railroad-built stops or stations along the line and used nearby streams and rivers to fill water tanks at these locations. The engines took on water and fuel at the stations.

Old Stone Dam – Cottonwood Creek
(Photograph by Sharlyn Mesch)

On August 12, 1873, the Houston and Texas Central Railroad paid Isaac Rhine $275 for a strip of land 150 feet wide "over and upon which said company has built a railway." The train tracks extended from Dallas through Collin County to the Red River. When the line passed through Collin County, the locomotives needed a place to add water to the engine boiler. In 1874, the railroad obtained an easement[777] from J.W. Franklin to dam Cottonwood Creek for a water stop. The railroad sent water from the dam to a tower and from there to water tanks serving the steam locomotives.

The railroad's executives decided to name the station Allen in honor of Ebenezer Allen who obtained the line's original charter.[778]

Allen Train Depot
(Photograph by Sharlyn Mesch)

On November 21, 1874, the Houston and Texas Central bought land for a future town from Abraham Rhine for $1,370. The company made a down payment of $685 and paid the balance in 1887. At 11 o'clock, February 10, 1876, the railroad filed a plat[779] for the town with the Clerk of Collin County. In 1874 the railroad established the town of Allen. Local farmers, tradesmen, and railroad officials laid out a town around the train station. A thriving community began to grow around the railroad post.

Original Plan of the Town of Allen - February 10, 1876
(Author's drawing based on map on page 236 of Lindy Fisher's, *Between the Creeks* in University of North Texas Libraries, The Portal to Texas History)[780]

The company gave the first lot in the northeast corner of town to school trustees for a school. J.W. Franklin, the town's first postmaster, bought the second lot for a general merchandise store. Franklin's twenty-five-foot wide establishment faced the railroad. Wilson Creek Baptist Church exchanged their land on the railroad right of way for a lot near the site of the new school. G.W. Patterson and S.K. Ingram bought business lots, and Dr. W. F. Wolford moved his medical office to the town. Within a year, Allen, Texas had a post office, school, church, doctor, and several businesses.[781]

The company sold lots to merchants and citizens. Less than 7,000 people lived in Collin County when the first steam engines traveled through it in 1872. On Christmas Eve 1873, a Missouri, Kansas and Texas steam locomotive crossed the Red River and met the Houston and Texas Central train at Denison, Texas. The cowcatchers[782] on the train engines touched one month after leaving St. Louis and Houston. Their steam whistles blew, and bells clanked to the cheers of the crowd.[783]

APPENDIX

The Annexation Process: 1836-1845

September 1836 - Texans vote on new government officers, national constitution, and the question of annexation to the United States. The citizens overwhelmingly select annexation.

January 11, 1837 - The U.S. Senate announces a resolution to recognize Texas.

March 3, 1837 - U.S. recognizes the Republic of Texas in the last act of Andrew Jackson's Presidency.

March 27, 1837 - U.S. Secretary of State reports treaty agreements with Mexico which prohibit the annexation of Texas.

August 4, 1837 – The Texas minister to the United States presents a formal offer from the Republic of Texas for annexation by the United States.

January 4, 1838 - Senator William C. Preston introduces a resolution for a tripartite treaty between the United States, Mexico, and Texas in the U.S. Senate.

June 14, 1838 - The Senate tables the proposed tripartite treaty.

June and July 1838 - John Quincy Adams speaks against the annexation of Texas all morning, every morning in the U.S. House of Representatives.

October 12, 1838 - Texas withdraws the offer of annexation because of the U.S. Congress' inaction on the proposal.

January 23, 1839 – The Texas Congress passes a joint resolution approving President Sam Houston's withdrawal of the annexation proposal.

March 3, 1843 - U.S. Senate passes a proposed commerce treaty with the Republic of Texas. However, the Senate's amendment to the terms of original treaty terms is unsatisfactory and the Texas Congress rejects the amended version of the treaty.

June 15, 1843 - Sam Houston issues a proclamation declaring armistice between Mexico and Texas.

January 1844 - President Houston presents the annexation question to the Texas Congress and instructs the Texas minister to the U.S. to resume annexation talks.

April 11, 1844 - Diplomats from the United States and Texas sign an annexation treaty.

June 8, 1844 - The U.S. Senate rejects the treaty, 35 to 16.

June 13, 1844 - The U.S. Senate votes to table the Benton Annexation Bill.

January 25, 1845 - The U.S. House of Representatives passes the Joint Resolution to annex Texas.

February 27, 1845 - The Senate approves the amended Joint Resolution, 27 to 25.

February 28, 1845 - The U.S. House adopts the Senate version of the joint resolution to annex the Republic of Texas, 132 to 76.

March 1, 1845 - President Tyler signs the annexation resolution.

March 3, 1845 - The annexation offer is sent to the Republic of Texas president Anson Jones.

May 19, 1845 - Mexico and Texas sign the Cuevas-Smith Treaty guaranteeing Texas independence if it remains a separate republic.

June 16, 1845 - The Texas Congress meets in a special session to consider both the proposed Mexican treaty and the annexation resolution from the U.S. Congress. The Texas Congress accepts the United States offer.

July 4, 1845 - A convention of representatives meets to consider both the Mexican treaty and the U.S. annexation resolution. The convention accepts the U.S. offer.

October 13, 1845 - The Texas government presents the annexation ordinance and state constitution to the Texas voters for approval. The vote tally on November 10, 1845 is 4,254 to 267 in favor of annexation. The vote on January 1, 1846, is 7,664 to 430 in favor of annexation.

December 16, 1845 - The U.S. House votes to annex Texas by Joint Resolution, 141 to 58 with 21 abstaining.

December 22, 1845 - The U.S. Senate approves the joint resolution for the admission of Texas as a state, 31 to 14 with 7 abstaining.

December 29, 1845 - President Polk signs the Joint Resolution and Texas officially becomes the twenty-eighth state.

February 19, 1846 - The transfer of government from the Republic to the state is completed when Governor J. Pinckney Henderson takes the oath of office. Anson Jones declares "The Republic of Texas is no more."[784]

Ordinance of Annexation

Ordinance of Annexation Approved by the Texas Convention on July 4, 1845

An Ordinance

Whereas,

the Congress of the United States of America has passed resolutions providing for the annexation of Texas to that Union, which resolutions were offered by the President of the United States on the first day of March, [sic] 1845; and

Whereas,

the President of the United States has submitted to Texas the first and second sections of said resolutions, as the basis upon which Texas may be admitted as one of the States of the said Union; and

Whereas,

the existing Government of the Republic of Texas, has assented to the proposals thus made, – the terms and conditions of which are as follows:

"Joint Resolutions for annexing Texas to the United States

Resolved by the Senate and House of Representatives of the United States of America in Congress assembled, That [sic] Congress doth consent that the territory properly included within and rightfully belonging to the Republic of Texas, may be erected into a new State to be called the State of Texas, with a republican form of government adopted by the people of said Republic, by deputies in convention assembled, with the consent of the existing Government in order that the same may be admitted as one of the States of this Union.

2nd. And be it further resolved, That the foregoing consent of Congress is given upon the following conditions, to wit: First, said state to be formed, subject to the adjustment by this government of all questions of boundary that may arise with other government, – and the Constitution thereof, with the proper evidence of its adoption by the people of said Republic of Texas, shall be transmitted to the President of the United States, to be laid before Congress for its final action on, or before the first day of January, one thousand eight hundred and forty-six. Second, said state when admitted into the Union, after ceding to the United States all public edifices, fortifications, barracks, ports and harbors, navy and navy yards, docks, magazines and armaments, and all other means pertaining to the public defense, belonging to the said Republic of Texas, shall retain funds, debts, taxes and dues of every kind which may belong to, or be due and owing to the said Republic; and shall also retain all the vacant and unappropriated lands lying within its limits, to be applied to the payment of the debts and liabilities of said Republic of Texas, and the residue of said lands, after discharging said debts and liabilities, to be disposed of as said State may direct; but in no event are said debts and liabilities to become a charge upon the Government of the United States. Third – New States of convenient size not exceeding four in number, in addition to said State of Texas and having sufficient population, may, hereafter by the consent of said State, be formed out of the territory thereof, which shall be entitled to admission under the provisions of the Federal Constitution; and such states as may be formed out of the territory lying south of thirty-six degrees thirty minutes north latitude, commonly known as the Missouri Compromise Line, shall be admitted into the Union, with or without slavery, as the people of each State, asking admission shall desire; and in such State or States as shall be formed out of said territory, north of said Missouri compromise Line, slavery, or involuntary servitude (except for crime) shall be prohibited."

Now in order to manifest the assent of the people of this Republic, as required in the above recited portions of said resolutions, we the deputies of the people of Texas, in convention assembled, in their name and by their authority, do ordain and declare, that we assent to and accept the proposals, conditions and guarantees, contained in the first and second sections of the Resolution of the Congress of the United States aforesaid.

In testimony whereof, we have hereunto subscribed our names
Thomas J. Rusk
President
followed by 61 signatures
Attest James H. Raymond
Secretary of the Convention.[785]

Joint Resolution for Annexing Texas to the United States

Joint Resolution for Annexing Texas to the United States Approved March 1, 1845

1. Resolved by the Senate and House of Representatives of the United States of America in Congress assembled, That Congress doth consent that the territory properly included within and rightfully belonging to the Republic of Texas, may be erected into a new State to be called the State of Texas, with a republican form of government adopted by the people of said Republic, by deputies in convention assembled, with the consent of the existing Government in order that the same may be admitted as one of the States of this Union.

2. And be it further resolved, That the foregoing consent of Congress is given upon the following conditions, to wit: First, said state to be formed, subject to the adjustment by this government of all questions of boundary that may arise with other government, – and the Constitution thereof, with the proper evidence of its adoption by the people of said Republic of Texas, shall be transmitted to the President of the United States, to be laid before Congress for its final action on, or before the first day of January, one thousand eight hundred and forty-six. Second, said state when admitted into the Union, after ceding to the United States all public edifices, fortifications, barracks, ports and harbors, navy and navy yards, docks, magazines and armaments, and all other means pertaining to the public defense, belonging to the said Republic of Texas, shall retain funds, debts, taxes and dues of every kind which may belong to, or be due and owing to the said Republic; and shall also retain all the vacant and unappropriated lands lying within its limits, to be applied to the payment of the debts and liabilities of said Republic of Texas, and the residue of said lands, after discharging said debts and liabilities, to be disposed of as said State may direct; but in no event are said debts and liabilities to become a charge upon the Government of the United States. Third – New States of convenient size not exceeding four in number, in addition to said State of Texas and having sufficient population, may, hereafter by the consent of said State, be formed out of the territory thereof, which shall be entitled to admission under the provisions of the Federal Constitution; and such states as may be formed out of the territory lying

south of thirty-six degrees thirty minutes north latitude, commonly known as the Missouri Compromise Line, shall be admitted into the Union, with or without slavery, as the people of each State, asking admission shall desire; and in such State or States as shall be formed out of said territory, north of said Missouri Compromise Line, slavery, or involuntary servitude (except for crime) shall be prohibited.

3. And be it further resolved, – That if the President of the United States shall in his judgment and discretion deem it most advisable, instead of proceeding to submit the foregoing resolution of the Republic of Texas, as an overture on the part of the United States for admission, to negotiate with the Republic; then,

Be it resolved, That a State, to be formed out of the present Republic of Texas, with suitable extent and boundaries, and with two representatives in Congress, until the next appointment of representation, shall be admitted into the Union, by virtue of this act, on an equal footing with the existing States, as soon as the terms and conditions of such admission, and the cession of the remaining Texian territory to the United States shall be agreed upon by the governments of Texas and the United States: And that the sum of one hundred thousand dollars be, and the same is hereby, appropriated to defray the expenses of missions and negotiations, to agree upon the terms of said admission and cession, either by treaty to be submitted to the Senate, or by articles to be submitted to the two houses of Congress, as the President may direct.

Approved, March 1, 1845.[786]

An Act to Establish the Galveston and Red River Railway Company

Section 1. Be it enacted by the Legislature of the State of Texas, That a body politic and corporate be, and the same is hereby created and established, under the name and style of the Galveston and Red River Railway Company, with capacity to make contracts, to have succession and a common seal, to make by-laws for its government, and in its said corporate name to sue and be sued, to grant and to receive, and generally to do and perform all such acts and things as may be necessary or proper for, or incident to the fulfilment of its obligations, or the maintenance of its rights under this act. and consistent with the provisions of the Constitution of this State.

Sec. 2. That the said Company be, and hereby is invested with the right of making, owning and maintaining a railway from such point on Galveston Bay, or its contiguous waters, to such point upon Red River, between the eastern boundary line of Texas and Coffee's station, as the said company may deem most suitable, with the privilege of making, owning and maintaining such branches to the railway as they may deem expedient.

Sec. 3. That Ebenezer Allen, and such other persons as he may associate with him for the purpose, are hereby appointed Commissioners, and invested with the right and privilege of forming and organizing the said company, of obtaining subscriptions to the capital stock, and distributing the shares thereof: and generally of taking such lawful measures to secure the effectual organization and successful operation of said company, as they may deem expedient

Sec. 4. That the capital stock of said company shall be divided into shares of one hundred dollars each, and the holders of such shares shall constitute the said company, and each member shall be entitled to one vote in person or by proxy, for each and every share he may own: and such shares of stock shall be transferable alone upon the books of the company, which books shall be kept open for the inspection of any stockholder who may wish to examine them at the office of the company, in proper business hours.

Sec. 5. That the affairs and business of the said company shall be conducted and managed by a board of directors, not to exceed nine in number, who shall be elected by the company, at such time as the said commissioners may appoint, and annually thereafter: Provided, that in case of failure so to elect at the stated time, the board of directors incumbent shall continue in office until there be an election, the time for which may be fixed by said board, thereof reasonable notice shall be given.

Sec. 6. That no person shall be eligible as a director unless he be owner of at least five shares of the capital stock: the said board shall elect a President from their number, to fill vacancies occurring from death, resignation or otherwise: have power to appoint a secretary and such other officers as they may consider necessary, and to require security for the faithful performance of their duties: also, to prescribe the time for the payment of instalments, or assessments upon the stock, and the amount of such instalments or assessments, to declare the forfeiture of such stock for non-payment; and to do or cause to be done all other lawful acts or things which they may deem necessary or proper in conducting the business of said company. A majority of said board of directors shall constitute a quorum for doing business. All instruments in writing executed by the President and secretary, under the seal of the company, with the consent of the board of directors, shall be valid and binding.

Sec. 7. That the said company shall be empowered to occupy such portions of the public lands, not exceeding one hundred yards in width, as the said railway or any of its branches, to be constructed in accordance with this act, shall pass through, and to take from the public lands contiguous thereto such metals, timber and other materials as may be useful or necessary in the construction and maintenance of their works and the prosecution of their operations or business, the company paying a reasonable compensation to the State for the said privilege.

Sec. 8. That if the said company shall not commence its operations within two years from the first day of June, [sic] 1848, and shall not have completed at least one hundred miles of the said railway within five years thereafter, then, and in such case the rights, powers and privileges herein granted to the said company, for the construction of said railway shall cease and he determined.

Sec. 9. That the said company shall have the right of constructing bridges and other improvements upon and over any water course bordering upon or crossing the said railway, or any of its branches: Provided, that the navigation of such water course shall not be obstructed thereby.

Sec. 10. That if any person shall negligently or designedly injure or destroy any of the fixtures, buildings, machines or improvements of the company, or any portion of the said railway or its branches, he shall he subject to indictment therefor, and on conviction may be punished by fine and imprisonment, and shall be also liable to the said company in a civil action for damages.

Sec. 11. That no provision contained in this act shall be so construed as to grant or allow any banking privileges, or any privilege of issuing any species of paper to circulate as money to the aforesaid company.

Sec. 12. That the said company shall have the right to charge five cents per mile for passengers and no more, and shall have the right to charge not exceeding fifty cents on the hundred pounds for freight for every hundred miles that the same may be transported on said railway: Provided, however, that the Legislature of the State of Texas shall have the right to fix and regulate the price that said company shall charge for carrying the public mails of the United States.

Approved, March 11, 1848.[787]

Allen's Broadside on the Act Relating to Lands in Peters' Colony

Attorney-General's Office,
June 3rd, 1852.

Sir: The obvious importance of the subjects of inquiry contained in your communications addressed to me for opinions, under dates of 29th April and 18th ultimo, demanded mature investigation before preparing my answer. In this I trust you will find a satisfactory reason for any apparent want of promptness in forwarding to you my reply.

First. – My attention is directed by your earlier note to certain applications made for patents for lands lying within the unsurveyed portions of Peters' Colony, by virtue of recent locations and surveys upon headright certificates, and other evidences of rights to land, accruing under the general laws of Texas to individuals. You inform me that these patents are claimed under the provisions of the 3rd section of the act "relating to lands in Peters' Colony," approved the 10th of February, [sic] 1852, and inquire whether those applicants are entitled to the patents which they demand.

Without circumlocution, I reply that *they are not.* Four separate contracts made between the Republic of Texas and the individuals composing the Texan Emigration and Land Company, in relation to this colony, are in existence, bearing the successive dates of 30th August, [sic] 1841, 9th November, [sic] 1841, 26th of July, [sic] 1842, and 20th January, [sic] 1843. These contracts were authorized by the act of February 4, 1841, and the joint resolution of 16th January, [sic] 1843. They were framed and executed in conformity with the provisions of these enactments, and with them, have like force and effect, as *positive laws.* – Now what is this *effect,* with regard to that portion of the public domain designated and reserved by the provisions of these contracts?

By the first, it was stipulated that *all lands lying within limits of the tract designated and set apart for the contractors which should not be appropriated according to the terms of the contract, should after the expiration of three years revert to and remain the sole property of the Government of Texas as part of the public domain.* Each of the succeeding contracts extended the boundaries of the grant. The joint resolution referred to authorized a modification of the preceding agreements; and by the last contract executed under the provisions of this resolution, the reserve of all the lands lying within the designated limits of the colonial territory, was extended five years from the 1st day of July, [sic] 1843, "*or until the completion otherwise of the terms and conditions of this contract.*"

Now, the acts of 1st January 1850, and 10th February, [sic] 1852, conclusively show that those *terms and conditions* have not yet been fully completed, and by the third section of the latter, the reserve is expressly *continued* two years and six months from the passage of the act. At what time, then, since the date of the first legislation on the subject of this colony in 1841, can it reasonably be contended that this reservation was suspended? When, since that date, has this territory become a part of the vacant domain subject to promiscuous locations for all classes of certificate holders? The answer is, *at no time.* – It follows that all locations and surveys made under the provisions of the general land laws of this country are unauthorized and void. A patent cannot be lawfully predicated upon any of them. Until the State shall relinquish its reservation, this territory is not subject to general appropriation, like the residue of the public lands.

Secondly. –You inquire whether, under the 9th section of the act of 1852, the company or its assigns are entitled to more than a half section of land in one patent? – the agent having chosen half section certificates.

By the provisions of the 8th section, the agent is authorized to cause to be made, by any persons who he may designate, all such surveys as may be necessary to satisfy the certificates issued for the benefit of the company, in conformity with the requirements of the act. These surveys may each embrace in *one body* more than a half section or section. The boundaries and superficial contents of each survey are to be determined by the fieldnotes [sic] when duly returned to the Landoffice; and a patent for each *survey,* and not for each *certificate,* is required to be issued by the provisions of the act, whenever the company or its assigns surrender certificates corresponding in the number of acres with the survey, and pay the usual fees. So under the 9th section, the agent may select from the surveyed portions of the colony any number of sections and parts of sections *in one and the same body,* and upon surrendering certificates corresponding in amount to the number of acres contained in the entire tract, he would be entitled to a patent for land embraced in the entire tract. Thus, if ten sections were included in one tract, a patent would issue for the whole, inasmuch as it constitutes one undivided area of surface. The *survey* mentioned in the 8th section, and the *designation* in the 9th, are the criteria for determining the respective area for which a patent in each case may properly issue. The adoption of a rule compelling the company to receive and pay for a patent for every half section of their land, would be unjust and oppressive, and could not be defended, unless the requirements of the statute most unequivocally demanded it.

Thirdly. – With reference to the alternate sections reserved by the State, it is perfectly clear, under the provisions of the act of 1852, that the colonists have no right to appropriate them. "The lands and alternate sections reserved to the Government of Texas" by virtue of the contracts referred to, continued the sole property of the Government, until the right to locate them was expressly conceded to the company by the terms of the 2d section of the act. The relinquishment executed by the agent in pursuance of the requirements of the first section, so far from prejudicing or invalidating this right of the company, was a necessary prerequisite to its establishment and consummation. Until the tender of this relinquishment, the right to locate the alternate sections, or even to receive their certificates, did not vest in the company. The relinquishment in express terms, excepts from its operation all rights and privileges reserved, guaranteed or secured to the company in the several sections of the act. No certificates can be legally or properly located upon these reserved lands, excepting those issued for the benefit of the company under the provisions of the first section of the act.

Fourthly. – It is suggested that some of the colonists entertain the opinion that they are entitled to divide their claims so as to secure two surveys on one and the same certificate. The statute of the 4th February, [sic] 1841, Sec. 1, provides "that not more than one section of six hundred and forty acres *to be located in a square,* shall be given to any family," nor more than three hundred and twenty acres to a single man. By the 2d. section, the claims of single men are subject to the same conditions and restrictions as those of families. The conditions of cultivation, the erection of cabins, and three years' occupancy, are also attached to the tracts designated for the colonists. Thus, the idea of a division in the location of a single certificate appears palpably erroneous. These claims are made indivisible and applicable singly and alone to one and the same section or half section of land to be located in a square. It does not follow that, because the surveying in certain cases is directed to be performed by the district and deputy surveyors, under the regulations prescribed by the general land law, the colonist is entitled to divide his claim. To render such an interference legitimate, it would be necessary first to show, that those officers were not authorized to survey any claims, *except divisible ones*. To my mind nothing is clearer than that the colonist must confine his certificate to one location. He cannot be permitted to divide against the express provisions of the law, and in contravention to the conditions essential to the existence of his right to land within the colonial limits.

Fifthly. – It is asked whether the colonists in locating their certificates within the surveyed portions of the colony are bound by the lines of sections, etc., run by the contractors. The fourth section of the act of 1852 makes it the duty of the colonist, before the 4th of August next, to file with the agent of the company a full and particular description of the land he claims. This description must, if the land be within the surveyed limits, be made by stating the number of the section or part of section, the township and range, base and meridian, *as surveyed by the company.* The location and description must conform to and coincide with the lines and corners of the surveys made by the company and delineated upon the corresponding maps and plats deposited in the General Land Office. These surveys constitute a part of the colonial system. It is highly important and imperatively required by the law, that the locations should strictly conform to the lines of the surveys. A departure from this rule would be a very hazardous experiment on the part of any individual, inasmuch as special legislation would be required to make the location a valid one, and the Legislature would be reluctant to relieve a person under circumstances requiring an obvious departure from the general system adopted by the State.

Where the colonist chooses his land from the *unsurveyed terri-*

tory within the limits of the colony, the requisite *description* of his location must be made by the fieldnotes [sic] of its survey. To such cases, the preceding observations are, of course, not intended to apply.

Sixthly – I am of opinion that those colonists who are, by the provisions of the tenth section of the act, entitled to certificate from the county courts, possess equal privileges with other colonists. Whenever they obtain their certificates, if before the 4th day of July next, the *preference* or *rights of priority* over the company in making locations, secured by the terms of the eleventh section of the act, at once vests in them. – This class of colonists cannot, however, make their locations till [sic] they obtain their certificates. At the respective dates of these, the *preference* attaches, and the right may be exercised at any time prior to the 4th day of July, [sic] 1852. By the terms of the 11th section, this right is vested in every colonist who had not, at the time of the passage of the act, located his land, whether such colonist should be entitled to the same by virtue of *"Ward's certificate or otherwise."*

Trusting that the conclusions thus attained may be as satisfactory and useful as they may be found truthful and correct, I have the honor to remain your obedient servant,

EBENEZER ALLEN.

Hon. STEPHEN CROSBY,

Commissioner General Landoffice.[788]

An Act Relating to Lands in Peters' Colony

Whereas, the President of the Republic of Texas, by virtue of an act of the Congress of said Republic, entitled "an act granting lands to emigrants," dated February 4th, 1841, and a joint resolution of said Congress, approved January 16th, 1843, to modify the provisions of said act, entered into four contracts bearing date, the first contract August 30th, 1841, the second November 20th, 1841, the third, July 26th, 1842, and the fourth contract, January 20th, 1843; making together one contract with W. S. Peters and others, his associates and assigns and legal representatives, to colonize and settle a portion of the then vacant public domain of said Republic, lying upon the Trinity and Red rivers, being in said contracts particularly described by metes and bounds, and commonly called "Peters' Colony." Beginning at a point on Red River, in said fourth contract particularly defined, and running thence along the extreme eastern boundary of said grant, south one hundred miles; thence west one hundred and sixty-four miles; thence north to Red River; thence down said river by its course to the place of beginning; and, Whereas, said contractors, W. S. Peters and others, their heirs or assigns and legal representatives, have organized and formed themselves by articles of association, into a company known and designated by the name and style of the "Texan Emigration and Land Company," and in pursuance of said laws and contracts, have entered upon said Colony and surveyed a large portion thereof, as is shown by their maps of survey, and have settled upon the lands so surveyed a large number of emigrant families; and it is proposed that said company shall relinquish to the State of Texas all the rights and interests accruing and belonging to them by the contracts aforesaid, except such rights and interests as are hereinafter reserved to said company, and grant to the colonists by them settled as aforesaid, the right to locate their claims under the acts of 21st January 1850 relating to Peters' Colony, upon the lands which by said contract, are claimed to belong to said contractors, or their assigns, whereby said company allege they will be divested of a large amount of rich and valuable lands, and to receive therefor an equivalent in lands of less value; also, to release said colonists from the payment of a large amount now alleged to be due from them to said company for surveying fees, and generally for the relief of said colonists and company, and to settle, adjust and effectually quiet the titles to lands in said colony or grant: Therefore,

Section 1. Be it enacted by the Legislature of the State of Texas, That whenever the agent of said company shall tender to the Commissioner of the General Land Office of this State a relinquishment, under his hand and seal, of all the rights and interests whatever, which said company have in said colony to the State of Texas, except such rights and privileges as are reserved, guaranteed and secured to said company in the several sections of this act, together with a release of all fees now alleged to be due and owing said company by said colonists, in consideration of such relinquishment and release, the Commissioner of the General Land Office shall immediately thereafter, and he is hereby required and directed to issue without delay, to said agent, for the use and benefit of said company, and in the name of the Trustees thereof or to their successors in office, certificates to the amount of seventeen hundred sections of land, in certificates for sections of six hundred and forty acres each, or half sections of three hundred and twenty acres each, as said agent may choose or prefer; and the agent of said company or trustees of the same shall, upon the receipt of the certificates herein provided for, pay to the Commissioner of the General Land Office the sum of three hundred dollars as a fee for the issuing of the certificates for the above mentioned seventeen hundred sections of land; provided, the relinquishment and release to the State, named in this section, shall be tendered to the Commissioner of the General Land Office within twenty days after the passage of this act.

Sec. 2. That all and each of said certificates, when issued to said agent by the Commissioner of the General Land Office as aforesaid, may be located upon any of the lands which have been surveyed or caused to be surveyed by said company within said colony, and including all lands and alternate sections reserved to the government of Texas as in said contracts directed, which are not settled upon or claimed by a colonist or colonists who are entitled to the same as colonists, by virtue of "an act to secure to all actual settlers within the limits of the Colony granted to Peters and others, commonly known as Peters' colony, the land to which they are entitled as colonists," approved January 21, 1850, and also upon any of the lands within the limits of said colony which have not been surveyed by said company and which are not located upon or surveyed by any colonists of Peters' colony or his assigns, by virtue of any certificate given to said colonist by the Commissioner of that colony, Thos. Wm. Ward, or by virtue of certificates which may be issued to colonists of said colony as aforesaid, in pursuance of any act of the Legislature for the relief of any colonists not embraced and provided for in the act of January, [sic] 1850, or their assigns. Said certificates or any of them shall be assignable by endorsement of said agent or trustees of said company, by acknowledgement before any officer authorized by the laws of Texas to take acknowledgement of deeds.

Sec. 3. That all the lands lying within the limits and boundaries of said colony, and which by said contracts were reserved and set apart to the parties of the second part thereof, their associates and legal representatives, until the end of five years from and after the first day of July, [sic] 1843, shall continue to be reserved and set apart for the purposes herein named for the term or space of two years and six months from and after the passage of this act, and shall remain and be held by the State of Texas for the purposes herein provided until the expiration of said term. And the Commissioner of the General Land Office is hereby prohibited from issuing patents to any lands located in said colony other than those and surveyed, or caused to be surveyed therein by said company or their assigns, in virtue of said certificates to be issued as aforesaid to said company, as provided for in the first section of this act, and all old surveys excepted by said colony contracts, located and surveyed before the date of said contracts, unless by the authority of the decree of some court of competent jurisdiction, and the rights or remedies in law or equity of those who may have made locations or surveys of land within the limits of said colony contracts, shall not be impaired or changed by the passage of this act; provided, however, that one-half of the lands acquired by said company in virtue of the provisions of this act, shall be alienated by them within ten years after the passage of this act.

Sec. 4. That it shall be the duty of each and every colonist, before the fourth day of August, [sic] 1852, to file with the agent of said company a full and particular description, under their hand and seal, of the land they claim and are entitled to in said colony as colonists, by the number of the section or parts of a section, township and range, base and meridian, if located and claimed as surveyed by said company in their surveys aforesaid; but if otherwise, by the map and field-notes of their said survey correctly made out, which description of land and maps and fieldnotes [sic] of surveys made by said colonists with the names of the persons claiming the same, said agent shall return to the Commissioner of the General Land Office. And all lands lying within the limits of said colony a description or map and field-notes of which shall not be returned by the agent as aforesaid to the Commissioner of the General Land Office, shall then be deemed and considered vacant so far as to be open to the location and surveys of said company, according to the provisions of the second and eighth sections of this act. – Provided, that a failure of said agent to return any or all of said descriptions, and maps, and field notes as aforesaid, which shall be actually filed with him in his office as aforesaid, shall not render vacant any land the description and field-notes and maps of which he shall fail to return as aforesaid. And. provided, also, that all locations and surveys made in said colony prior to November, [sic] 1841, shall be exempted from location.

Sec. 5. That it shall be the duty of the agent of said company to file in the General Land Office of this State, and also in the several offices of each and every district or county surveyor, whose district or county is in whole or in part embraced within the limits of said colony, a map containing the surveys heretofore made by said company in said colony, certified to by said agent, and it shall be the duty of each of said district or county surveyors to mark and lay down upon the map so furnished to him by said agent correctly, all the surveys which have at this time been made in said colony, or which may be made before the fourth day of July, [sic] 1852, by said District or County Surveyor, or by any and all of his deputies, for any colonist or colonists of Peters' colony, as the land to which they are entitled as colonists in said colony as aforesaid; which maps, with his surveys, and all those made by his deputies, as aforesaid, correctly laid down thereon, and certified to by him as being true and correct, and containing all the surveys made by him and those made by his deputies as aforesaid, under his hand and seal, he shall return to said agent, on or before the 24th day of July, [sic] 1852, at the office of said agent in said colony. And for any failure, refusal or neglect on part of either of said District or County Surveyors, in the performance of this duty, hereby enjoined on them, such District or County Surveyor, so failing, refusing or neglecting, shall be liable upon his official bond to any colonist, and to said company in the amount of any damage or injury said colonist or said company may sustain by reason of such failure, neglect or refusal, to be recovered before any competent tribunal.

Sec. 6. That it shall be the duty of said agent, on or before the fourth day of September, [sic] 1852, to return all of said maps and said descriptions of the lands claimed as aforesaid, by said colonists, which may be returned or filed in his office as aforesaid. to the Commissioner of the General Land Office, who shall inspect the same, and if found by him to be correct, and in accordance with this act, he shall file the same in his office, and deliver a certified copy thereof to said agent, and when filed, he shall, in accordance with said maps, and the description of the land returned and claimed by the colonists as aforesaid, issue patents to the colonists or their assigns.

See. 7. That the agent aforesaid, in the performance of said duties, shall keep his office in said colony, as near the centre [sic] thereof as may be convenient to him, and shall keep in his office the maps or plats of the surveys of the lands heretofore surveyed by said company in said colony, and the books and registers and papers in his possession, at all times open to the inspection of the colonists. And for any services which he may perform as aforesaid, or for any writing or receipt which he may give to any colonist, or for making the returns as aforesaid to the Commissioner of the General Land Office, he shall make no charge, either to the colonists or to the State. And for the faithful and impartial performance of his duties therein, he shall take an oath before some Notary Public of this State, and enter into bond with the State of Texas in the sum of twenty thousand dollars, with at least two good securities; said bond to be approved by the Secretary of State and deposited in his office.

Sec. 8. That it shall be lawful for the agent of said company, from time to time, as he shall deem necessary, during said two years and six months after the passage of this act, to make, or cause to be made by any person or persons whom he may authorize and designate, all the surveys which, in the location of their said certificates, it shall be necessary for said company to make in said colony. And the agent aforesaid shall semi-annually make returns to the Commissioner of the General Land Office of the field-notes of all surveys made, or caused to be made by him as aforesaid, certified to by said agent and sworn to by the person making said survey or surveys. And if said survey or surveys shall be found not to interfere with the lands claimed by the colonists as aforesaid, the description and field-notes of which shall have been returned to said Commissioner, by said agent, as contemplated in the fourth section of this act, or with any legal grants and surveys previously made, the Commissioner of the General Land Office shall issue to said company, or their assigns, patents therefor, whenever said company or their assigns shall surrender to him certificates corresponding in the number of acres with such survey or surveys, and paying to him the usual fees for issuing patents.

Sec. 9. That said agent shall also make to said Commissioner semi-annual returns of all sections or parts of sections which he may choose out of the lands heretofore surveyed by said company in said colony, by designating to him said sections or parts of sections, by number, township, range, base and meridian, and patents shall be issued therefor to said company or their assigns, containing said designation without further description, whenever said company shall surrender to said Commissioner of the General Land Office, certificates corresponding in number of acres with such sections or parts of sections so chosen, and paying to him the usual fees for issuing patents.

Sec. 10. That every colonist who settled within the limits of said colony prior to the first day of July, [sic] 1848, and resided therein three years, but who was not residing therein on the 21st day of January, [sic] 1850, and who has not received certificate from the colony Commissioner, Thomas Wm. Ward, or if residing therein at that time, and now a resident of said colony, and who has not received a certificate as aforesaid, shall be entitled — heads of families, to six hundred and forty acres each, and single men, to three hundred and twenty acres each. And it shall be lawful for any colonist as aforesaid to prove such settlement and residence before any County Court within said colony, by his own oath, and the oath of two respectable witnesses, and declaring under oath that he has not received a certificate from Thos. Wm. Ward, as a colonist, nor as provided for in this section; and that he has never received any land as a headright from the Republic or State of Texas, the clerk of said court shall give to said colonist a certificate thereof under his hand and official seal, setting forth the amount of land to which such colonist is entitled, and upon said certificate, said colonist may locate and survey the land to which he is thereby entitled as aforesaid, as other colony certificates are located, agreeable to the provisions of this act, for which oaths, certificates and seal, said Clerk shall receive two dollars and fifty cents; and whenever said colonist or his assigns shall file said certificate and the field-notes of his said survey or a description thereof, by section or parts of section, township and range, in the General Land Office of this State, and his survey is found not to conflict with the locations and surveys of other colonists, or with any of those locations or surveys contemplated by this act, to be made or caused to be made by said agent or said company in said colony, the Commissioner of the General Land Office shall issue patents therefor to said colonist his assigns. Also, the certificates issued to the colonists by the Commissioner, Thos. Wm. Ward, shall be transferable, and all transfers of such certificates heretofore made are hereby legalized, and may be located upon any of the vacant or unappropriated public lands within the limits of said colony; provided, that any certificate or patent issued by virtue of this section, to any person who may have previously obtained land, or a certificate for land from Mexico, Coahuila and Texas, or the Republic or State of Texas, shall be null and void.

Sec. 11. That each and every colonist who has not yet located or surveyed his land, to which as a colonist he or she is entitled in said colony, either by Ward's certificate or otherwise. shall have preference over said company until the fourth day of July, [sic] 1852, wherein to make their locations or survey; provided, however, that any location or survey which shall hereafter be made by any such colonist upon any of the lands in said colony, which have been surveyed by such company, such location or survey shall be governed by, and confined to the lines and comers of said company's surveys as delineated upon their maps; but should their location and survey be made upon part of the unsurveyed lands in said colony, such survey or location may be made as required by law for other surveys.

See. 12. That at the same time said agent shall file the relinquishment as aforesaid, he shall, also, file with the Commissioner of the General Land Office. the certificates of the Clerk of the District Court of Travis county [sic], certifying that the suit of the Trustees of said company vs. the Commissioner of the General Land Office has been dismissed, which dismissal shall be without prejudice to the plaintiffs upon their bond: and upon the filing of said relinquishment and certification, it is hereby made the duty of the Attorney General of this State to dismiss the suit of "the Governor for the use of the State." now pending, ' 'against Carrol, Mercer and others," in the Navarro District Court of this State.

Sec. 13. That all those who have heretofore located upon any of the lands within said colony, by any headright certificate,[789] land scrip,[790] or bounty warrant,[791] other than those heretofore or hereafter to be issued to said colonists or contractors as hereinbefore mentioned or provided, shall not be placed in a better or worse condition than they are at present, anything in this act contained to the contrary notwithstanding. − And nothing in this act shall be so construed as to oblige any colonist who has, or may locate his claim upon the lands heretofore surveyed by said company in said colony, to re-survey his land; provided, his location is confined to the lines and corners of the surveys of said company; nor to allow any person to locate upon the section or part of a section upon which any colonist may at this time be residing, or was residing on the first day of July, [sic] 1848; provided, such resident shall locate his claim thereon before the fourth day of July, [sic] 1852; and that this act be in force from and after its passage.

Approved, February 10, 1852.[792]

Spiritualism in the Allen Family

The interest in spiritualism continued with Ebenezer and Sylvinia's son, William Pitt Allen. William was an early resident of the Spiritualist colony at Summerland, California. [Please see The Allen Family After Ebenezer's Death.] William's daughter, Sylvanna, was married to Robert Bell in 1895 at Summerland, by a Spiritualist minister, David Davis.

A former Treasury agent and Spiritualist, Henry Lafayette Williams, initially intended to raise pigs in Summerland when he bought this land in 1885. But when the Southern Pacific Railroad announced it was laying tracks north from Los Angeles, which would cross his pig ranch, he changed his plans and decided to sell lots and build a town next to the train line.

Williams and his wife persuaded fellow Spiritualists to settle in their town. Lots of 60 feet by 25 feet sold for $25 each. In 1889, the early settlers called the town Summerland, the name of the Spiritualists' heaven. According to town folklore, many of the homes built by the Spiritualists had hidden rooms from which the spirit of a dead relative would enter during séances. People from neighboring towns nicknamed Summerland "Spookville" because of the rumors of strange activities, abnormal occurrences, and ghosts.

The town's future improved significantly around 1890 when natural gas was discovered. Then in 1894, a man drilling a water well discovered oil. These finds turned Summerland into an oil boomtown.[793] Wildcatters built piers into the ocean, erected derricks, and discovered the first offshore oil field in the Western Hemisphere at Summerland Beach, north of Los Angeles. In the late 1890s, Williams and other Spiritualists started exploratory drilling onshore to recover oil and gas from seepages. They noticed the nearer the well was to the ocean the more it produced. In the tidal area, gas bubbled to the surface and indicated the underground reservoirs extended beyond the shoreline. The problem was finding a way to reach these fields.

Williams decided to build a wooden dock into the ocean and perpendicular to the beach, which would serve as a drilling platform. In 1897, Williams built a pier, placed a cable-tool drilling rig[794] at the end of it, and constructed the first offshore drilling and production platform. The power generators and other supporting equipment were placed on the beach. Williams first three piers extended 1,350 feet from the shoreline and reached water depths of 35 feet. Williams' crew drilled down 455 feet and discovered two oil sand[795] deposits.[796]

In 1898, during an inspection of his four producing onshore wells, Williams stumbled and fell into an abandoned well. Weakened by his injuries, he developed pneumonia. He went to San Francisco to receive medical treatment, but he died on January 13, 1899, at the age of 58. The community praised Williams for his pioneering work in oil drilling, but many Summerland residents avoided him and objected to his belief in Spiritualism.

Encouraged by Williams' success, other Summerland entrepreneurs built piers into the Pacific Ocean in search of oil. By 1900 twelve piers reached into the ocean and twenty-two operating companies explored for oil. The community had 198 operating wells by 1903. The fields continued to produce oil until the late 1930s.[797]

The oil discoveries produced caused an invasion of non-Spiritualist settlers and businesses and encouraged many of the Spiritualists to move to Santa Barbara.[798]

Ebenezer Allen and William Pitt Allen's descendants were the only members of the Allen family interested in Spiritualism. Most of Allen's siblings remained in the Congregational Church and two converted to the Mormon Church.[799]

The Ordinance of the Texas Convention

An Ordinance:
To dissolve the union between the State of Texas and the other States, united under the compact styled "The Constitution of the United States of America."

Adopted in Convention, at Austin City, the first day of February, A.D. 1861.

Whereas,

The Federal Government has failed to accomplish the purposes of the compact of union between these States, in giving protection either to the persons of our people upon an exposed frontier, or to the property of our citizens; and, whereas, the action of the Northern States of the Union is violative [sic] of the compact between the States and the guarantees of the Constitution; and whereas the recent developments in federal affairs, make it evident that the power of the Federal Government is sought to be made a weapon with which to strike down the interests and prosperity of the people of Texas and her Sister slave-holding States, instead of permitting it to be, as was intended, our shield against outrage and aggression:

Therefore,

Section 1

We, the People of the State of Texas, by Delegates in Convention assembled, do declare and ordain, that the Ordinance adopted by our Convention of Delegates, on the Fourth day of July, A.D. 1845, and afterwards ratified by us, under which the Republic of Texas was admitted into Union with other States and became a party to the compact styled "The Constitution of the United States of America" be, and is hereby repealed and annulled; That all the powers, which by said compact were delegated by Texas to the Federal Government, are revoked and resumed; That Texas is of right absolved from all restraints and obligations incurred by said compact, and is a separate Sovereign State, and that her citizens and people are absolved from all allegiance to the United States, or the Government thereof.

Section 2

This ordinance shall be submitted to the people of Texas for ratification or rejection by the qualified voters thereof, on the 23rd day of February 1861, and unless rejected by a majority of the votes cast, shall take effect and be in force on and after the 2nd day of March, A.D. 1861. Provided, that in the Representative District of El Paso, said election may be held on the 19th day of February, A.D. 1861.

Adopted in Convention, at Austin City, the first day of February, A.D. 1861.[800]

Texas Declaration of Causes

DECLARATION OF CAUSES: February 2, 1861

A declaration of the causes which impel the State of Texas to secede from the Federal Union.

The government of the United States, by certain joint resolutions, bearing date the 1st day of March, in the year A.D. 1845, proposed to the Republic of Texas, then a free, sovereign and independent nation, the annexation of the latter to the former as one of the co-equal States thereof,

The people of Texas, by deputies in convention assembled, on the fourth day of July of the same year, assented to and accepted said proposals and formed a constitution for the proposed State, upon which on the 29th day of December in the same year, said State was formally admitted into the Confederated Union.

Texas abandoned her separate national existence and consented to become one of the Confederated States to promote her welfare, insure domestic tranquility [sic] and secure more substantially the blessings of peace and liberty to her people. She was received into the confederacy with her own constitution, under the guarantee of the Federal Constitution and the compact of annexation, that she should enjoy these blessings. She was received as a commonwealth holding, maintaining and protecting the institution known as negro [sic] slavery – the servitude of the African to the white race within her limits – a relation that had existed from the first settlement of her wilderness by the white race, and which her people intended should exist in all future time. Her institutions and geographical position established the strongest ties between her and other slave-holding States of the confederacy. Those ties have been strengthened by association. But what has been the course of the government of the United States, and of the people and authorities of the non-slave-holding States, since our connection with them?

The controlling majority of the Federal Government, under various pretences [sic] and disguises, has so administered the same as to exclude the citizens of the Southern States, unless under odious and unconstitutional restrictions, from all the immense territory owned in common by all the States on the Pacific Ocean, for the avowed purpose of acquiring sufficient power in the common government to use it as a means of destroying the institutions of Texas and her sister slave-holding States.

By the disloyalty of the Northern States and their citizens and the imbecility of the Federal Government, infamous combinations of incendiaries and outlaws have been permitted in those States and the common territory of Kansas to trample upon the federal laws, to war upon the lives and property of Southern citizens in that territory, and finally, by violence and mob law, to usurp the possession of the same as exclusively the property of the Northern States.

The Federal Government, while but partially under the control of these our unnatural and sectional enemies, has for years almost entirely failed to protect the lives and property of the people of Texas against the Indian savages on our border, and more recently against the murderous forays of banditti from the neighboring territory of Mexico; and when our State government has expended large amounts for such purpose, the Federal Government has refused reimbursement therefor [sic], thus rendering our condition more insecure and harassing [sic] than it was during the existence of the Republic of Texas.

These and other wrongs we have patiently borne in the vain hope that a returning sense of justice and humanity would induce a different course of administration.

When we advert to the course of individual non-slave-holding States, and that [of] a majority of their citizens, our grievances assume far greater magnitude.

The States of Maine, Vermont, New Hampshire, Connecticut, Rhode Island, Massachusetts, New York, Pennsylvania, Ohio, Wisconsin, Michigan and Iowa, by solemn legislative enactments, have deliberately, directly or indirectly violated the 3rd clause of the 2nd section of the 4th article of the Federal Constitution,[801] and laws passed in pursuance thereof; thereby annulling a material provision of the compact, designed by its framers to perpetuate amity between the members of the confederacy and to secure the rights of the slave-holdings States in their domestic institutions – a provision founded in justice and wisdom, and without the enforcement of which the compact fails to accomplish the object of its creation. Some of those States have imposed high fines and degrading penalties upon any of their citizens or officers who may carry out in good faith that provision of the compact, or the federal laws enacted in accordance therewith.

In all the non-slave-holding States, in violation of that good faith and comity which should exist between entirely distinct nations, the people have formed themselves into a great sectional party, now strong enough in numbers to control the affairs of each of those States, based upon the unnatural feeling of hostility to these Southern States and their beneficent and patriarchal system of African slavery, proclaiming the debasing doctrine of the equality of all men, irrespective of race or color – a doctrine at war with nature, in opposition to the experience of mankind, and in violation of the plainest revelations of the Divine Law. They demand the abolition of negro [sic] slavery throughout the confederacy, the recognition of political equality between the white and the negro [sic] races, and avow their determination to press on their crusade against us, so long as a negro [sic] slave remains in these States.

For years past this abolition organization has been actively sowing the seeds of discord through the Union, and has rendered the Federal Congress the arena for spreading firebrands and hatred between the slave-holding and non-slave-holding States.

By consolidating their strength, they have placed the slave-holding States in a hopeless minority in the Federal Congress, and rendered representation of no avail in protecting Southern rights against their exactions and encroachments.

They have proclaimed, and at the ballot box sustained, the revolutionary doctrine that there is a "higher law" than the constitution and laws of our Federal Union, and virtually that they will disregard their oaths and trample upon our rights.

They have for years past encouraged and sustained lawless organizations to steal our slaves and prevent their recapture, and have repeatedly murdered Southern citizens while lawfully seeking their rendition.

They have invaded Southern soil and murdered unoffending citizens, and through the press their leading men and a fanatical pulpit have bestowed praise upon the actors and assassins in these crimes, while the governors of several of their States have refused to deliver parties implicated and indicted for participation in such offences, upon the legal demands of the States aggrieved.

They have, through the mails and hired emissaries, sent seditious pamphlets and papers among us to stir up servile insurrection and bring blood and carnage to our firesides.

They have sent hired emissaries among us to burn our towns and distribute arms and poison to our slaves for the same purpose.

They have impoverished the slave-holding States by unequal and partial legislation, thereby enriching themselves by draining our substance.

They have refused to vote appropriations for protecting Texas against ruthless savages, for the sole reason that she is a slave-holding State.

And, finally, by the combined sectional vote of the seventeen non-slave-holding States, they have elected as president and vice-president of the whole confederacy two men whose chief claims to such high positions are their approval of these long continued [sic] wrongs, and their pledges to continue them to the final consummation of these schemes for the ruin of the slave-holding States.

In view of these and many other facts, it is meet [fitting or proper] that our own views should be distinctly proclaimed.

We hold as undeniable truths that the governments of the various States, and of the confederacy itself, were established exclusively by the white race, for themselves and their posterity; that the African race had no agency in their establishment; that they were rightfully held and regarded as an inferior and dependent race, and in that condition only could their existence in this country be rendered beneficial or tolerable.

That in this free government all white men are and of right ought to be entitled to equal civil and political rights; that the servitude of the African race, as existing in these States, is mutually beneficial to both bond and free, and is abundantly authorized and justified by the experience of mankind, and the revealed will of the Almighty Creator, as recognized by all Christian nations; while the destruction of the existing relations between the two races, as advocated by our sectional enemies, would bring inevitable calamities upon both and desolation upon the fifteen slave-holding States.

By the secession of six of the slave-holding States, and the certainty that others will speedily do likewise, Texas has no alternative but to remain in an isolated connection with the North or unite her destinies with the South.

For these and other reasons, solemnly asserting that the Federal Constitution has been violated and virtually abrogated by the several States named, seeing that the Federal Government is now passing under the control of our enemies to be diverted from the exalted objects of its creation to those of oppression and wrong, and realizing that our own State can no longer look for protection, but to God and her own sons – We the delegates of the people of Texas, in Convention assembled, have passed an ordinance dissolving all political connection with the government of the United States of America and the people thereof and confidently appeal to the intelligence and patriotism of the freemen of Texas to ratify the same at the ballot box, on the 23rd day of the present month.

Adopted in Convention on the 2nd day of Feby [February], in the year of our Lord one thousand eight hundred and sixty-one and of the independence of Texas the twenty-fifth.[802]

Act to Admit Texas to the Confederate States of America

Chapter XXIV. An Act to admit Texas as a Member of the Confederate States of America.

March 2, 1861

The Congress of the Confederate States of America do enact, That [sic] the State of Texas be and is hereby admitted as a member of this Confederacy, upon an equal footing with the other Confederate States.

Approved March 2, 1861.[803]

Texas Ordinance of Secession

No. 5 – An Ordinance

In relation to a union of the State of Texas with the Confederate States of America.

March 22, 1861

Whereas,

the Convention of this State has received information that the Congress of the Confederate States of America, now in session at the city of Montgomery, in the State of Alabama, has adopted a Constitution for a Provisional Government, which Constitution is modelled [sic] on that of the United States of America, and, whereas, as a seceded State, it becomes expedient and proper that Texas should join said Confederacy and share its destinies; and, whereas, a delegation, consisting of seven members, has already been elected by the Convention to the Congress of the Confederacy aforesaid;

therefore,

Section 1. The People of Texas, in Convention assembled, have ordained and declared, and do hereby ordain and declare, that the delegation aforesaid, to the Congress aforesaid, be, and they are hereby instructed, and we do accordingly instruct them, in behalf of the State, and as representing its sovereign authority, to apply for the admission of this State into said Confederacy; and to that end and for that purpose, to give in the adhesion of Texas to the provisional Constitution of said Confederate States; and which said Constitution, this Convention hereby approves, ratifies and accepts.

Sec. 2. Be it further ordained, That the delegation appointed by this Convention to the Congress of the Confederate States, be and they are hereby authorized to act in said Congress as the duly accredited representatives of the State of Texas: provided, however, that any permanent Constitution which may be formed by said Congress shall not become obligatory on this State until approved by the people in such way as shall be determined upon.

Sec. 3. Be it further ordained, That the President of the Convention immediately transmit, through such channel as he may elect, a copy or copies of this ordinance to the Congress at Montgomery, and the members of Congress from this State.

Done at Austin City, March 5th, A.D. 1861.[804]

Ordinance to Ratify the Confederate Constitution

No. 18 -- An Ordinance

To ratify the Constitution of the Confederate States of America.
March 23, 1861

The people of the State of Texas assembled by delegates in Convention, ordain, That the Constitution of the Confederate States of America, adopted March 11th, 1861, by the Congress of the Provisional Government of said Confederacy, for the permanent government thereof, subject to ratification by the respective States, is hereby ratified, accepted, and adopted for the purposes therein expressed on the part of this State, acting in its sovereign and independent character.

Adopted in Convention, at the City of Austin, on the 23d day of March, A.D. 1861.[805]

Ebenezer Allen Will

Will − Life in this world, always of uncertain duration is rendered peculiarly so to myself, in common with thousands of others, by the present condition of things. The battle, upon the issue upon of which the fate of this City and in no trifling degree the fortunes of the Confederacy hung, must soon be decided I think proper therefore under these circumstances to make this my olagraphic[806] Will and I do accordingly bequeath and hereby devise unto my dear wife Sylvinia Josephine Allen all my property and Estate both real and personal wherever situated or found, whether in Texas or elsewhere whereof I may be profected [*benefited, profited, or advanced*] or entitled to at the time of my decease; and I appoint her Executive of this my last Will and Testament, with full power to execute the same in accordance with the forms of the State of Texas without being required to furnish any bond as Executrix or otherwise, by the County Court or any other Court having jurisdiction hereof. If from any cause however she should first act as such executrix then I will and desire that my Son William Pitt Allen serve as Executor hereof and I appoint him such Executor in that case, with full power to execute the same without bond as is above provided in case of his mother, written & signed wholly by me and with mine own hand at Richmond Va. This fourth day of June Anna [*Anno*] Domini Eighteen hundred and sixty-two. --- Ebenezer Allen

In open Court January 27, 1864 and appeared in open Court this this 27th Jany F. H. Merriman & J. M. Joseph, witnesses of Lawful age who having been sworn in The State of Texas[807]

Ebenezer Allen's Will
(Judith M. Johnson, Johnson-Morrow Family Tree, Ancestry.com[808])

Josephine Allen vs. William R. Baker

In 1873, Ebenezer's widow filed a lawsuit against William R. Baker

1. Though a receipt given by the wife for money due the husband was not binding on the husband when the payment was made in Confederate money without his consent or authority, yet where the husband died after such a payment, and the wife who had given the receipt became his executrix and sole heir, she is bound by her receipt in the absence of fraud, covin[809] [fraud, misrepresentation or undue influence.

2. One who has voluntarily executed a contract by paying or receiving Confederate money in satisfaction of a demand will not be relieved, but left where his own action has placed him.

Appeal from Harris. Tried below before the Hon. James Masterson.

This suit was instituted by Mrs. Josephine Allen[810] as executrix of the estate of her late husband, Ebenezer Allen, deceased, to recover $7,500, with eight per cent [sic] interest per annum from the thirtieth of June, [sic] 1864, upon the following obligation:

"Agreement between Wm. R. Baker and Ebenezer Allen, entered into this ninth day of July, A. D. 1859, witnesseth [sic]:

Whereas, on the thirtieth day of June, A. D. 1859, the Houston and Texas Central Railway Company issued to Ebenezer Allen three hundred shares of its stock, which the said Allen now holds; and whereas, the said Allen for the consideration hereinafter named, has transferred to the said Baker, by indorsement on the certificate of shares, being No. 575, the said three hundred shares of stock to the said Baker: Now, it is agreed and understood between the parties hereto that of the said three hundred shares one hundred and fifty shares are transferred to and held by said Baker in trust for the said Allen, the trust being as follows: Whereas, an association or joint stock company was formed on the thirtieth of June past, by articles of association, between said Baker, J. W. McDade, Wm. M. Rice, P. Bremond, and others, ten in number for the purpose of purchasing and owning the stock of the Houston and Texas Central Railway Company, to the amount of three thousand shares, with the provision to acquire all the stock issued over and above that amount - the stock so acquired to be managed and administered for the common benefit of the associates, in accordance with the provisions of said articles, each of said associates to have or represent three hundred shares: It is understood that the interest of said Allen in said association is one-twentieth, and that said Baker is to hold the one hundred and fifty shares in trust for said Allen, and the remaining one hundred and fifty shares are sold and assigned to said Baker as his own property, in consideration of which he agrees to pay said Allen the sum of seven thousand five hundred dollars on the 30th of June, A. D. 1864. The said Allen to have the benefit of the provisions in said articles contained, relating to the subscription of $350,000 made on the 27th and 28th of April, A. D. 1858, the subscription of Harvey Baldwin of $50,000 having been canceled.

"Witness our hands in duplicate.

(Signed) "W. R. Baker,

"Eben'r Allen."

Baker in his answer set up four several payments in full discharge, and a receipt subsequently taken, in which Mrs. Allen acknowledged, in her capacity of executrix, that she had before received $7,500 in full discharge of the debt against the estate.

Mrs. Allen craved over of this instrument, which being refused, she demurred to so much of Baker's answer, and filed an amended petition by way of replication, in which she stated under oath that she had no recollection of ever having given such a receipt: that she executed a receipt for certificates for certain railroad stock, which she did not read at the time, nor did the defendant read it to her, as she had full confidence in Baker, not supposing that he would ask her to sign anything wrong; that it was a deception practiced on her, and that it was not her act and deed: that the several payments set up by Baker were made in Confederate money at a time when it was dangerous to refuse it, her husband being a Union man[811] and a fugitive from the state: that Baker took advantage of her situation and forced the Confederate money upon her against her will, and that the same was illegal and wholly worthless.

Baker filed an amended answer, in which he set up that Mrs. Allen was the solo devisee under the will, that she had her acts, and to plead want of authority, when she had voluntarily received Confederate money in payment of an obligation due her testator.

WALKER, J. There has not been before this court a case precisely like the one at bar.

Mrs. Allen, first as the agent of her husband, Ebenezer Allen, and afterwards as the executrix of his will, received certain sums of money before the same became due, from the appellee. Ebenezer Allen sold to Baker one hundred and fifty shares of the capital stock in the Houston and Texas Central Railway Company under a contract dated July 9, 1859. Payment was to be made for the stock on the thirtieth of June, [sic] 1864.

The war coming on, Allen went into the service of the Confederacy, leaving his wife and child in Texas. Owing, perhaps, to the necessities of Mrs. Allen, she accepted the payments, under authority from her husband, in advance of maturity. In 1863 Allen died, leaving his entire property to his wife, and appointing her the executrix of his will. Mrs. Allen appears to have taken a considerable estate by the devise over and above what was necessary to debts.

The defendant paid off his indebtedness in Confederate money. The receipt of Confederate money by Mrs. Allen as the agent of her husband, without an express authority to receive Confederate money, would not have discharged the debt, nor would her receipt as executrix of her husband's will have discharged the debt if there were other heirs, legatees or creditors to complain; but Mrs. Allen is sole legatee under her husband's will, and a handsome estate remains to her, after the payment of debts; and in the absence of fraud, covin, misrepresentation or undue influence, she must be bound by her contracts; and though, in this case, the contract was executed in Confederate money, it is nevertheless an executed contract, against which this court can grant no relief.

The judgment of the district court is affirmed.

Affirmed

M. A. Long, for appellant, filed an able argument for rehearing, which being obtained, he submitted a brief contesting the authority and application of the case relied upon and reported in 32 Tex. 333, of Richie v. Sweet. "That decision was a mere dictum, the question of Confederate money not necessarily arising. The report itself shows that Sweet collected the note sued on in Confederate money when that currency was of par value, and like coin could purchase cotton at the current rate of nine cents per pound." The note having thus been once fully paid, should not have been again demanded. The second demand was unjust and absurd. There was therefore no occasion for the court to have uttered the dictum about an "illegal executed contract," or to speculate about the effect of substituting an illegal contract for a legal one, etc.

It was also contended that the case of Richie v. Sweet was not a decision of the supreme court of Texas but only by a provisional military tribunal of final resort, appointed by the general of the United States army commanding the department of Western Texas. The so-called judges, so appointed, held their offices during the pleasure of the officer commanding, and not for the term designated by the constitution of this state. In no proper sense could such a temporary military tribunal be respected as the supreme court of Texas, however learned and able its members.

McAdoo, J., *on rehearing.* Ebenezer Allen held a written obligation of the appellee, W. H. Baker, for the sum of $7.500, executed June 30, 1859, payable five years after date.

On December 11, 1862, Allen (who was at the time in the Confederate military service at Columbia, South Carolina) wrote the following letter:

"*W. R. Baker, Esq.:*

"SIR: Please pay to my wife, Mrs. S. J. Allen, all or any portion of the sum of $7,500, which will become due and payable from you to me, upon contract for railroad stock, sometime in June (say on or about the twenty-ninth day of that month), 1864, deducting, if you choose, ten per cent [sic]. from the day of payment until maturity of the debt, and her receipt or receipts shall be as good and valid to you thereafter as my own would be.

(Signed) "Ebenezer Allen."

Before Baker received this letter, he had paid a small portion of the debt to Mrs. Allen. Payments were made from time to time, until May 15, 1863, when the last payment was made, Mrs. Allen indorsing on the note the several payments. The payments were made in Confederate money.

In the fall of 1863, after the note had been paid off, Ebenezer Allen died at Richmond, Va. he left a will, his wife being sole executrix and sole devisee and legatee of his estate. She accepted the estate and filed an inventory. The will was proven up in 1864, and in April of that year she received from Baker one hundred and fifty shares of Central Railroad stock, which Baker held for Ebenezer Allen, as trustee, and which said shares of stock were mentioned in the same obligation of Baker for $7,500.

She executed to Baker the following receipt:

"Received of W. R. Baker the one hundred and fifty shares of Central Railroad stock named in above contract held by him as trustee; and the agreement to pay $7,500 having been heretofore paid, the above contract is declared settled, canceled and annulled."

"Houston, April 25, 1864.

(Signed) "Josephine Allen."

This last receipt was executed about a year after the last payment was made, and after the death of Ebenezer Allen – after the probate of the will, after the return of the inventory, and after she had taken charge of the estate as executrix and legatee.

The inventory (showing about $30,000 of assets) did not embrace the claim against Baker for $7,500, though it did include the one hundred and fifty shares of railroad stock embraced in the same contract.

The entire indebtedness of the estate of Ebenezer Allen amounted to less than $2,000.

It has been the uniform ruling of this court that contracts based on payment in Confederate money, or tainted with Confederate money considerations, would not and could not be enforced by the courts in this state. But we have also held, and see no reason to change the ruling, that those who have voluntarily executed their contracts, paid and received, in satisfaction of demands, Confederate money, would be left by the courts precisely where they had placed themselves. We see no reason and know no authority for interference in such a case.

This is not an action by creditors of Ebenezer Allen, but of his surviving wife, who acted as his authorized agent, who, in his absence long continued from the state, would have been competent, we think, to act without his special authority: who is his sole legatee; who ratified her own acts as agent after she became alone responsible for them, and who does not, in our judgment, present such equities as entitles her to any relief in this case.

We therefore affirm the judgment of the district court.

Affirmed.[812]

Ebenezer Allen Timeline[813]

Date	Event
April 8, 1804	Ebenezer Allen is born in Newport, Sullivan County, New Hampshire
1812	Sylvinia Morse is born in Maine
1826	Graduates from Dartmouth College
1826-1828	Teaches in Lewiston, New York
1828-1830	Works in Newport as a clerk and apprentice under Amasa Edes
1830	Moves to Orono, Maine
1830-1831	Allen's brother, David Allen, reads law with Ebenezer in Orono.
1831	Allen lives in Somerset County Maine
1832	Allen moves to Solon, Maine
March 23, 1833	Allen marries Sylvinia Morse in Bloomfield, Maine
1834	Starts law practice in Bloomfield, Somerset County, Maine
1834	Allens move to Skowhegan, Maine
1834-1835	Forms partnership with James T. Leavitt
June 1834	Bar in Somerset County, Maine admits Allen
August 1835	Birth of son Henry Allen in Maine
1836	Birth of son William Pitt Allen in Maine
March 3, 1836	Delegates sign Texas Declaration of Independence at Washington-on-the-Brazos
March 6, 1836	Mexican troops storm the Alamo and kill all the defenders in a battle lasting only ninety minutes
April 21, 1836	Texan troops led by Sam Houston defeat the Mexican army commanded by Santa Anna at San Jacinto
May 14, 1836	Mexico and Texas sign the Treaty of Velasco
October 1836	The first Congress of the Republic of Texas meets in Columbia and elects Sam Houston as the first president of Texas.
1837	Panic of 1837
August 1, 1839	First sale of town lots in the new capital of the Republic at Austin
1840	Birth of son Edward C. Allen in Maine
August 30, 1841	The Peters' Colony impresarios obtain first contract and establish community in North Central Texas
1840s	Immigrants move into the Peters' Colony
December 18, 1840	The Allen family arrives in the Republic of Texas and settles in Clarksville

December 27, 1840	Death of Allen's father, David Allen, in Newport, New Hampshire
August 2, 1841	Allen obtains "conditional land grant" in Clarksville, Texas
1841-1842	Allen teaches in Clarksville, Texas
April 2, 1842	Allen orders survey of a tract of land on the South Bank of Sulfur Ford River in Red River County
September 1842	Allen opens law practice in Clarksville
February 4, 1843	Allen joins the Masonic Friendship Lodge No. 16 in Clarksville
1843	Sylvinia writes poem "An Invitation to Texas"
August 5, 1844	Board of Land Commissioners for Red River County awarded Allen six hundred and forty acres
December 9, 1844	Sam Houston appoints Allen Attorney General of the Republic of Texas
1844	Anson Jones is sworn in as President of the Republic of Texas
December 1844	President Jones adds Allen to his cabinet as Attorney General
March 1, 1845	President Tyler signs a "Joint Resolution for Annexing Texas to the United States"
May 8, 1845	President Jones instructs Allen to issue a proclamation recommending the citizens of Texas elect deputies for a convention
July 1845	Allen appointed interim Secretary of State in place of Ashbel Smith
July 4, 1845	The Texas Constitutional Convention votes to accept the United States' annexation proposal
October 13, 1845	Texas voters overwhelmingly (7,664 to 430 in favor of annexation) approve annexation, the new state constitution and the annexation ordinance
December 29, 1845	The U.S. Congress approves, and President James K. Polk signs, the "Joint Resolution for the Admission of the State of Texas into the Union"
1846	Allen forms partnership with William Hale
February 1846	Allen resigns as Attorney General
February 19, 1846	President Anson Jones states, "The final chapter of this great drama is performed. The Republic of Texas is no more."
1846	The Allens move to Galveston
1846-1848	The Mexican War
1847	Birth of son Frederick Allen in Texas

February 2, 1848	The Treaty of Guadalupe Hidalgo is signed, ending the Mexican War
March 11, 1848	Texas grants Allen charter to form the Galveston and Red River Railroad Company
May 1850	Allen conveys property to Jacob DeCordova
August 1850	Allen elected Attorney General as a Democrat
October 13, 1850	Death of Allen's mother, Hannah Wilcox Allen, in Newport, New Hampshire
1850	Allen family lives in Galveston, Texas
1850	Sylvinia and Ebenezer become active in the Spiritualist movement
1850-1852	Allen is Attorney General under Governor Peter H. Bell from 1850 to 1852
June 3, 1852	Allen issues broadside on legality of law passed by Texas legislature
1850-1860	William Pitt Allen living in Galveston with family
September 1, 1851	Death of Ebenezer's brother, David Allen, Jr., in Newport, New Hampshire
February 14, 1852	Allen transfers railroad charter to Bremond and House Galveston and Red River Railroad Company becomes active
January 1, 1853	Construction of the Galveston and Red River Railroad begins in Houston
January 9, 1853	Allen visits Dartmouth classmate, Salomon B. Chase, in Washington, DC
1852-1859	Allen is a director of the Houston and Central Texas Railroad
April 8, 1855	Allen writes "Retrospect" to Sylvinia
February 22, 1856	The directors of the Houston and Texas Central Railroad name their first engine the "Ebenezer Allen"
September 1, 1856	Texas legislature approves renaming the Galveston and Red River Railroad to the Houston and Texas Central Railroad
July 1, 1858	Death of Ebenezer's brother, William Allen in Newport, New Hampshire
August 1859	Birth of son Ebenezer Allen, Jr. in Galveston, Texas
1860	Allens live in Ward 2 in Galveston, Texas
January 28, 1861	Texas Secession Commission votes to hold popular election
February 8, 1861	Allen appointed to the Galveston Commission on Public Safety
February 23, 1861	Texas votes to secede in a state-wide popular vote and becomes the seventh state to leave the Union

April 12, 1861	Confederate forces capture Fort Sumter
July 2, 1861	Federal ships blockade Galveston
June 4, 1862	Allen writes will in Richmond, Wise County, Virginia
September 26, 1862	Allen presents Creuzbaur's invention to the Committee on National Affairs of the Confederate Senate
October 4, 1862	Union forces seize Galveston Harbor
December 11, 1862	Allen stationed in Columbia, Richland County, South Carolina
January 1, 1863	Confederates recapture Galveston
August 20, 1863	Allen and Creuzbaur are appointed to the Confederate Engineer Bureau
October 15, 1863	Allen dies in Richmond, Wise County, Virginia
October 18, 1863	Allen buried in Hollywood Cemetery in Richmond
January 27, 1864	Will probated in Galveston, Galveston County, Texas Two female slaves are included in Allen's estate
April 9, 1865	Lee surrenders to Grant at Appomattox
June 18, 1865	Union forces reoccupy Galveston
May 13, 1865	The Battle of Palmetto Ranch is fought near Brownsville
1870	The 1870 U.S. Census shows Sylvinia Allen (60 years) and her son Ebenezer Allen Jr. (10) living in Skowhegan, Somerset County, Maine with her sister Hannah B. Leavitt and her family
December 2, 1873	Josephine Allen vs. W. R. Walker
1874	The Houston and Texas Central Railroad extends to McKinney, Texas and company executives name a watering station Allen Depot
1875	Tax records reveal Ebenezer, Jr. and Sylvinia Allen living in Galveston
1876	Residents of the Town of Allen file original map with the state
1889-1894	Henry Allen lives in Galveston.
September 7, 1897 or December 17, 1897	Sylvinia Allen dies and is buried in Lakeview Cemetery in Galveston.
September 8, 1900	Ebenezer Allen, Jr. and his wife die in Galveston flood
May 9, 1901	Frederick Allen dies and is buried at Lakeview Cemetery in Galveston
April 4, 1904	William Pitt Allen dies
July 23, 1921	Henry Allen dies
March 23, 1925	Edward Allen dies

ACKNOWLEDGEMENTS

During my senior year in high school, I received an award for the best history student. I planned to attend a local university and become a high school teacher. Unfortunately, my parents "guided" me into a different future. Finally, after forty-five years, I returned to my first love. Thank you, Mr. Fay Reed, Mr. Lester J. Szabo, and Mr. Fred Lang, for answering my questions and nurturing my interest in history.

My very special gratitude to Mrs. Judith M. Johnson, Ebenezer Allen's great, great, great- granddaughter, for allowing me access to information on Ebenezer Allen contained in the private family history on Ancestry. This book would not have been possible without her generosity and participation.

Special appreciation to Barbara Terry, Emily Powers, and the staff of Waldorf Publishing for their hard work in turning the manuscript into the book telling Ebenezer Allen's story.

Great thanks for information and images from the Texas State Historical Association, Texas State Library and Archives Commission, and Texas General Land Office. This material provided background on the people and places mentioned in Ebenezer Allen's biography.

Dr. Brett Derbes, Managing Editor, for permission to use information from the Texas State Historical Association's on-line Handbook of Texas.

Ms. Cait Burhans, Photograph Archivist in the Archives and Information Services Division of the Texas State Library and Archives Commission, for allowing use of several images and letters from the Library and Archives Commission.

Mr. Patrick Walsh, Research and Outreach Specialist, for granting access to records from the Archives and Records Program of Texas General Land Office.

My gratitude to the following:
- Historical associations in Newport, New Hampshire and Skowhegan, Maine.
- Rosenberg Library in Galveston, Texas supplied information on the Allen family.
- The Dolph Briscoe Center for American History at The Uni-

versity of Texas at Austin and the William G. Hale Letters and Legal Papers.
- National Park Service for information on Civil War battles and soldiers.

Mr. Ed Bryan of the Allen Heritage Guild was helpful in sharing documents he had collected. I am also indebted to Ken Byler for providing copies of his columns on Allen, Texas and the Houston and Central Texas Railroad from the *Allen American*.

Our dear friend Sharon Doty who came to Plano, Texas for a vacation and ended up proofreading this manuscript.

As she has for the past fifty-three years, my wonderful wife Sharlyn Williams Mesch, helped during this adventure. She served as driver, travel coordinator, researcher, administrative assistant, photographer, and publicist. Sharlyn gathered books from many libraries, copied and photographed documents, helped me through the perilous and difficult path of obtaining permissions, checking citations, editing drafts, and providing the emotional support all writers need.

ABOUT THE AUTHOR

Allen Mesch at Allen Depot
(Photograph by Sharlyn Mesch)

Allen Mesch is an author, educator, and historian.

He earned a master's degree in chemical engineering from the Massachusetts Institute of Technology and a bachelor's degree in chemical engineering from Clarkson University. He has additional course work in business and management from the University of Pittsburgh and the University of Houston.

After graduating from MIT, Allen began a forty-year career in the oil and gas industry. He has extensive experience in both technical and management positions with major multinational petroleum companies. During his career in the petroleum industry, he published papers on trends in the oil and gas industry, innovations in business planning, and spoke at many professional conferences. He served as a resource to media on oil and gas issues with appearances on local and national television and quotes in business publications ranging from *The Oil & Gas Journal* to *Business Week*.

Mr. Mesch also held adjunct faculty positions at the University of Texas at Dallas, Southern Methodist University, and Texas Woman's University. He was Director of the Maguire Energy Institute at Southern Methodist University where he developed the Institute's innovative Oil and Gas Education Initiative and other learning programs.

Allen taught classes on the Civil War in Collin College's SAIL program. He shares his 4,000-plus photographs from over 145 Civil War sites on his web site Civil War Journeys (http://www.civil-war-journeys.org). He also writes a blog on the Civil War called Salient Points (http://salient-points.blogspot.com).

He is the author of *Teacher of Civil War Generals: Major General Charles Ferguson Smith, Soldier and West Point Commandant*, McFarland Publishers, Inc., July 2015. In March 2016, he published the companion book, *Your Affectionate Father, Charles F. Smith*, with letters Smith wrote to his daughter. Also, in 2016, Allen wrote about his wife's ancestor, *Charles A. Marvin – "One Year, Six Months, and Eleven Days. Preparing for Disunion: West Point Commandants and the Training of Civil War Leaders*, McFarland Publishers, Inc. was released in November 2018., Allen also published a political thriller, *The Analyst*, in 2012.

Allen and his wife live in Plano, Texas next to the town named for the railroad entrepreneur and the subject of this biography, Ebenezer Allen. When not visiting Civil War battlefields or building sandcastles on South Padre Island, Allen enjoys fishing and travel. He and his wife have two children, six grandchildren, and one great-grandchild.

BIBLIOGRAPHY

"1837: The Hard Times." Harvard Business School Historical Collections. http://www.library.hbs.edu/hc/crises/1837.html.

"23rd Regiment, South Carolina Infantry. https://www.nps.gov/civilwar/search-battle-units-detail.htm?battleUnitCode=CSC0023RIhttps://www.nps.gov/civilwar/search-soldiers.htm#q=%2223rd

+Regiment,+South+Carolina+Infantry+(Hatch's+Coast+Rangers)%22&sort=Last_Name+asc,First_Name+asc.

"26a. Religious Revival." U.S. History. http://www.ushistory.org/us/26a.asp.

"44th Regiment. North Carolina Infantry. https://www.nps.gov/civilwar/search-soldiers-detail.htm?soldierId=12F3757A-DC7A-DF11-BF36-B8AC6F-5D926A https://www.nps.gov/civilwar/search-battle-units-detail.htm?battleUnitCode=CNC0044RI.

"A Hard-Earned Victory." Stones River National Battlefield. https://www.nps.gov/stri/index.htm.

Abbott, Karen. "The Fox Sisters and the Rap on Spiritualism." Smithsonian.com. October 30, 2012. https://www.smithsonianmag.com/history/the-fox-sisters-and-the-rap-on-spiritualism-99663697/. 62

"About Slave Owners in Texas." Classroom. https://classroom.synonym.com/about-slave-owners-in-texas-12078347.html.

Allen, Ebenezer Esq. *Dallas Weekly Herald*. July 10, 1858. Judith M. Johnson, Johnson-Morrow Family Tree. Ancestry.com.

Allen, E. "The Civil War." National Park Service. https://www.nps.gov/civilwar/search-soldiers-detail.htm?soldierId=-09C8587A-DC7A-DF11-BF36-B8AC6F5D926A.

Allen, E. Search Burial Records." Hollywood Cemetery. https://www.hollywoodcemetery.org/genealogy/burial-records.

Allen, Edmond. "The Civil War, National Park Service." "Forty-fourth Regiment – Infantry." Civil War Index. https://www.nps.gov/civilwar/search-soldiers-detail.htm?soldierId=11F3757A-DC7A-DF11-BF36-B8AC6F-5D926Ahttp://www.civilwarindex.com/armync/soldiers/44th_nc_infantry_soldiers.pdf.

"Allen Family History | Find Genealogy Records & Family Crest. Archives. https://www.archives.com/genealogy/family-history-allen.html.

"Allen, William Pitt." California Wills and Probate Records, 1850-1953. http://www.ancestry.com.

"American Civil War: A North-South Divide, The." *History Today*. https://www.historytoday.com/archive/contrarian/american-civil-war-north-south-divide.

"American Series of Popular Biographies Maine Edition." *Representative Citizens of the State of Maine.* Boston: New England Historical Publishing Company. 1903.

"Anaconda Plan." *War of the Rebellion: a compilation of the official records of the Union and Confederate Armies.* I, v. 51/1.

Angel, William D. Jr (1984). "Vantage on the Bay: Galveston and the Railroads." *East Texas Historical Journal*: Vol. 22: Issue 1, Article 5. Available at: http://scholarworks.sfasu.edu/ethj/vol22/iss1/5.

"Annexation Process: 1836-1845 - A Summary Timeline." Texas State Library and Archives Commission. https://www.tsl.texas.gov/ref/abouttx/annexation/timeline.html.

"Annexation." Texas State Library and Archives Commission. https://www.tsl.texas.gov/lobbyexhibits/mural-annexation.

"Anson Jones Valedictory Speech, February 19, 1846." Texas State Library and Archives Commission. https://www.tsl.texas.gov/treasures/earlystate/nomore-1.html, https://www.tsl.texas.gov/treasures/earlystate/nomore-2.htm and https://www.tsl.texas.gov/treasures/earlystate/nomore-3.html.

"Arsenic Poisoning." Patient. https://patient.info/doctor/Arsenic-Poisoning.

"Astounding Developments in the Case of Judge Watrous, of Texas." *The Dallas Daily Herald.* Dallas, Texas. February 23, 1859.

"Attorneys General." *Texas Almanac.* http://texasalmanac.com/topics/government/attorneys-general.

Barnhart, David. "Masonic Saboteurs." Warriors of the Lone Star State. April 20, 2016. http://warriorsofthelonestar.blogspot.com/2016/04/masonic-saboteurs.html.

Bassett, Norman L. ed. *Report of the Maine State Bar Association.* Augusta: Charles E. Nash & Son. 1921. Vol. 22.

"Battle of Bridgewater, The." http://www.warof1812-bicentennial.info/newspapers/plattsburghrepublican/pr08131814-pg1-c.php.

"Battle of Chancellorsville." Fredericksburg & Spotsylvania National Military Park. https://www.nps.gov/frsp/learn/historyculture/chist.htm.

"Battle of Chickamauga." Chickamauga & Chattanooga National Military Park. https://www.nps.gov/chch/learn/historyculture/battle-of-chickamauga.htm.

"Benton, Thomas Hart, (1782-1858)." Biographical Directory of the United States Congress. http://bioguide.congress.gov/scripts/biodisplay.pl?index=B000398.

"Betty, Gerald. "A Shellcrete Society: The Aransas-Copano Bay Community, 1830-1880." Presented at the 112th Annual Meeting of the Texas State Historical Association. Corpus Christi, TX. March 6, 2008. http://achs1985.org/

wp-content/uploads/2013/05/A_Shellcrete_Society-G_Betty.pdf.

Biographical Encyclopedia of Maine of Nineteenth Century. Boston: Metropolitan Publishing and Engraving Company. 1885.

"Biographies of the Secretaries of State: Abel Parker Upshur (1791–1844)." Office of the Historian. United States Department of State. https://history.state.gov/departmenthistory/people/upshur-abel-parker.

"Biographies of the Secretaries of State: Henry Clay (1777-1852)." Office of the Historian. U.S. Department of State. https://history.state.gov/departmenthistory/people/clay-henry.

"Biographies of the Secretaries of State: John Caldwell Calhoun (1782–1850)." Office of the Historian. U.S. Department of State. https://history.state.gov/departmenthistory/people/calhoun-john-caldwell.

Biography of Samuel H. Edes. Access Genealogy. https://www.accessgenealogy.com/new-hampshire/biography-of-samuel-h-edes.htm.

Bohonos, Jeremy. "Spiritualism and Gender: Questions of Leadership & Masculine Identity." Muncie: Ball State University, 2012. master's thesis.

Bowman, John S. ed. *The Civil War.* East Bridgewater: World Publications Group. 2006.

Bozic, William J. Bozic. "A Chronology of the U.S.-Mexican War." http://www.dmwv.org/mexwar/chrono1845-6.htm.

Brenoff, Ann. "History of High Spirits." *Los Angeles Times.* June 17, 2007. http://articles.latimes.com/2007/jun/17/realestate/re-guide17.

Brittan, S. B. ed. *The Spiritual Telegraph.* New York: Partridge & Brittan Publishers. 1855. "Remarkable Developments by Poetic Spirits." E. A. (Ebenezer Allen).

Brooks, Emily. "The Spooky Story of Summerland." *The Horizon.* November 8, 2011. http://blogs.westmont.edu/horizon/2011/11/08/the-spooky-story-of-summerland/.

Burial Records. Hollywood Cemetery. https://www.hollywoodcemetery.org/genealogy/burial-records.

Byer, Ken. "Ebenezer Allen." *Allen American, Star Local Media.* September 24, 2015.

- "Is that Art on the Tracks?" *Allen American, Star Local Media.* September 24, 2015.
- "Wouldn't Train Be Nice." *Allen American. Star Local Media.* May 23, 2010.

By-laws and List of Members of Richmond Lodge. no. 10. revised and adopted A.L. 5864, A.D. 1864. Richmond: James E. Goode. 1864.

C.S.S. *Denbigh.* "Archeology of a Civil War Blockade Runner." Institute of Nautical Archaeology at Texas A&M University. http://nautarch.tamu.edu/

PROJECTS/denbigh/galv01.htm.

"caribbee." Definitions.net. STANDS4 LLC, 2019. https://www.definitions.net/definition/caribbee.

Carroll, Bret E. *Spiritualism in Antebellum America.* Bloomington. Indiana University Press. 1997.

"Case of Judge Watrous; His Impeachment Imminent Extraordinary Disclosures, The." *The New York Times.* July 11, 1860. http://www.nytimes.com/1860/07/11/news/the-case-of-judge-watrous-his-impeachment-imminent-extraordinary-disclosures.html.

"Cass, Richard, (1782-1866)." Biographical Directory of the United States Congress. http://bioguide.congress.gov/scripts/biodisplay.pl?index=C000233.

"Centennial Celebration and Dedication of Town Hall, Orono, Maine." Portland: Bailey & Noyes. 1874.

"Centennial celebration by Orono, Me." [from old catalog] Published 1874 Topics Orono, Maine. History. [from old catalog]. Maine -- History Colonial period, ca. 1600-1775.

"Centennial Celebration." https://archive.org/details/centennialcelebr00orona.

"Certificate Granting Ebenezer Allen Six Hundred and Forty Acres of Land." Fourth Class Certificate. Number 9. File No. 00030. Texas General Land Office. http://www.glo.texas.gov/ncu/SCANDOCS/archives_webfiles/arcmaps/webfiles/landgrants/PDFs/1/0/6/2/1062501.pdf.

Chapman, George T. *Chapman's Sketches of the Alumni of Dartmouth College.* Cambridge: Riverside Press. 1867.

"chattel." Meriam-Webster. https://www.merriam-webster.com/dictionary/chattel.

Civil Government of the State of Maine for the Political Year, 1932. Augusta: I. Berry & Co., Printers to the State, 1832.

"clairvoyant." Dictionary.com. https://www.dictionary.com/browse/clairvoyant.

Coburn, Loise Helen. *Skowhegan on the Kennebec.* Skowhegan: Self Published. 1941. Vol. I and Vol. II.

Conditional Certificate Granting Ebenezer Allen Six Hundred and Forty Acres of Land. Fourth Class Certificate. Number 9. File No. 00030. Texas General Land Office. http://www.glo.texas.gov/ncu/SCANDOCS/archives_webfiles/arcmaps/webfiles/landgrants/PDFs/1/0/6/2/1062501.pdf.

Constitution of the State of Texas, The. as Amended in 1861. The Constitution of the Confederate States of America. The Ordinances of the Texas Convention. and An Address to the People of Texas. Austin: Printed by John Marshall, State Printer. 1861. https://www.tsl.texas.gov/ref/abouttx/secession/5march1861.html.

"covin." https://www.merriam-webster.com/dictionary/covin.

"cowcatcher." Meriam-Webster. https://www.merriam-webster.com/dictionary/cowcatcher.

Crapol, Edward P. *John Tyler, the Accidental President.* Chapel Hill: University of North Carolina Press. 2006.

Cushing, E. H. *The Weekly Telegraph.* Houston, Texas. Vol. 22, No. 50, Ed. 1. Wednesday, March 4, 1857. https://texashistory.unt.edu/ark:/67531/metapth235930/m1/3/?q=Spiritualism: University of North Texas Libraries. The Portal to Texas History. https://texashistory.unt.edu. crediting The Dolph Briscoe Center for American History.

- Vol. 22, No. 51. Ed. 1 Wednesday, March 11, 1857. Houston, Texas. https://texashistory.unt.edu/ark:/67531/metapth235931/m1/1/?q=spiritualism: University of North Texas Libraries. The Portal to Texas History. https://texashistory.unt.edu; crediting The Dolph Briscoe Center for American History.

- Vol. 24, No. 2, Ed. 1. Wednesday, March 31, 1858. https://texashistory.unt.edu/ark:/67531/metapth235986/m1/1/?q=spiritualism. University of North Texas Libraries. The Portal to Texas History. https://texashistory.unt.edu. crediting The Dolph Briscoe Center for American History.

- Vol. 24, No. 3, Ed. 1. Wednesday, April 7, 1858. https://texashistory.unt.edu.ark:/67531/metapth235987/m1/3/. University of North Texas Libraries. The Portal to Texas History. https://texashistory.unt.edu.

- Vol. 24, No. 7, Ed. 1. Wednesday, May 5, 1858. https://texashistory.unt.edu/ark:/67531/metapth235991/. University of North Texas Libraries. The Portal to Texas History. https://texashistory.unt.edu. crediting The Dolph Briscoe Center for American History.

- Vol. 24, No. 8, Ed. 1. Wednesday, May 12, 1858. https://texashistory.unt.edu/ark:/67531/metapth235992/. University of North Texas Libraries. The Portal to Texas History. https://texashistory.unt.edu. crediting The Dolph Briscoe Center for American History.

- Vol. 24, No. 14, Ed. 1. Wednesday, June 23, 1858. Houston, Texas. University of North Texas Libraries. The Portal to Texas History. https://texashistory.unt.edu/ark:/67531/metapth235998/. https://texashistory.unt.edu. crediting The Dolph Briscoe Center for American History.

- *Daily Union, The.* Washington DC. May 27, 1847. Chronicling America: Historic American Newspapers. Library of Congress. http://chroniclingamerica.loc.gov/lccn/sn82003410/1847-05-27/ed-1/seq-4/.

- June 10, 1848. http://chroniclingamerica.loc.gov/lccn/sn82003410/1848-06-10/ed-1/seq-4/;

- January 18, 1848. http://chroniclingamerica.loc.gov/lccn/sn82003410/1848-01-18/ed-1/seq-4/.

- February 22, 1848. http://chroniclingamerica.loc.gov/lccn/sn82003410/1848-02-22/ed-1/seq-4/.

Danforth, E. F. *Skowhegan Lawyers*. Hinckley: Good Will Publishing Co. 1928.

"Daniel Webster – Dartmouth's Favorite Son." http://www.dartmouth.edu/~dwebster/intro.html.

Dartmouth College. https://home.dartmouth.edu/.

David Allen, Jr. and Decedents of Gideon Allen. Marylou McGuire. Newport Historical Society. Ancestry.com.

de Cordova, P. *South-Western American*. Austin, Texas. Vol. 3, No. 2, Ed. 1. Wednesday, July 16, 1851. https://texashistory.unt.edu/ark:/67531/metapth79702/. https://texashistory.unt.edu; crediting The Dolph Briscoe Center for American History.

- Vol. 4, No. 15, Ed. 1. Wednesday, October 20, 1852. Austin, Texas. https://texashistory.unt.edu/ark:/67531/metapth79743/. https://texashistory.unt.edu. crediting The Dolph Briscoe Center for American History.

- Vol. 4, No. 13, Ed. 1. Wednesday, October 6, 1852. Austin, Texas. https://texashistory.unt.edu/ark:/67531/metapth79741/. https://texashistory.unt.edu. crediting The Dolph Briscoe Center for American History.

DeCredico, Mary. "Richmond Bread Riot." Encyclopedia Virginia in partnership with the Library of Virginia. https://www.encyclopediavirginia.org/bread_riot_richmond.

De Morse, Charles. *The Northern Standard*. Clarksville, Texas. Vol. 1, No. 5, Ed. 1. Saturday. September 17, 1842. https://texashistory.unt.edu/ark:/67531/metapth80456/. University of North Texas Libraries. The Portal to Texas History. https://texashistory.unt.edu. crediting The Dolph Briscoe Center for American History.

- Vol. 2, No. 1, Ed. 1. Saturday, November 4, 1843. https://texashistory.unt.edu/ark:/67531/metapth80502/. https://texashistory.unt.edu; crediting The Dolph Briscoe Center for American History.

- Vol. 3, No. 4, Ed. 1. Wednesday, December 4, 1844. Clarksville, Texas. https://texashistory.unt.edu/ark:/67531/metapth80542/. https://texashistory.unt.edu. crediting The Dolph Briscoe Center for American History.

- Vol. 3, No. 5, Ed. 1. Thursday, December 12, 1844. https://texashistory.unt.edu/ark:/67531/metapth80543/. https://texashistory.unt.edu. crediting The Dolph Briscoe Center for American History.

- Vol. 3, No. 7, Ed. 1. Thursday, December 26, 1844. https://texashistory.unt.edu/ark:/67531/metapth8045/m1/4/. https://texashistory.unt.edu.

- Vol. 3, No. 11, Ed. 1. Thursday, January 30, 1845. Clarksville, Texas. https://texashistory.unt.edu/ark:/67531/metapth80548/m1/3/?q=Ebenezer%20Allen. texashistory.unt.edu; crediting The Dolph Briscoe Center for American History.

- Vol. 3, No. 13, Ed. 1. Thursday, February 13, 1845. https://texashistory.unt.edu/

ark:/67531/metapth80550/. https://texashistory.unt.edu. crediting The Dolph Briscoe Center for American History

- "Proclamation." Vol. 3, No. 21, Ed. 1. Friday, May 30, 1845. https://texashistory.unt.edu/ark:/67531/metapth80557/. https://texashistory.unt.edu. crediting The Dolph Briscoe Center for American History.
- Vol. 5, No. 3, Ed. 1. Thursday, May 13, 1847. https://texashistory.unt.edu/ark:/67531/metapth80639/m1/4/?q=%22Wm.%20S.%20Todd%22. https://texashistory.unt.edu. crediting The Dolph Briscoe Center for American History.
- Vol. 7, No. 44, Ed. 1. Saturday, June 29, 1850. https://texashistory.unt.edu/ark:/67531/metapth80783/. https://texashistory.unt.edu. crediting The Dolph Briscoe Center for American History.
- Vol. 8, No. 4, Ed. 1. Saturday, September 21, 1850. https://texashistory.unt.edu/ark:/67531/metapth80795/. https://texashistory.unt.edu. crediting The Dolph Briscoe Center for American History.
- Vol. 8, No. 9, Ed. 1. Saturday, October 26, 1850. https://texashistory.unt.edu/ark:/67531/metapth80800/m1/2/?q =Texas+attorney+general+election+1850. texashistory.unt.edu. crediting The Dolph Briscoe Center for American History.

Directory of Richmond City Officials. http://www.newrivernotes.com/neighboring_ richmond_government_1861-65_cityofficials.htm.

"dispensation." Merriam-Webster. https://www.merriam-webster.com/dictionary/dispensation.

Distance Between Cities. https://www.distance-cities.com/distance-new-portland-me-to-solon-me and https://www.distance-cities.com/distance-new-portland-me-to-solon-me.

"easement." The Balance. https://www.thebalance.com/definition-of-easements-1798543.

Eisenhower, John D. *So Far from God - The U.S. War with Mexico* - 1846-1848. New York: Anchor Books. 1989.

"equity." The Free Dictionary. https://legal-dictionary.thefreedictionary.com/equity.

"ermine." Merriam-Webster. https://www.merriam-webster.com/dictionary/ermine.

"Everett, Edward, (1794-1865)." Biographical Directory of the United States Congress. http://bioguide.congress.gov/scripts/biodisplay.pl?index=E000264.

"extra-constitutional." *American Heritage® Dictionary of the English Language, Fifth Edition.* S. v. "extraconstitutional." https://www.thefreedictionary.com/extraconstitutional.

FamilySearch. "Allen, Ebenezer." *Mill Town Messenger.* Newport Historical Society. Vol.4, Issue 1. February 2010 and "Maine Marriages, 1771-1907." da-

tabase. https://familysearch.org/ark:/61903/1:1:F481-JVZ.
- Allen, Ebenezer, Esq. and Morse, Sylvinia. March 23, 1833. citing reference. FHL microfilm 12,061.
- Allen, Fred. 1894. "Texas, County Tax Rolls, 1837-1910." https://familysearch.org/ark:/61903/1:1:QJ85-5X3X. Fred Allen. 1891.
- "California Great Registers, 1866-1910." database. https://familysearch.org/ark:/61903/1:1:VNFL-12B. William Henry Allen. June 17, 1880. citing Voter Registration, Arcata, Humboldt, California, United States. county clerk offices, California. FHL microfilm 976,464.
- "Maine Marriages, 1771-1907." database. https://familysearch.org/ark:/61903/1:1:F4XS-44N. Edward C. Allen and Lillian D. Ham. 07 May 1890. citing Civil, Portland, Cumberland, Maine. Reference. FHL microfilm 12,026.
- "Maine Marriages, 1771-1907." database. https://familysearch.org/ark:/61903/1:1:F4F8-C9M: Edward C. Allen and Mary S. Bennett. 15 May 1858; citing Gray, Cumberland, Maine. Reference. FHL microfilm.
- "Maine, Civil War Enlistment Papers, 1862-1865." database with images. https://familysearch.org/ark:/61903/1:1:Q2QB-JDNF. Edward Allen. August 21, 1863. citing Bangor, Bangor, Penobscot, Maine. United States. Maine State Archives. Augusta. FHL microfilm.
- "Texas, County Tax Rolls, 1837–1910." database with images. https://familysearch.org/ark:/61903/1:1:QJ85-2YK7. E Allen. 1850.
- "Texas, County Tax Rolls, 1837-1910." database with images. https://familysearch.org/ark:/61903/1:1:QJ85-PXK3. Fred Allen. 1886.
- "Texas, County Tax Rolls, 1837-1910." database with images. https://familysearch.org/ark:/61903/1:1:QJ85-LJSG. Ebenezer Allen. 1849,1850, 1851, 1854, 1857, 1858, 1859, and 1861.
- "United States Census (Slave Schedule), 1850." database with images. https://familysearch.org/ark:/61903/1:1:MVC3-1CN. Ebenezer Allen. Galveston county, Galveston, Texas, United States. citing line number 19, NARA microfilm publication M432 Washington D.C. National Archives and Records Administration, n.d. FHL microfilm 444,920.
- "United States Census, 1850." database with images. https://familysearch.org/ark:/61903/1:1:MXLK-DV1. Ebenezer Allen. Galveston city, Galveston, Texas, United States. citing family 289, NARA microfilm publication M432. Washington, D.C.: National Archives and Records Administration, n.d.
- "United States Census, 1850." database with images. https://familysearch.org/ark:/61903/1:1:MXLK-DK3:). Frederick Allen in household of Ebenezer Allen. Galveston city, Galveston, Texas, United States. citing family 289, NARA microfilm publication M432. Washington, D.C. National Archives and Records Administration, n.d. and "United States Census, 1860." database with images. https://familysearch.org/ark:/61903/1:1:MXFB-FNP. Fred Allen in entry for W

Allen. 1860.

- "United States Census, 1860." database with images. https://familysearch.org/ark:/61903/1:1:MXFB-FZM. Henry Allen in entry for W Allen. 1860.
- "United States Census, 1860." database with images. https://familysearch.org/ark:/61903/1:1:MXFB-FZ9. William P Allen in entry for W Allen. 1860.
- "United States Census, 1860." database with images. https://familysearch.org/ark:/61903/1:1:MXFB-FNG. Edward Allen in entry for W Allen. 1860.
- "United States Census, 1860." database with images. https://familysearch.org/ark:/61903/1:1:MXFB-FNP. Fred Allen in entry for W. Allen. 1860.
- "United States Census, 1870." database with images. https://familysearch.org/ark:/61903/1:1:M66M-C96. Sylvia Allen in household of Hannah B Leavitt, Maine, United States. citing p. 43, family 385. NARA microfilm publication M593. Washington D.C. National Archives and Records Administration, n.d. FHL microfilm 552,058.
- "United States Census, 1870." database with images. https://familysearch.org/ark:/61903/1:1:M66M-C96. Sylvia Allen in household of Hannah B Leavitt, Maine, United States. family 385, NARA microfilm publication M593. Washington D.C. National Archives and Records Administration, n.d. FHL microfilm 552,058.
- "United States Census, 1880." database with images. https://familysearch.org/ark:/61903/3:1:33S7-9YY1-M66M-C96. Sylvia Allen in household of Hannah B Leavitt, Maine, United States. family 385, NARA microfilm publication M593. Washington D.C. National Archives and Records Administration, n.d. FHL microfilm 552,058.
- "United States Census, 1880." database with images. https://familysearch.org/ark:/61903/1:1:MFNZ-YZJ. Fred Allen. 1880; citing enumeration district ED 63, sheet 26C, NARA microfilm publication T9. Washington D.C.: National Archives and Records Administration, n. d. roll 1305; FHL microfilm 1,255,305.
- "United States Census, 1880." database with images. https://familysearch.org. Citing NARA microfilm publication T9. Washington, D.C. National Archives and Records Administration, n.d.
- "United States Census, 1900." database with images. https://familysearch.org/ark:/61903/1:1:M3GH-MVB. Fred Allen. Galveston City Ward 1. Galveston, Texas, United States. citing enumeration district (ED) 114, sheet 7A, family 128. NARA microfilm publication T623. Washington, D.C. National Archives and Records Administration. 1972. FHL microfilm 1,241,637.
- "United States Census, 1900." database with images. https://familysearch.org/ark:/61903/1:1:M9GG-7T3. William C Allen. Vallejo Township Vallejo city Ward 1. Solano, California, United States. citing enumeration district (ED) 152. sheet 6B. family 141, NARA microfilm publication T623. Washington, D.C. National Archives and Records Administration. 1972. FHL microfilm

1,240,113.

- "United States Civil War Soldiers Index, 1861-1865." database. https://familysearch.org/ark:/61903/1:1:FSL4-SM3. Henry Allen, Private, Company FD, 26th Regiment, Texas Cavalry (Debray's). Davis' Missouri. Confederate. citing NARA microfilm publication M227. Washington D.C. National Archives and Records Administration, n.d. roll 1; FHL microfilm 880,014.

- "United States Civil War Soldiers Index, 1861-1865." database. https://familysearch.org/ark:/61903/1:1:F9KL-QWP. William P. Allen, Second Lieutenant, Company F&S, 11th Regiment, Texas Infantry (Roberts'). Confederate. citing NARA microfilm publication M227. Washington D.C. National Archives and Records Administration, n.d. roll 1; FHL microfilm 880,014.

- "United States Civil War Soldiers Index, 1861-1865." database. https://familysearch.org/ark:/61903/1:1:F9KL-SX9. Edward Allen, Private, Company H, Waul's Texas Legion. Confederate. citing NARA microfilm publication M227. Washington D.C. National Archives and Records Administration, n.d. roll 1; FHL microfilm 880,014.

- "United States Migration to Texas 1820 to 1845." National Institute. https://www.family search.org.

"Father of Waters." The Free Dictionary. https://www.thefreedictionary.com/Mississippi.

Faulkner, Carol. "Spiritualism, Slavery, and Whiteness in the 1850s." *Religion in American History.* http://usreligion.blogspot.com/2013/08/spiritualism-slavery-and-whiteness-in.html.

Fayman, W. A. & Reilly, T. W. *Galveston City Directory, 1875-1876.* https://texashistory.unt.edu/ark:/67531/metapth636884/. University of North Texas Libraries. The Portal to Texas History. https://texashistory.unt.edu; crediting Rosenberg Library.

Find A Grave. database and images. https://www.findagrave.com. memorial page for Josephine S Allen (unknown–7 Sep 1897). Find A Grave Memorial no. 132948277. citing Lakeview Cemetery, Galveston, Galveston County, Texas, USA. Maintained by Floyd Lanny Martin (contributor 47610184).

- memorial page for Edward C. Allen (2 Oct 1836–23 Mar 1925). Find A Grave Memorial no. 113514069. citing Mayberry Cemetery. Windham Center, Cumberland County, Maine, USA. Maintained by Find A Grave contributor 8.

- memorial page for Frederick Allen (1849–9 May 1901). Find A Grave Memorial no. 128070640. citing Lakeview Cemetery, Galveston, Galveston County, Texas, USA. Maintained by Find A Grave (contributor 8).

Finkelman, Paul. *Millard Fillmore: The American Presidents Series: the 13th President, 1850-1853.* New York: Times Books. 2011.

"First Locomotive in Texas." *The Athens Post.* Athens, Tennessee. February 22,

1856. https://www.newspapers.com/image/72122273/?terms=First%2BLocomotive%2Bin%2BTexas.

Fisher, Lindy. *Between the Creeks*. July 2006; http://texashistory.unt.edu/ark:/67531/metapth752794/. University of North Texas Libraries. The Portal to Texas History. http://texashistory.unt.edu.

Ford, John Guthrie. "Our San Jose Island Neighbors." Port Aransas South Jetty. http://www.portasouthjetty.com/news/2011-06-02/Island_Life/HISTORY_CORNER.html.

Fort Bankhead." North American Forts. https://www.northamericanforts.com/West/tx-coast1.html#galv.

Fort Point." North American Forts. http://www.northamericanforts.com/West/tx-coast1.html#galv.

Freeling, William W. *The Road to Disunion: Volume I: Secessionists at Bay, 1776–1854*. Oxford University Press. 1991.

"Gettysburg National Military Park." National Park Service. https://www.nps.gov/gett/index.htm.

Hale, Mrs. Sarah J. and Godey, Louis A. eds. *Godey's Lady's Book and Magazine*. Philadelphia: Louis A. Godey. 1855. Vol. LI from July to December 1855.

Hale, Sarah Josepha (1788-1879). "Notable Natives." The Town of Newport. https://www.newportnh.gov/about-newport/pages/notable-natives.

Handbook of Texas Online

- Barker. Eugene C. "Austin. Stephen Fuller." http://www.tshaonline.org/handbook/online/articles/fau14.
- Barker. Nancy N. "Dubois De Saligny." http://www.tshaonline.org/handbook/online/articles/fdu02.
- Barr, Alwyn. "Galveston. Battle of." http://www.tshaonline.org/handbook/online/articles/qeg01.
- Barr, Alwyn. "Green. Thomas." http://www.tshaonline.org/handbook/online/articles/fgr38.
- Beazley, Julia. "House, Thomas William." http://www.tshaonline.org/handbook/online/articles/fho68.
- Beazley, Julia. "Hutchins, William J." http://www.tshaonline.org/handbook/online/articles/fhu51.
- Beazley, Julia. "Sherman, Sidney." http://www.tshaonline.org/handbook/online/articles/fsh27.
- Benham, Priscilla Myers. "Eve, Joseph." http://www.tshaonline.org/handbook/online/articles/fev09.
- Benham, Priscilla Myers. "La Branche, Alcee Louis." http://www.tshaonline.org/handbook/online/articles/fla06.

- Benham, Priscilla Myers. "Rusk, Thomas Jefferson." http://www.tshaonline.org/handbook/online/articles/fru16.
- Biesele, Rudolph L. "Fisher, Henry Francis." http://www.tshaonline.org/handbook/online/articles/ffi17.
- Blake, Robert Bruce "Ochiltree, William Beck." http://www.tshaonline.org/handbook/online/articles/foc02.
- Britton, Morris L. "Coffee's Station." http://www.tshaonline.org/handbook/online/articles/dfc01.
- Brownrigg, Steven A. "Cooke, William Gordon." http://www.tshaonline.org/handbook/online/articles/fcobv.
- Brunson, B. R. and Muir, Andrew Forest. "Morgan, James." http://www.tshaonline.org/handbook/online/articles/fmo50of New Washington.
- Buenger, Walter L. "Secession Convention." http://www.tshaonline.org/handbook/online/articles/mjs01.
- Buenger, Walter L. "Secession." http://www.tshaonline.org/handbook/online/articles/mgs02.
- Burkhalter, Lois Wood. "Lincecum, Gideon." http://www.tshaonline.org/handbook/online/articles/fli03.
- Burns, Chester R. "Epidemic Diseases." http://www.tshaonline.org/handbook/online/articles/sme01.
- Campbell, Randolph B. "Slavery." http://www.tshaonline.org/handbook/online/articles/yps01.
- Carroll, H. Bailey "Snively Expedition." http://www.tshaonline.org/handbook/online/articles/qys02.
- Carroll, H. Bailey "Snively, Jacob." http://www.tshaonline.org/handbook/online/articles/fsn07.
- Carroll, H. Bailey. "Texan Santa Fe Expedition." http://www.tshaonline.org/handbook/online/articles/qyt03.
- Christian, Carole E. "Hempstead, TX." http://www.tshaonline.org/handbook/online/articles/hgh07.
- Christian, Carole E. "Longpoint, TX." http://www.tshaonline.org/handbook/online/articles/hnl44.
- "Clarksville Female Academy." http://www.tshaonline.org/handbook/online/articles/kbc25.
- Conner, J. E. "Fort Marcy." http://www.tshaonline.org/handbook/online/articles/qcf08.
- Connor, Seymour V. "Ford, John Salmon [RIP]." http://www.tshaonline.org/handbook/online/articles/ffo11.
- Connor, Seymour V. "Hale, William G." http://www.tshaonline.org/handbook/

online/articles/fha14.
- Connor, Seymour V. "New Washington, TX." http://www.tshaonline.org/handbook/online/articles/hvn28.
- "Creuzbaur, Robert." http://www.tshaonline.org/handbook/online/articles/fcr17.
- Cutrer, Thomas W. "Flournoy, George M." http://www.tshaonline.org/handbook/online/articles/ffl19.
- Cutrer, Thomas W. "Hebert, Paul Octave." http://www.tshaonline.org/handbook/online/articles/fhe09.
- Cutrer, Thomas W. "Magruder, John Bankhead." http://www.tshaonline.org/handbook/online/articles/fma15.
- Cutrer, Thomas W. "Raymond, Charles H." http://www.tshaonline.org/handbook/online/articles/fra50.
- Cutrer, Thomas W. "Reily, James." http://www.tshaonline.org/handbook/online/articles/fre26.
- Cutrer, Thomas W. "Robertson, John C." http://www.tshaonline.org/handbook/online/articles/fro29.
- Cutrer, Thomas W. "Scurry, William Read." http://www.tshaonline.org/handbook/online/articles/fsc38.
- Cutrer, Thomas W. "Yell, Archibald." http://www.tshaonline.org/handbook/online/articles/fye02.
- Cutrer, Thomas W. "Smith, Edmund Kirby." http://www.tshaonline.org/handbook/online/articles/fsm09.
- Dickson, James G. Jr. "Attorney General." http://www.tshaonline.org/handbook/online/articles/mba03.
- Elliott, Claude. "Henderson, James Pinckney." http://www.tshaonline.org/handbook/online/articles/fhe14.
- "Elliot, Charles." http://www.tshaonline.org/handbook/online/articles/fel09.
- Ellis, Hugo. "Donelson, Andrew Jackson." http://www.tshaonline.org/handbook/online/articles/fdo13.
- Frantz, Joe B. "Borden, Gail, Jr." http://www.tshaonline.org/handbook/online/articles/fbo24.
- Gambrell, Herbert. "Jones, Anson." http://www.tshaonline.org/handbook/online/articles/fjo42.
- Gambrell, Herbert. "Lamar, Mirabeau Buonaparte." http://www.tshaonline.org/handbook/online/articles/fla15.
- Giles, Marie. "Clarksville Academy." http://www.tshaonline.org/handbook/online/articles/kbc24.
- Gray, Christina L. "Millican, TX." http://www.tshaonline.org/handbook/online/

articles/hlm71.

- Haller, Uli. "Tod, John Grant, Sr." http://www.tshaonline.org/handbook/online/articles/fto05.
- Hamilton, Margaret Bearden. "Campbell's Bayou, TX." http://www.tshaonline.org/handbook/online/articles/hvcbc.
- Harper, Cecil Jr. "Todd, William Smith." http://www.tshaonline.org/handbook/online/articles/fto08.
- Harper, Cecil Jr. "Boston, TX." http://www.tshaonline.org/handbook/online/articles/hlb45.
- Harper, Cecil Jr. "Bryan, John Neely." http://www.tshaonline.org/handbook/online/articles/fbran.
- Harper, Cecil Jr. "Runnels, Hardin Richard." http://www.tshaonline.org/handbook/online/articles/fru13.
- Hart, Brian. "Van Alstyne, TX." http://www.tshaonline.org/handbook/online/articles/hjv02.
- Hazlewood, Claudia. "Clarksville, TX (Red River County)." http://www.tshaonline.org/handbook/online/articles/hgc07.
- Hazlewood, Claudia. "Swain, William Jesse." http://www.tshaonline.org/handbook/online/articles/fsw01.
- Henson, Margaret Swett. "McKinney, Thomas Freeman." http://www.tshaonline.org/handbook/online/articles/fmc75.
- Henson, Margaret Swett. "Williams, Samuel May." http://www.tshaonline.org/handbook/online/articles/fwi35.
- "Hill, George Washington." http://www.tshaonline.org/handbook/online/articles/fhi20.
- Hinton, Harwood P. "Watrous, John Charles." http://www.tshaonline.org/handbook/online/articles/fwa71.
- Humphrey, David C. "Austin, TX (Travis County)." http://www.tshaonline.org/handbook/online/articles/hda03.
- Humphrey, David C. "Ward, Thomas William." http://www.tshaonline.org/handbook/online/articles/fwa52.
- Huson, Hobart. "Webb, James." http://www.tshaonline.org/handbook/online/articles/fwe04.
- Hyman, Carolyn. "Hockley, George Washington." http://www.tshaonline.org/handbook/online/articles/fho08.
- Jaschke, Melvin B. "Terrell, George Whitfield." http://www.tshaonline.org/handbook/online/articles/fte22.
- Kemp, L. W. "Latimer, Albert Hamilton." http://www.tshaonline.org/handbook/online/articles/fla44.

- Kemp, L. W. "Robinson, James W." http://www.tshaonline.org/handbook/online/articles/fro37.
- Kielman, Chester V. "Holland, John Henry." http://www.tshaonline.org/handbook/online/articles/fho26.
- Kleiner, Diana J. "Baker, William Robinson." http://www.tshaonline.org/handbook/online/articles/fba42.
- Kleiner, Diana J. "Hockley, TX." http://www.tshaonline.org/handbook/online/articles/hlh49.
- Laing, Wesley N. "Allen, John M." http://www.tshaonline.org/handbook/online/articles/fal22.
- Leatherwood, Art. "St. Joseph Island." http://www.tshaonline.org/handbook/online/articles/rrs09.
- Loeffler, Mark. "Sea King." http://www.tshaonline.org/handbook/online/articles/etslq.
- Long, Mary Cole Farrow. "Cole, James Pope" http://www.tshaonline.org/handbook/online/articles/fcobf.
- Maberry, Robert Jr. "Wharton, John Austin [1828-65]." http://www.tshaonline.org/handbook/online/articles/fwh04.
- Marten, James A. "Hamilton, Andrew Jackson." http://www.tshaonline.org/handbook/online/articles/fha33.
- Maxwell, Robert S. "Bremond, Paul." http://www.tshaonline.org/handbook/online/articles/fbr39.
- Maywald, Lonnie Ficklen. "Port Lavaca, TX." http://www.tshaonline.org/handbook/online/articles/hep07.
- McKnight, Joseph W. "Law." http://www.tshaonline.org/handbook/online/articles/jzlph.
- Miller, Aragorn Storm. "Cook, Joseph Jarvis." http://www.tshaonline.org/handbook/online/articles/fcofa.
- Miller, Aragorn Storm. "Shea, Daniel D." http://www.tshaonline.org/handbook/online/articles/fsh68.
- "Miller, Washington D." http://www.tshaonline.org/handbook/online/articles/fmi29.
- Mitchell, Louis. "Lubbock, Francis Richard." http://www.tshaonline.org/handbook/online/articles/flu01.
- Muir, Andrew Forest. "Gray, Edwin Fairfax." https://tshaonline.org/handbook/online/articles/fgr20.
- Muir, Andrew Forest. "Harrisburg, TX (Harris County)." http://www.tshaonline.org/handbook/online/articles/hvh27.
- Muir, Andrew Forest. "Rice, William Marsh." http://www.tshaonline.org/

- handbook/online/articles/fri03.
- Murphy, Victoria S. "Hedgcoxe War." http://www.tshaonline.org/handbook/online/articles/jch01.
- Nance, Joseph Milton. "Mier Expedition." https://tshaonline.org/handbook/online/articles/qym02.
- Nance, Joseph Milton. "Somervell Expedition." http://www.tshaonline.org/handbook/online/articles/qys03.
- Nance, Joseph Milton. "Republic of Texas." http://www.tshaonline.org/handbook/online/articles/mzr02.
- Neu, C. T. "Annexation." http://www.tshaonline.org/handbook/online/articles/mga02.
- Neu, C. T. "Hunt, Memucan." http://www.tshaonline.org/handbook/online/articles/fhu31.
- Neu, C. T. "Stockton, Robert Field." http://www.tshaonline.org/handbook/online/articles/fst61.
- Ornish, Natalie. "Kaufman, David Spangler." http://www.tshaonline.org/handbook/online/articles/fka12.
- Procter, Ben H. "Richardson, Sid Williams." http://www.tshaonline.org/handbook/online/articles/fri08.
- Register1862; CSN Register; Compiled Military Service Record for Robert Creuzbaur, at FOLD3 1880 U.S. Census; 1910 U.S. Census. "Creuzbaur, Robert." www.tshaonline.org/handbook/online/articles/fcr17.
- "Roberts, Oran Milo." http://www.tshaonline.org/handbook/online/articles/fro18.
- Sealy, Edward Coyle. "Galveston Wharves." http://www.tshaonline.org/handbook/online/articles/etg01.
- Silverthorne, Elizabeth. "Smith, Ashbel." http://www.tshaonline.org/handbook/online/articles/fsm04.
- Southwick, Leslie H. "Anderson, Kenneth Lewis." http://www.tshaonline.org/handbook/online/articles/fan08.
- "Stafford, William." http://www.tshaonline.org/handbook/online/articles/fst04.
- Steen, Ralph W. "Convention of 1845." http://www.tshaonline.org/handbook/online/articles/mjc13.
- Strickland, Rex W. "Jonesborough, TX." http://www.tshaonline.org/handbook/online/articles/hvj16.
- Sugg, Redding S. Jr. "Daingerfield, William Henry." http://www.tshaonline.org/handbook/online/articles/fda04.
- "Texas Railroad, Navigation, and Banking Company." http://www.tshaonline.org/handbook/online/articles/dft01.

- Vaughn, William Preston. "Freemasonry." http://www.tshaonline.org/handbook/online/articles/vnf01.
- Vigness, Winifred W. "Almonte, Juan Nepomuceno." http://www.tshaonline.org/handbook/online/articles/fal45.
- Wade, Harry E. "Peters' Colony." http://www.tshaonline.org/handbook/online/articles/uep02.
- Wallace, Ernest "Clarksville Standard." http://www.tshaonline.org/handbook/online/articles/eec15.
- Warren, Harris Gaylord. "Laffite, Jean." http://www.tshaonline.org/handbook/online/articles/fla12.
- Weir, Merle. "Wharton, William Harris." http://www.tshaonline.org/handbook/online/articles/fwh08.
- "Wells, James B." http://www.tshaonline.org/handbook/online/articles/fwe23.
- Werner, George C. "Buffalo Bayou, Brazos and Colorado Railway." http://www.tshaonline.org/handbook/online/articles/eqb16.
- Werner, George C. "Houston and Texas Central Railway." http://www.tshaonline.org/handbook/online/articles/eqh09.
- Werner, George C. "Railroads." http://www.tshaonline.org/handbook/online/articles/eqr01.
- Werner, George C. "Texas Western Railroad." http://www.tshaonline.org/handbook/online/articles/eqt20.
- White, W. W. "Green, Duff." http://www.tshaonline.org/handbook/online/articles/fgr32.
- Wilder, John B. "Van Zandt, Isaac." http://www.tshaonline.org/handbook/online/articles/fva12.
- Williams, Amelia W. "Yates, Andrew Janeway." http://www.tshaonline.org/handbook/online/articles/fya02.
- Wooster, Ralph A. "Civil War." http://www.tshaonline.org/handbook/online/articles/qdc02.
- Wooster, Ralph A. "Clark, Edward." http://www.tshaonline.org/handbook/online/articles/fcl04.
- Young, Nancy Beck. "Galveston and Red River Railroad." http://www.tshaonline.org/handbook/online/articles/eqg02.

Hanson, J. W. *History of the Old Towns Norridgewock and Canaan comprising Norridgewock, Canaan, Starks, Skowhegan, and Bloomfield from their early settlement to the Year 1849*. Boston: J. W. Hanson. 1849.

Hardinge, Emma (Britten). "Spiritualism in the South" and "Spiritualism in Texas." *Modern American Spiritualism: A Twenty Year's Record of the Communion between Earth and the World of Spirits*. New York: Emma Hardinge.

1870.

Harmony Lodge No. 6, The. http://harmonylodge6.com/history.html.

"Harrison, William Henry." The White House. https://www.whitehouse.gov/about-the-white-house/presidents/william-henry-harrison/.

Hayward, John. *The New England and New York Law Register for the Year 1835.* New York: John Hayward. 1834.

"headright certificate." The Law.com Dictionary. https://dictionary.thelaw.com/headright-certificate/.

Healy, James L. *Sam Houston.* Norman: The University of Oklahoma Press 2004.

Historic Lewiston, New York." http://historiclewiston.org/pictures/.

"Historic Skowhegan Building to be Restored." Archive Article. History House Association. Skowhegan History House. http://www.skowheganhistoryhouse.org/pdf/LeavittBlock.pdf.

Historical Chronology of Newport New Hampshire." http://www.newportnh.net/aynnyd/uploaded/pdfs/history_of_newport_20101019.pdf.

Historical Chronology of Newport, New Hampshire." The Town of Newport, New Hampshire. https://www.newportnh.gov/sites/newportnh/files/uploads/historical_chronology_story.pdf.

Historical Marker Application for the City of Allen." Ebenezer Allen. Collin County History. https://www.collincountyhistory.com/allen-ebenezer.html.

Historical Sketch of Skowhegan, Maine." History. Skowhegan, Maine. https://www.skowhegan.org/307/History and http://history.rays-place.com/me/skowhegan-me.htm.

"History of Harmony Lodge No. 6 A.F. & A.M." Harmony Lodge No. 6 A.F. & A.M. http://harmonylodge6.com/history.html.

"History of Killingworth. Connecticut. The." http://www.killingworthhistorical.org/town-history.html.

"History of Lewiston, NY." http://history.rays-place.com/ny/lewiston-ny.htm.

"History of Modern American Spiritualism, The." http://www.spiritualistdesertchurchlv.org/what-we-believe/the-history-of-spiritualism.

"History of the Houston & Texas Central Railway Company up to 1903; excerpted from the Yearbook for Texas." Texas Transportation Archive. https://www.ttarchive.com/library/Articles/Houston-Texas-Central_1903_Year-Book-TX.html.

"History of the United States Patent Office." http://www.myoutbox.net/popchapx.htm.

"Hollywood Cemetery." Richmond, Virginia. https://www.hollywoodcemetery.org/about/our-history.

Holt, Michael. *The Fate of Their Country: Politicians, Slavery Extension, and the Coming of the Civil War.* New York: Hill and Wang. 2005.

"Houston & Texas Central Stations." Confederate Railroads. http://www.csa-railroads.com/Houston_and_Texas_Central_Stations.htm.

Hurd, D. Hamilton, ed. *History of Cheshire and Sullivan Counties, New Hampshire.* Philadelphia: J. W. Lewis & Co. 1886.

Inglis-Arkell, Esther. "The Deadliest Poisons in History (And Why People Stopped Using Them)." *Gizmodo.* https://io9.gizmodo.com/5942161/the-deadliest-poisons-in-history-and-why-people-stopped-using-them.

Johnson, Judith M. Johnson-Morrow Family Tree. Ancestry.com.

Johnson, Judith M. Email on August 22, 2019.

Biography of Jonas Cutting, L.L.D." https://www.accessgenealogy.com/new-hampshire/biography-of-jonas-cutting-ll-d.htm.

Jones, Anson. "History of Freemasonry in early Texas and the Frontier." *Frontier Times Magazine.* April 9, 2011. http://frontiertimesmagazine.blogspot.com/2011/04/history-of-freemasonry-in-early-texas.html.

Jones, Anson. *Memoranda and Official Correspondence Relating to the Republic of Texas and its History and Annexation.* New York: D. Appleton and Company. 1859.

Jones, Anson. *The Republic of Texas – Its History and Annexation.* New York: D. Appleton and Company. 1859.

Journals of the Constitution Convention of Texas, 1845. pub. in Austin by Miner and Cruger, Printers to the Constitution. 1846. https://www.tsl.texas.gov/ref/abouttx/annexation/4july1845.html.

Katcher, Susan. "Legal Training in the United States: A Brief History." *Wisconsin International Law Journal.* July 26, 2006.

"land scrip." Merriam-Webster. https://www.merriam-webster.com/dictionary/land%20scrip.

Laws Passed by the Second Legislature of the State of Texas. Houston: Published by Authority. 1848. Vol. 2.

"League, John C." League City. County of Galveston. http://www.galvestoncountytx.gov/cm/Pages/History-League-City.aspx.

Leavitt, James T. Coburn, Loise Helen. *Skowhegan on the Kennebec.* Vol. II.

Leon Smith: Confederate Mariner." *East Texas Historical Journal*: Vol. 3, Issue. 1, Article 7. https://scholarworks.sfasu.edu/ethj/vol3/iss1/7/.

Letter from A. L Rives to E. Kirby Smith. *The War of Rebellion: A Compilation of the Official Records of the Union and Confederate Armies.* Washington: Government Printing Office. 1882. Series 1 - Volume 34 Part IV.

- Andrew Jackson Donelson to Ebenezer Allen. April 16, 1845. The

Southwestern Historical Society. Austin: The Texas State Historical Association. 1921. Vol. 24.

- Ebenezer Allen to Andrew Jackson Donelson. April 14, 1845. The Southwestern Historical Society. Austin: The Texas State Historical Association. 1921. Vol. 244.

- Ebenezer Allen to Andrew Jackson Donelson. June 23, 1845. Hard Road to Texas Annexation. United States Diplomatic Correspondence. Texas Secretary of State records. Archives and Information Services Division. Texas State Library and Archives Commission. https://www.tsl.texas.gov/exhibits/annexation/part5/eben_allen_june23_1845_1.html and https://www.tsl.texas.gov/exhibits/annexation/part5/eben_allen_june23_1845_2.html.

- Ebenezer Allen to Charles Elliott. *Diplomatic Correspondence of the Republic of Texas.* Washington: Government Printing Office. 1911. Volume II. Part II.

- Ebenezer Allen to Dr. Gideon Lincecum. November 10, 1853. Courtesy of the Rosenberg Library, 2310 Sealy Street, Galveston, Texas. MSS# 350001 Ebenezer Allen Papers, Box Sm. Coll.

- Ebenezer Allen to James Morgan. January 11, 1858. Rosenberg Library. Galveston, Texas. MSS# 31-0001 Morgan Papers. Box 1. Folder 1.

- Ebenezer Allen to Sam Houston. Original is in the Texas State Archives. Judith M. Johnson. Johnson-Morrow Family Tree. Ancestry.com.

- Ebenezer Allen to Samuel May Williams. April 10, 1854. Samuel May Williams Papers. Courtesy of the Rosenberg Library. 2310 Sealy Street, Galveston, Texas. MSS# 23-2956 S. M. Williams, Box 14, Folder 9.

- N. Guilbeau to William G. Hale. William G. Hale Papers, 1819-1931. Box 2D5. Letters and Legal Papers: 1819-1848. The Dolph Briscoe Center for American History. The University of Texas at Austin.

- Sam Houston to His Wife. January 2, 1853. *The Personal Correspondence of Sam Houston* – Volume IV: 1852-1863. Denton: University of North Texas Press. 2001.

- Thomas F. McKinney to Samuel M. Williams. August 29, 1850. Samuel May Williams Papers. Rosenberg Library. MSS# 23-2372 S. M. Williams. Box 12. Folder 9.

"Life Expectancy - 1800-1850." Legacy.com. http://www.legacy.com/life-and-death/the-antebellum-era.html.

Livingston, John. *Livingston's Law Register New York: Monthly Law Magazine.* 1851.

"Louis Antoine Godey (1804 – 1878) Publisher. http://godeysladysbook.com/louisagodey.htm.

Luraghi, Raimondo. *A History of the Confederate Navy.* Annapolis: Naval Institute Press. 1996.

"Mackenzie Rebellion." http://warfarehistorynetwork.com/daily/military-history/mackenzies-rebellion/.

Marriages. *The Advocate*. June 5, 1833. E. F. Danforth. Hinckley, Maine. Good Will Publishing Co. [1927?].

Martin, John H. *Saints, Sinners and Reformers*. The Burned-Over District Re-Visited. Chapter 7 - Charles Grandison Finney. http://www.crookedlakereview.com/books/saints_sinners/martin7.html.

Matheson, David. "Galveston in the Civil War." East Texas History. http://easttexashistory.org/items/show/160.

Matthews, James M. ed. Statutes at Large of the Provisional Government of the Confederate States of America from the Institution of the Government, February 8, 1861, to Its Termination, February 18, 1862, Inclusive....Richmond: R. M. Smith. Printer to Congress. 1864. https://www.tsl.texas.gov/ref/abouttx/secession/1march1861.html.

Mau, Mark and Edmundson, Henry. "First Steps Offshore." Engineering and Technology History Wiki. http://ethw.org/First_Steps_.

McKenzie College. Early Texas Methodism. SMU. Birdwell Library. Perkins School of Theology. https://www.smu.edu/Bridwell/SpecialCollectionsandArchives/Exhibitions/EarlyTexas/McKenzieCollege.

"Megginson, Joseph C." Megginhttps://co.jefferson.tx.us/Historical_Commission/files/History/Elected%20Officials/District_Judges_of_Jefferson_County.pdf.

Merk, Frederick. *History of the Westward Movement.* New York: Alfred A. Knopf. 1978.

Merrill, Eliphalet and Merrill, Phinehas. *Gazetteer of the State of New Hampshire.* Exeter: C. Norris & Co. 1847.

Mesch, Allen H. *Teacher of Civil War Generals – Major General Charles Ferguson Smith, Soldier and West Point Commandant*. Jefferson: McFarland & Company, Inc. Publishers. 2015.

"Meyer vs. Anderson et al." *The Southwestern Reporter*. March 19-May 21, 1888. Vol. 7.

Middleton, Annie. "Donelson's Mission to Texas in Behalf of Annexation." *The Southwestern Historical Quarterly* 24, no. 4 (1921). http://www.jstor.org/stable/30234808.

Mitchell, H. E. *The Skowhegan Register.* Brunswick: The H. E. Mitchell Company. 1905.

"Morse, Andrew." https://www.ancestry.com/genealogy/records/andrew-morse_12123779.

Morrissey, Charles T. "Expatriates: New Hampshire and Vermont in Texas." Dartmouth College Library Bulletin. November 1997. Volume XXXVIII(NS).

Number 1. http://www.dartmouth.edu/~library/Library_Bulletin/Nov1997/Morrissey.html?mswitch-redir=classic.

National Archives Compiled Service Records of Confederate Soldiers Who Served in Organizations Raised Directly by the Confederate Government. NARA Catalogue ID# 586957. NARA Catalogue Title: Carded Records Showing Military Service of Soldiers Who Fought in Confederate Organizations. Compiled 1903-1927, documenting the period 1861-1865. Record Group 109. Roll 0104. Military Unit Engineers CSA C-Di. 1863. Letter from Ebenezer Allen to Robert Creuzbaur.

NC Civil War Sailors Project. Identifying NC Sailors and Marines. http://rblong.net/sailor/cr.html.

"New Hampshire's Turnpike History." New Hampshire's History Blog. www.cowhampshireblog.com/2006/08/23/new-hampshires-turnpike-history/.

No. 824. *The Austin Weekly Statesman*. Austin, Texas. October 2, 1873.

"Notice." *The Galveston Daily News*. Galveston, Texas. August 3, 1866. Newspapers by Ancestry.

Newspapers.com. "Announcements - Attorney General." *The Texian Advocate*. Victoria, Texas. May 31, 1850. https://www.newspapers.com/image/436666332.

- *Bangor Daily Whig and Courier.* Bangor, Penobscot, Maine. February 7, 1839. https://www.newspapers.com/image/15360097. Newspapers.com.

- "Congressional." *Hartford Courant.* Hartford, Connecticut. February 20, 1849. https://www.newspapers.com/image/368957327.

- Cradock, Van. "Early School Left Lasting Contribution. *Longview News-Journal* .Longview, Texas. https://www.newspapers.com.A2.

- *Dallas Daily Herald. The.* Dallas, Texas. December 1, 1858. https://www.newspapers.com/image/168122675/?clipping_id=14074749.

- *Dallas Daily Herald, The.* Dallas, Texas. December 29, 1858. https://www.newspapers.com/image/168124689/?terms=Watrous.

- "Fiftieth Anniversary." *The Los Angeles Times*. April 5, 1898. 13.https://www.newspapers.com/image/378343982/.

- "Fine River Oysters." *Richmond Dispatch.* Richmond, Virginia. October 26, 1860. https://www.newspapers.com/image/80614991/?terms=%22Gem%2BSaloon%22.

- "Flotsam and Jetsam." *The Galveston Daily News.* Galveston, Texas. May 17, 1888. https://www.newspapers.com/image/22270672/?terms=Ebenezer%2BAllen.

- "From Texas." *The New Orleans Crescent*. New Orleans, Louisiana. December 24, 1855. https://www.newspapers.com/

- image/167473176/?terms=%22citizens%2Bof%2BHouston%22.
- "Galveston and Red River Railroad." *The Opelousas Patriot.* Opelousas, Louisiana. January 5, 1856. https://www.newspapers.com/image/367163685/?terms= The%2BOpelousas%2BPatriot.
- "Great Excitement." *Richmond Dispatch.* Richmond, Virginia. June 14, 1860. https://www.newspapers.com/image/80613440/?terms=%22Gem%2BSaloon%22.
- "Houston and Allen." *The Washington Union.* Washington, District of Columbia. May 10, 1847. https://www.newspapers.com/image/319288470/?clipping_id=16773439.
- "Later from Texas." *The Times-Picayune.* New Orleans, Louisiana. December 28, 1852. https://www.newspapers.com/image/25539223/?terms=%22Leon%2BPioneer%22.
- "Legal Business in Texas." *The Times-Picayune.* New Orleans, Louisiana. March 12, 1847. https://www.newspapers.com/image/25554712/?clipping_id=1159820.
- "Local Matters." *The Daily Dispatch.* September 10, 1862. https://www.newspapers.com/image/80615978. *Louisville Daily Courier. The.* Louisville, Kentucky. January 21, 1853. https://www.newspapers.com/image/119156485/?terms=the%2Blouisville%2Bdaily%2Bcourier.
- "Maine Patents." *Bangor Daily Whig and Courier.* Bangor, Maine. December 16, 1887. https://www.newspapers.com/image/7189994/?terms=%22Edward%2BAllen%22.
- "Maine Patents." *Bangor Daily Whig and Courier.* Bangor, Maine. June 16, 1888. https://www.newspapers.com/image/18339966/?terms=%22Edward%2BAllen%22.
- *New Orleans Crescent, The.* New Orleans, Louisiana. October 19, 1849. https://www.newspapers.com/image/321462185/?terms=The%2BNew%2BOrleans%2BCrescent.
- *New Orleans Crescent, The.* New Orleans, Louisiana. December 24, 1855. https://www.newspapers.com/image/167473176/?terms=%22New%2BOrleans%2BCrescent%22.
- *San Francisco Chronicle.* San Francisco, California. April 26, 1893. https://www.newspapers.com/image/27340796/?terms=W.%2BP.%2BAllen
- "The Impeachment Case in Congress – Judge Watrous." *The Daily Dallas Herald.* Dallas, Texas. December 1, 1858. https://www.newspapers.com/image/168122675/?terms=%22Judge%2BWatrous%22.
- *Times-Picayune, The.* New Orleans, Louisiana. July 20, 1856. https://www.newspapers.com/image/25762768/?terms=%22Galveston%2Band%2BRed%2BRiver%22.

- "U.S. Supreme Court." *The Times-Picayune*. December 16, 1852. https://www.newspapers.com/image/25535905.
- *Vicksburg Daily Whig*. Vicksburg, Mississippi. December 2, 1856. https://www.newspapers.com/image/225590529.
- *Weekly National Intelligencer*. Washington, District of Columbia. October 30, 1852. https://www.newspapers.com/image/334861373/?terms=Galveston%2Band%2BRed%2BRiver%2BRailroad.
- *Times-Picayune, The*. New Orleans, Louisiana. May 31, 1856. https://www.newspapers.com/clip/26303305/the_timespicayune/.
- *Times-Picayune, The*. New Orleans, Louisiana. November 29, 1852. https://www.newspapers.com/image/25551562/?terms=Allen.

Oakdale Graphic. The. Oakdale, California. May 17, 1893. https://www.newspapers.com/image/486996198/?terms=Oakdale%2BGraphic.

Officers of the State of Texas." *The Texas Almanac for 1858*. Galveston: Richardson & Co. 1857.

"Oil History." Petroleum History Institute. http://www.petroleumhistory.org/OilHistory/pages/Cable/cable.html.

"Old Times in Jefferson, Texas." *Jefferson Jimplecute*. Jefferson, Texas. March 4, 1905.

"olographic testament." Louisiana Civil Code 1575. info.legalzoom.com/handwritten-wills-legal-louisiana-not-notarized-4135.html.

"Organization of the Confederate Military." Cold Southern Steel. https://coldsouthernsteel.wordpress.com/2015/01/02/organization-of-the-confederate-military/.

"Overview - Hunley." https://www.hunley.org/overview/.

"Panic of 1837." America's Story from America's Library. Library of Congress. http://www.americaslibrary.gov/aa/buren/aa_buren_panic_1.html.

Papers. Headright Certificate Law and Legal Definition. USLegal.com. https://definitions.uslegal.com/h/headright-certificate%20/.

"Parks, Gorham (1794-1877)." Biographical Directory of the United States Congress. bioguide.congress.gov/scripts/biodisplay.pl?index=P000074.

Parmalee, Joseph W. *History of Sullivan County*, New Hampshire.

Personal communications with Mr. Bruce Mercer of the Masonic Lodge of Texas who supplied records for E. Allen. May 26, 2016.

Peters, Richard, ed. *The Public Statutes at Large of the United States of America*. Boston: Chas. C. Little and Jas. Brown. 1850. Vol.5. https://www.tsl.texas.gov/ref/abouttx/annexation/march1845.html.

Petitfils, Charles K. "History of Harmony Lodge No. 6. A. F. & A. M., Galveston, Texas - 1840-1997." http://www.harmonylodge6.com/history.html.

Pettit, Gwen and Fisher, Lindy. *Between the Creeks*. Allen: Lindy Fisher. 2005.

"Polk, James K." The White House. https://www.whitehouse.gov/about-the-white-house/presidents/james-k-polk/.

"Populist Caucus." *The Los Angeles Times*. Los Angeles, California. August 16, 1898. https://www.newspapers.com/image/378332636/?terms=W.%2BP.%2BAllen.

"Port Hudson." National Park Service. https://www.nps.gov/nr/travel/louisiana/por.htm.

"prore." Your Dictionary. https://www.yourdictionary.com/prore.

Prushankin, Jeffery S. *The Civil War in the Trans-Mississippi Theater – 1861-1865*. Washington: Center of Military History United States Army, 2015.

Ragan, Mark K. "Singer's Secret Service Corps: Causing Chaos During the Civil War."*Civil War Times* Magazine. November/December 2007. reprinted on HistoryNet web page. https://www.historynet.com/singers-secret-service-corps-causing-chaos-during-the-civil-war.htm.

Rains, Gabriel J. and Michie, Peter S. *Confederate Torpedoes*. Jefferson: McFarland & Company, Inc. Publishers. 2011.

Read, S. G. *A History of Texas Railroads and of Transportation Conditions under Spain and Mexico and The Republic and State*. Houston: The St. Clair Publishing Co. 1941.

"rectus in curia." Merriam-Webster. https://www.merriam-webster.com/dictionary/rectus%20in%20curia.

Report of Conditional Certificate issued by the Board of Land Commissioners of Red River County for the quarter ending September 2, 1841. Fourth Class Certificate, Number 9, File No. 00030. Texas General Land Office. http://www.glo.texas.gov/ncu/SCANDOCS/archives_webfiles/arcmaps/ web files/land grants/PDFs/1/0/6/2/1062501.pdf.

Richardson, James D. *A Compilation of the Messages and Papers of the Confederacy including the Diplomatic Correspondence, 1861-1865*. Nashville: United States Publishing Company, 1906.

Richmond Examiner, The. Saturday. October 17, 1863. Source: GenealogyBank.com.

Richmond Dispatch. December 17, 1861. quotes a report from the *Texas State Gazette*. https://www.newspapers.com/image/80624091.

"river bottoms." Merriam-Webster. https://www.merriam-webster.com/dictionary/river%20bottom.

Robert Flint Family Tree. James T. Leavitt. Ancestry.com.

Roberts, O. M. "The Experiences of an Unrecognized Senator." *The Quarterly of the Texas State Historical Association*. Austin: Texas Historical Association. 1909. vol. XII.

Rosenberg Library, 2310 Sealy Street, Galveston, Texas.

Schmidt, James M. *Galveston and the Civil War.* Charleston: The History Press. 2012.

"Search for Soldiers." The Civil War, National Park Service. https://www.nps.gov/civilwar/search-soldiers.htm#sort=score+desc&q=Edward+Allen&fq%5B%5D=State%3A%22Maine%22.

Selected Ordinance Patents. http://www.civilwarartillery.com/patents.htm.

"selectman." Merriam-Webster. https://www.merriam-webster.com/dictionary/selectman.

Sellers, Charles. *James K. Polk, Continentalist.* Princeton: Princeton University Press. 1966.

"Siege of Vicksburg, The." Vicksburg National Military Park. https://www.nps.gov/vick/learn/historyculture/vicksburgsiege.htm.

"skin discoloration – bluish." U.S. National Library of Medicine. https://www.nlm.nih.gov/medlineplus/ency/article/003215.htm.

Skowhegan History House Museum and Research Center. http://www.skowheganhistoryhouse.org/contact.shtml.

"Slavery in New Hampshire." Slavery in the North. Timeline of abolition of slavery and serfdom. http://slavenorth.com/newhampshire.htm.

"Slave Schedules." 1850-1860 Slave Schedule, Random Acts of Genealogical Kindness. https://www.raogk.org/census-records/slave-schedule/.

Smith, Baxter Perry. *The History of Dartmouth College.* Boston: The Riverside Press. 1878.

Smith, Justin Harvey. *The Annexation of Texas.* New York: The Baker and Taylor Co. 1911.

Soley, James Russel. "The Blockading of Southern Ports during the Civil War." American Battlefield Trust. https://www.battlefields.org/learn/articles/blockade.

"Sudden and Mysterious Death." *The Richmond Examiner.* October 16, 1863.1. Judith M. Johnson. Johnson-Morrow Family Tree. Ancestry.com.

"Summerland Libel Suit, The." *San Francisco Call.* January 19, 1894. https://www.newspapers.com/image/92934874/?terms=Summerland%2BLibel%2BSuit.

"Supreme Court Decisions." *The Galveston Daily News.* Galveston, Texas. October 30, 1872, Newspapers by Ancestry.

Survey of Land Granted by Conditional Certificate to Ebenezer Allen Fourth Class Certificate. Number 9, File No. 00030. Texas General Land Office. http://www.glo.texas.gov/ncu/SCANDOCS/archives_webfiles/arcmaps/webfiles/landgrants/PDFs/1/0/6/2/1062501.pdf.

Taylor, E. W. (1839–?). Camp Taylor. http://www.taylorcampscv.org/ewtaylor.

html.

"Taylor, Zachary." The White House. https://www.whitehouse.gov/about-the-white-house/presidents/zachary-taylor/.

"Teaser." Naval History and Heritage Command. https://www.history.navy.mil/research/histories/ship-histories/confederate_ships/teaser.html.

Texas Freemason History. Dallas Freemasonry. http://dallasfreemasonry.org/about-freemasonry/texas-freemason-history/.

"Texas Masonic History." Freemasons in Texas. The Grand Lodge of Texas. https://grandlodgeoftexas.org/texas-masonic-history/.

"Texas Railroads." *Washington Telegraph*. Washington, Arkansas. October 5, 1853. https://www.newspapers.com/image/262221516.

Texas State Library and Archives Commission. "Hard Road to Texas. "Texas Annexation 1836-1845." Letter from Sam Houston to James Pinckney Henderson. https://www.tsl.texas.gov/exhibits/annexation/part4/sam_houston_feb21_1844.html.

- "Part 1: Texas Breaks Away - Texas and Mexico." https://www.tsl.texas.gov/exhibits/annexation/part1/page1.html.
- "Part 2: On Our Own - Houston Keeps his Options Open." https://www.tsl.texas.gov/exhibits/annexation/part2/page1.html.
- "Part 2: On Our Own - Lamar and the Rise of Texas Nationalism." https://www.tsl.texas.gov/exhibits/annexation/part2/page2.html.
- "Part 2: On Our Own - Santa Anna Strikes Back." https://www.tsl.texas.gov/exhibits/annexation/part2/page3.html.
- "Part 3: An International Matter - Britain Makes Its Move." The Texas State Library and Archives. https://www.tsl.texas.gov/exhibits/annexation/part3/page1.html.
- "Part 3: An International Matter – Texas Finds a Champion." https://www.tsl.texas.gov/exhibits/annexation/part3/page2.html.
- "Part 4: A Treaty of Annexation - The Annexation Treaty." https://www.tsl.texas.gov/exhibits/annexation/part4/page1.htm.
- "Part 4: A Treaty of Annexation – Tyler's Failed Gamble." https://www.tsl.texas.gov/exhibits/annexation/part4/page2.html.
- "Part 5: The Final Showdown – Starting Over Again." https://www.tsl.texas.gov/exhibits/annexation/part5/page1.html.
- "Part 5: The Final Showdown - A Proclamation, President Anson Jones, May 8, 1845." *National Register Extra*. https://www.tsl.texas.gov/exhibits/annexation/part5/anson_jones_may8_1845_proclamation.html.

"Texas State Fair." *The Galveston Daily* News. Galveston, Texas. June 2, 1871. https://www.newspapers.com/image/23029131/?terms=%22Texas%2B-

State%2BFair%22.

"This Day in Texas." *The Austin American*. Austin, Texas. June 9, 1948. https://www.newspapers.com/image/385691634/?terms=Austin%2BAmerican.

"Timeline: 1844-1848." "A Continent Divided: The U.S. - Mexico War." Center for Greater Southwestern Studies. UT Arlington Library Special Collections. https://library.uta.edu/usmexicowar/timeline.

Times-Picayune, The. New Orleans, Louisiana. March 4, 1852. https://www.newspapers.com/image/25559374/?terms=Galveston.

"Thompson, Waddy Jr. (1798-1868)." *Biographical Directory of the U.S. Congress*. http://bioguide.congress.gov/scripts/biodisplay.pl?index=T000221.

Thrall, Reverend Homer S. *A Pictorial History of Texas*. St. Louis: N. D. Thompson & Co. 1879.

"tort." http://tort.laws.com/torts.

"Town of Canaan." http://www.townofcanaan.com/.

"This day in history." February 28, 1844. "Tyler narrowly escapes death on the USS *Princeton*." History.com. https://www.history.com/this-day-in-history/tyler-narrowly-escapes-death-on-the-uss-princeton.

U.S. Constitution - Article 4 - Section 2. https://www.usconstitution.net/xconst_A4Sec2.html.

Union Bank of Louisiana v. Stafford. 53 U.S. 327 (1851). *Justia U.S. Supreme Court*. https://supreme.justia.com/cases/federal/us/53/327/case.html. University of North Texas Libraries. The Portal to Texas History.

University of North Texas Libraries. The Portal to Texas History. Allen & Brocket. *The Weekly Telegraph*. Houston, Texas. Vol. 21, No. 51, Ed. 1. Wednesday, March 5, 1856. https://texashistory.unt.edu/ark:/67531/metapth235887/. University of North Texas Libraries. The Portal to Texas History. https://texashistory.unt.edu. crediting The Dolph Briscoe Center for American History.

- "Case 220 - Josephine Allen v. W. R. Baker." Term of 1873, Texas. Supreme Court. Cases argued and decided in the Supreme Court of the State of Texas, during the latter part of the term beginning December 2, 1872, and closing November 28, 1873, and during the term beginning December 1, 1873, and until the change of judges made under the amendments to the Constitution adopted on December 2, 1873. Volume 39. 1882. St. Louis, Missouri. https://texashistory.unt.edu/ark:/67531/metapth28534/. https://texashistory.unt.edu.

- *Civilian and Gazette Weekly*. Galveston, Texas. Vol. 21, No. 50, Ed. 1. Tuesday, March 15, 1859. https://texashistory.unt.edu/ark:/67531/metapth177437/m1/2/?q=spiritualism. crediting The Dolph Briscoe Center for American History.

- Crawford, G. W. & Hampton, J. W. *Civilian and Gazette*. Austin, Texas. Vol.

9, Ed. 1. June 26, 1847. https://texashistory.unt.edu/ark:/67531/metapth80290/m1/2.
- Crawford, G. W. & Hampton, J. W. *Texas State Gazette*. Austin, Texas. Vol. 4, No. 23, Ed. 1, Saturday, January 22, 1853. https://texashistory.unt.edu/ark:/67531/metapth81067/. crediting The Dolph Briscoe Center for American History.
- Crawford, G. W. & Hampton, J. W. *Texas State Gazette*. Austin, Texas. Vol. 4, No. 42, Ed. 1, Saturday, June 4, 1853. https://texashistory.unt.edu/ark:/67531/metapth81086/. crediting The Dolph Briscoe Center for American History.
- de Cordova, P. *The South-Western American*. Austin, Texas. Vol. 4, No. 10, Ed. 1. Wednesday, September 15, 1852. https://texashistory.unt.edu/ark:/67531/metapth79738/. crediting The Dolph Briscoe Center for American History.
- De Morse, Charles. "Spiritualism – Another Victim." *Saratoga Republican*. August 24, 1853. *The Standard*. Clarksville, Texas. Vol. 10, No. 49, Ed. 1 Saturday, October 8, 1853. https://texashistory.unt.edu/ark:/67531/metapth233977/m1/1/?q=spiritualism. crediting The Dolph Briscoe Center for American History.
- De Morse, Charles. *The Standard*. Clarksville, Texas. Vol. 20, No. 28, Ed. 1. Saturday, December 5, 1863. https://texashistory.unt.edu/ark:/67531/metapth234371/. crediting The Dolph Briscoe Center for American History.
- De Morse, Charles. *The Standard*. Clarksville, Texas. Vol. 3, No. 1, Ed. 1. Friday, November 11, 1881. https://texashistory.unt.edu/ark:/67531/metapth234733/. crediting The Dolph Briscoe Center for American History.
- Ford, John S. *The Texas State Times*. Austin, Texas. Vol. 2, No. 43, Ed. 1. Saturday, September 29, 1855. https://texashistory.unt.edu/ark:/67531/metapth235778/. crediting The Dolph Briscoe Center for American History.
- Ford, John S. *The Texas State Times*. Austin Texas. Vol. 4, No. 12, Ed. 1. Saturday, March 28, 1857. https://texashistory.unt.edu/ark:/67531/metapth235831/. crediting The Dolph Briscoe Center for American History.
- "Fred Allen & Co's." *The Galveston Daily News*. Galveston, Texas. Vol. 54, No. 259, Ed. 1. Sunday, December 8, 1895. https://texashistory.unt.edu/ark:/67531/metapth465597/. crediting Abilene Library Consortium.
- *Galveston City Directory, 1872*. 1872. Galveston, Texas. https://texashistory.unt.edu/ark:/67531/metapth636856/. https://texashistory.unt.edu. crediting Rosenberg Library.
- *Galveston Weekly News*. Galveston, Texas. Vol. 12, No. 9, Ed. 1. Tuesday, May 8, 1855. https://texashistory.unt.edu/ark:/67531/metapth79827.
- *Galveston Weekly News*. Galveston, Texas. Vol. 12, No. 45, Ed. 1. Tuesday, January 15, 1856. https://texashistory.unt.edu/ark:/67531/metapth79844/m1/1.
- *Galveston Daily News, The*. Galveston, Texas. Vol. 52, No. 171. Ed. 1 Sunday,

- September 10, 1893. https://texashistory.unt.edu/ark:/67531/metapth466495/. https://texashistory.unt.edu. crediting Abilene Library Consortium.
- *Galveston News, The*. Galveston, Texas. Vol. 14, No. 54, Ed. 1. Tuesday, October 30, 1855. https://texashistory.unt.edu/ark:/67531/metapth79958/. crediting The Dolph Briscoe Center for American History.
- *Galveston Weekly News*. Galveston, Texas. Vol. 13, No. 18, Ed. 1. Tuesday, July 22, 1856. https://texashistory.unt.edu/ark:/67531/metapth79862/. crediting The Dolph Briscoe Center for American History.
- *Galveston Weekly News*. Galveston, Texas. Vol. 15, No. 10, Ed. 1. Tuesday, June 15, 1858. https://texashistory.unt.edu/ark:/67531/metapth79881/. crediting The Dolph Briscoe Center for American History.
- *Galveston Weekly News*. Galveston, Texas. Vol. 18, No. 3, Ed. 1. Tuesday, April 23, 1861. https://texashistory.unt.edu/ark:/67531/metapth79916/. crediting The Dolph Briscoe Center for American History.
- Gammel, Hans Peter Mareus Neilsen. *The Laws of Texas, 1822-1897 Volume 3*, 1898. Austin, Texas. https://texashistory.unt.edu/ark:/67531/metapth6728/m1/961/.
- Gibson, J. M. *Weekly Journal*. Galveston, Texas. Vol. 2, No. 20, Ed. 1. Tuesday, July 8, 1851. https://texashistory.unt.edu/ark:/67531/metapth182202/. crediting The Dolph Briscoe Center for American History.
- Harrison, J. C. *Nacogdoches Chronicle*. Nacogdoches, Texas. Vol. 2, No. 12, Ed. 1. Tuesday, May 31, 1853. https://texashistory.unt.edu/ark:/67531/metapth714438/.
- Heller, John H. *Galveston City Directory, 1870*. Galveston, Texas. https://texashistory.unt.edu/ark:/67531/metapth636853. crediting Rosenberg Library.
- Heller, John H. *Galveston City Directory, 1872*. Galveston, Texas. https://texashistory.unt.edu/ark:/67531/metapth636856/. crediting Rosenberg Library.
- Heller, John H. *Heller's Galveston Directory, 1876-1877*. Galveston, Texas. https://texashistory.unt.edu/ark:/67531/. metapth636850/. crediting Rosenberg Library.
- Heller, John H. *Heller's Galveston Directory, 1878-1879*. Galveston, Texas. https://texashistory.unt.edu/ark:/67531/metapth636857/. crediting Rosenberg Library.
- Heller, John H. *Heller's Galveston Directory, 1880-1881*. https://texashistory.unt.edu/ark:/67531/metapth636851/.
- *Houston Post, The*. Houston, Texas. Vol. 37, No. 112, Ed. 1. Monday, July 25, 1921. https://texashistory.unt.edu/ark:/67531/metapth610063/. crediting Rosenberg Library.
- Huston, E. G. *San Antonio Texan*. San Antonio, Texas. Vol. 9, No. 21, Ed. 1. Thursday, March 26, 1857. https://texashistory.unt.edu/ark:/67531/

metapth232695/m1/1/?q=spiritualism./. crediting The Dolph Briscoe Center for American History.

- Huston, E. G. *San Antonio Texan.* San Antonio, Texas. Vol. 9, No. 25, Ed. 1. Thursday, April 23, 1857. https://texashistory.unt.edu/ark:/67531/metapth232697. crediting The Dolph Briscoe Center for American History.

- Lancaster, J. *The Lone Star, and Texas Ranger.* Washington, Texas. Vol. 5, No. 7, Ed. 1. Saturday, September 3, 1853. https://texashistory.unt.edu/ark:/67531/metapth48286/. crediting The Dolph Briscoe Center for American History.

- Latimer, J. W. *Dallas Herald.* Dallas, Texas. Vol. 6, No. 9, Ed. 1. Saturday. August 29, 1857. https://texashistory.unt.edu/ark:/67531/metapth294029/.

- Latimer, J. W. *Dallas Herald.* Dallas, Texas. Vol. 7, No. 5, Ed. 1. Saturday, July 31, 1858. https://texashistory.unt.edu/ark:/67531/metapth294034/.

- Latimer, J. W. "Progress of Spiritualism." *The Dallas Daily Herald.* Dallas, Texas. Vol. 7, No. 36, Ed. 1. Wednesday, March 9, 1859. https://texashistory.unt.edu/ark:/67531/metapth294063.

- Loughery, Robert W. "Candidates." *The Texas Republican.* Marshall, Texas. Vol. 2, No. 4, Ed. 1. Saturday, July 6, 1850. https://texashistory.unt.edu/ark:/67531/metapth1094681/.

- Marshalk, Andrew. *The Indianola Bulletin.* Indiana, Texas. Vol. 1, No. 4, Ed. 1. Thursday, April 26, 1855. https://texashistory.unt.edu/ark:/67531/metapth739363/m1/3.

- Marston, C. W. *Galveston City Directory, 1868-1869.* Galveston, Texas. https://texashistory.unt.edu/ark:/67531/metapth636855/. crediting Rosenberg Library.

- McGown, Andrew J. *Texas Presbyterian.* Houston, Texas. Vol. 1, No. 49, Ed. 1. Saturday, February 19, 1848. https://https://texas. history.unt.edu/ark:/67531/metapth89428/m1/1/.

- Moore, Francis, Jr. *Democratic Telegraph and Texas Register.* Houston, Texas. Vol. 13, No. 47, Ed. 1. Thursday, November 23, 1848. https://texashistory.unt.edu/ark:/67531/metapth48521/. crediting The Dolph Briscoe Center for American History.

- Moore, Francis, Jr. *Telegraph & Texas Register.* Houston, Texas. Vol. 9. No. 47. Ed. 1. Wednesday. November 20, 1844. Houston, Texas. https://texashistory.unt.edu/ark:/67531/metapth78075/m1/1/?q=George+Terrell. crediting The Dolph Briscoe Center for American History.

- Moore, Francis, Jr. *Democratic Telegraph and Texas Register.* Houston, Texas. Vol. 15, No. 32, Ed. 1. Thursday, August 8, 1850. https://texashistory.unt.edu/ark:/67531/metapth48597/. crediting The Dolph Briscoe Center for American History.

- Moore, Francis, Jr. *Telegraph & Texas Register.* Houston, Texas. Vol. 17, No. 29, Ed. 1. Friday, July 16, 1852. https://texashistory.unt.edu/ark:/67531/metapth233390/. crediting The Dolph Briscoe Center for American History.

- Moore, Francis Jr. *Telegraph & Texas Register.* Houston, Texas. Vol. 17, No. 41, Ed. 1. Friday, October 8, 1852. https://texashistory.unt.edu/ark:/67531/metapth233394/. crediting The Dolph Briscoe Center for American History.
- Moore, Francis, Jr. *Telegraph & Texas Register.* Houston, Texas. Vol. 17, No. 42, Ed. 1. Friday, October 15, 1852. https://texashistory.unt.edu/ark:/67531/metapth233395/. crediting The Dolph Briscoe Center for American History.
- Moore, Francis, Jr. *Telegraph & Texas Register.* Houston, Texas. Vol. 18, No. 2, Ed. 1. Friday, January 14, 1853. https://texashistory.unt.edu/ark:/67531/metapth233399/. crediting The Dolph Briscoe Center for American History.
- Morrison & Fourmy. *Morrison & Fourmy's General Directory of the City of Galveston: 1859.* Houston, Texas. https://texashistory.unt.edu/ark:/67531/metapth908994/m1/4/. crediting Rosenberg Library.
- Morrison & Fourmy. *Morrison & Fourmy's General Directory of the City of Galveston: 1881-1882.*
- Houston, Texas. https://texashistory.unt.edu/ark:/67531/metapth894032/. crediting Rosenberg Library.
- Morrison & Fourmy. *Morrison & Fourmy's General Directory of the City of Galveston: 1884-1885.*
- Houston, Texas. https://texashistory.unt.edu/ark:/67531/metapth894029/. crediting Rosenberg Library.
- Morrison & Fourmy. *Morrison & Fourmy's General Directory of the City of Galveston: 1886-1887.* Houston, Texas. https://texashistory.unt.edu/ark:/67531/metapth894033/. crediting Rosenberg Library
- Morrison & Fourmy. *Morrison & Fourmy's General Directory of the City of Galveston: 1891-1892.* Houston, Texas. https://texashistory.unt.edu/ark:/67531/metapth894028/. crediting Rosenberg Library.
- Morrison & Fourmy. *Morrison & Fourmy's General Directory of the City of Galveston: 1893-1894.* Houston, Texas. https://texashistory.unt.edu/ark:/67531/metapth894023/. crediting Rosenberg Library.
- Morrison & Fourmy. *Morrison & Fourmy's General Directory of the City of Galveston: 1895-1896.* Houston, Texas. https://texashistory.unt.edu/ark:/67531/metapth894034/. crediting Rosenberg Library.
- Morrison & Fourmy. *Morrison & Fourmy's General Directory of the City of Galveston: 1896-1897.*
- Houston, Texas. https://texashistory.unt.edu/ark:/67531/metapth894025/. crediting Rosenberg Library.
- Morrison & Fourmy. *Morrison & Fourmy's General Directory of the City of Galveston: 1898.* Houston, Texas. https://texashistory.unt.edu/ark:/67531/metapth894031/. crediting Rosenberg Library.
- Morrison & Fourmy. *Morrison & Fourmy's General Directory of the City of*

- *Galveston: 1899-1900*. Houston, Texas. https://texashistory.unt.edu/ark:/67531/metapth894022/. crediting Rosenberg Library.
- Morrison & Fourmy. *Morrison & Fourmy's General Directory of the City of Galveston: 1901-1902*. Houston, Texas. https://texashistory.unt.edu/ark:/67531/metapth894024/.crediting Rosenberg Library.
- "Much About Annexation." *The Galveston Daily News*. Galveston, Texas. Vol. 45. No. 257. Ed. 1 Saturday, January 8, 1887. https://texashistory.unt.edu/ark:/67531/metapth462757/. crediting Abilene Library Consortium.
- Oldham, W. S. & Marshall. John. *State Gazette*. Austin, Texas. Vol. 8, No. 37, Ed. 1. Saturday, May 2, 1857. https://texashistory.unt.edu/ark:/67531/metapth81294/. crediting The Dolph Briscoe Center for American History.
- Richardson, W. & D. *Galveston City Directory, 1859-1860*. Galveston, Texas. https://texashistory.unt.edu/ark:/67531/metapth636854/m1/8/. crediting Rosenberg Library.
- Richardson, W. & D. *Galveston City Directory, 1866-1867*. Galveston, Texas. https://texashistory.unt.edu/ark:/67531/metapth636854/. crediting Rosenberg Library.
- Schrimpf, J. W. *Writers' Program, Texas*. a history and guide, book. 1942. Houston, Texas. texashistory.unt.edu/ark:/67531/metapth5865/m1/279/.
- Smith, H. H. *Weekly Journal*. Galveston, Texas. Vol. 3, No. 37, Ed. 1. Friday, December 24, 1852. https://texashistory.unt.edu/ark:/67531/metapth182227/. crediting The Dolph Briscoe Center for American History.
- Smith, H. H. "Public Meeting." *The Galveston Journal*. Galveston, Texas. Vol. 4, No. 16, Ed. 1. Friday, August 12, 1853. https://texashistory.unt.edu/ark:/67531/metapth178679/. https://texashistory.unt.edu. crediting The Dolph Briscoe Center for American History.
- Smith, H. H. *The Galveston Journal*. Galveston, Texas. Vol. 5, No. 17, Ed. 1. Friday, April 28, 1854. https://texashistory.unt.edu/ark:/67531/metapth178684/. crediting The Dolph Briscoe Center for American History.
- *South-Western American*. Austin, Texas. Vol. 4, No. 2, Ed. 1. Wednesday, July 21, 1852. crediting The Dolph Briscoe Center for American History.
- *"Spiritualism." Weekly Telegraph, The*. Houston, Texas. Vol. 22, No. 52, Ed. 1. Wednesday, March 18, 1857. https://texashistory.unt.edu/ark:/67531/metapth235932/m1/3/zoom/?q=Spiritualism&resolution=4&lat=6722.799682617187&lon=1691.380371093751.
- Tarver, B. E. *The Semi-Weekly Journal*. Galveston, Texas. Vol. 1, No. 52, Ed. 1. Wednesday, August 7, 1850. https://texashistory.unt.edu/ark:/67531/metapth874057/m1/1/?q =Texas%20attorney%20general%20election%20in%201850. crediting San Jacinto Museum of History.
- *Texas Almanac for 1858* – 1857, *The*. The Portal to Texas History and The *Texas Almanac, for 1857, with Statistics, Historical and Biographical Sketches,*

- &c, *Relating to Texas*. 1966; Dallas, Texas. https://texashistory.unt.edu/ark:/67531/metapth123763/. crediting Texas State Historical Association.
- *Texas Almanac, 1859*. https://texashistory.unt.edu/ark:/67531/metapth123765/. crediting Texas State Historical Association.
- *Texas National Register*. Washington, Texas. Vol. 1, No. 2, Ed. 1. Saturday, December 14, 1844. https://texashistory.unt.edu/ark:/67531/metapth80096/. crediting The Dolph Briscoe Center for American History.
- *Texas National Register.* Washington, Texas. Vol. 1, No. 14, Ed. 1. Saturday, March 8, 1845. https://texashistory.unt.edu/ark:/67531/metapth80108/m1/3/?q=Ebenezer+Allen. crediting The Dolph Briscoe Center for American History.
- "Texas Railroads on White vs. Slave Labor." *The San Antonio Ledger*. San Antonio, Texas. Vol. 6, No. 41, Ed. 1. Saturday, November 8, 1856. https://texashistory.unt.edu/ark:/67531/metapth179432/. crediting The Dolph Briscoe Center for American History.
- *Texas State Gazette*. Austin, Texas. Vol. 2, No. 8, Ed. 1. Saturday, October 12, 1850. https://texashistory.unt.edu/ark:/67531/metapth80950/. crediting The Dolph Briscoe Center for American History.
- Texas, The Constitution of the State of Texas. 1850. texashistory.unt.edu/ark:/67531/metapth2416/:
- *Times-Picayune, The*. New Orleans, Louisiana. August 22, 1858. https://www.newspapers.com/image/25562784/?terms=%22Houston%2Band%2BTexas%2BCentral%22.
- United States. Congress. Senate. Message from the President of the United States to the Two Houses of Congress at the Commencement of the First Session of the Twenty-Ninth Congress. 1845; Washington. https://texashistory.unt.edu/ark:/67531/metapth2365/.
- *Weekly Journal.* Galveston, Texas. Vol. 2, No. 20, Ed. 1. Tuesday, July 8, 1851. https://texashistory.unt.edu/ark:/67531/metapth182202/m1/4/zoom/?q=%22Ebenezer%20Allen%22&resolution=3&lat=7071.554368069872&lon=3883.0663104209616.
- *Weekly Telegraph, The.* Houston, Texas. Vol. 23, No. 20, Ed. 1. Wednesday, August 5, 1857. https://texashistory.unt.edu/ark:/67531/metapth235952/m1/1/zoom/?q=Spiritualism&resolution=4&lat=2996.838103285335&lon=3262.794972154248.

"vacant domain." The Free Dictionary. https://financial-dictionary.thefreedictionary.com/vacant+land.

"Van Buren, Martin." The White House. https://www.whitehouse.gov/about-the-white-house/presidents/martin-van-buren/.

Varney, George J. "History of Orono Maine." *A Gazetteer of Maine.* Boston: B. B. Russell. 1886. http://history.rays-place.com/me/orono-me.htm.

"verdure." Merriam-Webster. https://www.merriam-webster.com/dictionary/verdure.

Volo, James M. and Volo, Dorothy Denneen. *Family Life in 19th-Century America*. Westport: Greenwood Publishing Group. 2007.

Walker, Robert J. (1801–1869)." History. U.S. Department of the Treasury. https://www.treasury.gov/about/history/Pages/rjwalker.aspx.

Washington Sentinel, The. Washington, District of Columbia. May 31, 1854. Chronicling America: Historic American Newspapers. Lib. of Congress. https://chroniclingamerica.loc.gov/lccn/sn82014835/1855-05-31/ed-1/seq-3/.

"Webster, Daniel (1782-1852)." Biographical Directory of the United States Congress. http://bioguide.congress.gov/scripts/biodisplay.pl?index=W000238.

"Webster–Ashburton Treaty, The." Webster Ashburton Treaty. Maine. https://maineanencyclopedia.com/webster-ashburton-treaty/.

"What is an oil sand?" Fuel Chemistry Division. https://www.ems.psu.edu/~pisupati/ACSOutreach/Oil_Sands.html.

"What is Bounty Land?" Fold3HQ. https://blog.fold3.com/what-is-bounty-land/.

"What is Floating Rate Certificate of Deposit (FRCD)?" The Law Dictionary. https://thelawdictionary.org/floating-rate-certificate-of-deposit-frcd/.

Wheeler, Edmund. *The History of Newport, New Hampshire from 1776 to 1878 with a Genealogical Register with Steel and Wood Engravings.* Concord: Republican Press Organization. 1879.

Wheelock, Rev. Eleazar." Wheelock Genealogy. http://www.wheelockgenealogy.com/pages/ew_bio.htm.

Wikimedia Commons contributors. "File: Anson Jones House.jpg." *Wikimedia Commons, the free media repository.* https://commons.wikimedia.org/w/index.php?title=File:Anson_Jones_House.jpg&oldid=351841662.

Wikipedia contributors, (accessed December 9, 2019).

Wikipedia contributors. *Wikipedia, The Free Encyclopedia.* "32nd parallel north." https://en.wikipedia.org/w/index.php?title=32nd_parallel_north&oldid=898205484.

- "Abolitionism." https://en.wikipedia.org/w/index.php?title=Abolitionism&oldid=916505228.
- "Jones, Anson." *Wikipedia, The Free Encyclopedia.* https://en.wikipedia.org/w/index.php?title=Anson_Jones&oldid=926165194.
- "Brazos River." https://en.wikipedia.org/w/index.php?title=Brazos_River&oldid=898298795.
- "Brazos Valley." https://en.wikipedia.org/w/index.php?title=Brazos_Valley&oldid= 852254258.

- "Buchanan, James." https://en.wikipedia.org/w/index.php?title=James_Buchanan&oldid=911835953.
- "Burned-over district." https://en.wikipedia.org/w/index.php?title=Burned-over_district&oldid=900268582.
- "Cameron County, Texas." https://en.wikipedia.org/w/index.php?title=Cameron_County,_Texas&oldid=915982665.
- "Canopus." https://en.wikipedia.org/w/index.php?title=Canopus&oldid=910911540.
- "clapboard (architecture)." https://en.wikipedia.org/w/index.php?title=Clapboard_(architecture)&oldid=894373139.
- "codification." https://en.wikipedia.org/w/index.php?title=Codification&oldid=888189921.
- "Commentaries on the Laws of England." https://en.wikipedia.org/w/index.php?title= Commentaries_on_the_Laws_of_England&oldid=910466893.
- "common school." https://en.wikipedia.org/w/index.php?title=Common_school&oldid=871899693.
- "Congregational Christian Churches." https://en.wikipedia.org/w/index.php?title= Congregational_Christian_Churches&oldid=900537411.
- "Cross Timbers." https://en.wikipedia.org/w/index.php?title=Cross_Timbers&oldid=905889434.
- "Cypress, Texas." https://en.wikipedia.org/w/index.php?title=Cypress,_Texas&oldid=906075912.
- "embarrassment." https://en.wikipedia.org/w/index.php?title=Embarrassment&oldid= 907181637.
- "Finney, Charles Grandison." https://en.wikipedia.org/w/index.php?title=Charles_Grandison_Finney&oldid=911674823.
- "Francis Lubbock." https://en.wikipedia.org/w/index.php?title=Francis_Lubbock&oldid=915350497.
- "Gilmer, Thomas Walker." https://en.wikipedia.org/w/index.php?title= Thomas_Walker_Gilmer&oldid=90190129.
- "Hale, Horatio." https://en.wikipedia.org/w/index.php?title=Horatio_Hale&oldid=904685001.
- "History of slavery in Texas." https://en.wikipedia.org/w/index.php?title=History_of_slavery_in_Texas&oldid=929174021.
- "hot air engine." https://en.wikipedia.org/w/index.php?title=Hot_air_engine&oldid=905264692.
- "house slave." https://en.wikipedia.org/w/index.php?title=House_slave&oldid=902276692.
- "Johnstown (city), New York." https://en.wikipedia.org/w/index.php?title=

- Johnstown_(city),_New_York&oldid=.
- "Joint resolution." https://en.wikipedia.org/w/index.php?title=Joint_resolution&oldid=892816000.
- "Jones, Anson." https://en.wikipedia.org/w/index.php?title=Anson_Jones&oldid=915235930.
- "Justice of the Peace." https://en.wikipedia.org/w/index.php?title=Justice_of_the_peace&oldid=910760854.
- "Kennebec River." https://en.wikipedia.org/w/index.php?title=Kennebec_River&oldid=908936586.
- "lathe." https://en.wikipedia.org/w/index.php?title=Lathe&oldid=909723009.
- "Marcy, William L." https://en.wikipedia.org/w/index.php?title=William_L._Marcy&oldid=907542022.
- "master (naval)." https://en.wikipedia.org/w/index.php?title=Master_(naval)&oldid=892470945.
- "Newport, Henry 3rd Earl of Bradford." https://en.wikipedia.org/w/index.php?title=Henry_Newport,_3rd_Earl_of_Bradford&oldid=901137107.
- "Newport, New Hampshire." https://en.wikipedia.org/w/index.php?title=Newport,_New_Hampshire&oldid=902273058.
- "Pacific Railroad Acts." https://en.wikipedia.org/w/index.php?title=Pacific_Railroad_Acts&oldid=912203871.
- "Pakenham, Richard." https://en.wikipedia.org/w/index.php?title=Richard_Pakenham&oldid=893843033.
- "People's Party (United States)." https://en.wikipedia.org/wiki/People%27s_Party_(United_States).
- "Perrysburg, Ohio." https://en.wikipedia.org/w/index.php?title=Perrysburg,_Ohio&oldid=905297020.
- "Plat." https://en.wikipedia.org/w/index.php?title=Plat&oldid=910604444.
- "Pro tempore." https://en.wikipedia.org/w/index.php?title=Pro_tempore&oldid=877065335.
- "Red River of the South." https://en.wikipedia.org/w/index.php?title=Red_River_of_the_South&oldid=908559612.
- "rotary saw." https://en.wikipedia.org/w/index.php?title=Rotary_saw&oldid=787794189.
- "Saint-Jean-Baptiste Day." https://en.wikipedia.org/w/index.php?title=Saint-Jean-Baptiste_Day&oldid=904921238.
- "Saint Lawrence River." https://en.wikipedia.org/w/index.php?title=Saint_Lawrence_River&oldid=908112116.
- "Sanbornton, New Hampshire." https://en.wikipedia.org/w/index.php?title=

Sanbornton,_New_Hampshire&oldid=905495344.

- "Second Great Awakening. " https://en.wikipedia.org/w/index.php?title= Second_Great_Awakening&oldid=913206250.
- "Section (United States land surveying)." https://en.wikipedia.org/w/index.php?title= Section_(United_States_land_surveying)&oldid=888600809.
- "Sirius. " https://en.wikipedia.org/w/index.php?title=Sirius&oldid=907586564.
- "Skowhegan, Maine." https://en.wikipedia.org/w/index.php?title=Skowhegan,_Maine&oldid=911702692.
- "Spiritual Wifery." https://en.wikipedia.org/w/index.php?title=Spiritual_wifery&oldid=883279784.
- "Texas in the American Civil War." https://en.wikipedia.org/w/index.php?title=Texas_in_the_American_Civil_War&oldid=927219267.
- "Vassar College." https://en.wikipedia.org/w/index.php?title=Vassar_College&oldid=911019319.
- "Summerland, California." https://en.wikipedia.org/w/index.php?title=Summerland,_California&oldid=846316765.

Wilentz, Sean. *The Rise of American Democracy: Jefferson to Lincoln.* New York: W.W. Horton and Company. 2008.

William G. Hale Papers, 1819-1931. Box 2D52. Letters and Legal Papers: 1819-1848. The Dolph Briscoe Center for American History. The University of Texas at Austin.

Winkler, Ernest William, ed. *Journal of the Secession Convention of Texas 1861.* Edited from the original in the Department of State. Austin: Texas Library and Historical Commission. 1912.

Wooster, Ralph A. "Notes on Texas' Largest Slaveholders, 1860." *The Southwestern Historical Quarterly.* Vol. 65, No. 1. July 1961. Texas State Historical Association.

"World of Sam Houston, The." The Texas State Library and Archives. https://www.tsl.texas.gov/exhibits/presidents/houston2/mrprez.html.

Year: 1810; Census Place: Newport, Cheshire, New Hampshire; Roll: 23; Page: 201; Image: 00144; Family History Library Film: 0218684.

Young, Dr. S. O. *Thumb-Nail History of Houston.* Houston: Rein & Sons Company. 1912.

INDEX

abolitionist 35, 56, 435
Allen, Albert G 1, 4
Allen, David xi, 1, 3, 8, 16, 28, 231, 296
Allen, David Jr. 1, 4, 5, 28, 231, 297
Allen, Ebenezer
  Childhood in Newport, New Hampshire 1-8
  Dartmouth College 9-13
  Teaching at Lewiston Academy 14-16
  Studying the Law 16-19
  Law Practice in Maine 20-21
  Sylvinia Morse 22-23
  James T. Leavitt 23-24
  Teaching at The Clarksville Academy 37-38
  Texas Lawyer 38-42
  Texas Freemasonry 168-169
  Sam Houston's Attorney General 64-65
  Republic of Texas Attorney General and Secretary of State 65-68
  Role in Annexation 74-96
  State of Texas Attorney General 115-124
  Galveston and Red River Railway Company 128-137
  The Houston and Texas Central Railroad 139-159
  Texas Lawyer 160-168
  Spiritualism 182-197
  Galveston and the Civil War 202-204
  Creuzbaur and the Sea King 213-226
  The Engineer Bureau 220-223
  Death 225-236
Allen, Ebenezer Jr. xviii, 236-238, 243-245, 297, 298
Allen, Edward C., Allen, Edward xviii, 233, 236-238, 240, 295, 298
Allen, Elvira 1
Allen, Frederick (Fred) xviii, 232, 236-238, 241-243, 296, 298
Allen, Hannah xi, 1, 3, 182, 297
Allen, Hannah Cordelia 1, 4, 447, 452
Allen, Harriet 1, 4
Allen, Harvey H. 115, 133, 140, 153, 422
Allen, Henry 35, 56, 435
Allen, John M 43, 45, 377
Allen, Nahum Wilcox 1, 4
Allen, Roxanna 1
Allen, Samuel 1, 8
Allen, Samuel Johnson 1, 4, 231
Allen, Sylvania Josephine xi, xiv, 22-24, 29, 30, 126, 182, 203, 234, 236-238,
    243-247, 247, 274, 287, 289, 290, 295-298, 367, 368, 474
Allen, Texas 247, 249, 250

Allen, Uriah Wilcox 1, 4
Allen, William 1, 4
Allen, William Pitt 197, 204, 215, 231, 236, 238-240, 246, 274, 275, 287, 295, 297, 298
Anaconda Plan 202
Anderson, Kenneth Lewis 45, 67, 378
annexation ix, xii. xiv, xvi, xvii, 45, 47, 48, 50-53, 55-64, 66, 67, 70-74, 76-78, 80, 81, 83-87, 89, 91, 93, 94, 97, 98, 101, 102,105-113, 165, 198, 252-254, 278, 296, 369, 377-382, 384, 385, 389, 390, 391-395, 398, 400-403, 417, 449, 470
Aransas County, Texas 125
Aransas, Texas 126
arsenal 201, 204, 211
Athens Post 150
Attorney General, Republic of Texas xii, 45, 64, 67, 75, 93, 100, 103, 105, 118-120, 165, 296, 298, 378, 392, 408, 412
Attorney General, State of Texas xii, 36, 115, 116, 118, 119, 121, 123, 124, 134, 171, 173, 226, 261, 273, 296, 297, 378, 408, 410, 414
Austin, Stephen 37, 42, 45, 49, 127, 372, 373, 378, 385, 393, 411, 418, 436, 443
Austin, Texas 36, 52, 65, 91, 107, 116, 121, 134, 136, 141, 142, 220, 276, 277, 285, 300, 393, 395, 405, 406, 443-445, 451, 454
Baker, Moseley xiii, 183, 409, 441, 442
Baker, William R. xv, 133, 140, 141, 158, 234, 246, 289-293, 423, 430, 474
Baldwin, Judge Harvey 144, 171, 194, 290
Belgium 52, 407
Benton, Thomas Hart 61, 71-73, 252, 390
black vomit 181
Blackstone's Commentaries 18, 364
Blockade, Federal Blockade, Proclamation of Blockade against Southern Ports xiv, 201, 202, 205, 209-211, 215, 219, 223, 236
Bloomfield, Maine 22, 23, 240, 295, 367
Board of Commissioners 152
Board of Land Commissioners 32, 34, 296
Brazos and Galveston Railroad 127
Brazos River 126, 141, 144, 150, 386, 397, 411, 416, 423-426, 441
Brazos Valley, Texas 127, 416
Bremond, Paul xvi, xiii, 115, 133, 139-141, 143, 144, 149, 151-153, 157, 158, 182, 183, 247, 289, 284, 409, 417
Brenham, Texas 81, 184, 443
Britain, British, England, Great Britain 10, 25, 26, 38, 50, 52, 53, 54-59, 61, 63, 67, 73, 74, 100, 101, 121, 198, 203, 209, 360, 362-365, 378, 383, 384, 385, 387, 389, 390, 391, 392, 395
Britten, Emma Hardinge 182
Bryan, Texas 148
Buchanan, James 75, 95, 98, 96, 399
Buffalo Bayou, Brazos, and Colorado Railway Company 128, 134, 138, 145, 149, 401, 416-419
Buffalo Bayou, Texas 212, 422

Burned-over district 15, 16, 175, 364, 437
Burnet, David G. 45, 391, 405
Burrell, I. S. 207
Calhoun, John C. 60-62, 70-72, 75, 389, 398
Calvert, Texas 148
Campbell's Bayou, Texas 443
Cass, Lewis 56, 386
Catlett, Fairfax 50, 390
Cedar Point tract 245, 246
Chambodut, Father Louis C. M. 205
charge d'affaires 50, 52, 55-57, 62, 64, 72, 74, 75, 80, 93, 95, 98, 100, 103, 380, 381, 382, 386, 385, 392, 395, 397, 400, 402
Chase, Salmon Portland xiii, 12, 13, 35, 171, 297
Civil War ix, xiii, xiv, xvii, xviii,4, 31, 36, 45, 126, 138, 146, 148, 160, 168, 169, 198, 201, 204, 209-212, 223, 234, 237-239, 245, 371, 376, 388, 395, 399, 401, 410, 416, 421, 436, 444-446, 449, 451, 453, 456
Civilian and Gazette 169
Civilian and Gazette Weekly, The 180
clairvoyant 185, 186, 443
Clark, Edward 201, 445
Clark, Orville 141, 144
Clarksville Academy xii, 37
Clarksville Female Academy 31, 371, 375
Clarksville Masonic Lodge 296
Clarksville, Texas xi, xvi, 30, 33, 37, 39, 41, 42, 44, 46, 64, 65, 114, 116, 295, 296, 370, 371, 375, 386, 408
Coffee's Station, Texas 258, 418
Collin County, Texas 124, 247-250
Committee of Public Protection 203
Committee of Public Safety xiv, 202, 203, 204, 297, 446
Committee on Roads and Canals 137
communication with departed spirits 175, 180, 181
Confederacy, Confederate, Confederation xiv, xviii, 36, 37, 46, 61, 147, 168, 201-214, 218-220, 222, 224, 229, 230, 232-236, 246, 278-281, 283, 284, 286, 287, 289-293, 298, 444, 445, 447, 448, 449, 450, 452, 454, 456, 473, 474
Confederate Army 203, 206, 207, 212, 215, 219, 224, 381, 109, 444, 445, 448-450, 453
Confederate Congress 210, 211, 213, 215, 284
Confederate Engineer Bureau xiv, 212, 213, 219-221, 223, 234, 236, 298
Confederate Secret Service 210, 222
Convention
    Annexation xii, 76, 80-87, 89, 91, 253-255, 276, 277, 296, 372, 382, 395, 408, 412
    Secession xiv, 199-201, 203-205, 278, 282, 284, 286, 375, 394, 412, 444, 445, 449
    Others 43, 44, 69, 74, 123, 134, 380, 393, 408, 410, 436, 451
Converse, Sherman 122
Cook, Joseph Jarvis 448

Cooke, William Gordon 45, 77, 399
Corps of Engineers 220
Corsicana, Texas 140, 148, 247
cottonclad, cotton clad 208
cotton, cotton-growing, cotton press, cotton trade 6, 25, 26, 31, 53, 56, 59, 127, 198, 199, 202, 204, 216, 243, 223, 376, 386, 401, 407, 411, 412, 416-418, 420, 451
Cottonwood Creek, Collin County, Texas xviii, 246
Court of the State 20
Creuzbaur, Robert xiv, xviii, 213-223, 298, 451
Crosby, Stephen 123, 265
Cross Timbers, Texas 122
Croydon Turnpike, New Hampshire 1, 6, 356, 360
CSS *Bayou City* 208, 449
CSS *H. L. Hunley* 219, 224
CSS *Neptune* 🗆🗆⊙
CSS *Teaser* 215, 217, 452
Cushing, Edward Hopkins 35, 152
cyanide 231, 232, 235
cyanosis 230, 231
Cypress, Texas 145-147, 426
Daingerfield, William Henry 96, 402
Dallas Daily Herald, The, Dallas Herald 115, 147, 409
Dallas Weekly Herald 153, 154
Dartmouth College iv, xi. xvi, 4, 9, 10, 14, 16, 21, 27, 35, 36, 171, 295, 297, 354, 358, 361, 366, 447, 452, 620
Davis, Jefferson 36, 201, 210, 224, 447, 448, 450
de Saligny, Alphonse 74
de Saligny, Dubois 398
de Santa Anna, Antonio Lopez 43, 49, 53-56, 63, 295, 383-388, 403, 416, 418, 441
Del Norte Company 68
Democratic Party, Democrats 48, 50, 62, 69-72, 74, 120, 199, 297, 369, 386, 390, 399, 408, 410, 412, 451, 451, 462
Democratic Telegraph and Texas Register 117, 132, 140
Denison, Texas 148, 247, 250
Diplomatic Act of 1844 63, 391
Donelson, Andrew Jackson xii, xvii, 62, 63, 74-81, 83, 85-87, 90-95, 97-103, 105-111, 113, 390, 391, 400
Dyer, Abia xvi, 39, 40
Eagle, Henry 206
Ebenezer Allen engine xviii, 150, 151, 297
Edes, Amasa xi, 4, 16, 18, 20, 21, 295, 357, 358
Eighteenth Texas Cavalry Regiment (Darnell's Regiment) 237
Elliot, Charles 55, 74, 79, 80, 88, 110, 385
Emancipation 56, 57, 199, 224
Evans, A. H. 116, 118, 165, 410, 457
Eve, Joseph 52, 381

Everett, Edward 56, 387
Father of Texas Education 52
Federal Court at Galveston 118, 161
Fisher, Henry F. 133, 140, 422
Flint, Michah P. 163
Florida 47, 209, 239
Flournoy, George M. 120, 200, 445
Force, A. E. xiii, 194, 195
Force, Henry 194
Ford, John S. 200, 203, 204, 444, 445, 451
Fort Bankhead, Galveston, Texas 206, 448
Fort Point, Galveston, Texas 206, 448
Fort Sumter, Charleston, South Carolina 201, 298
Forty-Second Massachusetts Infantry 208
Foster, Thomas Gales 178, 179
Fox, Kate and Margaret 175, 441
France 52, 56, 59, 63, 67, 73, 76, 100, 102, 121, 378, 391, 392, 395, 403
Fred Allen Company xviii, 241-243
Free Masons, Freemason, Mason xii, xviii, 7, 37, 42-46, 227, 228, 230, 232, 235, 245, 296, 372, 376, 408, 433
free-soil 71,178, 369
Fretwell, John xiv, 211-213, 222
Friendship Lodge No. 16 43, 46, 296
Galveston and Red River Railroad, Galveston and Red River Railroad Company 128, 131-134, 137, 139-141, 143-145, 150, 171, 247, 258, 297, 471
Galveston Bay 127, 131, 137, 146, 206, 258, 380, 401, 443
Galveston City Directory 238, 241, 243, 246
Galveston Daily News, The 227, 238, 241, 244, 245
Galveston Civilian 135, 205
Galveston News 89, 134, 154
Galveston Weekly News 150
Galveston, Texas, Galveston Island ix, xiii, xiv, xvii, 35-37, 44, 23, 56, 68, 74, 81, 82, 85, 90, 91, 95-99, 111, 115, 117, 118, 127, 128, 131-137, 139, 143, 166, 168, 169, 170, 171, 173, 180-184, 187, 188, 192-194, 198, 202-208, 211, 212, 223, 227, 235, 236, 238, 242-245, 258, 296-299, 362, 365, 377, 380, 386, 395, 401, 402, 405, 407, 409, 415-419,436, 443, 444, 447-450, 452
Gem Saloon, Richmond, Virginia xviii, 225, 229, 230
German American, German, Germany 169, 198, 244, 245, 422
Gilmer, Thomas Walker 56, 57, 387, 388
Goliad, Texas 53, 441
Gorda, Montgomery County, California 239
Grand Lodge of Louisiana 42
Grand Lodge of Texas 42-46, 377
Grand Master 42, 44, 168, 372, 377
Gray, Edwin Fairfax 379
Great Hurricane and Flood of 1900 ix, 243, 245
Green, Duff xii, 56, 68, 69, 106, 107, 386
Green, Thomas 208, 449, 452

Gulf of Mexico 103, 104, 125, 245, 443
gunboat 211, 213, 214, 448, 454
Hale, Horatio   19, 365
Hale, Sarah Joseph xi, 7, 356, 361, 363
Hale, William G. xiii, xvii, 19, 125, 126, 137, 160-162, 167, 168, 173, 296, 300, 362, 365
Hamilton, Andrew Jackson 117, 118, 120, 168, 410
Hanover, New Hampshire 10, 354, 362
Harrisburg and Brazos Rail Road 127
Harrisburg Rail Road and Trading Company 416
Harrisburg, Texas 127, 128, 138, 407, 416
Hebert, Paul Octave 447
Hedgcoxe, Henry O. 122, 123, 124
Heller's Galveston Directory 243
Hempstead, Texas 146, 147,   157, 426
Henderson, James Pinckney xvi, 45, 59-61, 110, 114, 120, 253, 378, 388, 444
Hill, George W. 67, 395
Hockley, George 55, 385
Hockley, Texas 146, 147, 428
Holland 52
Holland, John H. 42, 377
Holland Lodge 42, 43
Hollywood Cemetery, Richmond, Virginia xiv, 228, 232, 233, 298, 456
House, Thomas William xvii, 139, 140, 144, 297, 421, 422
Houston and Texas Central Railroad, The xiii, xvii, 134, 136, 139, 141, 143, 145, 147-151, 153, 154, 156-158, 173, 183, 246-250, 289, 291, 297, 298, 408, 419, 421-423, 426-428, 430
Houston Morning Star 143
Houston Tap Road Company, Houston Tap and Brazoria 128, 134, 145
Houston Telegraph 35, 136, 144, 177, 238
Houston, Samuel xii, xiii, xvi, xvii, 36, 43, 45, 48, 54-56, 58, 59, 61-66, 72, 81, 85-87, 90, 106-108, 111, 127, 168, 161, 162, 199-205, 245, 245, 252, 295, 296, 373, 378-382, 384-386, 388, 392-394, 395, 412, 418, 436, 441, 442, 444, 445, 450-452, 454
Houston, Texas 112, 115, 127, 133-137, 139-147, 149, 150, 162, 171, 178, 179, 182, 183, 198, 202, 205, 219, 238, 293, 297, 393, 394, 405, 407, 409, 417, 419, 422, 423, 426, 427, 428, 436, 451, 458
Hunley, Horace L. 219
Hunt, Memucan 50, 380
Hutchins, W. J. 133, 138, 140, 141, 149, 419
impeachment xiii, 164, 166, 401, 441
impressed 190, 214
Jackson, Andrew 18, 26, 48-50, 62, 369, 380, 386, 391
Jacksonian Democracy 18, 390
Johnson, Joseph 15, 222
Johnstown, New York 359
joint resolution xii, xiv, 63, 66, 69-73, 75, 77-81, 91, 93, 93, 252-254, 256, 261, 266, 278, 296, 391, 398, 471

Jones, Anson xii, xviii, 35, 42, 43, 45, 58, 61, 62, 64, 65, 66, 67, 68, 72, 74, 76-82, 84-88, 91, 95-100, 105-107, 110-112, 114, 127, 158, 168, 222, 253, 296, 372, 385, 391, 392, 395, 399
Kaufman, David Spangler 96, 402, 403
Kennebec River 23, 24, 30, 354, 367
Kennedy, William 67, 170
Killingworth, Connecticut 1, 5, 360
Kuhn's Wharf, Galveston, Texas 207, 208, 448
La Branche, Alcee Louis 50, 380
La Grange Monument 136
La Vaca (Lavaca), Texas 211,
Lafitte, Jean xiii, 183, 184, 443
Lamar, Mirabeau B. xii, xvi, 45, 51, 52, 66, 380, 394, 412, 436
Latimer, Albert Hamilton 115, 408
league 33, 246, 422, 442
Leavitt, Hannah B. 238, 245, 298, 311, 460, 461, 475
Leavitt, James T. xi, 23, 24, 27, 295, 368
Lee, Robert E. 210, 224, 298
Lee, William D. 95, 402
Leon Pioneer, The 140
Lewiston Academy xvi, 14, 15
Lewiston, New York xi, 15, 16, 182, 295, 354
Lincecum, Dr. Gideon 183, 187, 442, 443
Lincoln, Abraham 7, 13, 18, 35, 199, 201, 205, 224
Linwood House, Richmond, Virginia 225, 229
Lone Star State vi, 110, 150, 178
Longpoint, Texas 442
Louisiana 30, 31, 47, 113, 134, 162, 222, 224, 355, 359, 417, 447, 449, 453, 474
Magruder, John Bankhead 208, 212, 219, 448, 449, 452
Maine iv, ix, xi, xvi, 5, 19-24, 27, 28, 30, 52, 144, 176, 177, 226, 237, 238, 240, 245, 279, 295, 298, 354, 358, 366, 368, 369, 459
Malone, E. 203
manifestations 95, 102, 187, 189
Marcy, William L. 96, 112, 113, 403
Martin, Bennett H. 38, 373
Masonic Harmony Lodge No. 6, A. F. & A.M., Masonic Lodge, Harmony Masonic Lodge xiii, 10, 44, 168, 169
Massachusetts 8, 19, 24, 27, 36, 177, 279, 357, 362, 372, 387
Matagorda Island, Texas 125, 211, 450
Maury, Matthew F. 215, 217, 218
McCulloch, Benjamin 203
McKenzie Institute 31, 39, 371
McKinney, Texas 148, 247, 298
McKinney, Thomas F. 116, 117, 172, 377, 386, 411
medium 176, 177, 183, 184, 186, 188, 189, 191, 192, 194, 195
Mexico, Mexican 25, 27, 36-38, 42, 43, 47-56, 59, 63, 66, 68, 70, 71, 74, 78, 79, 88-91, 94, 97-106, 109, 112-114, 126, 163, 169, 198, 252, 253, 272, 279, 295-297, 369, 372, 373, 378, 379, 383-387, 389, 390, 393, 395, 399, 402-405, 408,

412, 415, 417, 426, 436, 442, 443, 449, 448, 451, 453
Mier Expedition 54, 383, 385, 404, 405
Miller, Washington D. 107, 108, 221, 422, 454
Millican, Texas 147, 148, 247, 426, 427
Mississippi and Pacific Act 138
Mississippi River 30, 128, 202, 222, 236, 355, 449, 452, 453
Moore, Francis Jr. 127, 136, 392
Moore, John C. 202
Morrison & Fourmy's General Directory of the City of Galveston 241, 243
Morse, Hannah B. 23, 24, 245
Morse, Sylvinia xi, 22, 23, 295
Mr. Gough, Proprietor of Gem Saloon 225, 229
Mustang Island, Texas 125
Negroes 41, 149, 163
New Hampshire xi, xvi, xviii, 1, 3, 5, 6, 9, 10, 16, 19, 27, 35-37, 170, 177, 279, 295-297, 354, 356-359, 360, 362, 366, 368, 455
New Orleans Crescent 143
New Orleans, Louisiana 90, 30, 31, 35, 43, 86, 103, 116, 134, 192, 202, 205, 239, 365, 372, 400, 405, 417
New York xi, 5, 9, 14-17, 19, 143, 144, 165, 171, 175, 177, 182, 203, 279, 295, 354, 359, 361, 364, 369, 372, 403, 407, 417, 436, 437, 441
New York City, New York 19, 26, 112, 143, 165, 171, 179, 203, 220, 407, 417, 451
New York Land Company 165
Newport Academy 3-5, 16, 358
Newport, New Hampshire xi, xvi, 1, 3-8, 16, 19, 21, 295-297, 354, 356, 358--360, 365
Nichols, Ebenezer B. 204, 417
non-slaveholders 198
Northern Democrats 70, 71
Northern Standard, The, Clarksville Northern Standard 31, 37, 39-42, 64, 65, 116
Nueces River 70
Ochiltree, William Beck 45, 67, 395
Opelousas Patriot, The 144
Orono, Maine xi, 5, 20, 21, 22, 296, 366
Packenham, Richard 55
Panic of 1837, The xi, xvi, 24-27, 295, 369
Paschal, George W. 116, 118, 161
Penobscot County, Maine xvi, 21, 22, 366
Penobscot River, Maine 21
Perrysburg, Ohio 4, 5, 358, 447, 452
Peters, William S. 121, 122, 266, 267
Peters' Colony ix, xii, xiv, 121, 122, 124, 160, 165, 236, 261, 266, 267, 269, 295, 365, 406, 471
physical manifestations, manifestations 94, 101, 186, 188, 189, 190, 193
plantation society 60, 170, 198
planters 58, 169, 170, 199
Polk, James Knox xii, xvi, 62, 63, 66, 69-75, 91, 95-98, 100, 103, 106, 109, 111,

112, 114, 165, 253, 296, 389, 390, 397, 400, 402, 403
Potomac River 60, 387
Railroad Convention 134
Rains, Gabriel iii, xiv, xviii, 209, 210
Randolph, George W. 210
Raymond, Charles H. 72, 73, 397
re-annexation xii, 47, 48
Red River County 31, 33, 34, 67, 117, 296, 370, 380, 408,
Red River of the South, Texas Red River, Red River vi, ix, 30, 31, 121, 131, 248, 250, 266, 355, 370, 380, 412, 418, 449
Refugio, Texas 53
Reily, James 52, 381, 382
religion 5, 12, 15, 170, 174, 175, 182, 442
Renshaw, William B. 206-208
Republican Party, Republicans 120, 199
Rhine, Isaac 248, 249
Rice, William Marsh 127, 135, 138, 140, 141, 149, 153, 289, 417
Richardson, Sid Williams 416
Richardson, Willard 134-137
Richmond Dispatch 214 215, 225
Richmond Examiner, The 225, 226, 229, 230
Richmond, Virginia xviii, 210, 214, 215, 224, 230, 232, 233, 235, 236, 238, 287, 293, 298, 452, 454, 456
Rio Grande River 35, 43, 51, 54, 63, 70, 109, 113, 114, 126, 198, 383
Rives, Alfred L. xvii, 220-222
Roberts, Oran M. 200, 444
Robertson County, Texas 133, 140, 143, 397, 416
Robertson, John C. 203, 446
Robinson, James W. 54, 55, 384
Rusk, Thomas Jefferson 43, 45, 91, 111, 117, 255, 378
Sabine River 47, 183, 380
Saint Lawrence River iv, 354, 363
Saint-Jean-Baptiste Day 434
San Antonio, Texas 35, 43, 53, 54, 201, 204, 383, 416, 446
Sanbornton, New Hampshire 5, 359
Sanxay, Richard D. 225, 229, 230
Schrimpf, J. W. 140, 423
Scott, Winfield 202
Scurry, William R. 45, 208, 449, 450
Sea King 213-215, 218
Secession Convention 199, 200, 203-205, 395, 410, 412, 444, 445, 449
Secession, secede xiii, xiv, 35, 63, 198-205, 282, 284, 297, 376, 389, 410, 412, 445, 446
Second Great Awakening 16, 175, 364, 437, 438
Secretary of State, Republic of Texas xii, 45, 56, 58, 60, 61, 64, 66, 67, 69, 72, 74, 76, 77, 81, 82, 95, 98, 106, 118, 159, 226, 296, 373, 378, 389, 392, 393, 412
Secretary of State, State of Texas 412, 454
Seddon, J. A. 213, 220, 222

Shea, Daniel D 211, 212, 450
Sheldon, Henry 194
Sherman, Sidney xii, 90, 97, 98, 127, 128, 138, 204, 401, 417
sickly season 181
Singer, Edgar C. xiv, 211-213, 222
Skowhegan, Somerset County, Maine xi, 22-24, 30, 238, 295, 298, 299, 354, 367-369
Slack, Henry Richmond 225, 229, 230, 235
Slavery, slaves xiii, 25, 35, 36, 549 50, 52-61, 63, 70-72, 149, 162-164, 169-171, 173, 182, 198-200, 203, 204, 224, 255, 257, 276, 278, 279-282, 298, 369, 373, 375, 385-389, 408, 410, 412, 417, 435, 442, 451
slave-soil 71
Smith, Ashbel 67, 76, 96, 112, 296, 394, 407
Smith, E. Kirby 221-223, 453, 454
Smith, Leon 208, 449
Solon, Maine 20, 22, 23, 295, 368
Somerset County, Maine v, xvi, 22, 23, 24, 238, 295, 298, 354, 368, 369
Somervell Expedition 54, 383
South Carolina 199, 205, 219, 233, 234, 292, 298, 389, 457, 468
Southern Pacific Railroad Company 128, 138, 274
South-Western American 124, 133, 134
spirits 174-176, 180, 182, 185, 186, 193, 196
Spiritual Register 177
Spiritual Telegraph 182, 187, 194
Spiritual, Spiritualism, Spiritualist xiii, xiv, xviii, 15, 16, 170, 174-183, 187, 188, 193, 194, 196, 197, 239, 274, 275, 297, 409, 437, 438, 441, 472
Springfield, Texas 140, 145
St. Joseph Island, Texas xiii, xvii, 125, 223, 415, 416
Stafford, J. S. xiii, 162-164
Stafford, William 418
states' rights 53, 167, 198, 279, 280, 389, 444
Stillwater River 21, 22
Stockton, Robert F. xii, 90, 97, 98, 100, 401, 402
Stone, Ada xiii, 187-189, 191-193
Stuart, Hamilton 136
Sugar River 6
Summerland, California xviii, 239, 246, 274, 275
Swain, William Jesse 89, 401
Telegraph and Texas Register 140
Terrell, George Whitfield 64, 120, 392, 446
Texan Santa Fe expedition 66, 394, 405
Texas Agricultural, Commercial, and Manufacturing Company 122
Texas Congress 165, 252, 253, 266, 295, 370, 382, 393, 395, 397, 401, 408, 411, 412, 419, 441, 442, 445, 449, 454
Texas Emigration and Land Company 122, 123, 165, 261, 266
Texas Freemasonry xii, 37, 42, 44
Texas Hill Country 169
Texas Land Company 68

Texas Land Office, Texas General Land Office 32, 34, 45, 213, 214, 262, 264, 265, 267-273, 299, 396, 405, 406, 451
Texas Rail Road, Navigation, and Banking Company 65, 127, 393, 441
Texas State Gazette 215
Texas Supreme Court 36, 41, 44, 118, 200, 246, 247, 386, 412, 444
Texas True Evangelist 178
Texas Twenty-sixth Regiment (Debray's Regiment) 237
Texas Senate 44, 59, 379, 393, 408, 410, 445
Texas Western Railroad 137, 138
Thomas, Isaac. 163
Thompson, Waddy 56, 387
Thumb-Nail History of Houston 158
Times-Picayune, The 36, 89, 157
Tod, John Grant, Sr. 127, 138, 477
Todd, William Smith xvii, 41, 42, 65, 116, 375, 410
Torpedo xviii, 209, 210, 212, 213, 217, 219-223, 452
Torpedo Bureau ix, xiv, xviii, 209, 210, 213, 215, 222, 223
Town of Allen, Texas xiv, xviii, 247, 249, 250, 298, 302
Trans-Mississippi Department 220, 223, 453
Trinity River 126, 132, 141, 247, 266, 469
Tyler, John xii, xvi, 53, 56, 57, 59-62, 66, 68-72, 74, 78, 253, 296, 362, 387, 389, 391, 409, 400
union, unionist, Union lxiv, xvii, 4, 6, 8, 35-37, 48, 50, 54, 72, 73, 76, 80, 91, 94, 95, 101-106, 110, 114, 120, 126, 129, 132, 147, 199-211, 213, 214, 219, 220, 224, 230, 232, 234-237, 254-257, 276, 278, 280, 284, 290, 296-298, 355, 376, 382, 389, 402, 408, 410, 412, 436, 444, 448, 449, 453, 454, 458, 459, 474
Union Bank of Louisiana, The xiii, 162-164
United States Census 170, 236, 238, 239, 242, 245, 298, 435
United States Congress 48, 50, 52, 59, 63, 70, 72-76, 78, 82, 91, 95, 99, 100, 104, 105, 166, 168, 252, 254-257, 296, 398, 399
United States House of Representatives 70-72, 165, 167 168, 252-254, 256, 362, 390, 391, 397, 399, 400, 410. 449
United States Senate 48, 50, 56, 59-63, 66, 70-72, 78, 111, 216, 219, 224, 252, 253, 256, 257, 378, 386, 389-391, 394, 404, 405
United States Supreme Court 10, 13, 161, 164, 165, 171
Upshur, Abel Parker xvi, 56-58, 60, 387, 389
USS *Harriet Lane* 206, 208
USS *Housatonic* 219
USS *Princeton* 60, 387, 389
USS *Santee* 206
USS *South Carolina* 202
USS *Star* 166
USS *Westfield* 208
vacant domain 124, 262, 266, 415
van Alystyne, W. W. 140, 422
van Buren, Martin 26, 50, 51, 53, 369
Van Zandt, Isaac xvi, 52, 56-61, 72, 378, 382, 388, 397
Vassar College 7, 361

Vicksburg and El Paso Railroad Company 138
Vicksburg Daily Whig 149
Victoria Advocate 177
Victoria, Texas 36, 53, 393
Walker, Robert J. 60, 96, 388, 389, 445, 450
Ward, Thomas William 45, 67, 107, 268, 271, 272, 406, 417
Washington City, Texas, Washington, Texas, New Washington 44, 88, 100, 143, 295, 401, 407
Washington County, Texas 416, 443
Washington, DC xii, 5, 50, 52, 56, 60, 68, 72, 86, 88, 93, 95, 96, 104, 107, 114, 171, 232, 297, 369, 378, 380, 381, 382, 385, 391, 397, 402, 403
Washington-on-the-Brazos, Texas 89, 110, 295, 454
Watrous, John C. xiii, 120, 159-161, 164-168, 236, 365
Webb, James 45, 116, 117, 412
Webster, Daniel 10, 35, 53, 362, 381
Webster-Ashburton Treaty 56, 387
Weekly Telegraph, The 151, 152, 177, 179, 180
Wells, James B. 126, 415
Wharton, John Austin 200, 445, 452
Wharton, William Harris 50, 66, 379, 380, 393, 394, 418
Wheelock, Eleazar 9, 10, 34, 362
Whig Party, Whigs 53, 69-71, 199, 369
Williams, Henry Lafayette 239, 274
Williams, Samuel May 116, 117, 169, 171, 173, 377, 385, 386, 411, 412, 436
Yankee ix, 177, 178, 203, 264
Yates, Joseph A. 132, 418, 417
Yell, Archibald 83, 400
Yellow Fever xiii, 181, 182, 395, 442

ENDNOTES

1   A Retrospect Arcturus is the second brightest star in the northern sky. Note by Judith M. Johnson.

2   The St. Lawrence River flows in a roughly north-easterly direction, connecting the Great Lakes with the Atlantic Ocean. It traverses the Canadian provinces of Quebec and Ontario, and is part of the international boundary between Ontario, Canada, and the U.S. state of New York. Wikipedia contributors, *The Free Encyclopedia,* "Saint Lawrence River," *Wikipedia, The Free Encyclopedia,* https://en.wikipedia.org/w/index.php?title=Saint_Lawrence_River&oldid=908112116 (accessed August 20, 2019).

3   Wesserunsett is a lake in western Maine. Note by Judith M. Johnson.

4   Sunapee's mountain is in New Hampshire near Newport. Note by Judith M. Johnson.

5   Dartmouth College is an Ivy League College in Hanover, New Hampshire, Dartmouth College, accessed January 11, 2017, https://home.dartmouth.edu/.

6   The Battle of Bridgewater occurred on July 25, 1812 near Niagara Falls, accessed January 11, 2017, http://www.warof1812-bicentennial.info/newspapers/plattsburghrepublican/pr08131814-pg1-c.php.

7   Lewistown, New York is located in western New York and borders the Niagara River. History of Lewiston, NY, accessed January 11, 2017, http://history.raysplace.com/ny/lewiston-ny.htm.

8   Ermines refers to a rank or office whose ceremonial or official robe is ornamented with ermine fur. Ermine, Merriam-Webster, accessed January 11, 2017, https://www.merriam-webster.com/dictionary/ermine.

9   Somerset is a county in Maine. Note by Judith M. Johnson.

10   Kennebec River flows from Moosehead Lake by Skowhegan, Waterville, Augusta, and Gardiner into the Gulf of Maine. Wikipedia contributors, "Kennebec River," *Wikipedia, The Free Encyclopedia,* https://en.wikipedia.org/w/index.php?title=Kennebec_River&oldid=908936586 (accessed August 20, 2019).

11   The "Father of Waters" is the Mississippi River. Mississippi, The Free Dictionary, accessed January 11, 2017, https://www.thefreedictionary.com/Mississippi.

12   Caribbee refers to the Caribbean Islands. Definitions.net, STANDS4 LLC, 2019. "caribbee." accessed July 26, 2019. https://www.definitions.net/definition/caribbee.

13   Canopus is the brightest star in the Southern constellation of Carina. Wikipedia contributors, "Canopus," *Wikipedia, The Free Encyclopedia,* https://en.wikipedia.org/w/index.php?title=Canopus&oldid=910911540 (accessed August 20, 2019). https://en.wikipedia.org/w/index.php?title=Plagiarism&oldid=5139350

14   Sirius is the brightest star in the Earth's night sky. Wikipedia contributors, "Sirius," *Wikipedia, The Free Encyclopedia,* https://en.wikipedia.org/w/index.php?title=Sirius&oldid=907586564 (accessed August 20, 2019).

15   The "Antarctic Crown" (Corna Australis), "Antares", (Cor Scorpiones), and "Phaet" are visible in most parts of the Union; but Mr. Burritt observes, in his "Classbook of Astronomy" that "Canopus," the principle star in the constellation Argo Navis, cannot, owing to its great southern declination, be seen in the United States He is mistaken, however, for I have often, from my piazza, admired its brilliancy (but little inferior to that of Sirius) while it seemed to hang like a magnificent diamond a few degrees above the southern horizon. A few of the stars belonging to the "Cross" may also be seen, but not the whole of this beautiful constellation, with the dark southern "cloud," for its background. Note by Ebenezer Allen.

16   The Red River is the second-largest river basin in the southern Great Plains. It rises in two branches (forks) in the Texas Panhandle and flows east, where it acts as the border between the states of Texas and Oklahoma. It forms a short border between Texas and Arkansas before entering Arkansas, turning south near Fulton, Arkansas and flowing into Louisiana, where it flows into the Atchafalaya River. The total length of the river is 1,360 miles. Wikipedia contributors, "Red River of the South," *Wikipedia, The Free Encyclopedia,* https://en.wikipedia.org/w/index.php?title=Red_River_of_the_South&oldid=908559612 (accessed August 21, 2019).

17   Loup-cervier is a French word for a civet, fox, or lynx. Note by Judith M. Johnson.

18   Verdure means greenness, especially of flourishing vegetation, and lush green vegetation. Verdure, Merriam-Webster, accessed August 21, 2019, https://www.merriam-webster.com/dictionary/verdure.

19   The phrase, "the voice of the turtle," is a Biblical quote from the Song of Solomon, or Song of Songs, Chapter 2, verse 12. The "turtle" refers to a turtledove. Note by Judith M. Johnson.

20   Prore is a term for the prow of a ship. The prow is the forward-most part of a ship's bow that cuts through the water. The prow is the part of the bow above the waterline. The terms prow and bow are often used interchangeably to describe the most forward part of a ship and its surrounding parts. Prore, Your Dictionary, accessed August 21, 2019, https://www.yourdictionary.com/prore.

21   This poem was published in *Godey's Lady's Book and Magazine*. Mrs. Sarah J. Hale and Louis A. Godey, eds., *Godey's Lady's Book and Magazine* (Philadelphia: Louis A. Godey,1855), Vol. LI from July to December 1855, 510-511. Godey's was the most popular women's magazine of the day. Its editor, Sarah Josepha Hale, famous for writing "Mary had a Little Lamb," was the mother of Allen's law partner, William Hale. Courtesy of Judith M. Johnson, Johnson-Morrow Family Tree, accessed May 20, 2016, Ancestry.com.

CHILDHOOD IN NEWPORT, NEW HAMPSHIRE

22   The Croydon Turnpike Road was incorporated on June 21, 1804. The road went from Lebanon to, Grantham, Croydon, Newport, and Lempster. The road connected to the Second New Hampshire Turnpike in Washington, 34 miles, at an expense of $35,948. The Second New Hampshire Turnpike was chartered in 1799 and completed in 1801. This was the connecting route between Boston and Vermont. accessed February 6, 2017, New Hampshire's Turnpike History, http://www.cowhampshireblog.com/2006/08/23/new-hampshires-turnpike-history/.

23   Edmund Wheeler, *The History of Newport, New Hampshire from 1776 to 1878 with a Genealogical Register with Steel and Wood Engravings* (Concord: Republican Press Organization, 1879), 73.

24   A selectman is one of a board of officials elected in towns of all New England states except Rhode Island to serve as the chief administrative authority of the

town. "Selectman," Merriam-Webster, accessed August 22, 2019, https://www.merriam-webster.com/dictionary/selectman.

25 Wheeler, 287.

26 Wheeler, 206.

27 Wheeler, 288.

28 Year: 1810; Census Place: Newport, Cheshire, New Hampshire; Roll: 23; Page: 201; Image: 00144; Family History Library Film: 0218684, accessed May 20, 2016.

29 Descendants of Gideon Allen, Courtesy of Judith M. Johnson, Johnson-Morrow Family Tree, accessed May 20, 2016, Ancestry.com.

30 James M. Volo and Dorothy Denneen Volo, *Family Life in 19th-Century America*. (Westport: Greenwood Publishing Group, 2007), .

31 A common school was a public school in the United States during the nineteenth century. Horace Mann (1796–1859) was a strong advocate for public education and the common school. In 1837, the state of Massachusetts appointed Mann as the first secretary of the State Board of Education where he began a revival of common school education, the effects of which extended throughout America during the 19th century. Wikipedia contributors, "Common school," Wikipedia contributors, "Common school," *Wikipedia, The Free Encyclopedia*, https://en.wikipedia.org/w/index.php?title=Common_school&oldid=871899693 (accessed August 21, 2019).

32 "Historical Chronology of Newport New Hampshire," accessed May 19, 2016, http://www.newportnh.net/aynnyd/uploaded/pdfs/history_of_newport_20101019.pdf, 17-18.

33 Wheeler, 162-163.

34 "Historical Chronology of Newport, New Hampshire," The Town of Newport, New Hampshire, accessed April 14, 2016, https://www.newportnh.gov/sites/newportnh/files/uploads/historical_chronology_story.pdf, 18.

35 Amasa Edes (1792–1883) was born in Antrim, New Hampshire on March 21, 1792. He spent most of his youth at Peterborough. After he graduated from Dart-

mouth in 1817, Edes read law for one year in the office of Wilson & Porter at Belfast, Maine and two years with James Wilson, senior, at Keene. After the state bar admitted him in 1822, Edes traveled to Newport in 1823 and set up his practice. Colleagues said he had "naturally a legal mind." When Amasa was a young law student, "the more advanced students in the same law office would submit to him cases laid down, in the books for opinion, and that his decisions, from his intuitive sense of justice, were almost uniformly in accordance with those given by the court." During his law career, he was one of the pioneers in the temperance movement and its "earnest advocate." He was also a "warm friend of education," and for several years served as principal of the New Ipswich Academy. He was a trustee of the academy, principal of the Newport Academy, and a member of the superintending school committee of Newport. Edes was a successful lawyer and represented Newport in the state legislature in 1834. He practiced law for over sixty years until his death in 1883. Biography of Samuel H. Edes, Access Genealogy, https://www.accessgenealogy.com/new-hampshire/biography-of-samuel-h-edes.htm, accessed April 14, 2016 and Wheeler, 175-176.

36 D. Hamilton Hurd, ed., *History of Cheshire and Sullivan Counties*, New Hampshire. (Philadelphia: J. W. Lewis & Co., 1886) and Joseph W. Parmalee, *History of Sullivan County*, New Hampshire, 273.

37 Wheeler, 221-222.

38 Perrysburg was situated along the south side of the Maumee River. It was a center for shipbuilding and commerce. In 1833, Perrysburg had a courthouse and jail, a schoolhouse, two stores, two taverns, two physicians, two lawyers, about sixty houses, and two hundred and fifty inhabitants. In 1854, a cholera epidemic decimated the population in which more than one hundred people died. Wikipedia contributors, "Perrysburg, Ohio," *Wikipedia, The Free Encyclopedia,* https://en.wikipedia.org/w/index.php?title=Perrysburg,_Ohio&oldid=905297020, (accessed August 21, 2019).

39 In 1839, Dr. Thomas Sanborn began studies to qualify for the practice of medicine. He received his medical degree from Dartmouth College in 1841 and began practice in Goshen, continuing there until August 1843, when he came to this town. In 1847, he was induced to remove to New London, but soon became satisfied that this change was not for his interest. After an absence of less than one year, he returned to Newport, where the residue or his life was passed. He now, more than ever, bent his whole energies to the duties of his profession, was prompt in reply to calls, and faithful in ministering to the necessities or the sick. His leisure hours were spent in studying his cases, and in making himself familiar with the improvements of the times, and he was soon in the possession of a full and lucrative business, which he prosecuted until his last sickness, a period of more than twenty-five years. In 1853, he visited Europe, and was absent four or five months, availing himself of the advantages of observation in the hospitals of Edinburg, Paris, and other cities. In 1857 and 1858, he stood for Newport in the legislature. In 1862, the Army appointed him surgeon of the 16th N. H. Regiment Volunteers and went with General Banks' division to Louisiana. On his return, the Army appointed him as U.S. army surgeon for this locality. Wheeler, 49-50.

40   Wheeler, 288.

41   Wheeler, 288.

42   Dr. Samuel J. Allen. Find A Grave Index, 1600s-Current. accessed September 5, 2016, http://www.ancestry.com.

43   Johnstown is the county seat of Fulton County in New York. Wikipedia contributors, "Johnstown (city), New York," *Wikipedia, The Free Encyclopedia,* https://en.wikipedia.org/w/index.php?title=Johnstown_(city),_New_York&oldid=911474751 (accessed August 21, 2019).

44   Wheeler, 178-184.

45   "Sanbornton is a town in Belknap County, New Hampshire." Wikipedia contributors, "Sanbornton, New Hampshire," *Wikipedia, The Free Encyclopedia,* https://en.wikipedia.org/w/index.php?title=Sanbornton,_New_Hampshire&oldid=905495344 (accessed August 21, 2019).

46   David Allen, Jr. Find a Grave Index, 1600s-Current, accessed September 5, 2016, and Decedents of Gideon Allen, Marylou McGuire, Newport Historical Society. Ancestry.com.

47   Henry Newport (1683-1734) was the 3rd Earl of Bradford. He was educated at Christ Church, Oxford and was a Member of Parliament. Wikipedia contributors, "Henry Newport, 3rd Earl of Bradford," *Wikipedia, The Free Encyclopedia,* https://en.wikipedia.org/w/index.php?title=Henry_Newport,_3rd_Earl_of_Bradford&oldid=901137107, (accessed August 21, 2019).

48   Killingworth, Connecticut, Killingworth was established from the area called Hammonasset, taken from the local Native American tribe of the same name. The area originally incorporated the town of Clinton, which was separated along ecclesiastical borders. Part of New London County prior to May 1785, Killingworth was then included in the newly formed Middlesex County, where it remains today. The town was named after Kenilworth, England in honor of one of the first settlers, Edward Griswold. Kenilworth's name was more like "Killingworth" during the American colonial period, and over time the pronunciation and spelling drifted towards the modern one. In the late 17th century, Killingworth became the birthplace of what would eventually become Yale University. Eventually the school was moved to its present-day home in New Haven. "The History of Killingworth, Connecticut," accessed February 11, 2019, http://www.killingworthhistorical.org/town-history.html.

49   Newport, New Hampshire is a town in and the county seat of Sullivan County, New Hampshire. Wikipedia contributors, "Newport, New Hampshire," *Wikipedia, The Free Encyclopedia,* https://en.wikipedia.org/w/index.php?title=Newport,_New_Hampshire&oldid=902273058 (accessed August 21, 2019).

50   The Branch Road and Bridge Company was incorporated June 16, 1802 and went from Keene, corner of Swanzey, Marlborough, to north line of Fitzwilliam, for 7 miles, 195 rods. The road cost $7,510 to build. "New Hampshire's Turnpike History," New Hampshire's History Blog, accessed September 10, 2018, www.cowhampshireblog.com/2006/08/23/new-hampshires-turnpike-history/.

51   The Fourth Turnpike connected Lebanon to the seacoast, and by the incorporation of the Croydon Turnpike in 1804, allowed fast transport of food products. The convergence of the rivers and these turnpikes in Lebanon, along with the White River Turnpike and the Hanover Branch Turnpike supported several inns and public houses in towns along the routes and provided an excellent location for industrial development. "New Hampshire's Turnpike History," New Hampshire's History Blog, accessed September 10, 2018, www.cowhampshireblog.com/2006/08/23/new-hampshires-turnpike-history/.

52   Eliphalet Merrill and Phinehas Merrill, *Gazetteer of the State of New Hampshire* (Exeter: C. Norris & Co., 1847), 11.

53   Wheeler, 262.

54 Wheeler, 151-153.

55 Congregational Churches are Protestant Christian churches where the congregations govern themselves independently and autonomously. With their insistence on independent local bodies, they became important in many social reform movements, including abolitionism, temperance, and women's suffrage. Congregationalists founded some of the first colleges and universities in America, including Harvard, Yale, Dartmouth, Williams, Bowdoin, Middlebury, and Amherst. Wikipedia contributors, "Congregational Christian Churches," *Wikipedia, The Free Encyclopedia*, https://en.wikipedia.org/w/index.php?title=Congregational_Christian_Churches&oldid=900537411 (accessed August 21, 2019).

56 Wheeler, 115-116.

57 Louis Antoine Godey (1804 - 1878) was an American editor and publisher, known as the founder of Godey's Lady's Book, the first successful American women's fashion magazine. In 1830, he published the first edition of the Lady's Book, composed of reprinted articles and illustrations from French magazines. Godey hired Sarah Josepha Hale to be editor of *Godey's Lady's Book* in 1837. She remained the editor until her retirement in 1877. The magazine became extremely popular, becoming America's highest circulated magazine in the 1840s and reaching over 150,000 subscribers by 1858. 858

58 Vassar College is a private, coeducational, liberal arts college in Poughkeepsie, New York. Founded in 1861 by Matthew Vassar, it was the first degree-granting institution of higher education for women in the United States. Wikipedia contributors, "Vassar College," *Wikipedia, The Free Encyclopedia,* https://en.wikipedia.org/w/index.php?title=Vassar_College&oldid=911019319 (accessed August 21, 2019).

59 Sarah Josepha Hale (1788-1879), "Notable Natives," The Town of Newport, accessed May 7, 2018, https://www.newportnh.gov/about-newport/pages/notable-natives.

60 Wheeler, 288.

61 Wheeler, 214.

62 Wheeler, 216.

DARTMOUTH COLLEGE

63   Fellow native son, William G. Hale, graduated from Harvard University in 1842 and admitted to the Virginia bar in 1845. He moved to Texas in 1846, formed a partnership with Ebenezer Allen, and practiced law in Galveston, specializing in land suits. *Handbook of Texas Online*, Seymour V. Connor, "Hale, William G.," accessed July 21, 2016, http://www.tshaonline.org/handbook/online/articles/fha14.

64   "Newport Residents attending Dartmouth," Wheeler, 164-165.

65   Eleazar Wheelock (1711–1779) was an American Congregational minister, orator, and educator in Lebanon, Connecticut, for 35 years before founding Dartmouth College in New Hampshire. The college was primarily for the sons of English colonists. After sending Occom and another minister on a speaking tour of England to raise money for the charity school, Wheelock decided to enlarge it, as well as adding college classes for the education of English colonists in the classics, philosophy, and literature. He began to search for another location for the schools. Wheelock obtained a charter from King George III on December 13, 1769. Having worked and raised funds for the education of Native Americans, Occom and the British Board of Trustees headed by Lord Dartmouth opposed the addition of the college to advance colonists' sons. Wheelock kept the lord's donation and named the college after him, as Dartmouth College. He chose Hanover, New Hampshire, for the location and became the college's president. In 1771, four students were graduated in Dartmouth's first commencement, including Wheelock's son John. While some Native Americans attended Dartmouth, it primarily served the sons of English colonists. Wheelock died during the Revolutionary War, on April 24, 1779 "Rev. Eleazar Wheelock," Wheelock Genealogy, accessed February 11, 2019, http://www.wheelockgenealogy.com/pages/ew_bio.htm.

66   "Daniel Webster – Dartmouth's Favorite Son," accessed February 11, 2019, http://www.dartmouth.edu/~dwebster/intro.html.

67   Daniel Webster (1782–1852) was an American politician who represented New Hampshire (1813–1817) and Massachusetts (1823–1827) in the United States House of Representatives; served as a Senator from Massachusetts (1827–1841, 1845–1850); and was the United States Secretary of State under Presidents William Henry Harrison (1841), John Tyler (1841–1843), and Millard Fillmore (1850–1852). "WEBSTER, Daniel (1782-1852)," Biographical Directory of the United

States congress, accessed February 12, 2019, http://bioguide.congress.gov/scripts/biodisplay.pl?index=W000238.

68   Charles T. Morrissey, "Expatriates: New Hampshire and Vermont in Texas," Dartmouth College Library Bulletin, accessed March 22, 2016, http://www.dartmouth.edu/~library/Library_Bulletin/Nov1997/Morrissey.html?mswitch-redir=classic 51.

69   Baxter Perry Smith, *The History of Dartmouth College* (Boston: The Riverside Press, 1878), 84-85.

70   George T. Chapman, *Chapman's Sketches of the Alumni of Dartmouth College (Cambridge: Riverside Press, 1867)*, 226-233.

TEACHER AND LAW STUDENT

71   "Historic Lewiston, New York," accessed December 29, 2016, http://historiclewiston.org/pictures/.

72   Mackenzie Rebellion. In December 1837, 400 men armed with muskets, pitchforks, and staves marched against the city of Toronto and the British government. Intercepted by pickets, the undisciplined and ill-trained farmers, shopkeepers and students were driven back at gunpoint. One man was killed, and the rest fled. The rebellion spread from the Toronto streets all the way to an island in the Niagara River and on to the St. Lawrence River, with periodic raids launched from American soil against Canadian authorities. Before the rebellion ended, a wellspring of sentiment had arisen in the United States in favor of the Canadian rebels, reawakening memories of the War of 1812 and bringing the American government perilously close to the third war in 70 years with Great Britain. accessed July 6, 2017, http://warfarehistorynetwork.com/daily/military-history/mackenzies-rebellion/.

73   "History of Lewiston, New York," accessed April 14, 2016, http://history.rays-place.com/ny/lewiston-ny.htm. 24.

74   This poem was published in *Godey's Lady's Book and Magazine*. Mrs. Sarah J. Hale and Louis A. Godey, eds., Godey's Lady's Book and Magazine (Philadelphia: Louis A. Godey, 1855), Vol. LI from July to December 1855, 510-511.

75   The burned-over district refers to the western and central regions of New York in the early 19th century, where religious revivals and the formation of new religious movements of the Second Great Awakening took place. Wikipedia contributors, "Burned-over district," *Wikipedia, The Free Encyclopedia,* https://en.wikipedia.org/w/index.php?title=Burned-over_district&oldid=900268582, (accessed August 21, 2019).

76   "The History of Modern American Spiritualism," accessed December 29, 2016, http://www.spiritualistdesertchurchlv.org/what-we-believe/the-history-of-spiritualism.

77   "26a. Religious Revival," U.S. History, accessed December 29, 2016, http://www.ushistory.org/us/26a.asp.

78   Charles Grandison Finney (1792 - 1875) was an American Presbyterian minister and leader in the Second Great Awakening in the United States. He has been called The Father of Modern Revivalism. Finney was best known as an innovative revivalist during the period 1825–1835 in upstate New York and Manhattan, an opponent of Old School Presbyterian theology, an advocate of Christian perfectionism, and a religious writer. Wikipedia contributors, "Charles Grandison Finney," Wikipedia contributors, *Wikipedia, The Free Encyclopedia,* https://en.wikipedia.org/w/index.php?title=Charles_Grandison_Finney&oldid=911674823 (accessed August 21, 2019).

79   John H. Martin, *Saints, Sinners and Reformers*, The Burned-Over District Re-Visited, Chapter 7 - Charles Grandison Finney, accessed December 29, 2016, http://www.crookedlakereview.com/books/saints_sinners/martin7.html.

80   Wheeler, 287.

81   Susan Katcher, "Legal Training in the United States: A Brief History," *Wisconsin International Law Journal,* July 26, 2006, accessed December 29, 2016. 335-336.

82   Katcher, 336-338, 340.

83   Blackstone's Commentaries or more formally the Commentaries on the Laws of England are an influential eighteenth-century treatise on the common law of England by Sir William Blackstone, originally published by the Clarendon Press at Oxford, 1765–1769. The work is divided into four volumes, on the rights of

persons, the rights of things, of private wrongs and of public wrongs. For decades, a study of the Commentaries was required reading for all first-year law students. Wikipedia contributors, "Commentaries on the Laws of England," *Wikipedia, The Free Encyclopedia,* https://en.wikipedia.org/w/index.php?title=Commentaries_on_the_Laws_of_England&oldid=910466893 (accessed August 21, 2019).

84   Katcher, 71.

85   Katcher, 345-346.

86   Horatio Emmons Hale (1817–1896) was an American Canadian ethnologist, philologist and businessman who studied language in order to classify ancient peoples and trace their migrations. He was the first to discover that the Tutelo language of Virginia belonged to the Siouan family, and to identify the Cherokee language as a member of the Iroquoian family of languages. In addition, he published a work Iroquois Book of Rites (1883), based on interpreting the Iroquois wampum belts, as well as his studies with tribal leaders. He was the son of Sarah Hale and brother of William Hale. Wikipedia contributors, "Horatio Hale," *Wikipedia, The Free Encyclopedia,* https://en.wikipedia.org/w/index.php?title=Horatio_Hale&oldid=904685001 (accessed August 21, 2019).

87   William G. Hale (1822–1876). was an attorney, son of Sarah Hale, and law partner with Ebenezer Allen. Like Allen, Hale was born in Newport, New Hampshire. His mother was the editor of *Godey's Lady's Book*. He graduated from Harvard University in 1842 and was admitted to the Virginia bar in 1845. He moved to Texas in 1846, formed a partnership with Ebenezer Allen, and practiced law in Galveston, specializing in land suits. Hale was attorney for the Peters' Colony, handled much of the litigation in Cameron County, and had among his clients several of the former clients of Judge John C. Watrous. This connection caused Hale to be accused of being special counsel for the land speculators with whom Watrous was said to be involved. About 1873, Hale moved to New Orleans, where he was counsel for the Mixed Commission on British and American Claims. *Handbook of Texas Online*, Seymour V. Connor, "Hale, William G.," accessed August 17, 2018, http://www.tshaonline.org/handbook/online/articles/fha14.

88   Wheeler, 201a.

MARRIAGE AND EARLY CAREER

89 "Chapman, 231-232.

90 Norman L. Bassett, ed, *Report of the Maine State Bar Association* (Augusta: Charles E. Nash & Son, 1921), vol. 22, 32-35.

91 Jonas Cutting graduated from Dartmouth in 1823 and read law two years with Henry Hubbard in Charlestown and one year with Reuel Williams in Augusta. The Maine bar admitted Cutting in 1826. He moved to Orono, in Penobscot county, and set up his law practice. He stayed in Orono until October 1831, when he moved to Bangor. In 1854, the government appointed Cutting as Judge of the Supreme Judicial Court of Maine. In 1858, Dartmouth conferred upon him the honorary degree of Doctor of Law Biography of Jonas Cutting, L.L.D., accessed January 6, 2017, https://www.accessgenealogy.com/new-hampshire/biography-of-jonas-cutting-ll-d.htm. Wheeler, 201.

92 Other lawyers in Orono prior to 1834 were John Perley, John H. Hilliard, Frederick A. Fuller, and Thomas J. Goodwin. *Centennial Celebration and Dedication of Town Hall, Orono, Maine* (Portland: Bailey & Noyes, 1874), 108.

93 Wheeler, 288.

94 David Allen, Jr., Ancestry.com, U.S., Find a Grave Index, 1600s-Current, accessed September 5, 2016, http://www.ancestry.com and Decedents of Gideon Allen, Marylou McGuire, Newport Historical Society.

95 George J. Varney, "History of Orono Maine," *A Gazetteer of Maine* (Boston: B. B. Russell, 1886), accessed May 10, 2018, http://history.rays-place.com/me/orono-me.htm.

96 A lathe is a tool that rotates the workpiece about an axis of rotation to perform various operations such as cutting, sanding, knurling, drilling, deformation, facing, and turning, with tools that are applied to the workpiece to create an object with symmetry about that axis. Lathes are used in woodturning, metalworking, metal spinning, thermal spraying, parts reclamation, and glass working. Wikipedia contributors, "Lathe," *Wikipedia, The Free Encyclopedia,* https://en.wikipedia.org/w/index.php?title=Lathe&oldid=909723009 (accessed August 21, 2019).

97 Clapboard is a narrow board usually thicker at one edge than the other used

for siding. Wikipedia contributors, "Clapboard (architecture)," *Wikipedia, The Free Encyclopedia,* https://en.wikipedia.org/w/index.php?title=Clapboard_(architecture)&oldid=894373139 (accessed August 21, 2019).

98 A rotary saw, spiral cut saw, or cut out tool is a type of mechanically powered saw used for making accurate cuts without the need for a pilot hole in wallboard, plywood, or another thin, solid material. Wikipedia contributors, "Rotary saw," *Wikipedia, The Free Encyclopedia,* https://en.wikipedia.org/w/index.php?title=Rotary_saw&oldid=787794189 (accessed August 21, 2019).

99 Varney, accessed May 10, 2018, http://history.rays-place.com/me/orono-me.htm.

100 Varney, accessed May 10, 2018, http://history.rays-place.com/me/orono-me.htm.

101 "Centennial Celebration," accessed May 10, 2018, https://archive.org/details/centennialcelebr00orona.

102 Mrs. Allen's name is spelled two different ways. In some cases, Sylvinia was written as Sylvina. The author has chosen the spelling used in Ebenezer Allen's hand-written will. [Please see Ebenezer Allen Will in the Appendix.]

103 Skowhegan was across the Kennebec River from Bloomfield. Wikipedia contributors, "Skowhegan, Maine," *Wikipedia, The Free Encyclopedia,* https://en.wikipedia.org/w/index.php?title=Skowhegan,_Maine&oldid=911702692(accessed August 21, 2019).

104 "Andrew Morse," accessed April 11, 2017, https://www.ancestry.com/genealogy/records/andrew-morse_12123779.

105 Mr. Morse and Abraham Wyman erected a stone grist mill on Mill Street in 1829. Andrew Morse bought a fulling and-mill on Mill Street in 1821. Also owned part of a sawmill. Loise Helen Coburn, *Skowhegan on the Kennebec*, (Skowhegan: Self Published, 1941) vol. I - 430, vol. II. - 716, 938-940.

106 From poem by Ebenezer Allen that was published in *Godey's Ladies' Magazine and Book.* Courtesy of Judith M. Johnson, Johnson-Morrow Family Tree, accessed May 20, 2016, Ancestry.com.

107 "Ebenezer Allen," *Mill Town Messenger*, Newport Historical Society, Vol.4, Issue 1, February 2010, accessed March 9, 2016, 1 and "Maine Marriages, 1771-1907," database, *FamilySearch*, (https://familysearch.org/ark:/61903/1:1:F481-JVZ: accessed 9 March 2016), Ebenezer, Esq. Allen and Sylvinia Morse, 23 Mar 1833; citing, reference; FHL microfilm 12,061.

108 Marriages, *The Advocate*, June 5, 1833, E. F. Danforth (Hinckley, Me.: Good Will Publishing Co., 1927?).

109 James T. Leavitt (1804-1857) was born in Lee, New Hampshire on July 9, 1804. He received his Bachelor of Arts degree from Bowdoin College on September 5, 1827. Leavitt began his law practice in Skowhegan in 1834. Maine admitted Leavitt to practice law in the court of Common Pleas in 1832 and the Supreme Judicial Court in Somerset County in 1834. Mr. Leavitt stood for his district in the Maine House of Representatives in 1848 and 1855. He served his county in the Maine Senate in 1851 and 1852. He was also Attorney for the State in Somerset County for several years. He practiced law in Skowhegan for about thirty years. Coburn, vol. II, 790.

110 *Civil Government of the State of Maine for the Political Year, 1932* (Augusta: I. Berry & Co., Printers to the State, 1832), 370.

111 J. W. Hanson, *History of the Old Towns Norridgewock and Canaan comprising Norridgewock, Canaan, Starks, Skowhegan, and Bloomfield from their early settlement to the Year 1849* (Boston: J. W. Hanson, 1849), 332.

112 New Portland is twenty miles from Skowhegan and thirteen miles from Solon. Distance Between Cities, accessed January 23, 2019, https://www.distance-cities.com/distance-new-portland-me-to-solon-me and https://www.distance-cities.com/distance-new-portland-me-to-solon-me.

113 John Hayward, *The New England and New York Law Register for the Year 1835* (New York: John Hayward, 1834), 49 & 51.

114 E. F. Danforth, *Skowhegan Lawyers*, 1806-1827 (Hinckley: Good Will Publishing, Inc, 1928), 775.

115 Robert Flint Family Tree, James T. Leavitt, accessed September 12, 2016, Ancestry.com.

116   Coburn, vol. II, 719.

117   "Historic Skowhegan Building to be Restored," Archive Article, History House Association, Skowhegan History House, accessed December 19, 2016, http://www.skowheganhistoryhouse.org/pdf/LeavittBlock.pdf.

118   American Series of Popular Biographies Maine Edition, *Representative Citizens of the State of Maine*, (Boston: New England Historical Publishing Company, 1903), 429.

119   Canaan, Maine is a quiet suburban town located between Skowhegan and Pittsfield in Somerset County. "Town of Canaan," accessed February 23, 2018, http://www.townofcanaan.com/.

120   "Historical Sketch of Skowhegan, Maine," History, Skowhegan, Maine, accessed February 23, 2018, https://www.skowhegan.org/307/History and http://history.rays-place.com/me/skowhegan-me.htm.

121   Martin Van Buren (1782–1862) was the eighth President of the United States. He helped found the Democratic Party. He served as the ninth Governor of New York, the tenth Secretary of State, and the eighth Vice President. Van Buren won the 1836 presidential election based on the popularity of outgoing President Andrew Jackson and the organizational strength of the Democratic Party. He lost his 1840 reelection bid to Whig Party nominee William Henry Harrison due in part to the poor economic conditions of the Panic of 1837. Van Buren became an important anti-slavery leader and led the Free-Soil ticket in the 1848 presidential election. Van Buren sought peace abroad and harmony at home. He proposed a diplomatic solution to a long-standing financial dispute between American citizens and the Mexican government and rejected Jackson's threat to settle it by force. When the Texas minister at Washington, D.C., proposed annexation to the administration in August 1837, he was told the proposition could not be considered. Constitutional principles and fear of war with Mexico were the reasons given for the rejection. Van Buren was concerned Texas annexation would precipitate a clash over the extension of slavery undoubtedly influenced Van Buren and continued to be the chief obstacle to annexation. "Martin Van Buren," The White House, accessed February 12, 2019, https://www.whitehouse.gov/about-the-white-house/presidents/martin-van-buren/.

122   "Panic of 1837," America's Story from America's Library, Library of Con-

gress, accessed July 18, 2016, http://www.americaslibrary.gov/aa/buren/aa_buren_panic_1.html.

123 "1837: The Hard Times," Harvard Business School Historical Collections, accessed July 18, 2016, http://www.library.hbs.edu/hc/crises/1837.html.

124 "Centennial celebration by Orono, Me." [from old catalog] Published 1874 Topics Orono, Me. -- History. [from old catalog], Maine -- History Colonial period, ca. 1600-1775, 106.

125 Wheeler, 288.

GONE TO TEXAS

126 *The Galveston Daily News*, (Galveston, Tex.), Vol. 52, No. 171, Ed. 1 Sunday, September 10, 1893, newspaper, September 10, 1893; Galveston, Texas. (https://texashistory.unt.edu/ark:/67531/metapth466495. accessed August 27, 2019), University of North Texas Libraries, The Portal to Texas History, https://texashistory.unt.edu; crediting Abilene Library Consortium.

127 "United States Migration to Texas 1820 to 1845 (National Institute)," *Family Search*, accessed July 22, 2019, https://www.family search.org.

128 Jonesborough and Pecan Point were the first Anglo-American settlements in Texas. Jonesborough was located above the mouth of Lower Pine Creek. Jonesborough was named for Henry Jones, who hunted on the Red River as early as 1815. The Texas Congress incorporated Jonesborough in 1837. However, the county seat at Clarksville attracted many of its citizens. As late as 1841, Jonesborough retained some of its former activity, but the gradual westward movement of the frontier drew the trading companies to sites up the river. The spring thaw in 1843 flooded the town, ruined the buildings, and shifted the channel of the river a mile to the north of the old site. *Handbook of Texas Online*, Rex W. Strickland, "Jonesborough, TX," accessed January 19, 2017, http://www.tshaonline.org/handbook/online/articles/hvj16.

129 Report of Conditional Certificate issued by the Board of Land Commissioners of Red River County for the quarter ending September 2, 1841, Fourth Class Certificate, Number 9, File No. 00030, Texas General Land Office, http://www.glo.texas.gov/ncu/SCANDOCS/archives_webfiles/arcmaps/

web files/land grants/PDFs/1/0/6/2/1062501.pdf.

130 *Handbook of Texas Online*, Claudia Hazlewood, "Clarksville, TX (Red River County)," accessed January 19, 2017, http://www.tshaonline.org/handbook/online/articles/hgc07.

131 Clarksville Female Academy was first called Pine Creek Female Institute when it was established by Robert and Martha W. (Maum) Weatherred in 1840 on Pine Creek, fifteen miles north of Clarksville. The school was moved from Pine Creek to Clarksville in 1844, and the name was changed to Clarksville Female Academy, although the institution was often referred to as Mrs. Weatherred's School. Records show fifty-eight pupils were enrolled in 1846. A Mrs. Gattis bought the school in 1852 and continued to run it until the beginning of the Civil War, when a steady decrease in enrollment caused the school to close. *Handbook of Texas Online*, "Clarksville Female Academy," accessed March 10, 2016, http://www.tshaonline.org/handbook/online/articles/kbc25.

132 *Handbook of Texas Online*, Ernest Wallace, "Clarksville Standard," accessed December 05, 2016, http://www.tshaonline.org/handbook/online/articles/eec15.

133 *Handbook of Texas Online*, Claudia Hazlewood, "Clarksville, TX (Red River County)," accessed March 10, 2016, http://www.tshaonline.org/handbook/online/articles/hgc07.

134 *Handbook of Texas Online*, Claudia Hazlewood, "Clarksville, TX (Red River County)," accessed March 10, 2016, http://www.tshaonline.org/handbook/online/articles/hgc07.

135 McKenzie College, Early Texas Methodism, SMU, Birdwell Library, Perkins School of Theology, accessed January 22, 2018, https://www.smu.edu/Bridwell/SpecialCollectionsandArchives/Exhibitions/EarlyTexas/McKenzieCollege.

136 Conditional Certificate Granting Ebenezer Allen Six Hundred and Forty Acres of Land, Fourth Class Certificate, Number 9, File No. 00030, Texas General Land Office, http://www.glo.texas.gov/ncu/SCANDOCS/archives_webfiles/arc-maps/webfiles/landgrants/PDFs/1/0/6/2/1062501.pdf.

137 *Handbook of Texas Online*, Joseph Milton Nance, "Republic of Texas," accessed December 02, 2016, http://www.tshaonline.org/handbook/online/articles/mzr02.

138 Survey of Land Granted by Conditional Certificate to Ebenezer Allen Fourth Class Certificate, Number 9, File No. 00030, Texas General Land Office, http://www.glo.texas.gov/ncu/SCANDOCS/archives_webfiles/arcmaps/webfiles/landgrants/PDFs/1/0/6/2/1062501.pdf.

139 Certificate Granting Ebenezer Allen Six Hundred and Forty Acres of Land, Fourth Class Certificate, Number 9, File No. 00030, Texas General Land Office, http://www.glo.texas.gov/ncu/SCANDOCS/archives_webfiles/arcmaps/webfiles/landgrants/PDFs/1/0/6/2/1062501.pdf.

140 Anson Jones (1798–1858) was a doctor, congressman, and the last president of the Republic of Texas. He was born at Seekonkville, Massachusetts, on January 20, 1798. He hoped to become a printer but was persuaded to study medicine. In 1820 he received his license from the Oneida, New York, Medical Society and began practice at Bainbridge. He was not unsuccessful with his practice. He moved to Norwich, where he opened a drugstore that failed. He traveled to Philadelphia and opened a medical office and taught school. He went to Venezuela for two years. After he returned to Philadelphia, he opened a medical office and obtained an M.D. degree at Jefferson Medical College in 1827. He also became a Mason and an Odd Fellow. He became master of his Masonic lodge and grand master of the Independent Order of Odd Fellows in Pennsylvania. Unfortunately, his medical practice was not successful. In October 1832, he renounced medicine and became a commission merchant in New Orleans, where his businesses all failed leaving him despondent and broke. In October 1833, Jones traveled to Texas and opened a practice at Brazoria worth $5,000 a year. As tension between Texas and Mexico increased, he advocated forbearance and peace. In the summer of 1835, he ran out of patience and signed a petition for a convention. At a mass meeting at Columbia in December 1835, he presented resolutions calling for a convention to declare independence but declined to be nominated as a delegate. When war came, he enlisted and during the San Jacinto campaign served as judge advocate and surgeon of the Second Regiment. After brief service as apothecary general of the Texas army, Jones returned to Brazoria and resumed practice. "Jones, Anson," *Wikipedia*, accessed May 10, 2018, https://en.wikipedia.org/wiki/Anson_Jones.

141 Stephen Fuller Austin (1793-1836) was an American empresario. He was known as the "Father of Texas" and the "Founder of Texas." He led the second, and colonization of the region by bringing 300 families from the United States to the region in 1825. Throughout the 1820s, Austin tried to maintain good relations

with the Mexican government, and he helped suppress the Fredonian Rebellion. He also helped the introduction of slavery into Texas despite the attempts of the Mexican government to ban the institution. Texas settlers became increasingly dissatisfied with the Mexican government. Austin advocated conciliation with the Mexican government, but the dissent against Mexico escalated to the Texas Revolution. Austin led Texas forces at the Siege of Béxar before serving as a commissioner to the United States. Austin ran in the 1836 Texas presidential election but was defeated by Sam Houston. Houston appointed Austin as secretary of state for the new Republic, and Austin held the position until his death in December 1836. *Handbook of Texas Online*, Eugene C. Barker, "Austin, Stephen Fuller," accessed February 12, 2019, http://www.tshaonline.org/handbook/online/articles/fau14.

142 Charles T. Morrissey, "Expatriates: New Hampshire and Vermont in Texas," Dartmouth College Library Bulletin, November 1997, Volume XXXVIII(NS), Number 1.

143 Charles De Morse, *The Northern Standard*. Clarksville, Texas. Vol. 3, No. 4, Ed. 1, Wednesday, December 4, 1844. newspaper, December 4, 1844; Clarksville, Texas. https://texashistory.unt.edu/ark:/67531/metapth80542. accessed August 23, 2019), University of North Texas Libraries, The Portal to Texas History, https://texashistory.unt.edu; crediting The Dolph Briscoe Center for American History.

144 Bennett H. Martin was a judge of the sixth judicial district of Texas. de Cordova, P. *The South-Western American*. (Austin, Tex.), Vol. 4, No. 10, Ed. 1, Wednesday, September 15, 1852, newspaper, September 15, 1852; Austin, Texas. (texashistory.unt.edu/ark:/67531/metapth79738/: accessed August 22, 2018), University of North Texas Libraries, The Portal to Texas History, texashistory.unt.edu; crediting The Dolph Briscoe Center for American History. 2.

145 *Handbook of Texas Online*, Marie Giles, "Clarksville Academy," accessed August 02, 2016, http://www.tshaonline.org/handbook/online/articles/kbc24.

146 A tort is a civil wrong committed against someone, in which the injured party can sue for damages. In personal injury cases, the injured party will try to receive compensation to cover losses due to medical expenses and to pay for damages. accessed July 19, 2017, http://tort.laws.com/torts.

147 Chattels are personal property that are movable. Chattel includes livestock, slaves, furniture, and other property attached to the person and not the land or real

estate. Chattel, Meriam-Webster, accessed August 21, 2019, https://www.merriam-webster.com/dictionary/chattel.

148 Equity is fairness. As a legal system, it is a body of law that addresses concerns that fall outside the jurisdiction of Common Law. Equity also describes the money value of property in excess of claims, liens, or mortgages on the property. Equity and the common law represented opposing values in the English legal system. English common law judges considered equity arbitrary and a royal encroachment on the power of an independent judiciary. Despite this opposition, equity assumed a permanent place in the English legal system. Because of its association with the king, equity was viewed with suspicion in the American colonies. However, colonial legislatures understood the wisdom of allowing judges to fashion remedies in cases that were not covered by settled common law or statutes. The Framers of the U.S. Constitution recognized the providence of equity by writing in Article III, Section 2, Clause 1, that the "judicial Power shall extend to all Cases, in Law and Equity." All states eventually allowed for the judicial exercise of equity, and many states created Special Courts of equity, which maintained procedures distinct from those of courts of law. "Equity," The Free Dictionary, https://legal-dictionary.thefreedictionary.com/equity, assessed February 27, 2019.

149 Codification is the act, process, or result of arranging in a systematic form or code. In law, codification refers to the act, process, or result of stating the rules and principles applicable in a given legal order to one or more broad areas of life in this form of a code. It also is the reducing of unwritten customs or case law to statutory form. Wikipedia contributors, "Codification," *Wikipedia, The Free Encyclopedia,* https://en.wikipedia.org/w/index.php?title=Codification&oldid=888189921, (accessed August 21, 2019).

150 *Handbook of Texas Online*, Joseph W. McKnight, "Law," accessed December 02, 2016, http://www.tshaonline.org/handbook/online/articles/jzlph.

151 "Old Times in Jefferson, Texas," *Jefferson Jimplecute* (Jefferson, Texas), March 4, 1905, 2.

152 Van Cradock, "Early School Left Lasting Contribution," *Longview News-Journal* (Longview, Texas), January 17, 2016, https://www.newspapers.com, A2.

153   Charles DeMorse, *The Standard* (Clarksville, Tex.), Vol. 3, No. 1, Ed. 1 Friday, November 11, 1881, newspaper, November 11, 1881; Clarksville, Texas. (https://texashistory.unt.edu/ark:/67531/metapth234733/: accessed April 7, 2019), University of North Texas Libraries, The Portal to Texas History, https://texashistory.unt.edu; crediting The Dolph Briscoe Center for American History.

154   Charles De Morse, *The Northern Standard.* (Clarksville, Tex.), Vol. 1, No. 5, Ed. 1, Saturday, September 17, 1842, newspaper, September 17, 1842; Clarksville, Texas. (texashistory.unt.edu/ark:/67531/metapth80456/: accessed March 7, 2018), University of North Texas Libraries, The Portal to Texas History, texashistory.unt.edu; crediting The Dolph Briscoe Center for American History.

155   Charles De Morse, *The Northern Standard.*, (Clarksville, Tex.), Vol. 2, No. 1, Ed. 1, Saturday, November 4, 1843, newspaper, November 4, 1843; Clarksville, Texas. (texashistory.unt.edu/ark:/67531/metapth80502/: accessed January 27, 2019), University of North Texas Libraries, The Portal to Texas History, texashistory.unt.edu; crediting The Dolph Briscoe Center for American History.

156   Charles De Morse, *The Northern Standard,* (Clarksville, Tex.), Vol. 3, No. 11, Ed. 1, Thursday, January 30, 1845, newspaper, January 30, 1845; Clarksville, Texas. (texashistory.unt.edu/ark:/67531/metapth80548/m1/3/?q=Ebenezer%20Allen: accessed September 4, 2018), University of North Texas Libraries, The Portal to Texas History, texashistory.unt.edu; crediting The Dolph Briscoe Center for American History.

157   William Smith Todd was a lawyer and judge. He was born on a plantation in Caroline County, Virginia, in 1808. He received his early education at home from tutors and graduated from the University of Virginia in 1832. After graduating, he served two terms in the Virginia legislature and married Eliza Ann Hudgins. Around 1840 the Todds and their two small children moved to Texas. They settled in Boston, Bowie County, where Todd set up a law practice. In 1848, the couple moved to Clarksville, where Todd continued to practice law and Eliza opened the Clarksville Female Institute. In 1850, Todd was elected judge of the Eighth Judicial District. He had a reputation as a very competent judge and was reelected in 1854 and 1858. He moved his family to Jefferson in 1856, and in 1861 he was elected a delegate to the Secession Convention from Marion County. *Handbook of Texas Online*, Cecil Harper, Jr., "Todd, William Smith," accessed July 19, 2017, http://www.tshaonline.org/handbook/online/articles/fto08.

158 Boston, Texas is in Bowie County about forty-five miles from Clarksville. Bowie County was established in December 1840 and named for James Bowie, reduced to its present size in 1846. DeKalb was the temporary county seat, with Boston becoming the permanent county seat in 1841. Bowie County in the years leading up to the American Civil War was settled mostly by Southerners who brought their slave labor to work the cotton fields. By 1860, slaves outnumbered whites 2,651 to 2,401. The county voted 208-15 in favor of secession from the Union. While Bowie was never a battlefield in that war, it was nevertheless occupied during Reconstruction. Between 1860 and 1870, the population declined. The occupation, and the new legal equality of blacks, became a hostile situation that fostered Cullen Baker. *Handbook of Texas Online*, Cecil Harper, Jr., "BOSTON, TX," accessed August 21, 2019, http://www.tshaonline.org/handbook/online/articles/hlb45.

159 Charles De Morse, *The Northern Standard.* (Clarksville, Tex.), Vol. 3, No. 7, Ed. 1, Thursday, December 26, 1844, newspaper, December 26, 1844; (https://texashistory.unt.edu/ark:/67531/metapth8045/m1/4/: accessed March 7, 2018), University of North Texas Libraries, The Portal to Texas History, texashistory.unt.edu.

160 Charles De Morse, *The Northern Standard.* (Clarksville, Tex.), Vol. 3, No. 13, Ed. 1, Thursday, February 13, 1845, newspaper, February 13, 1845; Clarksville, Texas. (texashistory.unt.edu/ark:/67531/metapth80550/: accessed August 15, 2018), University of North Texas Libraries, The Portal to Texas History, texashistory.unt.edu; crediting The Dolph Briscoe Center for American History.

161 Charles De Morse, *The Northern Standard.* (Clarksville, Tex.), Vol. 5, No. 3, Ed. 1, Thursday, May 13, 1847, newspaper, May 13, 1847; Clarksville, Texas. (texashistory.unt.edu/ark:/67531/metapth80639/m1/4/?q=%22Wm.%20S.%20Todd%22: accessed April 27, 2018), University of North Texas Libraries, The Portal to Texas History, texashistory.unt.edu; crediting The Dolph Briscoe Center for American History.

162 Personal communications with Mr. Bruce Mercer of the Masonic Lodge of Texas who supplied records for E. Allen. May 26, 2016.

163 "Texas Masonic History," Freemasons in Texas, The Grand Lodge of Texas, accessed July 17, 2018, https://grandlodgeoftexas.org/texas-masonic-history/.

164 John M. Holland (1785-1864) was grand master of the Grand Lodge of Louisiana from 1825 to 1828 and again from 1830 to 1839. *Handbook of Texas Online*, Chester V. Kielman, "Holland, John Henry," accessed August 11, 2016, http://www.tshaonline.org/handbook/online/articles/fho26.

165 "Grand Lodge of Louisiana," accessed July 2, 2018, https://la-mason.com/.

166 Dispensation is a general state or ordering of things; a system of revealed commands and promises regulating human affairs. A privilege maintained under the new dispensation. An arrangement or provision especially of providence. Dispensation, Merriam-Webster, accessed August 22, 20198, https://www.merriam-webster.com/dictionary/dispensation.

167 John Allen (1802-1847) or Tampico Allen was a soldier and first mayor of Galveston. He joined the United States Navy in the support of the Greek revolution against Turkey. Allen came to Texas in 1830 and joined the Tampico expedition in 1835 but escaped imprisonment. He returned to Texas in December, enlisted in the revolutionary army, was appointed captain of infantry, and served as acting major at the battle of San Jacinto. He moved to Galveston, where he was elected mayor in March 1839. In 1840, Samuel May Williams tried to remove the threat Allen posed to the Galveston City Company, called for a new election with a change in the franchise. Allen, refusing to give up his office since his term was not over, removed the city archives to his home and the protection of two cannons. Thomas F. McKinney and a posse removed the archives after the district court ruled on the matter, and so ended the "charter war." Allen was re-elected annually until 1846. After annexation, he was appointed United States marshal for the Eastern District of Texas, an office he held until his death on February 12, 1847. Allen was a Mason. *Handbook of Texas Online*, Wesley N. Laing, "Allen, John M.," accessed April 17, 2016, http://www.tshaonline.org/handbook/online/articles/fal22.

168 Grand Lodge of Texas, Texas Masonic History, The Grand Lodge of Texas, accessed February 14, 2019, https://grandlodgeoftexas.org/texas-masonic-history/.

169 *Handbook of Texas Online*, William Preston Vaughn, "Freemasonry," accessed February 24, 2019, http://www.tshaonline.org/handbook/online/articles/vnf01.

170 Anson Jones, "History of Freemasonry in early Texas and the Frontier," *Frontier Times Magazine*, April 9, 2011, http://frontiertimesmagazine.blogspot.

com/2011/04/history-of-freemasonry-in-early-texas.html.

171   Texas Freemason History, Dallas Freemasonry, accessed April 21, 2016, http://dallasfreemasonry.org/about-freemasonry/texas-freemason-history/.

172   General Thomas Jefferson Rusk (1803–1857) was an early political and military leader in the Republic of Texas. He served as its first Secretary of War and a general at the Battle of San Jacinto. He was later a U.S. politician and served as a Senator from Texas from 1846 until his death. He served as the President pro tempore of the United States Senate in 1857. *Handbook of Texas Online*, Priscilla Myers Benham, "Rusk, Thomas Jefferson," accessed February 12, 2019, http://www.tshaonline.org/handbook/online/articles/fru16.

173   James Pickney Henderson (1808–1858) was a United States and Republic of Texas lawyer, politician, soldier, and the first Governor of the State of Texas. Sam Houston became President of the Republic of Texas on September 5, 1836, and appointed Henderson as the Republic's Attorney General. In December 1836, Houston named Henderson to replace the recently deceased Stephen F. Austin as Secretary of State. In early 1837 Houston appointed Henderson as minister from the Republic of Texas to France and England. As minister, he was successful in securing recognition of the Republic of Texas and trade agreements with both countries. He went to Washington, D.C. in 1844 to work with Isaac Van Zandt to secure the annexation of Texas to the United States. Although the annexation treaty was signed, it was rejected by the United States Senate, and Henderson was recalled to Texas. In preparation for anticipated statehood, the Texas gubernatorial election, Henderson was elected in 1845 as its first governor. He took office on February 19, 1846. When the Mexican American War broke out in April of that year, Henderson took a leave of absence as governor to command a troop of Texas Rangers. He served with the rank of major general under Zachary Taylor. *Handbook of Texas Online*, Claude Elliott, "Henderson, James Pinckney," accessed February 14, 2019, http://www.tshaonline.org/handbook/online/articles/fhe14.

174   Kenneth Lewis Anderson (1805 – 1845) was a lawyer and the fourth and last Vice President of the Republic of Texas. *Handbook of Texas Online*, Leslie H. Southwick, "Anderson, Kenneth Lewis," accessed February 10, 2019, http://www.tshaonline.org/handbook/online/articles/fan08.

175   *Handbook of Texas Online*, William Preston Vaughn, "Freemasonry," accessed March 31, 2016, http://www.tshaonline.org/handbook/online/articles/vnf01.

THE LONG JOURNEY TO ANNEXATION

176 *Handbook of Texas Online*, C. T. Neu, "Annexation," accessed March 06, 2019, http://www.tshaonline.org/handbook/online/articles/mga02.

177 Justin Harvey Smith, *The Annexation of Texas* (New York: The Baker and Taylor Co., 1911) 1, 6, 248, and 300.

178 Hard Road to Texas Annexation 1836-1845, "Part 1: Texas Breaks Away," The Texas State Library and Archives, accessed February 16, 2017, https://www.tsl.texas.gov/exhibits/annexation/part1/page1.html.

179 William W. Freeling, *The Road to Disunion: Volume I: Secessionists at Bay, 1776–1854* (Oxford University Press. 1991), 365 and Paul Finkelman, *Millard Fillmore: The American Presidents Series: the 13th President, 1850-1853* (New York: Times Books, 2011), 29-30.

180 William Wharton (1802–1839) was a leader in the Texas Revolution. In November 1836, President Houston appointed Wharton as first minister to the United States. Houston hoped he gain recognition by and possibly annexation to the United States. After he resigned as minister in early 1837, Wharton was captured at sea by a Mexican ship and transported to Matamoros, where he was imprisoned. He escaped and made his way back to Texas in time to be elected to the Texas Senate in 1838. In December 1838, he introduced a bill to modify the flag and the seal of the Republic. *Handbook of Texas Online*, Merle Weir, "Wharton, William Harris," accessed July 2, 2018, http://www.tshaonline.org/handbook/online/articles/fwh08.

181 Edwin Fairfax Gray (1829–1884) was a military officer and railroad engineer. He moved to Texas in 1838 and in 1841 obtained an appointment as midshipman in the Texas Navy. After the annexation of Texas, Gray was transferred to the U.S. Navy. He graduated with honors from the Naval Academy at Annapolis in June 1852 and accompanied Commodore Matthew G. Perry to Japan in 1853. On September 16, 1858, he was appointed Texas state engineer responsible for supervision of river improvements and inspection of railroad properties. In 1860, he became secretary and treasurer of the Houston Tap and Brazoria Railway Company. He served throughout the Civil War in the Third Texas Infantry and rose to the rank of lieutenant colonel. *Handbook of Texas Online*, Andrew Forest Muir, "Gray, Edwin Fairfax," accessed July 02, 2018, https://tshaonline.org/handbook/online/

articles/fgr20.

182 Memucan Hunt (1807–1856) was a legislator and secretary of the Texas Navy. President Sam Houston appointed Hunt as an agent to the United States to assist William H. Wharton in obtaining recognition of Texas. Hunt became Texan minister at Washington. His 1837 annexation proposal was rejected by the United States, but he succeeded in negotiating a boundary convention in 1838. He promoted a railroad from Galveston Bay to Red River. Under President Mirabeau B. Lamar, Hunt was secretary of the navy from December 1838 to May 1839, when he became the Texas representative on the joint United States-Texas boundary commission. *Handbook of Texas Online*, C. T. Neu, "Hunt, Memucan," accessed July 02, 2018, http://www.tshaonline.org/handbook/online/articles/fhu31.

183 Hard Road to Texas Annexation 1836-1845, "Part 2: On Our Own," The Texas State Library and Archives, accessed February 17, 2017, https://www.tsl.texas.gov/exhibits/annexation/part2/page1.html.

184 Alcée la Branche (1806–1861) was the United States *chargé d'affaires* to the Republic of Texas. On March 3, 1837, President Andrew Jackson appointed him to be the first diplomat from the United States to the Republic of Texas. Texas received him enthusiastically, eager to hear about the question of the annexation of Texas to the United States. As United States *chargé d'affaires*, La Branche negotiated a temporary commerce agreement. He aggressively defended the United States claim to disputed territory in Red River County. On April 25, 1838, the two countries signed the Convention of Limits, which recognized Texas claims to the contested county and the Sabine River as the eastern boundary of Texas. *Handbook of Texas Online*, Priscilla Myers Benham, "La Branche, Alcee Louis," accessed July 02, 2018, http://www.tshaonline.org/handbook/online/articles/fla06.

185 Hard Road to Texas, Texas Annexation 1836-1845, "Part 2: On Our Own," "Houston Keeps his Options Open," Texas State Library and Archives Commission, accessed March 12, 2019, https://www.tsl.texas.gov/exhibits/annexation/part2/page1.html.

186 *Handbook of Texas Online*, C. T. Neu, "Annexation," accessed March 20, 2019, http://www.tshaonline.org/handbook/online/articles/mga02.

187 "Annexation," Texas State Library and Archives Commission, accessed March 12, 2019, https://www.tsl.texas.gov/lobbyexhibits/mural-annexation.

188 *Handbook of Texas Online*, Herbert Gambrell, "Lamar, Mirabeau Buonaparte," accessed January 26, 2017 02, 2018, http://www.tshaonline.org/handbook/online/articles/fla15.

189 *Handbook of Texas Online*, Herbert Gambrell, "Lamar, Mirabeau Buonaparte," accessed January 26, 2017, http://www.tshaonline.org/handbook/online/articles/fla15.

190 *Handbook of Texas Online*, Herbert Gambrell, "Lamar, Mirabeau Buonaparte," accessed January 26, 2017, http://www.tshaonline.org/handbook/online/articles/fla15.

191 Hard Road to Texas Annexation 1836-1845, "Part 2: On Our Own," "Lamar and the Rise of Texas Nationalism," The Texas State Library and Archives, accessed February 17, 2017, https://www.tsl.texas.gov/exhibits/annexation/part2/page2.html.

192 *Handbook of Texas Online*, Herbert Gambrell, "Lamar, Mirabeau Buonaparte," accessed January 26, 2017, http://www.tshaonline.org/handbook/online/articles/fla15.

193 Joseph Eve (1784–1843) was a Kentucky legislator, judge, and chargé d'affaires of the United States to the Republic of Texas. Eve helped negotiate the boundary between the Republic of Texas and the United States. Eve failed to negotiate a new commercial treaty with Texas. Future negotiations were dropped when America renewed interest in annexation. *Handbook of Texas Online*, Priscilla Myers Benham, "Eve, Joseph," accessed March 20, 2019, http://www.tshaonline.org/handbook/online/articles/fev09.

194 Hard Road to Texas Annexation 1836-1845, "Part 2: On Our Own," "Santa Anna Strikes Back," The Texas State Library and Archives, accessed February 17, 2017, https://www.tsl.texas.gov/exhibits/annexation/part2/page3.html.

195 James Reily (1811–1863) was lawyer, diplomat, legislator, and Confederate Army officer. Reily represented Harris County in the House of Representatives in the Texas Republic. Sam Davis appointed him as *chargé d'affaires* for the Republic in Washington, DC. He negotiated with Secretary of State Daniel Webster in a failed attempt to obtain a treaty of amity, commerce, and navigation with the United States. Although Houston reappointed him to the same post, Reily's confirma-

tion failed because of his outspoken opposition to annexation. *Handbook of Texas Online*, Thomas W. Cutrer, "Reily, James," accessed July 17, 2018, http://www.tshaonline.org/handbook/online/articles/fre26.

196 Isaac Van Zandt (1813−1847). Isaac Van Zandt, lawyer, legislator, and diplomat. He represented Harrison County in the House of the Fifth and Sixth congresses, 1840−1842. In 1842 Sam Houston appointed him *chargé d'affaires* to the United States. During his tenure in Washington, Van Zandt worked for the annexation of Texas to the Union. He attended the Convention of 1845. *Handbook of Texas Online*, John B. Wilder, "Van Zandt, Isaac," accessed July 17, 2018, http://www.tshaonline.org/handbook/online/articles/fva12.

197 Hard Road to Texas Annexation 1836-1845, "Part 2: On Our Own," "Lamar and the Rise of Texas Nationalism," The Texas State Library and Archives, accessed February 17, 2017, https://www.tsl.texas.gov/exhibits/annexation/part2/page2.html.

198 William Henry Harrison (1773−1841) was an American military officer, politician, and ninth President of the United States. Harrison served as the first congressional delegate from the Northwest Territory and the first Governor of Indiana Territory. He gained national fame for leading U.S. forces against Native Americans at the Battle of Tippecanoe in 1811, where he earned the nickname "Old Tippecanoe". He was promoted to major general in the War of 1812 and fought in the Battle of the Thames. "William Henry Harrison," The White House, accessed February 12, 2019, https://www.whitehouse.gov/about-the-white-house/presidents/william-henry-harrison/.

199 Justin Harvey Smith, *The Annexation of Texas* (New York: The Baker and Taylor Co., 1911), 103-104.

200 Hard Road to Texas, Texas Annexation 1836-1845, "Part 3: An International Matter," "Texas Finds a Champion," Texas State Library and Archives, accessed July 17, 2018, https://www.tsl.texas.gov/exhibits/annexation/part3/page2.html.

201 Edward P. Crapol, *John Tyler, the Accidental President* (Chapel Hill: University of North Carolina Press, 2006), 24-25; Frederick Merk *History of the Westward Movement* (New York: Alfred A. Knopf, 1978), 280-281; and Smith, 105-106.

202 Hard Road to Texas, Texas Annexation 1836-1845, "Part 2: On Our Own," "Santa Anna Strikes Back," Texas State Library and Archives, accessed July 17, 2018, https://www.tsl.texas.gov/exhibits/annexation/part2/page3.html.

203 Hard Road to Texas, Texas Annexation 1836-1845, "Part 2: On Our Own," "Santa Anna Strikes Back," Texas State Library and Archives, accessed July 17, 2018, https://www.tsl.texas.gov/exhibits/annexation/part2/page3.html.

204 The Somervell expedition was an expedition against Mexico in retaliation for three Mexican raids on Texas in 1842. On October 3, 1842, President Sam Houston ordered Alexander Somervell to organize the militia and volunteers and invade Mexico if the strength, equipment, and discipline of the army offered a reasonable hope of success. Seven hundred men left San Antonio on November 25. The Texans captured Laredo on December 8. The size of the expedition dwindled as men returned home. Somervell and the five hundred remaining men took Guerrero. On December 19, Somervell realized the expedition was a failure and ordered his men to disband and return home. The Texans were so disappointed with the order to disband that only 189 men and officers obeyed. Around 308 men under the command of William S. Fisher continued to Mexico on the Mier expedition. *Handbook of Texas Online*, Joseph Milton Nance, "Somervell Expedition," accessed February 21, 2017, http://www.tshaonline.org/handbook/online/articles/qys03.

205 The Mier expedition was an attack by a Texian militia against Mexican border settlements. The attack followed the unsuccessful Somervell expedition in December 1842. Although the Texians were ordered to retreat from the Rio Grande to Gonzales, 308 men remained in the area captured Ciudad Mier on December 20, 1842. However, the Texians did not know there were 3,000 Mexican troops in the area. In the ensuing battle, the Mexicans defeated the Texians. Although the Texians inflicted heavy casualties on the Mexicans, they were forced to surrender on December 26. The Mexicans marched the 243 Texian prisoners toward Mexico City. On February 11, 1843, 181 Texians escaped but 176 of them were captured. When the prisoners reached Saltillo, they learned Santa Anna had ordered the 176 escapees to be executed. General and Governor Francisco Mexía refused to follow the order. The new commander, Colonel Domingo Huerta, moved the prisoners to El Rancho Salado. Diplomatic efforts by the foreign ministers of the United States and Great Britain led Santa Anna to compromise. He said one in ten of the prisoners would be killed. To help determine who would die, Huerta had 159 white beans and 17 black beans placed in a pot. In what came to be known as the Black Bean

Episode, the Bean Lottery, the Texans were blindfolded and ordered to draw beans. The seventeen men who drew black beans were allowed to write letters home before being executed by firing squad. *Handbook of Texas Online*, Joseph Milton Nance, "Mier Expedition," accessed February 21, 2017, https://tshaonline.org/handbook/online/articles/qym02.

206 "The World of Sam Houston," The Texas State Library and Archives, accessed February 17, 2017, https://www.tsl.texas.gov/exhibits/presidents/houston2/mrprez.html.

207 Hard Road to Texas Annexation 1836-1845, "Part 2: On Our Own," "Santa Anna Strikes Back," The Texas State Library and Archives, accessed February 17, 2017, https://www.tsl.texas.gov/exhibits/annexation/part2/page3.html.

208 James W. Robinson (1790–1857) was a judge, attorney, and veteran of the Battle of San Jacinto. He was in San Antonio when it was captured by Mexico in September 1842 and was sent to Mexico as a prisoner. While in prison, Robinson began a secret correspondence with Antonio López de Santa Anna and reached an agreement under which the Mexican government released him from prison and allowed him to return to Texas. He carried a Mexican proposal for an agreement between Texas and Mexico. Robinson presented the offer to Mexico conferred with President Sam Houston and may have been responsible for the negotiations which resulted in a brief armistice. *Handbook of Texas Online*, L. W. Kemp, "Robinson, James W.," accessed July 03, 2018, http://www.tshaonline.org/handbook/online/articles/fro37.

209 Hard Road to Texas Annexation 1836-1845, "Part 3: An International Matter," "Britain Makes Its Move," The Texas State Library and Archives, accessed February 17, 2017, https://www.tsl.texas.gov/exhibits/annexation/part3/page1.html.

210 *Handbook of Texas Online*, C. T. Neu, "Annexation," accessed August 3, 2016, http://www.tshaonline.org/handbook/online/articles/mga02.

211 Sir Richard Pakenham (1797–1868) was a British diplomat. He served as Ambassador to the United States from 1835 until 1847. He unsuccessfully worked to prevent U.S. annexation of Texas and California by establishing British forces there instead. On December 14, 1843, he was appointed envoy extraordinary and minister plenipotentiary to the United States of America. He resolved the Oregon

boundary dispute. In this negotiation, though he did not carry the British points, he obtained the approval of his government, which signed the Oregon Treaty in 1846. The attitude of Great Britain regarding Texas proved of greater difficulty. Wikipedia contributors, "Richard Pakenham," *Wikipedia, The Free Encyclopedia*, https://en.wikipedia.org/w/index.php?title=Richard_Pakenham&oldid=893843033 (accessed August 23, 2019).

212 Charles Elliot (1801–1875) was a British knight and admiral. As British *chargé d'affaires* to Texas, Elliot advocated the abolition of slavery in Texas, worked for the establishment of free trade, and emphasized the importance of securing peace with Mexico. He worked with the British minister in Mexico City for an armistice between Texas and Mexico in 1843 and was instrumental in securing the release of some of the prisoners of the Mier expedition. Elliot opposed the annexation of Texas to the United States. In 1845, with the approval of President Jones, he went to Mexico to obtain a treaty guaranteeing Texas independence on condition that Texas not be annexed. He brought the treaty back to Texas, but Texans voted for annexation instead of Mexican recognition and protection by England. *Handbook of Texas Online*, "Elliot, Charles," accessed September 15, 2016, http://www.tshaonline.org/handbook/online/articles/fel09.

213 George Hockley (1802–1854) was chief of staff of the Texas army during the Texas Revolution. Sam Houston convinced him to move to Tennessee when Houston became governor there in 1828. Hockley followed Houston to Texas in 1835 and was made chief of staff upon Houston's election as commander-in-chief of the Texas army. Hockley commanded the artillery at the battle of San Jacinto. Later he was one of those who accompanied Antonio López de Santa Anna and Juan N. Almonte to Washington, DC. Hockley and Houston remained friends after the revolution. Houston appointed him colonel of ordnance on December 22, 1836, and secretary of war on November 13, 1838, and again on December 23, 1841. Houston also sent Hockley with Samuel M. Williams in 1843 to arrange an armistice with Mexico. *Handbook of Texas Online*, Carolyn Hyman, "Hockley, George Washington," accessed August 17, 2018, http://www.tshaonline.org/handbook/online/articles/fho08.

214 Samuel May Williams (1795–1858) was an entrepreneur and associate of Stephen F. Austin. In 1823, Austin hired him as translator and clerk. For the next thirteen years Williams was Austin's assistant. He wrote deeds, kept records, and directed colonial activities during the Austin's absences. He entered a partnership with Thomas F. McKinney in 1833 to establish their firm. The commission house dominated the Brazos cotton trade until 1838, when they moved to Galveston. The firm of McKinney and Williams used its credit to purchase arms and raise funds for the Texas Revolution. Neither the Republic nor the state was able to repay the $99,000 debt in full, and the partners realized only a small portion of their investment in addition to the passage of favorable relief legislation. As investors in the Galveston City Company, McKinney and Williams helped develop the city by constructing the Tremont Hotel and the commission house and wharf. In 1848, Williams opened the Commercial and Agricultural Bank of Galveston. Antibanking enemies attacked the bank because it violated constitutional prohibitions against banks. The Texas Supreme Court sustained the bank in 1852, The bank was forced to close in 1859. In 1838, he received a commission to negotiate a $5 million loan in the United States and to purchase seven ships for the Texas Navy. President Houston sent him to Matamoros in 1843 in an unsuccessful attempt to obtain an armistice with Mexico. *Handbook of Texas Online*, Margaret Swett Henson, "Williams, Samuel May," accessed August 5, 2016, http://www.tshaonline.org/handbook/online/articles/fwi35.

215 Hard Road to Texas Annexation 1836-1845, "Part 3: An International Matter," The Texas State Library and Archives, accessed March 19, 2017, https://www.tsl.texas.gov/exhibits/annexation/part3/page1.html.

216 Hard Road to Texas Annexation 1836-1845, "Part 3: An International Matter," The Texas State Library and Archives, accessed March 19, 2017, https://www.tsl.texas.gov/exhibits/annexation/part3/page1.html.

217 Duff Green (1791–1875) was a real estate promoter and speculator. *Handbook of Texas Online*, W. W. White, "Green, Duff," accessed March 19, 2017, http://www.tshaonline.org/handbook/online/articles/fgr32.

218 Lewis Cass (1782–1866) was an American military officer, politician, and statesman. He represented Michigan in the United States Senate and served in the Cabinets of two U.S. Presidents, Andrew Jackson and James Buchanan. He was also the 1848 Democratic presidential nominee and a leading spokesman for the Doctrine of Popular Sovereignty, which held the people in each territory should decide whether to permit slavery. "Cass, Richard, (1782-1866), Biographical Directory of the United States Congress, accessed February 12, 2019, http://bioguide.congress.gov/scripts/biodisplay.pl?index=C000233.

219 Abel Parker Upshur (1790–1844) was an American lawyer, judge and politician from Virginia. Upshur was active in Virginia state politics and served as Secretary of the Navy and Secretary of State during the Tyler administration. Upshur was instrumental in negotiating the secret treaty which led to the 1845 annexation of Texas to the United States and played a key role in ensuring Texas was admitted to the United States as a slave state. He was killed on February 28, 1844, when a gun exploded during a Potomac River cruise on the USS *Princeton*. "Biographies of the Secretaries of State: Abel Parker Upshur (1791–1844)," Office of the Historian, United States Department of State, accessed February 12, 2019, https://history.state.gov/departmenthistory/people/upshur-abel-parker.

220 Edward Everett (1794–1865) was an American politician, pastor, educator, diplomat, and orator from Massachusetts. Everett served as U.S. Representative, US. Senator, the 15th Governor of Massachusetts, Minister to Great Britain, and U.S. Secretary of State. He also taught at Harvard University and served as its president. Everett, Edward, (1794-1865)," Biographical Directory of the United States Congress, accessed February 12, 2019, http://bioguide.congress.gov/scripts/biodisplay.pl?index=E000264.

221 "Waddy Thompson, Jr. (1798-1868)" was a Representative from South Carolina. He was elected as an Anti-Jacksonian. He was reelected to the Twenty-fifth and Twenty-sixth Congresses and served from September 10, 1835, to March 3, 1841. He was appointed Envoy Extraordinary and Minister Plenipotentiary to Mexico and served from February 10, 1842, to March 9, 1844. *Biographical Directory of the U.S. Congress,* accessed February 28, 2019, http://bioguide.congress.gov/scripts/biodisplay.pl?index=T000221.

222 The Webster–Ashburton Treaty, signed August 9, 1842, was a treaty resolving several border issues between the United States and the British North American colonies. Webster Ashburton Treaty, Maine, accessed March 12, 2019, https://maineanencyclopedia.com/webster-ashburton-treaty/.

223 Crapol, 180.

224 Thomas W. Gilmer (1802–1844) was an American statesman. He served in several political positions in Virginia, including election as the 28th Governor of Virginia. Gilmer's final political office was as the 15th Secretary of the Navy, but he died in an accident ten days after assuming the position. Wikipedia contributors, "Thomas Walker Gilmer," *Wikipedia, The Free Encyclopedia,* https://en.wikipedia.org/w/index.php?title=Thomas_Walker_Gilmer&oldid=901901291 (accessed August 22, 2019).

225 North-South Conflict was over slavery. The South wanted to maintain slavery as a key element of its economy and society. The South also wanted to extend slavery to other territories and states. The North wanted to stop the expansion of slavery. "The American Civil War: A North-South Divide," *History Today*, accessed August 22, 2019, https://www.historytoday.com/archive/contrarian/american-civil-war-north-south-divide.

226 Merk, 281 and Crapol, 180-181.

227 Hard Road to Texas Annexation 1836-1845, "Part 3: An International Matter," The Texas State Library and Archives, accessed February 21, 2017, https://www.tsl.texas.gov/exhibits/annexation/part3/page1.html.

228 Hard Road to Texas Annexation 1836-1845, "Part 3: An International Matter," The Texas State Library and Archives, accessed February 21, 2017, https://www.tsl.texas.gov/exhibits/annexation/part3/page2.html.

229 Hard Road to Texas Annexation 1836-1845, "Part 4: A Treaty of Annexation," The Texas State Library and Archives, accessed February 21, 2017, https://www.tsl.texas.gov/exhibits/annexation/part4/page1.htm.

230 Hard Road to Texas Annexation 1836-1845, "Part 4: A Treaty of Annexation," The Texas State Library and Archives, accessed February 21, 2017, https://www.tsl.texas.gov/exhibits/annexation/part4/page1.htm.

231 Houston wrote to Henderson on February 21, 1844: "Consider, therefore that you and Van Zandt have all the needful powers to conclude the treaty of annexation or alliance with the Government of the United States, on just and reciprocal principles between the contracting parties – thereby fully securing the interest of Texas as an integral part of the United States, as a State or Territory, and the individual rights and privileges of its citizens, without innovation upon our fundamental institutions." Hard Road to Texas Annexation 1836-1845, "Sam Houston Letter to James Pinckney Henderson," accessed January 14, 2019, https://www.tsl.texas.gov/exhibits/annexation/part4/sam_houston_feb21_1844.html.

232 Robert J. Walker (1801–1869) was a lawyer, economist, and politician. He was a senator from Mississippi from 1835 until 1845, Secretary of the Treasury from 1845 to 1849 during the administration of President James K. Polk, and briefly as Territorial Governor of Kansas in 1857. Senator Walker vigorously supported the annexation of Texas. As Secretary of the Treasury, he was responsible for the management of funds relating to the Mexican American War and was involved in a bank scandal. He contributed to a bill called the Walker Tariff, which reduced rates to some of the lowest in history. "Robert J. Walker (1801–1869)," History, U.S. Department of the Treasury, accessed February 12, 2019, https://www.treasury.gov/about/history/Pages/rjwalker.aspx.

233 Hard Road to Texas Annexation 1836-1845, "Part 4: A Treaty of Annexation," The Texas State Library and Archives, accessed February 21, 2017, https://www.tsl.texas.gov/exhibits/annexation/part3/page2.html.

234 "Tyler narrowly escapes death on the USS Princeton," "This day in history," February 28, 1844, "Tyler narrowly escapes death on the USS *Princeton*," History.com, accessed February 14, 2019, https://www.history.com/this-day-in-history/tyler-narrowly-escapes-death-on-the-uss-princeton.

235 John Caldwell Calhoun (1782–1850) was a statesman and politician from South Carolina. He was the seventh Vice President of the United States from 1825 to 1832. He defended slavery and advanced the concept of minority rights in politics. He became a leading proponent of states' rights, limited government, nullification, and opposition to high tariffs. Calhoun believed the Northern states had to accept these policies to keep the South in the Union. His beliefs and warnings influenced the South's secession from the Union in 1860–1861. President Tyler named Calhoun Secretary of State on following the death of Abel P. Upshur. Calhoun championed Texas acquisition. Secretary of State Calhoun worked to see the presidency was placed in the hands of a southern extremist, who would put the expansion of slavery at the center of national policy. Secretary Calhoun was directed to honor former Secretary Upshur's verbal assurances of protection which Calhoun put in writing and to provide U.S. military intercession if Mexico attacked Texas. On April 22, 1844, Secretary Calhoun signed the treaty of annexation and ten days later delivered it to the Senate for consideration. In a letter to British ambassador Richard Pakenham, Calhoun claimed slavery contributed to the physical and mental well-being of Southern slaves. By linking Texas annexation to the expansion of slavery, Calhoun had alienated many senators who might previously have supported the treaty. On June 8, 1844, the Senate rejected the Tyler-Texas treaty by a vote of 35–16. "Biographies of the Secretaries of State: John Caldwell Calhoun (1782–

1850)," Office of the Historian, accessed March 8, 2019, https://history.state.gov/departmenthistory/people/calhoun-john-caldwell.

236 Hard Road to Texas Annexation 1836-1845, "Part 4: A Treaty of Annexation," The Texas State Library and Archives, accessed February 22, 2017, https://www.tsl.texas.gov/exhibits/annexation/part4/page1.html.

237 Hard Road to Texas Annexation 1836-1845, "Part 4: A Treaty of Annexation," The Texas State Library and Archives, accessed February 21, 2017, https://www.tsl.texas.gov/exhibits/annexation/part4/page2.html.

238 Thomas Hart Benton (1782–1858) was a United States Senator from Missouri. He was a Democrat and was an architect and champion of westward expansion by the United States or Manifest Destiny. Benton served in the Senate from 1821 to 1851, becoming the first senator to serve five terms. Benton's prime concern was the westward expansion of the United States. He supported annexation of the Republic of Texas. He advocated compromise in the partition of Oregon Country with the British and supported the 1846 Oregon Treaty, which divided the territory along the 49th parallel. He also authored the first Homestead Act, which granted land to settlers willing to farm it. "Benton, Thomas Hart, (1782-1858)," Biographical Directory of the United States Congress, accessed March 12, 2019, http://bioguide.congress.gov/scripts/biodisplay.pl?index=B000398.

239 James Knox Polk (1795–1849) was the eleventh President of the United States (1845–1849). Previously he was Speaker of the House of Representatives (1835–1839) and Governor of Tennessee (1839–1841). A protégé of Andrew Jackson, he was a member of the Democratic Party and an advocate of Jacksonian democracy. During Polk's presidency, the United States expanded significantly with the annexation of the Republic of Texas, the Oregon Territory, and the Mexican Cession following the American victory in the Mexican American War. "James K. Polk," The White House, accessed February 21, 2017, https://www.whitehouse.gov/about-the-white-house/presidents/james-k-polk/.

240 Hard Road to Texas Annexation 1836-1845, "Part 4: A Treaty of Annexation," The Texas State Library and Archives, accessed February 23, 2017, https://www.tsl.texas.gov/exhibits/annexation/part4/page2.html.

241 Andrew Jackson Donelson (1799–1871) was a diplomat and Army officer. He attended Cumberland College, Nashville, and graduated from the United States

Military Academy in 1820. He spent two years as aide-de-camp to his uncle, General Andrew Jackson, before resigning his commission to study law. In 1829, President Jackson appointed Donelson as his private secretary. Donelson served as the president's private secretary in Washington until the end of his uncle's second term on March 4, 1837.

In 1844, President John Tyler appointed Donelson *chargé d'affaires* of the United States to the Republic of Texas. His duties were to present American propositions to President Anson Jones and to further the cause of annexation of the Republic to the United States. After this work, he was minister to Prussia and in 1852 a candidate for the vice presidency of the United States. *Handbook of Texas Online*, Hugo Ellis, "Donelson, Andrew Jackson," accessed, August 02, 2017, http://www.tshaonline.org/handbook/online/articles/fdo13

242 Hard Road to Texas Annexation 1836-1845, "Part 5: The Final Showdown," The Texas State Library and Archives, accessed February 23, 2017, https://www.tsl.texas.gov/exhibits/annexation/part5/page1.html.

243 In the United States Congress, a joint resolution is a legislative measure which requires approval by the Senate and the House and is presented to the president for his approval or disapproval. Wikipedia contributors, "Joint resolution," *Wikipedia, The Free Encyclopedia,* https://en.wikipedia.org/w/index.php?title=Joint_resolution&oldid=892816000 (accessed August 22, 2019).

244 Hard Road to Texas Annexation 1836-1845, "Part 5: The Final Showdown," The Texas State Library and Archives, accessed February 23, 2017, https://www.tsl.texas.gov/exhibits/annexation/part5/page1.html.

245 The so-called "Diplomatic Act" provided that Great Britain and France would guarantee the peace at the Rio Grande. Hard Road to Texas Annexation 1836-1845, "Part 5: The Final Showdown," The Texas State Library and Archives, accessed February 23, 2017, https://www.tsl.texas.gov/exhibits/annexation/part5/page1.html.

246 Hard Road to Texas Annexation 1836-1845, "Part 5: The Final Showdown," The Texas State Library and Archives, accessed February 23, 2017, https://www.tsl.texas.gov/exhibits/annexation/part5/page1.html.

247 Hard Road to Texas Annexation 1836-1845, Part 5: The Final Showdown,

The Texas State Library and Archives, accessed February 23, 2017, https://www.tsl.texas.gov/exhibits/annexation/part5/page1.html.

ALLEN'S ROLE IN ANNEXATION

248 George Whitfield Terrell (?–1846) was district attorney of San Augustine County in 1840 and later served as district judge. Terrell was secretary of state of the Republic of Texas under David G. Burnet in 1841. In December 1841, he was made Attorney General of the Republic by Sam Houston. From 1842 to 1844, Terrell was Indian commissioner and as such negotiated the Indian treaty at Bird's Fort on September 29, 1843. He was appointed *chargé d'affaires* to France, Great Britain, and Spain in December 1844 and continued in that capacity under President Anson Jones. Upon his return to Texas in 1845, Terrell was again made Indian commissioner. He was an opponent of annexation. He died on May 13, 1846. *Handbook of Texas Online*, Melvin B. Jaschke, "Terrell, George Whitfield," accessed January 23, 2017, http://www.tshaonline.org/handbook/online/articles/fte22.

249 Francis, Jr. Moore, *Telegraph and Texas Register* (Houston, Tex.), Vol. 9, No. 47, Ed. 1, Wednesday, November 20, 1844, newspaper, November 20, 1844; Houston, Texas. (texashistory.unt.edu/ark:/67531/metapth78075/m1/1/?q=George+Terrell: accessed September 4, 2018), University of North Texas Libraries, The Portal to Texas History, texashistory.unt.edu; crediting The Dolph Briscoe Center for American History.

250 *Texas National Register*, (Washington, Tex.), Vol. 1, No. 2, Ed. 1, Saturday, December 14, 1844, newspaper, December 14, 1844; Washington, Texas. (texashistory.unt.edu/ark:/67531/metapth80096/: accessed September 4, 2018), University of North Texas Libraries, The Portal to Texas History, texashistory.unt.edu; crediting The Dolph Briscoe Center for American History.

251 *Texas National Register,* (Washington, Tex.), Vol. 1, No. 14, Ed. 1, Saturday, March 8, 1845, newspaper, March 8, 1845; Washington, Texas. (texashistory.unt.edu/ark:/67531/metapth80108/m1/3/?q=Ebenezer+Allen: accessed September 4, 2018), University of North Texas Libraries, The Portal to Texas History, texashistory.unt.edu; crediting The Dolph Briscoe Center for American History.

252 Charles De Morse, *The Northern Standard.* (Clarksville, Tex.), Vol. 3, No. 5,

Ed. 1, Thursday, December 12, 1844, newspaper, December 12, 1844; Clarksville, Texas. (https://texashistory.unt.edu/ark:/67531/metapth80543/: accessed August 23, 2019), University of North Texas Libraries, The Portal to Texas History, https://texashistory.unt.edu; crediting The Dolph Briscoe Center for American History.

253 In 1839, Austin was chosen to replace Houston as the capital of the Republic of Texas and was incorporated under the name "Waterloo." Shortly afterward, the name was changed to Austin in honor of Stephen F. Austin, the "Father of Texas" and the Republic's first secretary of state. *Handbook of Texas Online*, David C. Humphrey, "Austin, TX (Travis County)," accessed February 12, 2019, http://www.tshaonline.org/handbook/online/articles/hda03.

254 The Texas Railroad, Navigation, and Banking Company was chartered by the First Congress of the Republic of Texas on December 16, 1836. The company was authorized to connect Gulf ports by canal, to construct railroads wherever desirable, and to have banking privileges as soon as one-fifth of its capital stock of $5,000,000 had been subscribed. *Handbook of Texas Online*, "Texas Railroad, Navigation, and Banking Company," accessed January 31, 2019, http://www.tshaonline.org/handbook/online/articles/dft01.

255 *Handbook of Texas Online*, Herbert Gambrell, "Jones, Anson," accessed March 31, 2016, http://www.tshaonline.org/handbook/online/articles/fjo42.

256 William Harris Wharton (1802–1839) was a speaker and leader in the Texas Revolution. William Wharton established Eagle Island Plantation. Wharton supported colonists requesting a more vigorous policy toward Mexico. He was a signer of the surrender document. He was a delegate from Victoria to the Convention of 1832, which asked for separate statehood for Texas and drew up a provisional constitution for a state government. Wharton wrote the petition to Mexico asking for statehood. He was president at the Convention of 1833. Wharton was chosen judge advocate. He served with the army in the Siege of Bexar. He resigned after his appointment as a commissioner to the United States to obtain aid for the Texans. In November of 1836 President Houston appointed Wharton first minister to the United States to obtain recognition by and possibly annexation. Recognition was won on March 3, 1837. After he resigned as minister in early 1837, Wharton was captured at sea by a Mexican ship and imprisoned at Matamoros. He escaped and reached Texas in time to be elected to the Texas Senate in 1838. Though he resigned before the beginning of the Adjourned Session in May 1838, he was reelected the same year. Wharton was killed on March 14, 1839, when he accidentally discharged a pistol while dismounting his horse. *Handbook of Texas Online*, Merle Weir, "Wharton, William Harris," accessed September 16, 2018, http://www.tshaonline.org/handbook/online/articles/fwh08.

257 The Santa Fe Expedition was a commercial and military expedition in 1841 to secure Republic of Texas's claims to parts of Northern New Mexico. The expedition was unofficially initiated by President Mirabeau B. Lamar, to gain control over the lucrative Santa Fe Trail and further develop the trade links between Texas and New Mexico. The initiative was a major component of Lamar's ambitious plan to turn the Republic into a continental power. President Lamar wanted to expand Texas as quickly as possible to stave off the growing movement demanding the annexation of Texas to the United States. Lamar's administration had already started courting the New Mexicans, sending out a commissioner in 1840, and many Texans thought they might be favorable to the idea of joining the Republic of Texas. The expedition was a complete failure. *Handbook of Texas Online*, H. Bailey Carroll, "Texan Santa Fe Expedition," accessed February 10, 2019, http://www.tshaonline.org/handbook/online/articles/qyt03.

258 Pro tempore, abbreviated pro tem or p. t. is a Latin phrase which best translates to "for the time being" in English. This phrase often describes a person who acts as a locum tenens (placeholder) in the absence of a superior, such as the President pro tempore of the United States Senate, who acts in place of the President of the United States Senate, the Vice President of the United States. Wikipedia contributors, "Pro tempore," *Wikipedia, The Free Encyclopedia*, https://en.wikipedia.org/w/index.php?title=
Pro_tempore&oldid=877065335 (accessed August 22, 2019).

259 Wikipedia contributors, "Anson Jones," *Wikipedia, The Free Encyclopedia*, https://en.wikipedia.org/w/index.php?title=Anson_Jones&oldid=926165194 (accessed December 9, 2019).

260 Ashbel Smith (1805–1886) was a doctor and leader in the development of Texas. He has been called "the father of Texas medicine" and "the father of the University of Texas." Sam Houston appointed Smith surgeon general of the Army of the Republic of Texas on June 7, 1837. As surgeon, Smith set up an efficient system of operation and established the first hospital in Houston. He also served as the first chairman of the Board of Medical Censors established in December 1837. During the Yellow Fever epidemic in Galveston in 1839, he treated the sick, published factual reports of the progress of the disease, and wrote the first treatise on yellow fever in Texas. In 1848, Smith met with ten other Galveston doctors to begin working for the formation of the Medical and Surgical Society of Galveston. Houston recognized Smith's diplomatic ability and in 1838 sent him to negotiate a treaty with the Comanche Indians. In 1842, Smith was appointed the *chargé d'affaires* of Texas to England and France. In 1845, Anson Jones selected him as secretary of state, but he gave up the role to serve *chargé d'affaires* of Texas to England and France. He negotiated the Smith-Cuevas Treaty with Mexico in which Mexico acknowledged the independence of Texas. Smith served in Mexican and Civil Wars. Smith devoted much time and energy to the cause of education. He urged Texas to underwrite the education of every child in the state. He was a charter member and first vice president of the Philosophical Society of Texas. One of that organization's first acts was to draw up a memorial to the Texas Congress urging the establishment of a system of public education in Texas. He championed public education for blacks and women and was one of three commissioners appointed by Governor Richard Coke to establish an "Agricultural and Mechanical College of Texas, for the benefit of the Colored [sic] Youths." This school is now Prairie View A&M University. He spent his last years trying to establish a state university with a first-class medical branch. *Handbook of Texas Online*, Elizabeth Silverthorne, "Smith, Ashbel," accessed September 07, 2018, http://www.tshaonline.org/handbook/online/articles/fsm04.

261 George Washington Hill (1814–1860) secretary of war and secretary of the navy in Sam Houston's cabinet. *Handbook of Texas Online*, "Hill, George Washington," accessed February 01, 2019, http://www.tshaonline.org/handbook/online/articles/fhi20.

262 William Beck Ochiltree (1811–1867) was judge of the Fifth Judicial District, secretary of the treasury in 1844, adjutant general in 1845, and delegate to the Convention of 1845. After annexation, he was a representative in the Sixth Legislature in 1855 and delegate to the Secession Convention in 1861. *Handbook of Texas Online*, Robert Bruce Blake, "Ochiltree, William Beck," accessed February 01, 2019, http://www.tshaonline.org/handbook/online/articles/foc02.

263 Thomas William "Peg Leg" Ward (1807–1872) was the second commissioner of the General Land Office, three-time mayor of Austin, and United States consul to Panama. Ward systematized the process for transferring land from public to private ownership and initiated important reforms, such as permanent land districts and centralization of land mapping in the General Land Office. During his seven years in office, almost 11,000 patents (legal titles to land) were issued to those Texans promised free land, whereas when Ward took office, not a single such patent had been issued. *Handbook of Texas Online*, David C. Humphrey, "Ward, Thomas William," accessed February 01, 2019, http://www.tshaonline.org/handbook/online/articles/fwa52.

264 Anson Jones, *Republic of Texas*, 74.

265 Annie Middleton, "Donelson's Mission to Texas in Behalf of Annexation." *The Southwestern Historical Quarterly* 24, no. 4 (1921): 270. http://www.jstor.org/stable/30234808.

266 Ebenezer Allen Letter to Charles Elliott, *Diplomatic Correspondence of the Republic of Texas* (Washington: Government Printing Office, 1911), Volume II, Part II, 1169.

267 Middleton, 258. 87

268 *Handbook of Texas Online*, W. W. White, "Green, Duff," accessed March 19, 2017, http://www.tshaonline.org/handbook/online/articles/fgr32.

269 Anson Jones, *Memoranda and Official Correspondence Relating to the Republic of Texas and its History and Annexation* (New York: D. Appleton and Company, 1859), 417-418.

270 "Biographies of the Secretaries of State: Henry Clay (1777-1852)," Office of the Historian, U.S. Department of State, accessed March 14, 2019, https://history.state.gov/departmenthistory/people/clay-henry.

271 Middleton, 262-264.

272 Middleton, 251-252.

273 Freeling, 440; Michael Holt, *The Fate of Their Country: Politicians, Slavery Extension, and the Coming of the Civil War* (New York: Hill and Wang, 2005), 13; and Merk, 286.

274 Freeling, 440 & 455 and Sean Wilentz, *The Rise of American Democracy:*

Jefferson to Lincoln (New York: W.W. Horton and Company, 2008), 575.

275 Holt, 13. and Charles Sellers, *James K. Polk, Continentalist* (Princeton: Princeton University Press, 1966), 205.

276 Freeling, 443.

277 Wilentz, 572 & 575 and Freeling, 446.

278 Sellers, 170 and Wilentz, 578.

279 Crapol, 220; Freeling, 447-448; Holt, 14-15; and Sellers, 215.

280 Middleton, 265.

281 *Handbook of Texas Online*, Joseph Milton Nance, "Republic of Texas," accessed March 07, 2019, http://www.tshaonline.org/handbook/online/articles/mzr02.

282 Charles H. Raymond (1816–?) was a lawyer, soldier, and diplomat. Raymond moved to Texas in 1839 and settled in Robertson's colony. He formed a partnership with John Hilphill and set up a law practice in Milam and Robertson counties. On November 23, 1840, he was appointed a commissioner to inspect land offices east of the Brazos River. He was elected to represent Robertson County in the House of Representatives of the Sixth Congress. He served as a second lieutenant in a campaign against the Comanches in 1841. He was appointed secretary of the Texas legation in Washington, DC, in July 1842. When Van Zandt resigned Raymond was appointed to be *chargé d'affaires*. *Handbook of Texas Online*, Thomas W. Cutrer, "Raymond, Charles H.," accessed August 02, 2017, http://www.tshaonline.org/handbook/online/articles/fra50.

283 "Much About Annexation," *The Galveston Daily News*. (Galveston, Tex.), Vol. 45, No. 257, Ed. 1 Saturday, January 8, 1887, newspaper, January 8, 1887; Galveston, Texas. (https://texashistory.unt.edu/ark:/67531/metapth462757/: accessed August 24, 2019), University of North Texas Libraries, The Portal to Texas History, https://texashistory.unt.edu; crediting Abilene Library Consortium.

284 "Much About Annexation," *The Galveston Daily News*. (Galveston, Tex.), Vol. 45, No. 257, Ed. 1 Saturday, January 8, 1887, newspaper, January 8, 1887; Galveston, Texas. (https://texashistory.unt.edu/ark:/67531/metapth462757/: accessed August 24, 2019), University of North Texas Libraries, The Portal to Texas

History, https://texashistory.unt.edu; crediting Abilene Library Consortium.

285 "Much About Annexation," *The Galveston Daily News*. (Galveston, Tex.), Vol. 45, No. 257, Ed. 1 Saturday, January 8, 1887, newspaper, January 8, 1887; Galveston, Texas. (https://texashistory.unt.edu/ark:/67531/metapth462757/: accessed August 24, 2019), University of North Texas Libraries, The Portal to Texas History, https://texashistory.unt.edu; crediting Abilene Library Consortium.

286 "Much About Annexation," *The Galveston Daily News*. (Galveston, Tex.), Vol. 45, No. 257, Ed. 1 Saturday, January 8, 1887, newspaper, January 8, 1887; Galveston, Texas. (https://texashistory.unt.edu/ark:/67531/metapth462757/: accessed August 24, 2019), University of North Texas Libraries, The Portal to Texas History, https://texashistory.unt.edu; crediting Abilene Library Consortium.

TEXAS CONSIDERS HER OPTIONS

287 President Tyler appointed Andrew Jackson Donelson in March 1845. *Handbook of Texas Online*, Joseph Milton Nance, "Republic of Texas," accessed March 07, 2019, http://www.tshaonline.org/handbook/online/articles/mzr02.

288 Dubois de Saligny (1809 – 1888) was a French diplomat in the Republic of Texas. While at this last post, he was instructed by the French government to go to Texas to investigate the conditions and prospects of the new republic. Dubois returned in January 1844 to serve as the French representative until the annexation of Texas to the United States. *Handbook of Texas Online*, Nancy N. Barker, "Dubois De Saligny," accessed February 01, 2019, http://www.tshaonline.org/handbook/online/articles/fdu02.

289 Middleton, 255-256.

290 The evidence required by Mr. Calhoun was approval of the Congressional joint resolution for annexation by the Texas executive and legislature and preparing a new state constitution.

291 Jones, *Memoranda*, 505.

292 Middleton, 265.

293 James Buchanan Jr. (1791–1868) was 15th President of the United States

(1857–1861) prior to the Civil War. He was a member of the Democratic Party, 17th United States Secretary of State. He served in the Senate and House of Representatives before becoming president. In 1845, he accepted appointment as President James K. Polk's Secretary of State. During Buchanan's tenure as Secretary of State, the United States grew immensely with the conclusion of the Oregon Treaty and victory in the Mexican American War. Wikipedia contributors, "James Buchanan," *Wikipedia, The Free Encyclopedia,* https://en.wikipedia.org/w/index.php?title=James_Buchanan&oldid=911835953 (accessed August 23, 2019).

294 Middleton, 266.

295 Cooke was appointed by President Anson Jones in December 1844 to replace Morgan Calvin Hamilton as secretary of war. Cooke, who had become the last commander of the regular Texas army when the troops were disbanded in 1841, was now responsible for raising troops and supplies for the United States army of occupation under Gen. Zachary Taylor. He served in this office until the spring of 1846, when he ran unsuccessfully for the Congress of the United States. *Handbook of Texas Online,* Steven A. Brownrigg, "Cooke, William Gordon," accessed February 05, 2019, http://www.tshaonline.org/handbook/online/articles/fcobv.

296 Jones, *Memoranda*, 74.

297 Extra-constitutional - not authorized by or based on a constitution; beyond the provisions of a constitution. *American Heritage® Dictionary of the English Language, Fifth Edition.* S. v. "extraconstitutional." Retrieved August 23, 2019 from https://www.thefreedictionary.com/extraconstitutional.

298 Middleton, 258.

299 Smith, *The Annexation of Texas*, 436-437.

300 Middleton, 258.

301 Middleton, 258-259.

302 Letter from Mr. Allen to Mr. Donelson, April 14, 1845, The Southwestern Historical Society (Austin: The Texas State Historical Association, 1921), Vol. 24, 54.

303 Letter from Mr. Donelson to Mr. Allen, April 16, 1845, The Southwestern Historical Society (Austin: The Texas State Historical Association, 1921), Vol. 24,

54.

304 Jones, *Memoranda*, 453.

305 Jones, *Memoranda*, 453-455.

306 *Handbook of Texas Online*, Herbert Gambrell, "Jones, Anson," accessed May 25, 2016, http://www.tshaonline.org/handbook/online/articles/fjo42.

307 Jones, *Memoranda*, 458.

308 Archibald Yell (1797? −1847) was a soldier, congressman, and governor of Arkansas. On March 10, 1845, Yell's close friend and political mentor, President James K. Polk, sent the congressman-elect to Texas with instructions to the American *chargé d'affaires*, Andrew Jackson Donelson, confirming John Tyler's choice of the House of Representatives' plan to bring about annexation. Yell went with Donelson from New Orleans to Texas to accept the Republic's offer of annexation. He was active in stimulating public meetings, and he was unstinting in his promises of the benefits to Texas and Texans should the measure be consummated. *Handbook of Texas Online*, Thomas W. Cutrer, "Yell, Archibald," accessed January 15, 2018, http://www.tshaonline.org/handbook/online/articles/fye02.

309 Jones, *Memoranda*, 459-461.

310 Jones, *Memoranda*, 459-461.

311 Jones, *Memoranda*, 461-462.

312 Jones, *Memoranda*, 461-462.

313 Hard Road to Texas, Texas Annexation 1836-1845, "Part 5: The Final Showdown," National Register Extra --- Extra, Texas State Library and Archives Commission, accessed February 6, 2019, https://www.tsl.texas.gov/exhibits/annexation/part5/anson_jones_may8_1845_proclamation.html.

314 *Handbook of Texas Online*, Herbert Gambrell, "Jones, Anson," accessed May 25, 2016, http://www.tshaonline.org/handbook/online/articles/fjo42.

315 Charles De Morse "Proclamation, *The Northern Standard*. (Clarksville, Tex.), Vol. 3, No. 21, Ed. 1, Friday, May 30, 1845, newspaper, May 30, 1845; Clarksville, Texas. (https://texashistory.unt.edu/ark:/67531/metapth80557/: accessed March 26,

2019), University of North Texas Libraries, The Portal to Texas History, https://texashistory.unt.edu; crediting The Dolph Briscoe Center for American History.

316 New Washington, Texas was at the point where Buffalo Bayou entered San Jacinto Bay, at the northwestern extremity of Galveston Bay in eastern Harris County. *Handbook of Texas Online*, Seymour V. Connor, "New Washington, TX," accessed June 01, 2016, http://www.tshaonline.org/handbook/online/articles/hvn28.

317 William Jesse Swain (1839–1904) was a soldier and legislator. *Handbook of Texas Online*, Claudia Hazlewood, "Swain, William Jesse," accessed September 18, 2018, http://www.tshaonline.org/handbook/online/articles/fsw01.

318 The phrase "rectus in curia" is a legal term meaning "right in court," free from charge or impeachment, and free from any offence. "rectus in curia," Merriam-Webster, accessed August 22, 2019, https://www.merriam-webster.com/dictionary/rectus%20in%20curia.

319 Sidney Sherman (1805–1873) was a soldier and entrepreneur. Sherman was a successful manufacturer in Kentucky. He formed the first company to make cotton bagging by machinery, and he was the first maker of sheet lead west of the Alleghenies. Sherman sold his cotton bagging plant and used the money to equip a company of fifty-two volunteers for the Texas Revolution. Sherman held various command positions in the Texas Army and fought with other volunteers through the Battle of San Jacinto. The battle cry, "Remember the Alamo" was attributed to Sherman. After the battle, he acted as president of the board of officers which distributed captured property among the soldiers. Sherman was Harris County's representative in the Seventh Congress of the Republic and served as chairman of the committee on military affairs. In 1843, he was elected major general of militia, a position he held until annexation. After annexation, Sherman moved to Harrisburg and with the financial support of investors bought the town and the local railroad company. A new town was laid out, and he organized the Buffalo Bayou, Brazos and Colorado Railway Company. When the Civil War began, Sherman was appointed commandant of Galveston. *Handbook of Texas Online*, Julia Beazley, "Sherman, Sidney," accessed September 08, 2018, http://www.tshaonline.org/handbook/online/articles/fsh27.

320 Robert Field Stockton was a U. S. Navy officer. He was instructed to take his fleet to Galveston, display the American flag, and try to determine the sentiment

of the people regarding annexation. Stockton was so eager to bring Texas into the Union and to extend its limits at the expense of Mexico, and his superiors felt it necessary to warn him against rashness. His presence at Galveston had some influence in determining the action taken by Texas, the first news of which was brought to President James K. Polk by Stockton. *Handbook of Texas Online*, C. T. Neu, "Stockton, Robert Field," accessed March 16, 2019, http://www.tshaonline.org/handbook/online/articles/fst61.

321 Jones, *Memoranda*, 466-468.

322 *Handbook of Texas Online*, Ralph W. Steen, "Convention of 1845," accessed February 07, 2019, http://www.tshaonline.org/handbook/online/articles/mjc13.

323 "Jones to Polk," Annual Report of the American Historical Association for the Year 1908 (Washington: Government Printing Office, 1911), Vol. II, Part II, 386-387.

324 *Handbook of Texas Online*, C. T. Neu, "Annexation," accessed March 16, 2019, http://www.tshaonline.org/handbook/online/articles/mga02.

325 Ebenezer Allen Letter to Andrew Jackson Donelson, June 23, 1845. Hard Road to Texas Annexation, United States Diplomatic Correspondence, Texas Secretary of State records, Archives and Information Services Division, Texas State Library and Archives Commission, accessed June 9, 2016, https://www.tsl.texas.gov/exhibits/annexation/part5/eben_allen_june23_1845_1.html (page 1) and https://www.tsl.texas.gov/exhibits/annexation/part5/eben_allen_june23_1845_2.html. (page 2)

326 William D. Lee was Secretary to the Legation to the United States and served as acting *chargé d'affaires* to the United States until Mr. David S. Kaufman reached Washington. Jones, Letters, 487-489.

327 Jones, *Memoranda*, 487-489.

328 Jones, *Memoranda*, 490-491.

329 *Handbook of Texas Online*, C. T. Neu, "Annexation," accessed March 16, 2019, http://www.tshaonline.org/handbook/online/articles/mga02.

330 William H. Daingerfield - *chargé d'affaires* to the Netherlands. *Handbook of Texas Online*, Redding S. Sugg, Jr., "Daingerfield, William Henry," accessed Feb-

ruary 16, 2019, http://www.tshaonline.org/handbook/online/articles/fda04.

331 David S. Kaufman was *chargé d'affaires* to the United States. *Handbook of Texas Online*, Natalie Ornish, "Kaufman, David Spangler," accessed February 16, 2019, http://www.tshaonline.org/handbook/online/articles/fka12.

332 William L. Marcy (1786 – 1857) was an American lawyer, politician, and judge who served as U.S. Senator, Governor of New York, U.S. Secretary of War and U.S. Secretary of State. In the latter office, he negotiated the Gadsden Purchase, the last major acquisition of land in the continental United States. He served as Secretary of War under James K. Polk from 1845 to 1849, overseeing the Mexican American War. Wikipedia contributors, "William L. Marcy," *Wikipedia, The Free Encyclopedia,* https://en.wikipedia.org/w/index.php?title=William_L._Marcy&oldid=907542022 (accessed August 22, 2019).

333 Jones, *Memorand054=-067a*, 505.

IMMEDIATE AND AGGRESSIVE PROTECTION

334 Jones, *Memoranda*, 46.

335 John D. Eisenhower, *So Far from God - The U.S. War with Mexico* - 1846-1848 (New York: Anchor Books, 1989), 24-26.

336 Jones, *Memoranda*, 53.

337 Jones, *Memoranda*, 67.

338 General Juan Nepomuceno Almonte (1803–1809) was a Mexican official and diplomat. In 1834, Almonte inspected Texas and wrote a detailed and comprehensive report on what he found. When he went with Antonio López de Santa Anna to Texas in 1836, they were taken prisoner at San Jacinto. Santa Anna and Almonte were sent to the United States and returned to Mexico in February 1837. He continued in diplomatic and military service and rose to the rank of general of a division. In 1839, he headed the Mexican legation in Belgium but in 1840 returned to the War Department. Almonte was minister plenipotentiary to Washington from 1841 to 1845. After the annexation of Texas, he returned to Mexico and appointed minister to France. He joined Santa Anna in Havana and returned to Mexico. During the Mexican War, Almonte served for a time as secretary of war. *Handbook*

of Texas Online, Winifred W. Vigness, "Almonte, Juan Nepomuceno," accessed August 13, 2018, http://www.tshaonline.org/handbook/online/articles/fal45.

339 Jones, *Memoranda,* 457.

340 The use of "embarrassment" may refer to "dilemma," "awkwardness," "unease," or "predicament." Wikipedia contributors, "Embarrassment," *Wikipedia, The Free Encyclopedia,* https://en.wikipedia.org/w/index.php?title=Embarrassment&oldid=907181637, (accessed August 22, 2019).

341 Jones, *Memoranda,* 458.

342 Jones, *Memoranda,* 53.

343 Jones, *Memoranda,* 468.

344 Jones, *Memoranda,* 46-47.

345 The Snively Expedition was one of a series of raids by Texan and Mexican forces to revenge the failures of the Texan Santa Fe Expedition and the Mier Expedition. In January 1843, Jacob Snively received permission from the Texas government to organize and equip an expedition to intercept and seize the property of Mexican traders passing through territory claimed by Texas on the Santa Fe Trail. The Texans attacked a Mexican convoy protected by 100 Mexican soldiers. Seventeen Mexicans were killed and eighty-two taken prisoner in the raid. Following the attack, the men waited for another opportunity. Spies indicated there was no prospect of encountering a caravan in the immediate future. Friction in the command developed, and many of the men wanted to return home. Finally, on June 28, the Mexican prisoners were released, and the battalion dissolved. A small group commanded by Snively marched to the Arkansas River where they were intercepted by U.S. dragoons. The Texans were captured and ordered to return home. The Texas government complained the dragoons had invaded Texas territory in arresting Snively's forces. Finally, the United States made a trifling appropriation for the Texans engaged in the expedition. *Handbook of Texas Online,* H. Bailey Carroll, "Snively Expedition," accessed September 05, 2018, http://www.tshaonline.org/handbook/online/articles/qys02.

346 United States, Congress, Senate, Message from the President of the United States to the Two Houses of Congress at the Commencement of the First Session of the Twenty-Ninth Congress., book, 1845; Washington. (texashistory.unt.edu/

ark:/67531/metapth2365/: accessed March 9, 2018), University of North Texas Libraries, The Portal to Texas History, texashistory.unt.edu; 61-62.

347 Jacob Snively (1809–1871) was a military officer in the Republic of Texas. On May 13, 1837, he was appointed paymaster general of the Army of the Republic of Texas with the rank of colonel, and during June and July of 1837, was acting secretary of war. Snively resigned from the army in September 1837, but in 1839 he again served as paymaster general under Albert Sidney Johnston and in 1843 was quartermaster of the army and assistant inspector general of the Republic. In January 1843, Snively petitioned the Texas Department of War and Marine for permission to intercept a party of Mexican traders who would reportedly be crossing Texas territory by way of the Santa Fe Trail and to appropriate their goods in retaliation for the Mexican raids on San Antonio in 1842 and for the alleged mistreatment of Texas prisoners captured at the battle of Mier and on the Texan Santa Fe Expedition. *Handbook of Texas Online*, H. Bailey Carroll, "Snively, Jacob," accessed July 10, 2018, http://www.tshaonline.org/handbook/online/articles/fsn07.

348 United States. Congress. Senate. Message from the President of the United States to the Two Houses of Congress at the Commencement of the First Session of the Twenty-Ninth Congress., book, 1845; Washington. (texashistory.unt.edu/ark:/67531/metapth2365/: accessed March 9, 2018), University of North Texas Libraries, The Portal to Texas History, texashistory.unt.edu; 62-63.

349 Jones, *Memoranda*, 465-466.

350 Jones, *Memoranda*, 52.

351 Jones, *Memoranda*, 102.

352 Thomas William Ward (1807–1872) was the second commissioner of the General Land Office, three-time mayor of Austin, and U. S. consul to Panama. Ward recruited men from New Orleans for the Texas revolution. As a result of his military service, Ward acquired rights to almost 8,000 acres of Texas land, including 4,428 acres in recognition of the disability he sustained in battle. In 1837, Ward constructed a two-story capitol for Texas in Houston. Then in late 1839, he was elected as chief clerk in the Texas House of Representatives. He was elected Austin's second mayor in August 1840. In January 1841, Texas President David G. Burnet appointed Ward second commissioner of the General Land Office. He systematized the process for transferring land from public to private ownership and

created permanent land districts and centralized land mapping in the General Land Office. During his seven years in office, almost 11,000 land titles were issued to those Texans promised free land. In early 1848, Ward's critics in the Legislature voted him out of office. He lost statewide elections for land commissioner in 1849 and 1851. In 1850, Governor Peter Bell appointed him temporary special land commissioner to the Peters Colony, where he reviewed colonists' disputed land claims. In December 1852, Austin voters again elected Ward mayor, but he resigned in August 1853 after President Franklin Pierce appointed him United States consul to Panama. During his term from October 1853 to August 1856 80,000 Americans crossed the Isthmus on their way to and from California. In November 1864, Ward was elected Austin's mayor for the third time. *Handbook of Texas Online*, David C. Humphrey, "Ward, Thomas William," accessed February 16, 2019, http://www.tshaonline.org/handbook/online/articles/fwa52.

353 Jones, *Memoranda*, 102-103.

354 Jones, *Memoranda*, 127-128.

355 Jones, *Memoranda*, 509.

356 Jones, *Memoranda*, 508.

357 "Anson Jones Valedictory Speech, February 19, 1846," Texas State Library and Archives Commission, accessed March 22, 2019, https://www.tsl.texas.gov/treasures/earlystate/nomore-1.html, https://www.tsl.texas.gov/treasures/earlystate/nomore-2.htm, and https://www.tsl.texas.gov/treasures/earlystate/nomore-3.html.

358 *Handbook of Texas Online*, Herbert Gambrell, "Jones, Anson," accessed May 25, 2016, http://www.tshaonline.org/handbook/online/articles/fjo42.

359 Jones, *Memoranda*, 44.

360 James L. Healy, *Sam Houston* (Norman: The University of Oklahoma Press 2004), 293.

361 Anson Jones, *The Republic of Texas – Its History and Annexation* (New York: D. Appleton and Company, 1859).

362 *Handbook of Texas Online*, Herbert Gambrell, "Jones, Anson," accessed July 04, 2016, http://www.tshaonline.org/handbook/online/articles/fjo42.

363 James Morgan (?–1866) was a merchant, land speculator, and officer in the Texas Revolution. In 1830, he opened a mercantile business in Texas. Morgan formed a partnership with John Reed, and they bought a schooner. In 1835, Morgan was appointed agent for the New Washington Association to develop Texas real estate. Morgan purchased many properties in Harrisburg and Liberty for the company. He bought land at the mouth of the San Jacinto River. He laid out a town where many Scottish highlanders and free blacks from New York settled. Morgan ran one of two ships belonging to the company. Texas used these ships during the Texas Revolution. Morgan also supplied the civil and military branches with merchandise from his store. From March 20, 1836, to April 1, 1837, he was colonel and commandant of Galveston Island. In 1843, Morgan and William Bryan managed the secret sale of the Texas Navy. During the 1850s, Morgan advocated improvement of what became the Houston Ship Channel. He owned extensive herds of cattle and reputedly imported the first Durham shorthorns into Texas. He also experimented with the cultivation of oranges, cotton, and sugarcane. *Handbook of Texas Online*, B. R. Brunson and Andrew Forest Muir, "Morgan, James," accessed July 04, 2016, http://www.tshaonline.org/handbook/online/articles/fmo50of New Washington.

364 Ebenezer Allen Letter to James Morgan, January 11, 1858, Rosenberg Library, Galveston, Texas, MSS# 31-0001 Morgan Papers, Box 1, Folder 1.

365 Mary Jones obtained the help of Ashbel Smith and Ebenezer Allen to have the book published. Smith took the manuscript to New York and arranged for D. Appleton and Company to publish it within three months. The printers thought one thousand books five hundred pages in length might cost as much as $600. They were ordered to go ahead. The books had not been delivered by late 1861, and Allen prepared to file suit against D. Appleton Company. Then the books were shipped, and Mrs. Jones received a bill for $1,744.50. She settled the account in July 1861. She explained what happened in a letter to a friend: "I of course was instructed by Allen not to receive them. I have learned that the boxes were broken open during the war and books were taken by anyone who felt curious enough to read them. Allen died in the summer of 1862 [actually October 15, 1863]." Jones, ix.

366 William J. Bozic, "A Chronology of the U.S.-Mexican War," accessed March 22, 2019, http://www.dmwv.org/mexwar/chrono1845-6.htm.

367 Zachary Taylor (1784 –1850) was the 12th president of the United States, serving from March 1849 until his death in July 1850. Taylor previously was a career officer in the United States Army, rose to the rank of major general and became a national hero as a result of his victories in the Mexican American War. As a result, he won election to the White House despite his vague political beliefs. His top priority as president was preserving the Union, but he died sixteen months into his term, before making any progress on the status of slavery, which had been inflaming tensions in Congress. accessed March 18, 2019, https://www.whitehouse.gov/about-the-white-house/presidents/zachary-taylor/.

368 Allen H. Mesch, *Teacher of Civil War Generals – Major General Charles Ferguson Smith, Soldier and West Point Commandant* (Jefferson: McFarland & Company, Inc., Publishers, 2015), 47.

369 Mesch, 51-52.

370 Eisenhower, 63, 64, 65, and 66.

STATE OF TEXAS SERVICE

371 Please see "Texas Lawyer" chapter. The railroad venture is discussed in more detail in the chapters titled "Entrepreneur" and "The Houston and Texas Central Railroad."

372 Albert Latimer (1800? –1877) was an influential politician from Red River County. In 1834, Latimer moved northeast of Clarksville and helped found the town of La Grange. Latimer represented Red River County in the lower house of the Fifth and Sixth congresses of the Republic of Texas from 1840 to 1842. He was a delegate to the Convention of 1845. Latimer was a member of the Senate of the Third Legislature from 1849 to 1851. By 1860, he was a wealthy planter. Latimer was a member of DeKalb Masonic Lodge. His position in Red River County and membership in the Masons might have helped propel Ebenezer from new Texas emigrant in 1840 to Republic of Texas Attorney General in 1845. *Handbook of Texas Online*, L. W. Kemp, "Latimer, Albert Hamilton," accessed March 28, 2018, http://www.tshaonline.org/handbook/online/articles/fla44.

373 The Waco Convention was held in 1857 to select a Democratic nominee for governor and other state positions and federal political campaigns. The convention also favored the acquisition of Cuba and a direct importing trade. Oldham, W. S. & Marshall, John. *State Gazette*. (Austin, Tex.), Vol. 8, No. 37, Ed. 1, Saturday, May 2, 1857, newspaper, May 2, 1857; Austin, Texas. (https://texashistory.unt.edu/ark:/67531/metapth81294/: accessed August 27, 2019), University of North Texas Libraries, The Portal to Texas History, https://texashistory.unt.edu; crediting The Dolph Briscoe Center for American History.

374 Paul Bremond (1810–1885) was a businessman, entrepreneur, and spiritualist. In 1839, he moved to Galveston and opened an auction and commission house. Bremond relocated to Houston around 1842 and expanded his business interests and associates. Bremond was a spiritualist and organized a Houston society to study spiritualism. He believed he was spiritually guided by Moseley Baker, a soldier of the Texas Revolution, to build another railroad. He secured a charter in 1875 for the Houston, East and West Texas Railway to run from Houston to Shreveport. Unfortunately, local funds and the state land grant did not supply enough capital, and Bremond mortgaged the railroad to borrow the necessary money from eastern bankers. Bremond died on May 8, 1885 before the railroad was completed. *Handbook of Texas Online*, Robert S. Maxwell, "Bremond, Paul," accessed April 26, 2016, http://www.tshaonline.org/handbook/online/articles/fbr39.

375 E. W. Taylor (1839–?) emigrated to Texas in 1846 where he was employed by the J. C. Preston & Company, who were druggists at Jefferson. In January 1855, he studied the U. S. Dispensatory, and a year and a half later, he was placed in charge of a new drug store established by Dr. R. W. Walker. After two years, he started a business with Dr. H. Witherspoon, under the firm name of Taylor and Witherspoon. In 1861, he sold his drug business and enlisted in the Army of the Confederate States, Company A, Nineteenth Texas Infantry. He was elected major and, in a few months, succeeded Colonel R. H. Graham as lieutenant colonel of the regiment. After the battle of Jenkins' Ferry, Arkansas, Colonel Richard Waterhouse was made brigadier general and Mr. Taylor was promoted to the colonelcy of the regiment. Camp Taylor, accessed April 29, 2018, http://www.taylorcampscv.org/ewtaylor.html.

376 *The Daily Dallas Herald* newspaper.

377 J. W. Latimer, *Dallas Herald*. (Dallas, Tex.), Vol. 6, No. 9, Ed. 1 Saturday, August 29, 1857, newspaper, August 29, 1857; Dallas, Texas, https://texashistory.unt.edu/ark:/67531/metapth294029/, accessed August 25, 2019, University of

North Texas Libraries, The Portal to Texas History, https://texashistory.unt.edu; .

378 William Todd won the 1850 judicial election. He earned a reputation as a highly competent judge and the was reelected in 1854 and 1858. In 1856, the Todds moved to Jefferson, Texas. He was elected as a delegate to the Secession Convention in 1861. Todd retired from the bench because of ill health in 1862. He died in Jefferson on May 20, 1864. *Handbook of Texas Online*, Cecil Harper, Jr., "Todd, William Smith," accessed December 07, 2016, http://www.tshaonline.org/handbook/online/articles/fto08.

379 A. H. Evans was a "practicing lawyer" who lived in San Augustine, Texas. O. M. Roberts, "The Experiences of an Unrecognized Senator," *The Quarterly of the Texas State Historical Association* (Austin: Texas Historical Association, 1909), vol. XII, 92.

380 Charles De Morse, *The Northern Standard*. (Clarksville, Tex.), Vol. 7, No. 44, Ed. 1, Saturday, June 29, 1850, newspaper, June 29, 1850; Clarksville, Texas. (https://texashistory.unt.edu/ark:/67531/metapth80783/: accessed August 23, 2019), University of North Texas Libraries, The Portal to Texas History, https://texashistory.unt.edu; crediting The Dolph Briscoe Center for American History.

381 Andrew Jackson Hamilton (1815–1875) was a lawyer, state representative, military governor of Texas, and Governor of Texas during Reconstruction. In 1849 Hamilton was appointed as the acting state attorney general by Governor Peter H. Bell. In 1850, he was elected to the Texas House of Representatives representing Travis County. He was part of a group of southern politicians in the Democratic Party who opposed secession and the reopening of the slave trade. In 1858, Hamilton was elected to the U.S. House of Representatives as an Independent Democrat representing the western district of Texas. During his term, he served on a House committee in 1860 to solve the growing sectional feud between the North and South. He chose not to run for re-election in 1860. He returned to Texas in 1861 and won a special election to the State Senate. Hamilton was later forced to resign this post after his life was threatened for his pro-Union statements. During the Civil War, Hamilton sided with the Union. He went on a speaking tour of the Northeast. He spoke out in favor of the Union and criticized the "slave power" of the South. Hamilton was regarded as a hero by the North, though he was generally viewed as a traitor at home. *Handbook of Texas Online*, James A. Marten, "Hamilton, Andrew Jackson," accessed February 13, 2019, http://www.tshaonline.org/

handbook/online/articles/fha33.

382 "Announcements," "Attorney General," *The Texian Advocate* (Victoria, Texas), May 31, 1850, accessed August 21, 2018, 2, https://www.newspapers.com/image/436666332.

383 "Candidates," Loughery, Robert W. *The Texas Republican*. (Marshall, Tex.), Vol. 2, No. 4, Ed. 1 Saturday, July 6, 1850, newspaper, July 6, 1850; Marshall, Texas. (https://texashistory.unt.edu/ark:/67531/metapth1094681/: accessed August 21, 2018), University of North Texas Libraries, The Portal to Texas History, https://texashistory.unt.edu; .

384 Thomas Freeman McKinney (1801–1873) was a Texas trader and stock raiser. In 1834, he became senior partner with Samuel May Williams in McKinney and Williams. Williams supplied the bookkeeping and commercial contacts in the United States, while McKinney collected and shipped the cotton. The firm developed Quintana at the mouth of the Brazos River in 1835 and used its credit to help finance $99,000 for the Texas Revolution. *Handbook of Texas Online*, Margaret Swett Henson, "McKinney, Thomas Freeman," accessed December 07, 2016, http://www.tshaonline.org/handbook/online/articles/fmc75.

385 Samuel May Williams (1795–1858) was an entrepreneur and associate of Stephen F. Austin. In 1823, Austin hired him as translator and clerk. For the next thirteen years Williams was Austin's lieutenant. He wrote deeds, kept records, and directed colonial activities during the impresario's absences. In 1826, he was named postmaster of San Felipe and was appointed revenue collector and dispenser of stamped paper by the state of Coahuila and Texas the following year. He became secretary to the town council of San Felipe in 1828. He entered a partnership with Thomas F. McKinney in 1833 and used his family's mercantile contacts in the U.S. to secure credit for the firm. McKinney and Williams purchased arms and raised funds for the Texas Revolution. Neither the Republic nor state was able to repay the entire $99,000 debt. The partners received a small portion of their investment and passage of favorable relief legislation. Sam Williams concentrated on banking after 1841. Williams' commission house received special permission from the Texas Congress to establish a bank to issue and circulate paper money to promote commerce. In 1848, he opened the Commercial and Agricultural Bank of Galveston. Jacksonian antibanking sentiment inspired his enemies to attack the bank through the state courts because it violated constitutional prohibitions against banks. The Texas Supreme Court sustained the bank in 1852, but subsequent suits caused its demise in 1859. Williams represented the Brazos district in the Coahuila and Texas legislature in 1835 and Galveston County in the lower House of the Texas Congress in 1839. He was an unsuccessful candidate for the United States Congress in 1846. In 1838, he received a commission to negotiate a $5 million loan in the United States to purchase seven ships for the Texas Navy. President Houston sent him to Matamoros in 1843 to seek an armistice with Mexico. *Handbook of Texas Online*, Margaret Swett Henson, "Williams, Samuel May," accessed August 5, 2016, http://www.tshaonline.org/handbook/online/articles/fwi35.

386 Judge James Webb (1792–1856) was a Texas legislator and judge. He was a friend and adviser of Mirabeau B. Lamar, who appointed him secretary of the treasury and then Secretary of State. Webb also held the post of attorney general from November 18, 1839 to March 20, 1841. Webb represented the Travis-Bastrop-Fayette-Gonzales district as senator in the Sixth, Seventh, and Eighth congresses (1841–1844) and served as chairman of the Judiciary Committee and was a member of the Foreign Relations Committee. He was a representative at the Convention of 1845. The attendees endorsed him for United States district judge for Texas. From 1846 to 1849, Webb and Thomas H. Duval were reporters for the state Supreme Court and produced the first three volumes of the Texas Reports. Governor Peter H. Bell appointed Webb Secretary of State, and he held that post from December 28, 1849, until his resignation in July 1851. *Handbook of Texas Online*, Hobart Huson, "Webb, James," accessed April 28, 2018, http://www.tshaonline.org/handbook/online/articles/fwe04.

387 Hardin R. Runnels (1820–1873) was a Texas governor and legislator. His family owned a cotton plantation on the Red River. From 1847 to 1855, Runnels was a representative in the Texas legislature. In 1855 he was elected lieutenant governor. In May 1857, the Democratic party nominated Runnels as its gubernatorial candidate. Runnels won by a vote of 38,552 to 23,628 and became the only person ever to defeat Sam Houston in an election. Runnels thought Texas might be forced to secede from the Union, supported the unsuccessful effort to put the Texas legislature on record in favor of reopening the African slave trade, and signed a bill allowing free blacks to choose a master and become slaves. He also signed into law the bill which appropriated financial support to establish the University of Texas and the bill establishing the State Geological Survey. He was a vigorous supporter of the secession resolution at the Secession Convention in 1861. *Handbook* *of Texas Online*, Cecil Harper, Jr., "Runnels, Hardin Richard," accessed August 05, 2016, http://www.tshaonline.org/handbook/online/articles/fru13.

388   Thomas F. McKinney Letter to Samuel M. Williams, August 29, 1850, Samuel May Williams Papers, Rosenberg Library, MSS# 23-2372 S. M. Williams, Box 12, Folder 9.

389   Charles De Morse, *The Northern Standard,* (Clarksville, Tex.), Vol. 8, No. 9, Ed. 1, Saturday, October 26, 1850. texashistory.unt.edu/ark:/67531/metapth80800/m1/2/?q=Texas+attorney+general+election+1850. accessed August 21, 2018, University of North Texas Libraries, The Portal to Texas History, texashistory.unt.edu; crediting The Dolph Briscoe Center for American History.

390   *Texas State Gazette.* (Austin, Tex.), Vol. 2, No. 8, Ed. 1, Saturday, October 12, 1850. Austin, Texas. texashistory.unt.edu/ark:/67531/metapth80950/: accessed August 21, 2018, University of North Texas Libraries, The Portal to Texas History, texashistory.unt.edu; crediting The Dolph Briscoe Center for American History.

391   B. E. Tarver, *The Semi-Weekly Journal.* (Galveston, Tex.), Vol. 1, No. 52, Ed. 1 Wednesday, August 7, 1850, newspaper, August 7, 1850; Galveston, Texas. (texashistory.unt.edu/ark:/67531/metapth874057/m1/1/?q=Texas%20attorney%20general%20election%20in%201850: accessed August 21, 2018), University of North Texas Libraries, The Portal to Texas History, texashistory.unt.edu; crediting San Jacinto Museum of History.

392   Francis Moore, Jr., *Democratic Telegraph and Texas Register* (Houston, Tex.), Vol. 15, No. 32, Ed. 1, Thursday, August 8, 1850, newspaper, August 8, 1850; Houston, Texas. (https://texashistory.unt.edu/ark:/67531/metapth48597/: accessed August 26, 2019), University of North Texas Libraries, The Portal to Texas History, https://texashistory.unt.edu; crediting The Dolph Briscoe Center for American History.

393   Officers of the State of Texas, *The Texas Almanac for 1858* (Galveston: Richardson & Co., 1857), 102.

394   Charles De Morse, *The Northern Standard.* (Clarksville, Tex.), Vol. 8, No. 4, Ed. 1, Saturday, September 21, 1850, newspaper, September 21, 1850; Clarksville, Texas. (https://texashistory.unt.edu/ark:/67531/metapth80795/: accessed August 26, 2019), University of North Texas Libraries, The Portal to Texas History,

https://texashistory.unt.edu; crediting The Dolph Briscoe Center for American History.

395 *Handbook of Texas Online*, James G. Dickson, Jr., "Attorney General," accessed February 27, 2019, http://www.tshaonline.org/handbook/online/articles/mba03.

396 Texas, The Constitution of the State of Texas, book, 1850; texashistory.unt.edu/ark:/67531/metapth2416/: accessed August 22, 2018), University of North Texas Libraries, The Portal to Texas History, texashistory.unt.edu; 16.

397 Texas, The Constitution of the State of Texas, 29.

398 Texas, The Constitution of the State of Texas, 11.

399 Texas, The Constitution of the State of Texas, 28.

400 "Attorneys General," Texas Almanac, accessed January 5, 2018, http://texasalmanac.com/topics/government/attorneys-general.

401 First elected attorney general in the State of Texas.

402 A section of land is 640 acres. Wikipedia contributors, "Section (United States land surveying)," *Wikipedia, The Free Encyclopedia,* https://en.wikipedia.org/w/index.php?title=Section_(United_States_land_surveying)&oldid=888600809, (accessed August 22, 2019).

403 The term Cross Timbers or the Central Oklahoma/Texas Plains describes a strip of land that runs from southeastern Kansas across Central Oklahoma to Central Texas. The region has a mixture of prairie, savanna, and woodland. Cross Timbers forms part of the boundary between the more heavily forested eastern country and the almost treeless Great Plains. Wikipedia contributors, "Cross Timbers," *Wikipedia, The Free Encyclopedia,* https://en.wikipedia.org/w/index.php?title=Cross_Timbers&oldid=905889434, (accessed August 22, 2019).

404 A floating certificate of deposit is issued by a bank which pays a monthly, quarterly, semiannual, or annual coupon based on a floating interest rate. "What is Floating Rate Certificate of Deposit (FRCD)?" The Law Dictionary, accessed August 20, 2018, https://thelawdictionary.org/floating-rate-certificate-of-deposit-frcd/.

405 Vacant domain or vacant land is land with no houses, offices or other permanent structures. Vacant land may be available for development, or it maybe set aside by a government or a private owner to remain vacant. The Free Dictionary, accessed August 6, 2019, https://financial-dictionary.thefreedictionary.com/vacant+land.

406 *South-Western American* (Austin, Tex.), Vol. 4, No. 2, Ed. 1, Wednesday, July 21, 1852 - Page: 2 of 4 . The Portal to Texas History.

407 *Handbook of Texas Online*, Victoria S. Murphy, "Hedgcoxe War," accessed February 13, 2019, http://www.tshaonline.org/handbook/online/articles/jch01.

408 *Handbook of Texas Online*, Harry E. Wade, "Peters' Colony," accessed April 06, 2018, http://www.tshaonline.org/handbook/online/articles/uep02.

ENTREPRENEUR

409 *Handbook of Texas Online*, Art Leatherwood, "St. Joseph Island," accessed May 20, 2016, http://www.tshaonline.org/handbook/online/articles/rrs09.

410 James B. Wells (ca. 1812–1880) was a Texas naval officer. He raised a company of men who fought in the Texas Revolution. After the battle of San Jacinto, he used his seafaring experience as a lieutenant in the Texas Navy and as sailing master of the *Brutus*. He is best known for his destruction of a Mexican supply depot at Cox's Point. In 1837, Wells became the first commandant of the new navy yard at Galveston; but he left government service, settled on St. Joseph Island, and became a successful cattle raiser. *Handbook of Texas Online*, "Wells, James B.," accessed September 16, 2018, http://www.tshaonline.org/handbook/online/articles/fwe23.

411 Gerald Betty, "A Shellcrete Society: The Aransas-Copano Bay Community, 1830-1880," Presented at the 112th Annual Meeting of the Texas State Historical Association, Corpus Christi, TX, March 6, 2008. accessed May 20, 2016, http://achs1985.org/wp-content/uploads/2013/05/A_Shellcrete_Society-G_Betty.pdf, 11.

412 Betty, 11.

413 John Guthrie Ford, "Our San Jose Island Neighbors," Port Aransas South Jetty, accessed February 2, 2017, http://www.portasouthjetty.com/news/2011-06-02/

Island_Life/HISTORY_CORNER.html.

414 Texas oilman, Sid W. Richardson, purchased the island and used it as his private hunting resort. He built an extravagant hunting lodge. Richardson invited businessmen and politicians, including Senator Lyndon B. Johnson and President Franklin D. Roosevelt, to enjoy the resort. *Handbook of Texas Online*, Ben H. Procter, "Richardson, Sid Williams," accessed February 13, 2019, http://www.tshaonline.org/handbook/online/articles/fri08.

415 Courtesy of Judith M. Johnson, Johnson-Morrow Family Tree, accessed May 20, 2016, Ancestry.com.

416 River bottoms are low-lying lands along rivers. "River bottoms," Merriam-Webster, accessed August 6, 2019, https://www.merriam-webster.com/dictionary/river%20bottom.

417 Harrisburg, Texas was established before 1825 on the right bank of Buffalo Bayou in eastern Harris County. On April 16, 1836, Antonio López de Santa Anna burned the town. After the Texas Revolution, the city of Houston was laid out on the bayou above Harrisburg and became the seat of Harrisburg (later Harris) County and the capital of the Republic of Texas. Harrisburg incorporated on June 5, 1837. The Republic chartered the Harrisburg Railroad and Trading Company, and citizens offered the town to the Republic as capital. The Buffalo Bayou, Brazos and Colorado Railway Company bought the town property in 1847 for $150,000. By 1853, Harrisburg had a steam saw and grist mill, several stores, three hotels, and a railroad terminal with shops and yards. The construction of the road to Alleyton and the establishment of steamship connections with Galveston, made Harrisburg the first railroad terminal in Texas. After the Civil War, the railroad became the Galveston, Harrisburg and San Antonio and extended its track to San Antonio. Harrisburg remained important until fire destroyed the railroad shops. Afterwards, the railroad rebuilt the shops in Houston during the 1870s. *Handbook of Texas Online*, Andrew Forest Muir, "Harrisburg, TX (Harris County)," accessed October 14, 2016, http://www.tshaonline.org/handbook/online/articles/hvh27.

418 The Brazos Valley is a region in Central Texas consisting of the counties of Brazos, Burleson, and Robertson, and the neighboring counties of Grimes, Leon, Madison, and Washington. Although the Brazos River lies at the center of the region, not all areas of the region are a part of the Brazos watershed. Wikipedia contributors, "Brazos Valley," *Wikipedia, The Free Encyclopedia,* https://en.wikipedia.

org/w/index.php?title=Brazos_Valley&oldid=852254258, (accessed August 22, 2019).

419 William Marsh Rice (1816–1900) was an American businessman who bequeathed his fortune to found Rice University in Houston, Texas. In 1838, Rice traveled to Texas in search of new business opportunities. He founded the Rice and Nichols general store with his business partner Ebenezer Nichols. This business was the foundation for what would later become William M. Rice and Company. Rice made his fortune by investing in land, real estate, lumber, railroads, cotton, and other projects in Texas and Louisiana. In 1860, his total property, including fifteen slaves, was worth $750,000. In 1850, Rice married Margaret Bremond, daughter of Paul Bremond and Harriet Martha Sprouls, in Houston, Texas. He moved to New York in 1865. He built a house on a 160-acre estate in Dunellen, New Jersey, and moved there in 1872. On January 28, 1882, Rice drafted a will, assigning funds from his estate for the establishment of "The William M. Rice Orphans Institute." In the late 1980s, Rice established the William M. Rice Institute for the Advancement of Literature, Science and Art in Houston. *Handbook of Texas Online*, Andrew Forest Muir, "Rice, William Marsh," accessed February 13, 2019, http://www.tshaonline.org/handbook/online/articles/fri03.

420 John Grant Tod, Sr. (1808–1877) was a naval officer and one of the founders of the Buffalo Bayou, Brazos and Colorado Railway. He obtained a commission as a midshipman in the United States Navy. He received a commission in the Texas Navy, which only consisted of three vessels. Tod was appointed a naval inspector in 1838, charged with investigating supply purchases at the Galveston naval station, and from 1838 to 1840 was one of the Texas Navy's purchasing agents in Baltimore. In July 1839, he was appointed a commander in the navy and the following year was placed in command of the naval station at Galveston. From November to December of 1840, he also served as acting secretary of the navy for the Republic. In 1842, Tod resigned his post and went to Washington to lobby for annexation and other issues. In 1845, he returned to Texas carrying the official notification of annexation. During the Mexican War, Tod served in the United States Navy and as an agent of the United States quartermaster general at the Brazos Santiago Depot and at New Orleans. In 1852, Sidney Sherman and Tod, with support from eastern capitalists, founded the Buffalo Bayou, Brazos and Colorado Railway. Tod remained a principal in the company until the late 1860s. *Handbook of Texas Online*, Uli Haller, "Tod, John Grant, Sr.," accessed March 27, 2018, http://

www.tshaonline.org/handbook/online/articles/fto05.

421 William Stafford (1780–1840) established a plantation with a cane mill and a horse-powered cotton gin in 1830. During the Texas Revolution, Antonio López de Santa Anna's forces burned the plantation. Stafford rebuilt his plantation and lived there until his death in 1840. A settlement called "Stafford's Point" established itself around the plantation; it became a townsite in August 1853 when the Buffalo Bayou, Brazos and Colorado Railway began stopping there. In 1884, Stafford had 50 residents, two general stores, and a grocer. *Handbook of Texas Online*, "Stafford, William," accessed February 13, 2019, http://www.tshaonline.org/handbook/online/articles/fst04.

422 *Handbook of Texas Online*, George C. Werner, "Buffalo Bayou, Brazos and Colorado Railway," accessed May 09, 2018, http://www.tshaonline.org/handbook/online/articles/eqb16.

423 *Handbook of Texas Online*, George C. Werner, "Railroads," accessed July 19, 2018, http://www.tshaonline.org/handbook/online/articles/eqr01.

424 Courtesy of the Judith M. Johnson, Johnson-Morrow Family Tree, accessed May 20, 2016, Ancestry.com.

425 Coffee's Station or Coffee's Trading Post was on the Red River from 1834 to 1846. *Handbook of Texas Online*, Morris L. Britton, "Coffee's Station," accessed January 15, 2018, http://www.tshaonline.org/handbook/online/articles/dfc01.

426 Courtesy of the Judith M. Johnson, Johnson-Morrow Family Tree, accessed May 27, 2016, Ancestry.com.

427 *Laws Passed by the Second Legislature of the State of Texas* (Houston, Published by Authority, 1848), vol. 2, 372.

428 A. J. Yates (1803-1856) Before he moved to Texas in 1835, he was highly regarded as a lawyer, college professor, and author. He soon had won the confidence of Stephen F. Austin, Sam Houston, John A. and William H. Wharton. When the Texas Revolution broke out, Yates immediately joined the army, but late in December 1835, he was appointed loan commissioner and served under Austin. Yates focused on the legal and clerical details of the loan negotiations and to purchase boats, munitions, and other supplies for the newly declared Republic of Texas. After the revolution, he moved to Galveston, published the *Daily Advertiser,* and practiced law. He took an active part in enterprises of city and county. Yates prepared an elaborate and sensible plan for a system of public schools. He also developed a course of study for training and certification of teachers. Yates was also the first signer of a memorial petitioning Congress to establish a system of popular education. *Handbook of Texas Online*, Amelia W. Williams, "Yates, Andrew Janeway," accessed March 30, 2019, http://www.tshaonline.org/handbook/online/articles/fya02.

429 Francis, Jr. Moore, *Democratic Telegraph and Texas Register* (Houston, Tex.), Vol. 13, No. 47, Ed. 1, Thursday, November 23, 1848, newspaper, November 23, 1848; Houston, Texas. (https://texashistory.unt.edu/ark:/67531/metapth48521/: accessed August 23, 2019), University of North Texas Libraries, The Portal to Texas History, https://texashistory.unt.edu; crediting The Dolph Briscoe Center for American History.

430 William J. Hutchins (1813–1884) was a government official, merchant, and railroad developer. He ran a private bank and owned a large mercantile business in Houston. In the 1850s, Hutchins was a partner in the Houston Navigation Company, which controlled steamboat traffic between Houston and Galveston. He was an incorporator of the Brazos Plank Road Company and the Buffalo Bayou, Brazos and Colorado Railway. In 1860, Hutchins, Abram Morris Gentry, and others incorporated the State Star Telegraph Company to build lines throughout the state. His estate was worth $700,000 in 1860. In 1861, he built Hutchins House, which was then the state's largest hotel. In 1861, he and David H. Paige bought the Houston and Texas Central Railway for $10,000. Hutchins served as president and general manager of this line for seven years. Hutchins was alderman of Houston for several terms and mayor in 1861. He was one of the organizers of the Houston Cotton Compress Company in 1860 and of the City Cotton Mills in 1865. The Board of Trade and Cotton Exchange chose him its first vice president. *Handbook of Texas Online*, Julia Beazley, "Hutchins, William J.," accessed March 12, 2017, http://www.tshaonline.org/handbook/online/articles/fhu51.

431 P. de Cordova, *South-Western American* (Austin, Tex.), Vol. 4, No. 15, Ed. 1, Wednesday, October 20, 1852, newspaper, October 20, 1852; Austin, Texas. (https://texashistory.unt.edu/ark:/67531/metapth79743/: accessed August 26, 2019), University of North Texas Libraries, The Portal to Texas History, https://texashistory.unt.edu; crediting The Dolph Briscoe Center for American History.

432 H. H. Smith, *Weekly Journal*. (Galveston, Tex.), Vol. 3, No. 37, Ed. 1 Friday, December 24, 1852, newspaper, December 24, 1852; Galveston, Texas. (https://texashistory.unt.edu/ark:/67531/metapth182227/: accessed August 23, 2019), University of North Texas Libraries, The Portal to Texas History, https://texashistory.unt.edu; crediting The Dolph Briscoe Center for American History.

433 P. de Cordova, *South-Western American* (Austin, Tex.), Vol. 4, No. 13, Ed. 1, Wednesday, October 6, 1852, newspaper, October 6, 1852; Austin, Texas. (https://texashistory.unt.edu/ark:/67531/metapth79741/: accessed August 22, 2019),University of North Texas Libraries, The Portal to Texas History, https://texashistory.unt.edu; crediting The Dolph Briscoe Center for American History.

434 William D. Angel, Jr (1984), "Vantage on the Bay: Galveston and the Railroads," *East Texas Historical Journal*: Vol. 22: Issue 1, Article 5. Available at: http://scholarworks.sfasu.edu/ethj/vol22/iss1/5, 4-5.

435 *The Civilian and Galveston Gazette*. (Galveston, Tex.), Vol. 10, Ed. 1, Friday, May 5, 1848, newspaper, May 5, 1848; Galveston, Texas. (https://texashistory.unt.edu/ark:/67531/metapth80299/: accessed November 17, 2019), University of North Texas Libraries, The Portal to Texas History, https://texashistory.unt.edu; crediting The Dolph Briscoe Center for American History.

436 Francis Moore, Jr., *Telegraph & Texas Register* (Houston, Tex.), Vol. 17, No. 41, Ed. 1 Friday, October 8, 1852, newspaper, October 8, 1852; Houston, Texas, https://texashistory.unt.edu/ark:/67531/metapth233394/:, accessed April 6, 2019, University of North Texas Libraries, The Portal to Texas History, https://texashistory.unt.edu; crediting The Dolph Briscoe Center for American History.

437 Angel, 5.

438 Francis Moore, Jr., *Telegraph & Texas Register* (Houston, Tex.), Vol. 17, No. 29, Ed. 1 Friday, July 16, 1852, newspaper, July 16, 1852; Houston, Texas. (https://texashistory.unt.edu/ark:/67531/metapth233390/: accessed August 23, 2019), University of North Texas Libraries, The Portal to Texas History, https://texashistory.unt.edu; crediting The Dolph Briscoe Center for American History.

439 *Galveston Weekly News* (Galveston, Tex.), Vol. 12, No. 9, Ed. 1, Tuesday, May 8, 1855, newspaper, May 8, 1855; Galveston, Texas. (https://texashistory.unt.edu/ark:/67531/metapth79827/: accessed December 6, 2019), University of North

Texas Libraries, The Portal to Texas History, https://texashistory.unt.edu; crediting The Dolph Briscoe Center for American History.

440 Angel, 11-12.

441 "Congressional," *Hartford Courant* (Hartford, Connecticut), February 20, 1849, 2, accessed August 28, 2019, https://www.newspapers.com/image/368957327.

442 Hans Peter Mareus Neilsen Gammel, *The Laws of Texas, 1822-1897*, Volume 3, book, 1898; Austin, Texas. (https://texashistory.unt.edu/ark:/67531/metapth6728/: accessed March 19, 2019), University of North Texas Libraries, The Portal to Texas History, https://texashistory.unt.edu.

443 The Mississippi and Pacific Railroad was an attempt by the State of Texas to encourage the construction of a southern transcontinental railroad through Texas. On December 21, 1853, the legislation authorized Governor Peter H. Bell to request proposals for a railroad from the eastern boundary of Texas to, at, or near El Paso. *Handbook of Texas Online*, George C. Werner, "Mississippi and Pacific Railroad," accessed August 07, 2019, http://www.tshaonline.org/handbook/online/articles/eqm05. Wikipedia contributors, "Pacific Railroad Acts," *Wikipedia, The Free Encyclopedia,* https://en.wikipedia.org/w/index.php?title=Pacific_Railroad_Acts&oldid=912203871 (accessed March 29, 2019).

444 *Handbook of Texas Online*, George C. Werner, "Texas Western Railroad," accessed March 29, 2019, http://www.tshaonline.org/handbook/online/articles/eqt20.

445 *Handbook of Texas Online*, George C. Werner, "Buffalo Bayou, Brazos and Colorado Railway," accessed March 29, 2019, http://www.tshaonline.org/handbook/online/articles/eqb16.

THE HOUSTON AND TEXAS CENTRAL RAILROAD

446 Thomas William House (1814–1880) moved to Houston. House bought the dry goods and grocery company, James H. Stevens & Company, in 1835 and opened a baking and confectionary business.in 1838. T. W. House & Company became the largest dry goods and groceries business in Texas. Only a few banks operated in Texas before the Civil War, and banking was conducted by the larger merchants. Mr. House's company began receiving deposits around 1840 and

later the company started issuing exchange. These activities grew into House's banking business. For about fifteen years, the company conducted business in wholesale dry-goods and groceries, cotton dealing and banking. In addition, Mr. House became a major land holder including a large sugar plantation and stock ranch. He helped organize the Protection Fire Company and was a board member until his death. In 1857 and 1861, he was elected to the Board of Aldermen of the city. In 1862, he was elected mayor. He was a charter member of the Ship Channel Company. He was one of the originators of the Houston Gas Company, and he was president and its largest stockholder for many years. He was a director of the Houston & Texas Central Railroad and helped finance the line. He was also a stockholder in several other railroads in the state. He was a large investor in the Houston Direct Navigation Company, the Houston City Street Railway Company, and the first two newspapers. *Handbook of Texas Online*, Julia Beazley, "House, Thomas William," accessed August 13, 2018, http://www.tshaonline.org/handbook/online/articles/fho68.

447 *The Times-Picayune* (New Orleans, Louisiana), March 4, 1852, 2, accessed August 13, 2018, https://www.newspapers.com/image/25559374/?terms=Galveston.

448 Henry F. Fisher (1805–1867) was a German Texan. He came to Houston in 1837 or 1838 where he served as Hanseatic (Bremen) consul to Texas. He became interested in the exploration and colonization of the San Saba, Texas area and in 1839 was acting treasurer of the San Saba Company, which was later reorganized as the San Saba Colonization Company. He was a key party in the Fisher-Miller Land Grant. *Handbook of Texas Online*, Rudolph L. Biesele, "Fisher, Henry Francis," accessed February 13, 2019, http://www.tshaonline.org/handbook/online/articles/ffi17.

449 W. A. Van Alystyne was a civil engineer with the Houston and Texas Central Railway railroad who surveyed the right-of-way and the townsite for Van Alystyne, Texas. *Handbook of Texas Online*, Brian Hart, "Van Alstyne, TX," accessed July 25, 2018, http://www.tshaonline.org/handbook/online/articles/hjv02.

450 Harvey H. Allen (?–1862) was one of the five Allen brothers who lived in Houston. A. C. and J. K. Allen came to Texas in 1832, and in 1836 bought a league of land on Buffalo Bayou and laid out the city of Houston. Harvey H. Allen was the Chief Justice of Harris County. Reverend Homer S. Thrall, *A Pictorial History* *of Texas* (St. Louis: N. D. Thompson & Co., 1879), 477.

451 William Robinson Baker (1820–1890) was a railroad executive, Texas State Senator and Mayor of Houston, TX. In 1852, Baker became the Secretary of the Texas Central Railroad, and in 1856, Secretary of the Houston and Texas Central Railroad. He eventually became Director and the Vice President of the line. From 1868 to 1871, Baker was President of the railroad, and from 1873 to 1875, served as Vice-President and Manager. *Handbook of Texas Online*, Diana J. Kleiner, "Baker, William Robinson," accessed February 13, 2019, http://www.tshaonline.org/handbook/online/articles/fba42.

452 J. W. Schrimpf was a Houston businessman in the packing and selling of meat products. *Writers' Program* (Tex.). Houston, a history and guide, book, 1942; Houston, Texas. (texashistory.unt.edu/ark:/67531/metapth5865/m1/279/: accessed August 27, 2018), University of North Texas Libraries, The Portal to Texas History, texashistory.unt.edu.

453 Moore, Francis, Jr. *Telegraph & Texas Register* (Houston, Tex.), Vol. 17, No. 42, Ed. 1 Friday, October 15, 1852, newspaper, October 15, 1852; Houston, Texas. (https://texashistory.unt.edu/ark:/67531/metapth233395/: accessed August 22, 2019),University of North Texas Libraries, The Portal to Texas History, https://texashistory.unt.edu; crediting The Dolph Briscoe Center for American History.

454 *Weekly National Intelligencer* (Washington, District of Columbia), October 30, 1852, 4, accessed August 22, 2019, https://www.newspapers.com/image/334861373/?terms=Galveston%2Band%2BRed%2BRiver%2BRailroad.

455 "Later from Texas," *The Times-Picayune* (New Orleans, Louisiana), January 11, 1853, 3, accessed August 22, 2019, https://www.newspapers.com/image/25542725/?terms=Later%2Bfrom%2BTexas.

456 "Later from Texas," *The Times-Picayune* (New Orleans, Louisiana), December 28, 1852, 2, accessed August 22, 2019, https://www.newspapers.com/image/25539223/?terms=%22Leon%2BPioneer%22.

457 S. G. Read, *A History of Texas Railroads and of Transportation Conditions under Spain and Mexico and The Republic and State* (Houston: The St. Clair Publishing Co., 1941), 72.

458 The Brazos River is the longest river in Texas. It is sometimes used to mark the boundary between East and West Texas. Wikipedia contributors, "Brazos River," *Wikipedia, The Free Encyclopedia,* https://en.wikipedia.org/w/index.php?title=Brazos_River&oldid=898298795, (accessed August 22, 2019).

459 J. C. Harrison, *Nacogdoches Chronicle*. (Nacogdoches, Tex.), Vol. 2, No. 12, Ed. 1 Tuesday, May 31, 1853, newspaper, May 31, 1853; Nacogdoches, Texas. (https://texashistory.unt.edu/ark:/67531/metapth714438/: accessed August 23, 2019), University of North Texas Libraries, The Portal to Texas History, https://www.texashistory.unt.edu.

460 G. W. Crawford, & J. W. Hampton, *Texas State Gazette*. (Austin, Tex.), Vol. 4, No. 42, Ed. 1, Saturday, June 4, 1853, newspaper, June 4, 1853; Austin, Texas. (https://texashistory.unt.edu/ark:/67531/metapth81086/: accessed August 26, 2019), University of North Texas Libraries, The Portal to Texas History, https://texashistory.unt.edu; crediting The Dolph Briscoe Center for American History.

461 J. Lancaster, *The Lone Star, and Texas Ranger*. (Washington, Tex.), Vol. 5, No. 7, Ed. 1, Saturday, September 3, 1853, newspaper, September 3, 1853; Washington, Texas. (https://texashistory.unt.edu/ark:/67531/metapth48286/: accessed August 26, 2019), University of North Texas Libraries, The Portal to Texas History, https://texashistory.unt.edu; crediting The Dolph Briscoe Center for American History.

462 *The Washington Sentinel* (Washington, District of Columbia), May 31, 1854, 3. Washington sentinel. [volume] (City of Washington [D.C.]), 31 May 1855. Chronicling America: Historic American Newspapers. Lib. of Congress. accessed August 26, 2019 <https://chroniclingamerica.loc.gov/lccn/sn82014835/1855-05-31/ed-1/seq-3/>.

463 John S. Ford, *The Texas State Times* (Austin, Tex.), Vol. 2, No. 43, Ed. 1 Saturday, September 29, 1855, newspaper, September 29, 1855; Austin, Texas. (https://texashistory.unt.edu/ark:/67531/metapth235778/: accessed April 7, 2019), University of North Texas Libraries, The Portal to Texas History, https://texashistory.unt.edu; crediting The Dolph Briscoe Center for American History.

464 *The Times-Picayune* (New Orleans, Louisiana), May 31, 1856, 1, accessed April 7, 2019, https://www.newspapers.com/clip/26303305/the_timespicayune/.

465 *New Orleans Crescent* (New Orleans, Louisiana), December 24,

1855, 1, accessed April 7, 2019, https://www.newspapers.com/image/167473176/?terms=%22New%2BOrleans%2BCrescent%22.

466 Francis Moore, Jr., *Telegraph & Texas Register* (Houston, Tex.), Vol. 18, No. 2, Ed. 1 Friday, January 14, 1853, newspaper, January 14, 1853; Houston, Texas. (https://texashistory.unt.edu/ark:/67531/metapth233399/: accessed August 22, 2019), University of North Texas Libraries, The Portal to Texas History, https://texashistory.unt.edu; crediting The Dolph Briscoe Center for American History.

467 G. W. Crawford, & J. W. Hampton, *Texas State Gazette* (Austin, Tex.), Vol. 4, No. 23, Ed. 1, Saturday, January 22, 1853, newspaper, January 22, 1853; Austin, Texas. (https://texashistory.unt.edu/ark:/67531/metapth81067/: accessed August 26, 2019), University of North Texas Libraries, The Portal to Texas History, https://texashistory.unt.edu; crediting The Dolph Briscoe Center for American History.

468 *The Louisville Daily Courier* (Louisville, Kentucky), January 21, 1853, 2, accessed August 26, 2019, https://www.newspapers.com/image/119156485/?terms=the%2Blouisville%2Bdaily%2Bcourier.

469 "Texas Railroads," *Washington Telegraph* (Washington, Arkansas), October 5, 1853, 1, accessed August 26, 2019, https://www.newspapers.com/image/262221516.

470 *Handbook of Texas Online*, Nancy Beck Young, "Galveston and Red River Railroad," http://www.tshaonline.org/handbook/online/articles/eqg02.

471 "Later from Texas," *The Times-Picayune* (New Orleans, Louisiana), May 2, 1855, 2, accessed August 26, 2019, https://www.newspapers.com/image/28056062/?terms=%22running%2Border%22.

472 *The Galveston News* (Galveston, Tex.), Vol. 14, No. 54, Ed. 1, Tuesday, October 30, 1855, newspaper, October 30, 1855; Galveston, Texas. (https://texashistory.unt.edu/ark:/67531/metapth79958/: accessed August 26, 2019), University of North Texas Libraries, The Portal to Texas History, https://texashistory.unt.edu; crediting The Dolph Briscoe Center for American History.

473 "Galveston and Red River Railroad," *The Opelousas Patriot* (Opelousas, Louisiana), January 5, 1856, 2, accessed August 26, 2019, https://www.newspapers.com/image/367163685/?terms=The%2BOpelousas%2BPatriot.

474 *Handbook of Texas Online*, George C. Werner, "Houston and Texas Central," accessed December 13, 2018, http://www.tshaonline.org/handbook/online/articles/eqh09.

475 *Handbook of Texas Online*, George C. Werner, "Railroads," accessed September 15, 2018, http://www.tshaonline.org/handbook/online/articles/eqr01.

476 *The Times-Picayune* (New Orleans, Louisiana), July 20, 1856, 3, accessed August 22, 2019, https://www.newspapers.com/image/25762768/?terms=%22Galveston%2Band%2BRed%2BRiver%22.

477 In the United States, the parallel defines part of the border between New Mexico and Texas. It was the proposed route of the Texas Pacific Railroad. Wikipedia contributors, "32nd parallel north," *Wikipedia, The Free Encyclopedia*, https://en.wikipedia.org/w/index.php?title=32nd_parallel_north&oldid=898205484 (accessed August 22, 2019).

478 "Texas Railroads," *Washington Telegraph* (Washington, Arkansas), October 5, 1853, 1, accessed August 22, 2019, https://www.newspapers.com/image/262221516.

479 Cypress is approximately twenty-five miles northwest of downtown Houston in Harris County. Wikipedia contributors, "Cypress, Texas," *Wikipedia, The Free Encyclopedia*, https://en.wikipedia.org/w/index.php?title=Cypress,_Texas&oldid=906075912 (accessed August 22, 2019).

480 On December 29, 1856, Dr. Richard Rodgers Peebles and James W. McDade organized the Hempstead Town Company to sell lots in the newly established community of Hempstead. Hempstead was at the projected terminus of Houston and Texas Central Railway. Peebles and Mary Ann Groce Peebles, his wife, contributed 2,000 acres of the Jared E. Groce estate for the community. On June 29, 1858, the Houston and Texas Central Railway reached Hempstead. The community became a distribution center between the Gulf Coast and the interior of Texas. On November 10, 1858, the Texas legislature incorporated Hempstead. *Handbook of Texas Online*, Carole E. Christian, "Hempstead, TX," accessed February 14, 2019, http://www.tshaonline.org/handbook/online/articles/hgh07.

481 Millican is located between the Brazos and Navasota Rivers fifteen miles southeast of College Station in southern Brazos County. The town was settled in

1820 and by 1850 it had a post office and stagecoach service from Houston. From 1860 to around 1867, the town was the terminus of the Houston and Texas Central Railways. At that time, Millican was the largest city north of Houston and Galveston. *Handbook of Texas Online*, Christina L. Gray, "Millican, TX," accessed July 25, 2018, http://www.tshaonline.org/handbook/online/articles/hlm71.

482 "Houston & Texas Central Stations," Confederate Railroads, accessed April 25, 2016, http://www.csa-railroads.com/Houston_and_Texas_Central_Stations.htm.

483 *Handbook of Texas Online*, George C. Werner, "Railroads," accessed January 09, 2019, http://www.tshaonline.org/handbook/online/articles/eqr01.

484 "History of the Houston & Texas Central Railway Company up to 1903; excerpted from the Yearbook for Texas." Texas Transportation Archive, accessed January 09, 2019, https://www.ttarchive.com/library/Articles/Houston-Texas-Central_1903_Year-Book-TX.html.

485 Ken Byler, "Wouldn't Train Be Nice," *Allen American*, *Star Local Media*, May 23, 2010. Courtesy of Ken Byler.

486 "Houston & Texas Central Locomotives," Confederate Railroads, accessed April 25, 2016, http://www.csa-railroads.com/.

487 "Houston & Texas Central Locomotives," Confederate Railroads, accessed April 25, 2016, http://www.csa-railroads.com/.

488 "Texas Railroads on White vs. Slave Labor," *The San Antonio Ledger*. (San Antonio, Tex.), Vol. 6, No. 41, Ed. 1 Saturday, November 8, 1856, newspaper, November 8, 1856; San Antonio, Texas. (https://texashistory.unt.edu/ark:/67531/metapth179432/: accessed September 3, 2019), University of North Texas Libraries, The Portal to Texas History, https://texashistory.unt.edu; crediting The Dolph Briscoe Center for American History.

489 *Vicksburg Daily Whig* (Vicksburg, Mississippi), December 2, 1856, 4, accessed April 25, 2016, https://www.newspapers.com/image/225590529.

490 "From Texas," *The New Orleans Crescent* (New Orleans, Louisiana), December 24, 1855, 1, accessed September 15, 2018, https://www.newspapers.com/image/167473176/?terms=%22citizens%2Bof%2BHouston%22.

491 *Handbook of Texas Online*, George C. Werner, "Railroads," accessed September 15, 2018, http://www.tshaonline.org/handbook/online/articles/eqr01.

492 Hockley, Texas is thirty-six miles northwest of Houston. Sam McCurley was the earliest settler. George Washington Hockley set up the community in 1835. The Texas army camped near the settlement in April 1836. The Houston and Texas Central Railway began service to the community in May 1857. A post office was set up there as Houseville in 1858, but the name was changed to Hockley before the end of the year. *Handbook of Texas Online*, Diana J. Kleiner, "Hockley, TX," accessed October 15, 2016, http://www.tshaonline.org/handbook/online/articles/hlh49.

493 *Galveston Weekly News* (Galveston, Tex.), Vol. 12, No. 45, Ed. 1, Tuesday, January 15, 1856, newspaper, January 15, 1856; (https://texashistory.unt.edu/ark:/67531/metapth79844/m1/1; accessed March 4. 2018), University of North Texas Libraries, The Portal to Texas History, texashistory.unt.edu;/.

494 "First Locomotive in Texas," *The Athens Post* (Athens, Tennessee), February 22, 1856, 1, accessed March 4. 2018, https://www.newspapers.com/image/72122273/?terms=First%2BLocomotive%2Bin%2BTexas.

495 Allen & Brocket. *The Weekly Telegraph* (Houston, Tex.), Vol. 21, No. 51, Ed. 1 Wednesday, March 5, 1856, newspaper, March 5, 1856; Houston, Texas. (https://texashistory.unt.edu/ark:/67531/metapth235887/: accessed March 4. 2018),University of North Texas Libraries, The Portal to Texas History, https://texashistory.unt.edu; crediting The Dolph Briscoe Center for American History.

496 "This Day in Texas," *The Austin American* (Austin, Texas), June 9, 1948, 13, accessed March 4. 2018, https://www.newspapers.com/image/385691634/?terms=Austin%2BAmerican.

497 *The Times-Picayune* (New Orleans, Louisiana), November 29, 1852, 2, accessed March 4. 2018, https://www.newspapers.com/image/25551562/?terms=Allen.

498 E. H. Cushing, *The Weekly Telegraph* (Houston, Tex.), Vol. 24, No. 7, Ed. 1 Wednesday, May 5, 1858, newspaper, May 5, 1858; Houston, Texas. (https://texashistory.unt.edu/ark:/67531/metapth235991/: accessed June 5, 2019), University of North Texas Libraries, The Portal to Texas History, https://texashistory.unt.edu;

crediting The Dolph Briscoe Center for American History.

499 E. H. Cushing, *The Weekly Telegraph* (Houston, Tex.), Vol. 24, No. 8, Ed. 1 Wednesday, May 12, 1858, newspaper, May 12, 1858; Houston, Texas. (https://texashistory.unt.edu/ark:/67531/metapth235992/: accessed May 24, 2019), University of North Texas Libraries, The Portal to Texas History, https://texashistory.unt.edu; crediting The Dolph Briscoe Center for American History.

500 E. H. Cushing, *The Weekly Telegraph* (Houston, Tex.), Vol. 24, No. 14, Ed. 1 Wednesday, June 23, 1858, newspaper, June 23, 1858; Houston, Texas. (https://texashistory.unt.edu/ark:/67531/metapth235998/: accessed May 29, 2019), University of North Texas Libraries, The Portal to Texas History, https://texashistory.unt.edu; crediting The Dolph Briscoe Center for American History.

501 *Texas Almanac, 1859*, book, 1859~; (https://texashistory.unt.edu/ark:/67531/metapth123765/: accessed June 3, 2019), University of North Texas Libraries, The Portal to Texas History, https://texashistory.unt.edu; crediting Texas State Historical Association.

502 *Galveston Weekly News* (Galveston, Tex.), Vol. 15, No. 10, Ed. 1, Tuesday, June 15, 1858, newspaper, June 15, 1858; Galveston, Texas. (https://texashistory.unt.edu/ark:/67531/metapth79881/: accessed June 4, 2019), University of North Texas Libraries, The Portal to Texas History, https://texashistory.unt.edu; crediting The Dolph Briscoe Center for American History.

503 Ebenezer Allen, Esq., *Dallas Weekly Herald*, July 10, 1858, Courtesy of Judith M. Johnson, Johnson-Morrow Family Tree, accessed May 20, 2016, Ancestry.com.

504 J. W. Latimer, *Dallas Herald*. (Dallas, Tex.), Vol. 7, No. 5, Ed. 1 Saturday, July 31, 1858, newspaper, July 31, 1858; Dallas, Texas. (https://texashistory.unt.edu/ark:/67531/metapth294034/: accessed September 3, 2019), University of North Texas Libraries, The Portal to Texas History, https://texashistory.unt.edu.

505 *The Times-Picayune* (New Orleans, Louisiana), August 22, 1858, 3, accessed April 10, 2019, https://www.newspapers.com/image/25562784/?terms=%22Houston%2Band%2BTexas%2BCentral%22.

506 *The Texas Almanac for 1858* – 118-119. The Portal to Texas History and The Texas Almanac, for 1857, with Statistics, Historical and Biographical Sketches,

&c., Relating to Texas., book, 1966; Dallas, Texas. (https://texashistory.unt.edu/ark:/67531/metapth123763/: accessed April 10, 2019), University of North Texas Libraries, The Portal to Texas History, https://texashistory.unt.edu; crediting Texas State Historical Association.

507 Dr. S. O. Young, *Thumb-Nail History of Houston* (Houston: Rein & Sons Company, 1912), 68-69.

508 In 1852, William R. Baker (1820–1890) was the Secretary of the Texas Central Railroad, and in 1856, Secretary of the Houston and Texas Central Railroad, and became Director and the Vice President of the line. From 1868 to 1871, he was President of the railroad, and from 1873 to 1875, served as Vice-President and Manager. He sold his interests and retired from the railroad business in 1877. In 1841, Baker successfully ran for County Clerk of Harris County, a position he held for 16 years. *Handbook of Texas Online*, Diana J. Kleiner, "Baker, William Robinson," accessed February 11, 2019, http://www.tshaonline.org/handbook/online/articles/fba42.

TEXAS LAWYER

509 H. H. Smith, *The Galveston Journal*. (Galveston, Tex.), Vol. 5, No. 17, Ed. 1 Friday, April 28, 1854, newspaper, April 28, 1854; Galveston, Texas. (texashistory.unt.edu/ark:/67531/metapth178684/: accessed September 11, 2018), University of North Texas Libraries, The Portal to Texas History, texashistory.unt.edu; crediting The Dolph Briscoe Center for American History.

510 *Handbook of Texas Online*, Seymour V. Connor, "Hale, William G.," accessed March 18, 2019, http://www.tshaonline.org/handbook/online/articles/fha14

511 William G. Hale Papers, 1819-1931, Box 2D52, Letters and Legal Papers: 1819-1848, The Dolph Briscoe Center for American History, The University of Texas at Austin.

512 "Legal Business in Texas," March 12, 1847, 1, accessed March 18, 2019, https://www.newspapers.com/image/25554712/?clipping_id=1159820.

513 N. Guilbeau Letter to William G. Hale, William G. Hale Papers, 1819-1931, Box 2D52, Letters and Legal Papers: 1819-1848, The Dolph Briscoe Center for American History, The University of Texas at Austin.

514 John Livingston, *Livingston's Law Register* (New York: Monthly Law Magazine, 1851), 181.

515 "U.S. Supreme Court," *The Times-Picayune*, December 16, 1852, 2, accessed March 18, 2019, https://www.newspapers.com/image/25535905.

516 "Houston and Allen," *The Washington Union* (Washington, District of Columbia), May 10, 1847, 4. 13, accessed March 18, 2019, https://www.newspapers.com/image/319288470/?clipping_id=16773439.

517 *The Daily Union* (Washington [D.C.]), 10 June 1848. Chronicling America: Historic American Newspapers. Lib. of Congress. http://chroniclingamerica.loc.gov/lccn/sn82003410/1848-06-10/ed-1/seq-4/; *The Daily Union*. (Washington [D.C.]), 22 Feb. 1848. Chronicling America: Historic American Newspapers. Lib. of Congress. http://chroniclingamerica.loc.gov/lccn/sn82003410/1848-02-22/ed-1/seq-4/; *The Daily Union*. (Washington [D.C.]), 18 Jan. 1848. Chronicling America: Historic American Newspapers. Lib. of Congress. http://chroniclingamerica.loc.gov/lccn/sn82003410/1848-01-18/ed-1/seq-4/; and *The Daily Union*. (Washington [D.C.]), 27 May 1847. Chronicling America: Historic American Newspapers. Lib. of Congress, accessed March 18, 2019, http://chroniclingamerica.loc.gov/lccn/sn82003410/1847-05-27/ed-1/seq-4/.

518 *The New Orleans Crescent* (New Orleans, Louisiana), October 19, 1849, 1, accessed March 18, 2019, https://www.newspapers.com/image/321462185/?terms=The%2BNew%2BOrleans%2BCrescent.

519 Ebenezer Allen Letter to Sam Houston. The original is in the Texas State Archives. Courtesy of Judith M. Johnson, Johnson-Morrow Family Tree, accessed May 20, 2016, Ancestry.com.

520 Sam Houston Letter to His Wife, January 2, 1853, *The Personal Correspondence of Sam Houston – Volume IV: 1852-1863* (Denton: University of North Texas Press, 2001), 17.

521 Union Bank of Louisiana v. Stafford, 53 U.S. 327 (1851), *Justia U.S. Supreme Court*, accessed August 10, 2016, https://supreme.justia.com/cases/federal/us/53/327/case.html.

522 William G. Hale Papers, 1819–1931, Box 2D52, Letters and Legal Papers: 1819-1848, The Dolph Briscoe Center for American History, The University of

Texas at Austin.

523 In the laws of the Republic of Texas, a certificate issued under authority of an act of 1839, which provided every person immigrating to the Republic between October 1, 1837, and January 1, 1840, who was the head of a family and actually resided within the government with his or her family should be entitled to a grant of 640 acres of land, to be held under such a certificate for three years, and then conveyed by absolute deed to the settler, if in the meantime he had resided permanently within the Republic and performed all the duties required of citizens. Headright Certificate, The Law.com Dictionary, accessed March 8, 2019, https://dictionary.thelaw.com/headright-certificate/, 5.

524 "The Case of Judge Watrous; His Impeachment Imminent Extraordinary Disclosures," *The New York Times*, July 11, 1860, accessed January 17, 2018, http://www.nytimes.com/1860/07/11/news/the-case-of-judge-watrous-his-impeachment-imminent-extraordinary-disclosures.html.

525 "The Impeachment Cas in Congress – Judge Watrous," *The Daily Dallas Herald* (Dallas, Texas), December 1, 1858, 1, accessed September 5, 2019, https://www.newspapers.com/image/168122675/?terms=%22Judge%2BWatrous%22.

526 *The Dallas Daily Herald* (Dallas), December 1, 1858, 1, accessed March 19, 2019, https://www.newspapers.com/image/168122675/?clipping_id=14074749.

527 *The Dallas Daily Herald* (Dallas), December 29, 1858, 1, accessed January 17, 2018, https://www.newspapers.com/image/168124689/?terms=Watrous.

528 *Weekly Journal* (Galveston, Tex.), Vol. 2, No. 20, Ed. 1 Tuesday, July 8, 1851, accessed July 14, 2016, https://texashistory.unt.edu/ark:/67531/metapth182202/m1/4/zoom/?q=%22Ebenezer%20Allen%22&resolution=3&lat=7071.554368069872&lon=3883.0663104209616.

529 *Weekly Journal* (Galveston, Tex.), Vol. 2, No. 20, Ed. 1 Tuesday, July 8, 1851 - Page: 4 of 4. Magnified. The Portal to Texas History, accessed March 27, 2019.

530 P. de Cordova, *South-Western American* (Austin, Tex.), Vol. 3, No. 2, Ed. 1, Wednesday, July 16, 1851, newspaper, July 16, 1851; Austin, Texas. (https://texashistory.unt.edu/ark:/67531/metapth79702/: accessed May 30, 2019), University of North Texas Libraries, The Portal to Texas History, https://texashistory.unt.edu; crediting The Dolph Briscoe Center for American History.

531 J. M. Gibson, *Weekly Journal* (Galveston, Tex.), Vol. 2, No. 20, Ed. 1 Tuesday, July 8, 1851, newspaper, July 8, 1851; Galveston, Texas. (https://texashistory.unt.edu/ark:/67531/metapth182202/: accessed March 26, 2019), University of North Texas Libraries, The Portal to Texas History, https://texashistory.unt.edu; crediting The Dolph Briscoe Center for American History.

532 John S. Ford, *The Texas State Times* (Austin, Tex.), Vol. 4, No. 12, Ed. 1 Saturday, March 28, 1857, newspaper, March 28, 1857; Austin, Texas. (https://texashistory.unt.edu/ark:/67531/metapth235831/: accessed May 31, 2019), University of North Texas Libraries, The Portal to Texas History, https://texashistory.unt.edu; crediting The Dolph Briscoe Center for American History.

533 "Astounding Developments in the Case of Judge Watrous, of Texas," *The Dallas Daily Herald* (Dallas, Texas), February 23, 1859, 2.

534 *Handbook of Texas Online*, Harwood P. Hinton, "Watrous, John Charles," accessed September 21, 2018, http://www.tshaonline.org/handbook/online/articles/fwa71.

535 The Master Masons were F. M. Gibson, Nicholas Lynch, Amassa Turner, W. Thomas Brannum, Samuel M. Williams, James P. Boylen and Thomas M. Thompson. Charles K. Petitfils et al, "History of Harmony Lodge No. 6 A.F. & A.M.," Harmony Lodge No. 6 A.F. & A.M., accessed May 19, 2016, http://harmonylodge6.com/history.html.

536 The Harmony Lodge No. 6, accessed May 19, 2016, http://harmonylodge6.com/history.html.

537 Charles K. Petitfils, "History of Harmony Lodge No. 6. A. F. & A. M., Galveston, Texas - 1840-1997," accessed June 26, 2016, http://www.harmonylodge6.com/history.html.

538 *Civilian and Gazette.* June 26, 1847, vol. 9, ed. 1. https://texashistory.unt.edu/ark:/67531/metapth80290/m1/2, accessed March 4, 2018. University of North Texas Libraries. The Portal to Texas History. texashistory.unt.edu. St. John the Baptist Day is celebrated on June 24. The date is the anniversary of when the first Grand Lodge was formed. June 24 is the feast day of John the Baptist in 1717. This may arise from a very old tradition, since the Baptist appears to have been regarded as the

patron of stonemasons in continental Europe during the Middle Ages. The guild of masons and carpenters attached to Cologne Cathedral was known as the Fraternity of St. John the Baptist. Wikipedia contributors, "Saint-Jean-Baptiste Day," *Wikipedia, The Free Encyclopedia,* https://en.wikipedia.org/w/index.php?title=Saint-Jean-Baptiste_Day&oldid=904921238 (accessed August 22, 2019).

539 *Handbook of Texas Online,* Randolph B. Campbell, "Slavery," accessed February 24, 2019, http://www.tshaonline.org/handbook/online/articles/yps01.

540 "About Slave Owners in Texas," Classroom, accessed February 2, 2018, https://classroom.synonym.com/about-slave-owners-in-texas-12078347.html.

541 Ralph A. Wooster, "Notes on Texas' Largest Slaveholders, 1860," *The Southwestern Historical Quarterly,* Vol. 65, No. 1 (July 1961), 78-79 (8 pages) Texas State Historical Association.

542 *Handbook of Texas Online,* Randolph B. Campbell, "Slavery," accessed January 09, 2019, http://www.tshaonline.org/handbook/online/articles/yps01.

543 Galveston County Totals by County and Year 1837 – 1845, Texas Slavery Project, accessed January 15, 2019, http://www.texasslaveryproject.org/database/list.php?begin_year=1837 &end_year=1845&county=Galveston&group=&include_estimated_data=1&submit=Submit 24.

544 "Galveston and Slavery," accessed February 2, 2018, http://civilwarmed.blogspot.com/2013/04/galveston-and-slavery-2-39-lashes.html and "Texas, County Tax Rolls, 1837-1910", database with images, *FamilySearch,* (https://familysearch.org/ark:/61903/1:1:QJ85-LJSG : 19 July 2017), Ebenezer Allen, 1849,1850, 1851, 1854, 1857, 1858, 1859, and 1861.

545 "United States Census (Slave Schedule), 1850," database with images, *FamilySearch,* (https://familysearch.org/ark:/61903/1:1:MVC3-1CN : 4 August 2017), Ebenezer Allen, Galveston county, Galveston, Texas, United States; citing line number 19, NARA microfilm publication M432 (Washington D.C.: National Archives and Records Administration, n.d.); FHL microfilm 444,920.

546 "Texas, County Tax Rolls, 1837–1910", database with images, *FamilySearch,* (https://familysearch.org/ark:/61903/1:1:QJ85-2YK7 : 19 July 2017), E Allen, 1850.

547 Slave Schedules were used in two U.S. Federal Censuses: The 1850 U.S. Federal Census and the 1860 U.S. Federal Census. Slaves were usually not named but were enumerated separately and usually only numbered under the slave owner's name. The National Archives has microfilmed all the original manuscripts for applicable states. 1850-1860 Slave Schedule, Random Acts of Genealogical Kindness, accessed April 25, 2018, https://www.raogk.org/census-records/slave-schedule/.

548 "Texas, County Tax Rolls, 1837-1910", database with images, *FamilySearch*, https://familysearch.org/ark:/61903/1:1:QJ85-LJSG : 19 July 2017, Ebenezer Allen, 1849,1850, 1851, 1854, 1857, 1858, 1859, and 1861.

549 An abolitionist is someone who wants a practice stopped. At this time, abolitionists wanted to end slavery. "abolitionist," accessed July 19, 2017, https://www.bing.com/search?q=define%20abolitionist&tf=U2VydmljZT1EaWN0aW9uYXJ5QW5zd2VyVjIgU2NlbmFyaW89RGVmaW5pdGlvblNjZW5hcmlvIFBvc2l0aW9uPU5PUCBSYW5raW5nRGF0YT1UcnVlIEZvcmNlUGxhY2U9RmFsc2UgUGFpcnM9RGljdGlvbmFyeVdvcmQ6YWJvbGl0aW9uaXN0O3NjbjbjpEZWZpbml0aW9uU2NlbmFyaW87cDpRQVM7IHw%3d&hs=0Hni27K%2fbHdyxxDnaoN8L%2bJrzhKcGPdwFXMjkaNvwhM%3d&FORM=DCNMOP

550 Carol Faulkner, "Spiritualism, Slavery, and Whiteness in the 1850s," *Religion in American History*, accessed September 20, 2018, http://usreligion.blogspot.com/2013/08/spiritualism-slavery-and-whiteness-in.html.

551 A commonly accepted date for the end of slavery in New Hampshire is 1857, when an act was passed stating: "No person, because of decent, should be disqualified from becoming a citizen of the state." "Slavery in New Hampshire," Slavery in the North, Timeline of abolition of slavery and serfdom. accessed February 16, 2019, http://slavenorth.com/newhampshire.htm.

552 A house slave was a slave who worked, and often lived, in the house of the slave-owner. House slaves had many duties such as cooking, cleaning, serving meals, and caring for children. Wikipedia contributors, "House slave," *Wikipedia, The Free Encyclopedia,* https://en.wikipedia.org/w/index.php?title=House_slave&oldid
=902276692 (accessed September 17, 2019).

553 Courtesy of Judith M. Johnson, Johnson-Morrow Family Tree, accessed May 20, 2016, Ancestry.com. This journal can be found online under "Samuel P. Chase Papers 1829-1872."

554 Joseph C. Megginson was a "special judge" in the Judicial Court of Jefferson County, accessed May 2, 2017, Megginhttps://co.jefferson.tx.us/Historical_Commission/files/History/Elected%20Officials/District_Judges_of_Jefferson_County.pdf.

555 Gail Borden, II (1801–1874) was a native New Yorker who settled in Texas in 1829. In Texas he worked as a land surveyor, newspaper publisher, and inventor. Borden is best known as the developer of condensed milk in 1853. Borden co-plotted the cities of Houston and Galveston in 1836. He returned to the East to market another product. Borden built factories for condensed milk in Connecticut, New York, and Illinois. Demand was high for his product by the Union Army during the Civil War. Borden was a delegate at the Convention of 1833, where he assisted in writing early drafts of a Republic of Texas constitution. He shared administrative duties with Samuel M. Williams during 1833 and 1834 when Stephen F. Austin was away in Mexico. President Sam Houston appointed Borden as the Republic of Texas Collector of Customs at Galveston in June 1837. He was popular and performed his job well, raising half of the government income through his taxation on imports. Houston's successor to the presidency, Mirabeau B. Lamar, removed Borden from office in December 1838. However, Borden was so well liked, the newcomer was resented. *The Galveston News* frequently criticized the new regime about malfeasance. After Houston was re-elected to the presidency, he reappointed Borden to the post, and he served from December 1841 to April 1843. He finally resigned after a dispute with Houston. Borden obtained a position at the Galveston City Company, where he served for twelve years as a secretary and agent. During that period, he helped sell 2,500 lots of land, for a total of $1,500,000. *Handbook of Texas Online*, Joe B. Frantz, "Borden, Gail, Jr.," accessed February 15, 2019, http://www.tshaonline.org/handbook/online/articles/fbo24.

556 John C. League, League City, County of Galveston, accessed May 2, 2017, http://www.galvestoncountytx.gov/cm/Pages/History-League-City.aspx.

557 Ebenezer Allen, Letter to Samuel May Williams, April 10, 1854, Samuel May Williams Papers, Courtesy of the Rosenberg Library, 2310 Sealy Street, Galveston, Texas, MSS# 23-2956 S. M. Williams, Box 14, Folder 9.

558 "Texas, County Tax Rolls, 1837-1910", database with images, *FamilySearch,* (https://familysearch.org/ark:/61903/1:1:QJ85-LJSG : 19 July 2017), Ebenezer Allen, 1849,1850, 1851, 1854, 1857, 1858, 1859, and 1861.

559 Cameron County is the southernmost county in Texas. The county seat is in Brownsville. The county was founded in 1848. Wikipedia contributors, "Cameron County, Texas," *Wikipedia, The Free Encyclopedia,* https://en.wikipedia.org/w/index.php?title=Cameron_County,_Texas&oldid=915982665 (accessed September 17, 2019).

SPIRITUALISM

560 Bret E. Carroll, *Spiritualism in Antebellum America* (Bloomington: Indiana University Press, 1997), 2-4.

561 Jeremy Bohonos, "Spiritualism and Gender: Questions of Leadership & Masculine Identity" (Muncie: Ball State University, 2012), master's thesis, 5-6.

562 The burned-over district refers to the western and central regions of New York in the early nineteenth century, where religious revivals and the formation of new religious movements of the Second Great Awakening took place. Charles G. Finney coined the term to denote an area in central and western New York State during the Second Great Awakening. He felt the area had been so heavily evangelized as to have no "fuel" (unconverted population) left over to "burn" (convert). Wikipedia contributors, "Burned-over district," *Wikipedia, The Free Encyclopedia,* https://en.wikipedia.org/w/index.php?title=Burned-over_district&oldid=900268582, (accessed September 1, 2019).

563 The Second Great Awakening was a Protestant religious revival movement during the early 19th century in the United States. The movement began around 1790, gained momentum by 1800 and, after 1820, membership rose rapidly among Baptist and Methodist congregations whose preachers led the movement. It was past its peak by the late 1850s. The Second Great Awakening reflected Romanticism characterized by enthusiasm, emotion, and an appeal to the super-natural. It rejected the skeptical rationalism and deism of the Enlightenment. The revivals enrolled millions of new members in existing evangelical denominations and led to the formation of new denominations. Many converts believed the Awakening heralded a new millennial age. The Second Great Awakening stimulated the establishment of many reform movements designed to remedy the evils of society before the anticipated Second Coming of Jesus Christ. Wikipedia contributors, "Second Great Awakening," *Wikipedia, The Free Encyclopedia,* https://en.wikipedia.org/w/index.php?title=Second_Great_Awakening&oldid=913206250 (accessed September 1, 2019).

564 Karen Abbott, "The Fox Sisters and the Rap on Spiritualism," Smithsonian.com, October 30, 2012, https://www.smithsonianmag.com/history/the-fox-sisters-and-the-rap-on-spiritualism-99663697/. 62

565 E. G. Huston, *San Antonio Texan* (San Antonio, Tex.), Vol. 9, No. 25, Ed. 1 Thursday, April 23, 1857, newspaper, April 23, 1857; San Antonio, Texas. (https://texashistory.unt.edu/ark:/67531/metapth232697/: accessed March 26, 2019), University of North Texas Libraries, The Portal to Texas History, https://texashistory.unt.edu; crediting The Dolph Briscoe Center for American History.

566 "Spiritualism – Another Victim," *Saratoga Republican*, August 24, 1853, Charles De Morse, *The Standard*. (Clarksville, Tex.), Vol. 10, No. 49, Ed. 1 Saturday, October 8, 1853, newspaper, October 8, 1853;(texashistory.unt.edu/ark:/67531/metapth233977/m1/1/?q=spiritualism: accessed May 2, 2018), University of North Texas Libraries, The Portal to Texas History, texashistory.unt.edu; crediting The Dolph Briscoe Center for American History.

567 E. H. Cushing, *The Weekly Telegraph* (Houston, Tex.), Vol. 22, No. 50, Ed. 1 Wednesday, March 4, 1857, newspaper, March 4, 1857; Houston, Texas, texashistory.unt.edu/ark:/67531/metapth235930/m1/3/?q=Spiritualism: accessed May 3, 2018, University of North Texas Libraries, The Portal to Texas History, texashistory.unt.edu; crediting The Dolph Briscoe Center for American History.

568 The spiritual wife system describes the idea that certain people are divinely destined to meet and share their love (at differing points along the carnal-spiritual spectrum, depending on the religious movement involved) after a receiving a spiritual confirmation, and regardless of previous civil marital bonds. The term "spiritual wifery" was to describe their religious doctrine of free love.

569 J. W. Latimer, "Progress of Spiritualism," *The Dallas Daily Herald* (Dallas, Texas), March 9, 1859, Vol. 7, No. 36, Ed. 1 Wednesday, March 9, 1859, newspaper, March 9, 1859; Dallas, Texas, (https://texashistory.unt.edu/ark:/67531/metapth294063/: accessed October 8, 2019), University of North Texas Libraries,

The Portal to Texas History, https://texashistory.unt.edu, 2.

570 E. H Cushing, *The Tri-Weekly Telegraph* (Houston, Tex.), Vol. 28, No. 59, Ed. 1 Friday, August 1, 1862, newspaper, August 1, 1862; Houston, Texas. https://texashistory.unt.edu/ark:/67531/metapth236408/:. accessed March 26, 2019. University of North Texas Libraries. The Portal to Texas History. https://texashistory.unt.edu. crediting The Dolph Briscoe Center for American History.

571 Andrew J. McGown, *Texas Presbyterian* (Houston, Tex.), Vol. 1, No. 49, Ed. 1, Saturday, February 19, 1848, newspaper, February 19, 1848; https://https://texashistory.unt.edu/ark:/67531/metapth89428/m1/1/:, accessed March 6, 2018, University of North Texas Libraries, The Portal to Texas History, texashistory.unt.edu.

572 Andrew Marshalk, *The Indianola Bulletin*. (Indiana, Tex.), Vol. 1, No. 4, Ed. 1 Thursday, April 26, 1855, newspaper, April 26, 1855; (https://texashistory.unt.edu/ark:/67531/metapth739363/m1/3:accessed March 6, 2, 2018), University of North Texas Libraries, The Portal to Texas History, texashistory.unt.edu;

573 *Galveston Weekly News* (Galveston, Tex.), Vol. 13, No. 18, Ed. 1, Tuesday, July 22, 1856, 1 of 4, The Portal to Texas History. Tuesday, July 22, 1856. https://texashistory.unt.edu/ark:/67531/metapth79862/; accessed March 6, 2018, University of North Texas Libraries, The Portal to Texas History, https://texashistory.unt.edu; crediting The Dolph Briscoe Center for American History.

574 E. H. Cushing, *The Weekly Telegraph* (Houston, Tex.), Vol. 24, No. 3, Ed. 1 Wednesday, April 7, 1858, newspaper, April 7, 1858; Houston, Texas. (https://texashistory.unt.edu/ark:/67531/metapth235987/: accessed March 26, 2019), University of North Texas Libraries, The Portal to Texas History, https://texashistory.unt.edu; crediting The Dolph Briscoe Center for American History.

575 E. H. Cushing, *The Weekly Telegraph* (Houston, Tex.), Vol. 22, No. 51, Ed. 1 Wednesday, March 11, 1857, newspaper, March 11, 1857; Houston, Texas. texashistory.unt.edu/ark:/67531/metapth235931/m1/1/?q=spiritualism: accessed May 2, 2018. University of North Texas Libraries, The Portal to Texas History. texashistory.unt.edu; crediting The Dolph Briscoe Center for American History.

576 *"Spiritualism," Weekly Telegraph, The,* Houston, Texas, Vol. 22, No. 52, Ed. 1 Wednesday, March 18, 1857, https://texashistory.unt.edu/ark:/67531/metapth235932/m1/3/zoom/?q=

Spiritualism&resolution=4&lat=6722.799682617187&lon=1691.380371093751, accessed March 26, 2019, University of North Texas Libraries, The Portal of Texas History.

577 *The Weekly Telegraph* (Houston, Tex.), Vol. 23, No. 20, Ed. 1 Wednesday, August 5, 1857, https://texashistory.unt.edu/ark:/67531/metapth235952/m1/1/zoom/?q=Spiritualism&resolution=4&lat=2996.838103285335&lon=3262.794972154248, accessed March 26, 2019, University of North Texas Libraries, The Portal of Texas History.

578 E. H. Cushing, *The Weekly Telegraph* (Houston, Tex.), Vol. 24, No. 2, Ed. 1 Wednesday, March 31, 1858, March 31, 1858; Houston, Texas. texashistory.unt.edu/ark:/67531/metapth235986/m1/1/?q=spiritualism. accessed May 2, 2018. University of North Texas Libraries, The Portal to Texas History, texashistory.unt.edu; crediting The Dolph Briscoe Center for American History.

579 E. G. Huston, *San Antonio Texan* (San Antonio, Tex.), Vol. 9, No. 21, Ed. 1 Thursday, March 26, 1857, newspaper, March 26, 1857; San Antonio, Texas. (texashistory.unt.edu/ark:/67531/metapth232695/m1/1/?q=spiritualism: accessed May 2, 2018), University of North Texas Libraries, The Portal to Texas History, texashistory.unt.edu; crediting The Dolph Briscoe Center for American History.

580 E. H. Cushing, *The Weekly Telegraph* (Houston, Tex.), Vol. 24, No. 3, Ed. 1 Wednesday, April 7, 1858, newspaper, April 7, 1858; https://texashistory.unt.edu.ark:/67531/metapth235987/m1/3/:, accessed March 6, 2018), University of North Texas Libraries, The Portal to Texas History, texashistory.unt.edu.

581 *Civilian and Gazette Weekly*. (Galveston, Tex.), Vol. 21, No. 50, Ed. 1 Tuesday, March 15, 1859, newspaper, March 15, 1859; Galveston, Texas. (https://texashistory.unt.edu/ark:/67531/metapth177437/m1/2/?q=spiritualism: accessed May 2, 2018), University of North Texas Libraries, The Portal to Texas History, texashistory.unt.edu; crediting The Dolph Briscoe Center for American History.

582 *Handbook of Texas Online*, Chester R. Burns, "Epidemic Diseases," accessed January 28, 2017, http://www.tshaonline.org/handbook/online/articles/sme01.

583 "Public Meeting," Smith, H. H. *The Galveston Journal*. (Galveston, Tex.), Vol. 4, No. [16], Ed. 1 Friday, August 12, 1853, newspaper, August 12, 1853; Galveston, Texas. (https://texashistory.unt.edu/ark:/67531/metapth178679/: accessed

August 29, 2019), University of North Texas Libraries, The Portal to Texas History, https://texashistory.unt.edu; crediting The Dolph Briscoe Center for American History.

584 Wheeler, 288.

585 Spiritualists consider March 31, 1848 the beginning of their movement. On that date, Kate and Margaret Fox, of Hydesville, New York, reported they had contacted a spirit. The spirit claimed to be a murdered peddler whose body was found in the house. However, no record of such a person was found. The spirit was said to have communicated through rapping noises. The "physical evidence" appealed to practically minded Americans, and the Fox sisters became a sensation. Karen Abbott, "The Fox Sisters and the Rap on Spiritualism," Smithsonian.com, accessed February 16, 2019, https://www.smithsonianmag.com/history/the-fox-sisters-and-the-rap-on-spiritualism-99663697/.

586 Emma Hardinge (Britten), "Spiritualism in the South" and "Spiritualism in Texas," *Modern American Spiritualism: A Twenty Year's Record of the Communion between Earth and the World of Spirits* (New York: Emma Hardinge, 1870), " 403-404.

587 Moseley (Mosly) Baker (1802-1848)", pioneer legislator and soldier, was born in Norfolk, Virginia, on September 20, 1802. Baker moved to San Felipe around 1833. He and his wife, Eliza (Ward), and their daughter certainly moved to Liberty, Texas, in March 1835. Baker claimed to have made the first speech in favor of disunion.
Baker was one of the military leaders of the Texas Revolution. On Houston's retreat into East Texas after the disasters at the Alamo and Goliad, Baker refused to abandon the line of the Brazos River. For several days his company, guarded the ford at San Felipe, where most of his men resided, thus preventing Santa Anna's army from turning Houston's left flank and forcing his retreat toward the San Jacinto River. Baker commanded Company D of the First Regiment of Texas Volunteers at the battle of San Jacinto.
After San Jacinto Baker helped to incorporate the Texas Railroad, Navigation, and Banking Company and was elected as a representative from Austin County to the First Congress of the Republic of Texas. During his term, which ran from October 3, 1836, to June 13, 1837, he drew up charges of impeachment, stemming from his earlier disagreements with Sam Houston, against the chief executive. Although the

proceedings against Houston failed, Baker was elected to the Third Congress from Galveston County, to which he had moved in 1837, and served from November 5, 1838, to January 24, 1839. He then moved to a league of land near Goose Creek in Harris County, where he established a plantation that he called Evergreen. In 1839, Congress appointed him a brigadier general in the militia of the republic for a campaign against the Indians on the Brazos. In 1842, he was reappointed brigadier general and raised a company in response to Mexican forces capturing San Antonio. On November 4, 1848, Baker died in Houston of yellow fever.
Handbook of Texas Online, Thomas W. Cutrer, "BAKER, MOSELEY," accessed March 02, 2020, http://www.tshaonline.org/handbook/online/articles/fba37.

588 *Handbook of Texas Online*, Robert S. Maxwell, "Bremond, Paul," accessed April 26, 2016, http://www.tshaonline.org/handbook/online/articles/fbr39.

589 Gideon Lincecum was a physician, philosopher, and naturalist. He moved to Texas in 1848 after years of practicing medicine with herbal remedies learned from Indians. He bought 1,828 acres of fertile prairie land. Lincecum, his wife, ten children, several grandchildren, and ten slaves arrived in Long Point on his fifty-fifth birthday. In Texas, Lincecum continued to practice medicine, made geological explorations, assembled a plant collection including 500 species with medicinal properties, kept a meteorological journal that charted drought cycles, and observed and recorded the daily activities of insect life. He was recognized as an astute naturalist, corresponded with internationally known scientists, and contributed valuable collections to the Philadelphia Academy of Science and the Smithsonian Institution. He was elected a corresponding member of the Philadelphia Academy. His writings appeared in publications such as the American Naturalist, the American Sportsman, and the Proceedings of the Academy of Natural Sciences. His views on a variety of subjects, including politics, appeared in the Texas Almanac and in newspapers. Charles Darwin sponsored the publication of Lincecum's controversial paper on the agricultural ant in the Journal of the Linnaean Society of London in 1862. Lincecum was opposed to organized religion and considered himself an atheist and freethinker. He was an ardent advocate of castration for criminals and mental misfits and led a vigorous campaign to legalize castration as the only method of improving humanity. *Handbook of Texas Online*, Lois Wood Burkhalter, "Lincecum, Gideon," accessed July 1, 2016. http://www.tshaonline.org/handbook/online/articles/fli03.

590 Long Point (Longpoint), Texas is on Farm Road 390 and Old Rocky Creek, ten miles northwest of Brenham and eighty-five miles east of Austin in northwestern Washington County. The settlement was founded in 1850 on land originally owned by Stephen F. Austin. Botanist Gideon Lincecum lived there on his plantation, Mount Olympus, from 1848 to 1874. He was attracted to the vicinity by its botanical diversity. *Handbook of Texas Online*, Carole E. Christian, "Longpoint, TX," accessed April 12, 2018, http://www.tshaonline.org/handbook/online/articles/hnl44.

591 Campbell's Bayou was across Galveston Bay from Galveston on an inlet now in southern Texas City, Galveston County. *Handbook of Texas Online*, Margaret Bearden Hamilton, "Campbell's Bayou, TX," accessed August 12, 2018, http://www.tshaonline.org/handbook/online/articles/hvcbc.

592 Mrs. Bradbury may be the wife of Captain D. Bradbury. Morrison & Fourmy. *Morrison & Fourmy's General Directory of the City of Galveston: 1859*, book, 1859; Houston, Texas. (texashistory.unt.edu/ark:/67531/metapth908994/m1/4/: accessed April 25, 2018), University of North Texas Libraries, The Portal to Texas History, texashistory.unt.edu; crediting Rosenberg Library.

593 Ms. McGuire may be the wife of Galveston dentist William McGuire W. & D. Richardson. *Galveston City Directory, 1859-1860*, book, 1859; Galveston, Texas. (texashistory.unt.edu/ark:/67531/metapth636854/m1/8/: accessed April 25, 2018), University of North Texas Libraries, The Portal to Texas History, texashistory.unt.edu; crediting Rosenberg Library.

594 Jean Lafitte was a French pirate and privateer who operated in the Gulf of Mexico during the early 19th century. Lafitte established a pirate stronghold and smuggling base on Galveston Island. Lafitte's colony grew to 100–200 men and several women. Lafitte created "letters of marque" from an imaginary nation to "authorize" all the ships sailing from Galveston as privateers. The letters gave the ships "permission" to attack ships from all nations. In 1821, the USS Enterprise was sent to Galveston to remove Lafitte from the Gulf. One of the pirate's captains had attacked an American merchant ship. As a result, Lafitte agreed to leave the island without a fight. In 1823, Lafitte was killed after a naval engagement with Spanish ships. *Handbook of Texas Online*, Harris Gaylord Warren, "Laffite, Jean," accessed February 15, 2019, http://www.tshaonline.org/handbook/online/articles/fla12.

595 A clairvoyant person has or claims to have the power of seeing objects or

actions beyond the range of natural vision. Dictionary.com, accessed February 15, 2019, https://www.dictionary.com/browse/clairvoyant.

596 Ebenezer Allen Letter to Dr. Gideon Lincecum, November 10, 1853, Courtesy of the Rosenberg Library, 2310 Sealy Street, Galveston, Texas, MSS# 350001 Ebenezer Allen Papers, Box Sm. Coll.

597 S. B. Brittan, ed., *The Spiritual Telegraph* (New York: Partridge & Brittan Publishers, 1855), "Remarkable Developments by Poetic Spirits," E. A. (Ebenezer Allen), 119-131.

598 Hardinge, 403-404.

599 Please see "Spiritualism in the Allen Family" in the Appendix.

GALVESTON AND THE CIVIL WAR

600 Wikipedia contributors, "History of slavery in Texas," *Wikipedia, The Free Encyclopedia,* https://en.wikipedia.org/w/index.php?title=History_of_slavery_in_Texas&oldid=929174021 (accessed December 9, 2019).

601 *Handbook of Texas Online*, Walter L. Buenger, "Secession," accessed January 18, 2019, http://www.tshaonline.org/handbook/online/articles/mgs02.

602 Oran M. Roberts (1815–1898) was appointed a district attorney by President Sam Houston in 1844. After Texas became a state, he was appointed district judge by Governor James Pinckney Henderson. In 1856, Roberts was elected to the Texas Supreme Court. Roberts became a spokesman for states' rights and a leader in the pro-Confederate faction. In January 1861, he was unanimously elected president of the Secession Convention in Austin. Roberts was influential in organizing the meeting. Along with colleagues, Roberts helped pass the 1861 ordinance which removed Texas from the Union. In 1862, he entered the Confederate army and was elected colonel of the Eleventh Texas infantry assigned to the Trans Mississippi Department. In 1864, Governor Roberts was elected Chief Justice of the Supreme Court. He held this position until he was removed along with other state officers in 1865. *Handbook of Texas Online*, Ford Dixon, "Roberts, Oran Milo," accessed February 13, 2019, http://www.tshaonline.org/handbook/online/articles/fro18.

603 John S. Ford (1815–1897), better known as "Rip" Ford, was a member of the

Republic of Texas Congress, Texas Senate, and mayor of Brownsville, Texas. He was additionally a Texas Ranger, a Confederate colonel, doctor, lawyer, journalist, and newspaper owner. Ford commanded men during the Antelope Hills Expedition and led Confederate forces in the last engagement of the Civil War, the Battle of Palmetto Ranch on May 12-13, 1865. *Handbook of Texas Online*, Seymour V. Connor, "Ford, John Salmon [RIP]," accessed February 13, 2019, http://www.tshaonline.org/handbook/online/articles/ffo11.

604 Wikipedia contributors, "Texas in the American Civil War," *Wikipedia, The Free Encyclopedia,* https://en.wikipedia.org/w/index.php?title=Texas_in_the_American_Civil_War&oldid=927219267 (accessed December 9, 2019).

605 John Austin Wharton (1828–1865) was a lawyer, plantation owner, and Confederate general during the American Civil War. He is considered one of the Confederacy's best tactical cavalry commanders. *Handbook of Texas Online*, Robert Maberry, Jr., "Wharton, John Austin [1828-65]," accessed February 15, 2019, http://www.tshaonline.org/handbook/online/articles/fwh04.

606 George M. Flournoy (1832–1889) helped organize the Secession Convention at Austin on December 3. He was a delegate to the convention and coauthored the declaration of causes for secession. He organized the Sixteenth Texas Infantry regiment of Walker's Texas Division. *Handbook of Texas Online*, Thomas W. Cutrer, "Flournoy, George M.," accessed May 10, 2018, http://www.tshaonline.org/handbook/online/articles/ffl19.

607 *Handbook of Texas Online*, Walter L. Buenger, "Secession Convention," accessed January 18, 2019, http://www.tshaonline.org/handbook/online/articles/mjs01.

608 Edward Clark (1815–1880) was the eighth Governor of Texas. When Sam Houston refused to take an oath of allegiance to the Confederacy, Clark was appointed governor. After losing the governor's race to Francis Lubbock, Clark became a colonel in the Texas militia. In 1863, he joined the Confederate States Army and was commissioned colonel of the 14th Texas Infantry Regiment. *Handbook of Texas Online*, Ralph A. Wooster, "Clark, Edward," accessed February 15, 2019, http://www.tshaonline.org/handbook/online/articles/fcl04.

609 *Handbook of Texas Online*, Walter L. Buenger, "Secession Convention," accessed March 31, 2016, http://www.tshaonline.org/handbook/online/articles/mjs01.

610 James Russel Soley, "The Blockading of Southern Ports during the Civil War," American Battlefield Trust, accessed August 30, 2016, https://www.battlefields.org/learn/articles/blockade.

611 Anaconda Plan, *War of the Rebellion: a compilation of the official records of the Union and Confederate Armies. I, v. 51/1*, 369–370, 387.

612 Soley, 116

613 C.S.S. *Denbigh*, "Archeology of a Civil War Blockade Runner," Institute of Nautical Archaeology at Texas A&M University. accessed June 27, 2016, http://nautarch.tamu.edu/PROJECTS/denbigh/galv01.htm. Galveston During the Civil War, accessed August 30, 2016, http://nautarch.tamu.edu/PROJECTS/denbigh/galv01.htm.

614 *Galveston Weekly News* (Galveston, Tex.), Vol. 18, No. 3, Ed. 1, Tuesday, April 23, 1861, Galveston, Texas., texashistory.unt.edu/ark:/67531/metapth79916/:, accessed February 25, 2019, University of North Texas Libraries, The Portal to Texas History, texashistory.unt.edu; crediting The Dolph Briscoe Center for American History.

615 John C. Robertson (1824- 1895) was a jurist and soldier. Three days after the secession ordinance was passed, Robertson was appointed chairman of the Committee of Public Safety and given the authority to meet with General David E. Twiggs, commander of the Department of Texas. This committee was given the power to demand, "in the name of the people of the State of Texas," the United States arms, stores, and munitions under Twiggs's control in San Antonio. After Twiggs's surrender on February 16, 1861, Robertson raised a company of cavalry which served in Arkansas. He returned to Texas and raised seven new companies for Alexander W. Terrell's regiment of Texas cavalry. Robertson was commissioned lieutenant colonel of Terrell's regiment in June 1863 and served throughout the Civil War. *Handbook of Texas Online*, Thomas W. Cutrer, "Robertson, John C.," accessed January 08, 2019, http://www.tshaonline.org/handbook/online/articles/fro29.

616 *Handbook of Texas Online*, Walter L. Buenger, "Secession," accessed March 31, 2016, http://www.tshaonline.org/handbook/online/articles/mgs02.

617 James M. Schmidt, *Galveston and the Civil War* (Charleston: The History

Press, 2012), 24.

618 *Handbook of Texas Online*, Mary Cole Farrow Long, "Cole, James Pope," accessed June 24, 2016, http://www.tshaonline.org/handbook/online/articles/fcobf.

619 William P. Allen Letter to John W. Comstock, December 8, 1889 in response to an inquiry from a librarian or historian at Dartmouth College. The request was sent to Ebenezer Allen's sister, Cordelia (Allen) Beach in Perrysburg, Ohio. William said he would send the letter to "my mother who is living in Galveston and doubtless you will receive more full and exact information as to my father's career from than from any other source." Courtesy of Judith M. Johnson, Johnson-Morrow Family Tree, accessed May 27, 2016, Ancestry.com.

620 *Handbook of Texas Online*, Ralph A. Wooster, "Civil War," accessed June 27, 2016, http://www.tshaonline.org/handbook/online/articles/qdc02.

621 Schmidt, 21.

622 C.S. *Denbigh*, "Archeology of a Civil War Blockade Runner," Institute of Nautical Archaeology at Texas A&M University. accessed June 27, 2016, http://nautarch.tamu.edu/PROJECTS/denbigh/galv01.htm. Galveston During the Civil War, accessed August 30, 2016, http://nautarch.tamu.edu/PROJECTS/denbigh/galv01.htm.

623 Schmidt, 24.

624 Schmidt, 37-38.

625 Paul O. Hébert (1818–1880) was posted to the Department of Texas in 1862. Jefferson Davis dismissed him as military commander of Texas on October 10, 1862 for imposition of martial law and harsh measures in enforcing conscription. He later took part in the defense of Vicksburg and fought at the Battle of Milliken's Bend in Louisiana in June 1863. *Handbook of Texas Online*, Thomas W. Cutrer, "Hebert, Paul Octave," accessed February 15, 2019, http://www.tshaonline.org/handbook/online/articles/fhe09.

626 David Matheson, "Galveston in the Civil War," East Texas History, accessed August 31, 2016, http://easttexashistory.org/items/show/160.

627 Joseph J. Cook (1826–1869) was a lieutenant colonel and raised an artillery company, the Active Company of Dixie Grays, for service in the Confederacy. In

July, Federal ships arrived off Galveston and Cook and his battalion were sent to help in the defense of the city. Cook served in the Galveston area throughout the war. On April 28, 1862, he led the First Texas Heavy Artillery Regiment. Cook was promoted to colonel and given command of this unit. He participated in the Battle of Galveston in October 1862, the New Year's Eve attempt to retake Galveston, and the repulse of Union forces at the battle of Sabine Pass on September 8, 1863. *Handbook of Texas Online*, Aragorn Storm Miller, "Cook, Joseph Jarvis," accessed March 12, 2018, http://www.tshaonline.org/handbook/online/articles/fco-fa.

628 Fort Point was an eight-gun sand works at Fort Point, Galveston Island. Fort Point was located on the northeast corner of Galveston Island. North American Forts, accessed March 12,2018, http://www.northamericanforts.com/West/tx-coast1.html#galv.

629 Fort Bankhead was a two-gun sand battery west of Fort Point, Galveston, accessed August 12, 2018, https://www.northamericanforts.com/West/tx-coast1.html#galv.

630 The first commercial wharves in Galveston were built by Ephraim W. McLean, who established his Kuhn's Wharf at the foot of Eighteenth Street in 1839. *Handbook of Texas Online*, Edward Coyle Sealy, "Galveston Wharves," accessed May 10, 2018, http://www.tshaonline.org/handbook/online/articles/etg01.

631 Galveston, CWSAC Battle Summaries, "Texas in the American Civil War," accessed August 12, 2018, https://www.nps.gov/abpp/battles/tx002.htm.

632 Schmidt, 45.

633 John Bankhead Magruder (1807–1871) served in the United States, Confederate States, and Mexican armies. He commanded Confederate forces at Yorktown, Virginia and deceived Union general George McClellan about the size of his force and delayed the Union army for weeks. He commanded the District of Texas, New Mexico, and Arizona in November 1862. In August 1864, he was transferred to the command of the Department of Arkansas. In March 1865, President Jefferson Davis returned Magruder to the command of the District of Texas, New Mexico, and Arizona. After the war, Magruder served with Emperor Maximilian's army in Mexico. *Handbook of Texas Online*, Thomas W. Cutrer, "Magruder, John Bankhead," accessed August 10, 2018, http://www.tshaonline.org/handbook/online/

articles/fma15.

634 Thomas Green (1814–1864) was elected colonel of the Fifth Texas Volunteer Cavalry, which, fought in the invasion of New Mexico in 1862. Green led the Confederate victory at the battle of Valverde in February. He led his men, aboard the river steamer *Bayou City*, to assist in the recapture of Galveston on January 1, 1863. In the spring of 1863, Green commanded the First Cavalry Brigade in fighting along Bayou Teche in Louisiana. On May 20, he became a brigadier general. In June, he captured a Union garrison at Brashear City but failed to seize Fort Butler on the Mississippi. At Cox's Plantation, he defeated a Union advance in July. In September, the First Cavalry captured another Union detachment at Stirling's Plantation. A similar success followed in November at Bayou Burbeaux. In four victories, Green's men inflicted about 3,000 casualties and suffered only 600. In April 1864, he led a division in successful attacks against Maj. Gen. Nathaniel P. Banks at the battle of Mansfield and against Maj. Gen. William H. Emory at the battle of Pleasant Hill. A few days later, on April 12, 1864, Green died while leading an attack on federal gunboats patrolling the Red River at Blair's Landing. *Handbook of Texas Online*, Alwyn Barr, "Green, Thomas," accessed August 12, 2018, http://www.tshaonline.org/handbook/online/articles/fgr38.

635 Leon Smith (?–1869) was a steamboat captain and soldier. In the Civil War, he served the Confederate States of America as a volunteer. He was named Commander of the Texas Marine Department under General John B. Magruder. Smith was involved in most major conflicts along the Texas coast during the war and was described by war-time governor of Texas Francis Lubbock as "undoubtedly the ablest Confederate naval commander in the Gulf waters." Day, James M. (1965) "Leon Smith: Confederate Mariner," *East Texas Historical Journal*: Vol. 3 : Issue. 1 , Article 7. https://scholarworks.sfasu.edu/ethj/vol3/iss1/7/.

636 William R. Scurry (1821–1864) was a public official, army officer, and representative in the Texas Congress. As a member of the House of Representatives in 1845, Scurry was energetic and effective in his support of the annexation of Texas to the United States. He served in the Mexican War he enlisted as a private in Col. George T. Wood's Second Regiment, Texas Mounted Volunteers, and was promoted to major on July 4, 1846. After representing Victoria, DeWitt, Jackson, and Calhoun counties in the Secession Convention, Scurry entered Confederate service in July 1861 as the lieutenant colonel of the Fourth Texas Cavalry and commanded Confederate forces at the battle of Glorieta. He was promoted to colonel on March

28, 1862, and to brigadier general on September 12, 1862, and played a vital role in the Confederate recapture of Galveston on January 1, 1863. He was assigned to command the Third Brigade of Walker's Texas Division in October 1863. Scurry was wounded at the battle of Jenkins Ferry, on April 30, 1864, but refused to be carried to the rear. A federal attack overran the place where he lay, and for two hours his wound was unattended. *Handbook of Texas Online*, Thomas W. Cutrer, "Scurry, William Read," accessed August 12, 2018, http://www.tshaonline.org/handbook/online/articles/fsc38.

637 *Handbook of Texas Online*, Alwyn Barr, "Galveston, Battle of," accessed June 27, 2016, http://www.tshaonline.org/handbook/online/articles/qeg01.

638 Schmidt, 25.

THE TORPEDO BUREAU

639 Raimondo Luraghi, *A History of the Confederate Navy* (Annapolis: Naval Institute Press, 1996), 234-235.

640 Gabriel J. Rains and Peter S. Michie, *Confederate Torpedoes* (Jefferson: McFarland & Company, Inc. Publishers, 2011), 3-5.

641 Luraghi, 242-243.

642 *Handbook of Texas Online*, Lonnie Ficklen Maywald, "Port Lavaca, TX," accessed April 04, 2019, http://www.tshaonline.org/handbook/online/articles/hep07.

643 Daniel J. Shea was a sailor and Confederate officer. Shea commanded artillery units in defense of the Matagorda-Corpus Christi area. *Handbook of Texas Online*, Aragorn Storm Miller, "Shea, Daniel D.," accessed March 08, 2018, http://www.tshaonline.org/handbook/online/articles/fsh68.

644 Mark K. Ragan, "Singer's Secret Service Corps: Causing Chaos During the Civil War,"*Civil War Times* Magazine, November/December 2007, reprinted on HistoryNet web page, https://www.historynet.com/singers-secret-service-corps-causing-chaos-during-the-civil-war.htm.

645 David Barnhart, "Masonic Saboteurs," Warriors of the Lone Star State, http://warriorsofthelonestar.blogspot.com/2016/04/masonic-saboteurs.html, April 20,

2016, accessed December 4, 2019.

646 Robert Creuzbaur (1823–1911) was a surveyor and draftsman who made maps for the General Land Office of Texas during the mid-1800s. In 1848, he was commissioned to compile topographic information for a map of Texas for Jacob de Cordova, a land promoter. Creuzbaur made a map from notes compiled by John S. (Rip) Ford on his exploring expedition in 1849 showing the route from Austin to Paso del Norte. This map was published for emigrants, and it gave the distances from one water hole to another, as well as pertinent landmarks and detailed descriptions of the nature of the soil and terrain. This map is included in *Creuzbaur's Guide to California and the Pacific Ocean* (1849). Creuzbaur drew a map of Austin in 1853. After the Civil War, he moved north and settled in Brooklyn, New York. *Handbook of Texas Online*, "Creuzbaur, Robert," accessed March 21, 2016, http://www.tshaonline.org/handbook/online/articles/fcr17.

647 A hot air engine is an engine that uses the expansion of heated air to drive a piston. Wikipedia contributors, "Hot air engine," *Wikipedia, The Free Encyclopedia,* https://en.wikipedia.org/w/index.php?title=Hot_air_engine&oldid=905264692 (accessed August 21, 2019).

648 Francis R. Lubbock (1815–1905) was governor of Texas and a Confederate officer in the Civil War. Lubbock moved to Texas in 1836. In 1837, Lubbock opened a general store in Houston, Texas. Lubbock was a lifelong Democrat. In Texas, he continued his political activities and President Sam Houston appointed him comptroller of the Republic of Texas. He was also elected clerk of the Harris County district court and served from 1841 to 1857. He was elected lieutenant governor in 1857 but lost his race for re-election in 1859. In 1860, Lubbock served as a Texas delegate to the national Democratic convention at Charleston. In 1861, Lubbock was elected governor of Texas. He staunchly supported the Confederacy and worked to improve the military capabilities of Texas. He chaired the state military board, which attempted to trade cotton and United States Indemnity Bonds for military goods through Mexico. He worked with the board to establish a state foundry and percussion-cap factory. Lubbock vigorously supported Confederate conscription, opposing draft exemptions for able-bodied men as unfair and the substitution system as advantageous to the wealthy. Viewing the use of whites in government contracting and cattle driving as wasteful, he encouraged their replacement with slaves to increase enlistment. He made aliens residing in Texas subject to the draft. Lubbock exempted frontier counties from the Confederate draft and enlisted their residents for local defence against Indian attack.

When his term ended, Lubbock entered military service. He was appointed lieutenant colonel and served as assistant adjutant general on the staffs of General Magruder, General Thomas Green, General. John A. Wharton. In August 1864, Lubbock was appointed aide-de-camp to Jefferson Davis and provided him with firsthand information on the war west of the Mississippi River. *Handbook of Texas Online*, Louis Mitchell, "Lubbock, Francis Richard," accessed August 21, 2019, http://www.tshaonline.org/handbook/online/articles/flu01.

649 *Richmond Dispatch.* December 17, 1861. quotes a report from the *Texas State Gazette.* https://www.newspapers.com/image/80624091.

650 The *Teaser* was built in Philadelphia and brought to Virginia in 1861. The Virginia Navy assigned her to the naval forces on the James River. After Virginia seceded, the *Teaser* became a part of the Confederate States Navy. The *Teaser* took part in the Battle of Hampton Roads in March 1862. On June 17, 1862, she laid mines in the James River to aid the Army of Northern Virginia in its defense of Richmond. The Confederate Navy assigned her to the Confederate Naval Submarine Battery Service to plant and service "torpedoes" in the James River. "Teaser," Naval History and Heritage Command, accessed May 27, 2016, https://www.history.navy.mil/research/histories/ship-histories/confederate_ships/teaser.html.

651 The master, or sailing master, was a historic term for a naval officer trained in and responsible for the navigation of a sailing vessel. Wikipedia contributors, "Master (naval)," *Wikipedia, The Free Encyclopedia,* https://en.wikipedia.org/w/index.php?title=Master_(naval)&oldid=892470945 (accessed August 21, 2019).

652 William P. Allen Letter to John W. Comstock, December 8, 1889 in response to an inquiry from a librarian or historian at Dartmouth College, the request was sent to Ebenezer Allen's sister, Cordelia (Allen) Beach in Perrysburg, Ohio. William said he would send the letter to "my mother who is living in Galveston and doubtless you will receive more full and exact information as to my father's career from than from any other source." Courtesy of Judith M. Johnson, Johnson-Morrow Family Tree, accessed May 27, 2016, Ancestry.com.

653 The source for this letter is the National Archives Compiled Service Records of Confederate Soldiers Who Served in Organizations Raised Directly by the Confederate Government, NARA Catalogue ID# 586957, NARA Catalogue Title:

Carded Records Showing Military Service of Soldiers Who Fought in Confederate Organizations, Compiled 1903-1927, documenting the period 1861-1865, Record Group 109, Roll 0104, Military Unit Engineers CSA C-Di, 1863, Robert Creuzbaur, letter from Ebenezer Allen.

654 *Handbook of Texas Online*, Mark Dallas Loeffler, "SEA KING," accessed January 08, 2019, http://www.tshaonline.org/handbook/online/articles/etslq.

655 James D. Richardson, *A Compilation of the Messages and Papers of the Confederacy including the Diplomatic Correspondence, 1861-1865* (Nashville, United States Publishing Company: 1906), vol. I, 266.

656 H. L. Hunley (submarine). "Overview," Hunley, accessed February 12, 2019, https://www.hunley.org/overview/.

657 Selected Ordinance Patents, accessed January 31, 2017, http://www.civilwarartillery.com/patents.htm.

658 History of the United States Patent Office, accessed January 31, 2017, http://www.myoutbox.net/popchapx.htm.

659 NC Civil War Sailors Project, Identifying NC Sailors and Marines, accessed May 5, 2017, http://rblong.net/sailor/cr.html.

660 Register1862; CSN Register; Compiled Military Service Record for Robert Creuzbaur, at FOLD3 1880 U.S. Census; 1910 U.S. Census; *Handbook of Texas Online*, "Creuzbaur, Robert," accessed May 5, 2017, www.tshaonline.org/handbook/online/articles/fcr17.

661 "Organization of the Confederate Military," Cold Southern Steel, accessed January 8, 2019, https://coldsouthernsteel.wordpress.com/2015/01/02/organization-of-the-confederate-military/.

662 Edmund Kirby Smith (1824–1893) was a career U. S. Army officer who fought in the Mexican American War and Civil War. He joined the Confederate States Army and was promoted to general in the first months of the war. He was notable for his command of the Trans-Mississippi Department after the fall of Vicksburg to the Union. On January 14, 1863, Smith was transferred to command the Trans-Mississippi Department and he remained west of the Mississippi River for the balance of the war, based part of this time in Shreveport, Louisiana. Smith's department never had the manpower or gunboats to challenge the Union Army and federal navy. *Handbook of Texas Online*, Thomas W. Cutrer, "Smith, Edmund Kirby," accessed February 11, 2019, http://www.tshaonline.org/handbook/online/articles/fsm09.

663 Washington D. Miller (1814–1866) was a legislator and editor. He moved to Texas in 1837 and settled in Gonzales to practice law. He stood for the county in the Congress of the Republic of Texas from November 1840 to February 1841. In 1841, he became Sam Houston's private secretary in Austin. In 1842, he was appointed postmaster general by Sam Houston. Miller and William H. Cushney published the *National Register* at Washington-on-the-Brazos. In 1845, Miller returned to Austin, where he served as secretary of state under Governor George T. Wood from 1848 to 1850. After government service, Miller, joined Cushney and edited and published the Austin *Texas Democrat. Handbook of Texas Online*, "Miller, Washington D.," accessed May 13, 2017, http://www.tshaonline.org/handbook/online/articles/fmi29.

664 A. L Rives Letter to E. Kirby Smith, *The War of Rebellion: A Compilation of the Official Records of the Union and Confederate Armies,* Washington: Government Printing Office, 1882. Series 1 - Volume 34 (Part IV). 973-974.

665 Jeffery S. Prushankin, *The Civil War in the Trans-Mississippi Theater – 1861-1865* (Washington: Center of Military History United States Army, 2015), 7- 9.

DEATH

666 "A Hard-Earned Victory," Stones River National Battlefield, accessed February 11, 2019, https://www.nps.gov/stri/index.htm.

667 Richmond bread riot occurred on April 2, 1863 motivated by shortages and hunger the Confederacy. DeCredico, Mary, "Richmond Bread Riot," Encyclopedia Virginia in partnership with the Library of Virginia, https://www.encyclopediavirginia.org/bread_riot_richmond.

668 "Battle of Chancellorsville," Fredericksburg & Spotsylvania National Military Park, accessed February 11, 2019, https://www.nps.gov/frsp/learn/historyculture/chist.htm.

669 "The Siege of Vicksburg," Vicksburg National Military Park, accessed February 11, 2019, https://www.nps.gov/vick/learn/historyculture/vicksburgsiege.htm.

670 "Gettysburg National Military Park," National Park Service, accessed February 11, 2019, https://www.nps.gov/gett/index.htm.

671 "Port Hudson," National Park Service, accessed February 11, 2019, https://www.nps.gov/nr/travel/louisiana/por.htm.

672 "Battle of Chickamauga," Chickamauga & Chattanooga National Military Park, accessed February 11, 2019, https://www.nps.gov/chch/learn/historyculture/battle-of-chickamauga.htm.

673 John S. Bowman, ed., *The Civil War* (East Bridgewater: World Publications Group, 2006), 90-123.

674 "Sudden and Mysterious Death," *The Richmond Examiner*, October 16, 1863, 1, Courtesy of Judith M. Johnson, Johnson-Morrow Family Tree, accessed May 20, 2016, Ancestry.com.

675 Ebenezer Allen was 59 years old.

676 Allen was born in New Hampshire.

677 *The Richmond Examiner*, Saturday, October 17, 1863, Source: GenealogyBank.com, accessed May 20, 2016.

678 Charles De Morse, *The Standard.* (Clarksville, Tex.), Vol. 20, No. 28, Ed. 1 Saturday, December 5, 1863, newspaper, December 5, 1863; (https://texashistory.unt.edu/ark:/67531/metapth234371/: accessed August 30, 2019), University of North Texas Libraries, The Portal to Texas History, https://texashistory.unt.edu; crediting The Dolph Briscoe Center for American History.

679 "Local Matters," *The Daily Dispatch*, September 10, 1862, accessed March 21, 2016, https://www.newspapers.com/image/80615978.

680 Directory of Richmond City Officials, accessed March 21, 2016, http://www.newrivernotes.com/neighboring_richmond_government_1861-65_cityofficials.htm.

681 *By-laws and List of Members of Richmond Lodge, no. 10*: revised and adopted A.L. 5864, A.D. 1864 (Richmond: James E. Goode, 1864), 11.

682 "Skin discoloration - bluish," U.S. National Library of Medicine, accessed May 22, 2106, https://www.nlm.nih.gov/medlineplus/ency/article/003215.htm.

683 "Life Expectancy," "1800-1850," Legacy.com, accessed August 14, 2018, http://www.legacy.com/life-and-death/the-antebellum-era.html.

684 William Pitt Allen, California Wills and Probate Records, 1850-1953, accessed September 5, 2016, http://www.ancestry.com.

685 Esther Inglis-Arkell, "The Deadliest Poisons in History (And Why People Stopped Using Them)," *Gizmodo*, accessed February 15, 2018, https://io9.gizmodo.com/5942161/the-deadliest-poisons-in-history-and-why-people-stopped-using-them.

686 Arsenic poisoning, Patient, accessed August 14, 2018, https://patient.info/doctor/Arsenic-Poisoning.

687 Two Richmond entrepreneurs visited Boston's Mount Auburn Cemetery, which was a model for the rural cemetery movement. In 1847, the men decided to design their new Hollywood Cemetery based on Mount Auburn. When the men returned to Richmond, they commissioned Philadelphia architect John Notman to design grounds for a new cemetery on a hilly, wooded plot on the western edge of town overlooking the James River. Public controversies delayed the project into the 1850s. The site developed its distinctiveness when President James Monroe's remains were reburied in 1858 and the later Confederate burials during and after the Civil War. accessed May 4, 2017, https://www.hollywoodcemetery.org/about/our-history.

688 "Allen, E., Search Burial Records," Hollywood Cemetery, accessed February 23, 2019, https://www.hollywoodcemetery.org/genealogy/burial-records.

689 Burial Records, Hollywood Cemetery, accessed January 5, 2018, https://www.hollywoodcemetery.org/genealogy/burial-records.

690 44th Regiment, North Carolina Infantry, 44th Infantry Regiment completed its organization in March 1862, at Camp Mangum, near Raleigh, North Carolina. Its companies were recruited in the counties of Granville, Edgecombe, Pitt, Chatham, Montgomery, Beaufort, and Franklin. It served in the Department of North Carolina, then was assigned to General Pettigrrew's, Kirkland's, and MacRae's Brigade, Army of Northern Virginia. En route to Gettysburg the 44th stayed at

Hanover Junction to guard the railroads. Later it fought at Bristoe, The Wilderness, Spotsylvania, and Cold Harbor. It was then involved in the Petersburg siege south of the James River and the Appomattox Campaign. The regiment reported 23 killed and 63 wounded at Bristoe, sustained heavy losses at The Wilderness and in front of Petersburg, and surrendered 8 officers and 74 men on April 9, 1865. Its commanders were Colonels G.B. Singeltary and T.C. Singeltary; Lieutenant Colonels Richard C. Cotton, Elisha Cromwell, and Tazewell L. Hargrove, and Major Charles M. Stedman. accessed May 4, 2017, https://www.nps.gov/civilwar/search-soldiers-detail.htm?soldierId=12F3757A-DC7A-DF11-BF36-B8AC6F-5D926A https://www.nps.gov/civilwar/search-battle-units-detail.htm?battleUnit-Code=CNC0044RI.

691 Burial Records, Hollywood Cemetery, accessed January 5, 2018, https://www.hollywoodcemetery.org/genealogy/burial-records.

692 23rd Regiment, South Carolina Infantry The 23rd Infantry Regiment (also called Hatch's Coast Rangers) was assembled at Charleston, South Carolina in November 1861. Most of the men were from Horry, Georgetown, Charleston, and Colleton Counties. After being stationed in South Carolina, the regiment moved to Virginia and during the war served in General Evans', Elliot's, and Wallace's Brigade. It participated in the conflicts at Second Manassas, South Mountain, and Sharpsburg, then was ordered to North Carolina and later to Mississippi. The unit skirmished at Jackson, was sent to Charleston, and in the spring of 1864 returned to Virginia. It continued the fight in the trenches of Petersburg and around Appomattox. During the Second Manassas operations, August 6-20, 1862, this regiment lost sixty-eight percent of the 225 engaged, and all its field officers were wounded. It reported 10 killed, 22 wounded, and 5 missing in the Maryland Campaign, totaled 297 men in October 1863, and had 49 killed or wounded at the Petersburg mine explosion. The 23rd had many disabled at Sayler's Creek and surrendered 5 officers and 103 men. Its commanders were Colonels Henry L. Benbow and Lewis M. Hatch; Lieutenant Colonels Allen J. Green, John M. Kinloch, Edgar O. Murden, and John Roberts; and Majors Matthew V. Bancroft, Henry H. Lesesne, L.P. Miller, and John M. Whilden. accessed May 4, 2017, https://www.nps.gov/civilwar/search-battle-units-detail.htm?battleUnitCode=CSC0023RIhttps://www.nps.gov/civilwar/search-soldiers.htm#q=%2223rd+Regiment,+South+Carolina+Infantry+(Hatch's+Coast+Rangers)%22&sort=Last_Name+asc,First_Name+asc.

693 Edmond Allen, "The Civil War, National Park Service," accessed February

23, 2019, "Forty-fourth Regiment - Infantry," Civil War Index, accessed January 5, 2018. https://www.nps.gov/civilwar/search-soldiers-detail.htm?soldierId=-11F3757A-DC7A-DF11-BF36-B8AC6F5D926Ahttp://www.civilwarindex.com/armync/soldiers/44th_nc_infantry_soldiers.pdf, 238.

694 E. Allen, The Civil War, National Park Service, accessed February 23, 2019, https://www.nps.gov/civilwar/search-soldiers-detail.htm?soldierId=-09C8587A-DC7A-DF11-BF36-B8AC6F5D926A.

695 The reference to Ebenezer Allen as "Union man and a fugitive from the state" is interesting. Did Allen change sides and work for the Union? This is the only reference to Allen as a wanted Union man.

696 The number of people with surname "Allen" complicated research on the family. *John Heller's Galveston City Directory, 1870* includes ten people. Heller, John H. *Galveston City Directory, 1870*, book, 1870; Galveston, Texas. (https://texashistory.unt.edu/ark:/67531/metapth636853/: accessed August 17, 2019), University of North Texas Libraries, The Portal to Texas History, https://texashistory.unt.edu; crediting Rosenberg Library. The Galveston City Directory, 1872 contains eighteen people. Heller, John H. Galveston City Directory, 1872, book, 1872; Galveston, Texas. (https://texashistory.unt.edu/ark:/67531/metapth636856/: accessed August 17, 2019), University of North Texas Libraries, The Portal to Texas History, https://texashistory.unt.edu; crediting Rosenberg Library. Mason & Fourmy's *General Directory of the City of Galveston, 1899-1900* lists sixty citizens. Morrison & Fourmy. *Morrison & Fourmy's General Directory of the City of Galveston: 1899-1900*, book, 1899/1900; Houston, Texas. (https://texashistory.unt.edu/ark:/67531/metapth894022/: accessed August 17, 2019), University of North Texas Libraries, The Portal to Texas History, https://texashistory.unt.edu; crediting Rosenberg Library.

697 Allen Family History Find Genealogy Records & Family Crest, Archives, accessed August 9, 2019, https://www.archives.com/genealogy/family-history-allen.html. The surname Allen is the twenty-seventh most common surname in the United States. There were sixty Texans named Allen in the 1900 city directory. Several famous Allens were Augustus Chapman Allen (1806–1864), founder of Houston, Charlotte Baldwin Allen (1805–1895), financed founding of Houston, known as the "mother of Houston" John Kirby Allen (1810-1838), founder of Houston.

698 "United States Census, 1850," database with images, *FamilySearch*, (https://

familysearch.org/ark:/61903/1:1:MXLK-DV1 : 12 April 2016), Ebenezer Allen, Galveston city, Galveston, Texas, United States; citing family 289, NARA microfilm publication M432 (Washington, D.C.: National Archives and Records Administration, n.d.).

699 "United States Census, 1860", database with images, *FamilySearch*, (https://familysearch.org/ark:/61903/1:1:MXFB-FZM : 12 December 2017), Henry Allen in entry for W Allen, 1860.

700 "United States Census, 1860", database with images, *FamilySearch*, (https://familysearch.org/ark:/61903/1:1:MXFB-FZ9 : 12 December 2017), William P Allen in entry for W Allen, 1860.

701 "United States Census, 1860", database with images, *FamilySearch*, (https://familysearch.org/ark:/61903/1:1:MXFB-FNG : 12 December 2017), Edward Allen in entry for W Allen, 1860.

702 "United States Census, 1860", database with images, *FamilySearch*, (https://familysearch.org/ark:/61903/1:1:MXFB-FNP : 12 December 2017), Fred Allen in entry for W Allen, 1860.

703 "United States Census, 1860", database with images, *FamilySearch*, (https://familysearch.org/ark:/61903/1:1:MXFB-FZM : 12 December 2017), Henry Allen in entry for W Allen, 1860.

704 "United States Civil War Soldiers Index, 1861-1865," database, *FamilySearch*, (https://familysearch.org/ark:/61903/1:1:FSL4-SM3 : 4 December 2014), Henry Allen, Private, Company FD, 26th Regiment, Texas Cavalry (Debray's) (Davis' Mo, Confederate; citing NARA microfilm publication M227 (Washington D.C.: National Archives and Records Administration, n.d.), roll 1; FHL microfilm 880,014.

705 "United States Civil War Soldiers Index, 1861-1865," database, *FamilySearch*, (https://familysearch.org/ark:/61903/1:1:F9KL-QWP : 4 December 2014), William P. Allen, Second Lieutenant, Company F&S, 11th Regiment, Texas Infantry (Roberts'), Confederate; citing NARA microfilm publication M227 (Washington D.C.: National Archives and Records Administration, n.d.), roll 1; FHL microfilm 880,014.

706 There were four Union soldiers from Maine. Two served in the artillery and

two in the infantry. They joined the army as privates and left as privates. "Search for Soldiers," The Civil War, National Park Service, accessed August 14, 2019, https://www.nps.gov/civilwar/search-soldiers.htm#sort=score+desc&q=Edward+Allen&fq%5B%5D=State%3A%22Maine%22.
"United States Civil War Soldiers Index, 1861-1865," database, *FamilySearch*, (https://familysearch.org/ark:/61903/1:1:F9KL-SX9 : 4 December 2014), Edward Allen, Private, Company H, Waul's Texas Legion, Confederate; citing NARA microfilm publication M227 (Washington D.C.: National Archives and Records Administration, n.d.), roll 1; FHL microfilm 880,014.

707 "Maine, Civil War Enlistment Papers, 1862-1865," database with images, *FamilySearch*, (https://familysearch.org/ark:/61903/1:1:Q2QB-JDNF : accessed 15 August 2019), Edward Allen, 21 Aug 1863; citing Bangor, Bangor, Penobscot, Maine, United States, Maine State Archives, Augusta; FHL microfilm.

708 Please see Ebenezer Allen Will in the Appendix.

709 *Find A Grave*, database and images (https://www.findagrave.com : accessed 19 August 2019), memorial page for Frederick Allen (1849–9 May 1901), Find A Grave Memorial no. 128070640, citing Lakeview Cemetery, Galveston, Galveston County, Texas, USA ; Maintained by Find A Grave (contributor 8) .

710 W. & D. Richardson. *Galveston City Directory, 1866-1867*, book, 1859; Galveston, Texas. (https://texashistory.unt.edu/ark:/67531/metapth636854/: accessed August 14, 2019), University of North Texas Libraries, The Portal to Texas History, https://texashistory.unt.edu; crediting Rosenberg Library.

711 "United States Census, 1870," database with images, *FamilySearch*, (https://familysearch.org/ark:/61903/1:1:M66M-C96: 17 October 2014), Sylvia Allen in household of Hannah B Leavitt, Maine, United States; citing p. 43, family 385, NARA microfilm publication M593 (Washington D.C.: National Archives and Records Administration, n.d.); FHL microfilm 552,058.

712 W. & D. Richardson, *Galveston City Directory, 1866-1867*, book, 1859; Galveston, Texas. (https://texashistory.unt.edu/ark:/67531/metapth636854/: accessed August 14, 2019), University of North Texas Libraries, The Portal to Texas History, https://texashistory.unt.edu; crediting Rosenberg Library.

713 C. W. Marston, *Galveston City Directory, 1868-1869*, book, 1868; Galveston,

Texas. (https://texashistory.unt.edu/ark:/67531/metapth636855/: accessed August 14, 2019), University of North Texas Libraries, The Portal to Texas History, https://texashistory.unt.edu; crediting Rosenberg Library.

714 "Texas State Fair." *The Galveston Daily News* (Galveston, Texas), June 2, 1871, accessed August 15, 2019, https://www.newspapers.com/image/23029131/?terms=%22Texas%2BState%2BFair%22.

715 "United States Census, 1880," database with images, *FamilySearch*, (https://familysearch.org/ark:/61903/3:1:33S7-9YY1-M66M-C96: 17 October 2014), Sylvia Allen in household of Hannah B Leavitt, Maine, United States; citing p. 43, family 385, NARA microfilm publication M593 (Washington D.C.: National Archives and Records Administration, n.d.); FHL microfilm 552,058.

716 Samuel Oliver Young, *A thumb-nail history of the city of Houston, Texas, from its founding in 1836 to the year 1912*, book, 1912; Houston, Texas. (https://texashistory.unt.edu/ark:/67531/metapth24649/: accessed August 14, 2019), University of North Texas Libraries, The Portal to Texas History, https://texashistory.unt.edu.

717 *The Houston Post*. (Houston, Tex.), Vol. 37, No. 112, Ed. 1 Monday, July 25, 1921,newspaper, July 25, 1921; Houston, Texas. (https://texashistory.unt.edu/ark:/67531/metapth610063/: accessed August 12, 2019), University of North Texas Libraries, The Portal to Texas History, https://texashistory.unt.edu.

718 Email from Judith M. Johnson on August 22, 2019.

719 "United States Census, 1900," database with images, *FamilySearch*, (https://familysearch.org/ark:/61903/1:1:M9GG-7T3 : accessed 20 August 2019), William C Allen, Vallejo Township Vallejo city Ward 1, Solano, California, United States; citing enumeration district (ED) 152, sheet 6B, family 141, NARA microfilm publication T623 (Washington, D.C.: National Archives and Records Administration, 1972.); FHL microfilm 1,240,113.

720 "California Great Registers, 1866-1910," database, *FamilySearch,* (https://familysearch.org/ark:/61903/1:1:VTXV-CDM : 25 July 2019), William Pitt Allen, 24 Sep 1892; citing Voter Registration, Summerland, Santa Barbara, California, United States, county clerk offices, California; FHL microfilm 1,548,299.

721 "California Great Registers, 1866-1910," database, *FamilySearch*, (https://

familysearch.org/ark:/61903/1:1:VTXV-CDM : 25 July 2019), William Pitt Allen, 24 Sep 1892; citing Voter Registration, Summerland, Santa Barbara, California, United States, county clerk offices, California; FHL microfilm 1,548,299.

722 *San Francisco Chronicle* (San Francisco, California), April 26, 1893, 1, accessed August 21, 2019, https://www.newspapers.com/image/27340796/?terms=W.%2BP.%2BAllen and *The Oakdale Graphic* (Oakdale, California), May 17, 1893, https://www.newspapers.com/image/486996198/?terms=Oakdale%2BGraphic.

723 "The Summerland Libel Suit," *San Francisco Call*, January 19, 1898, 2, accessed August 21, 2019, https://www.newspapers.com/image/92934874/?terms=-Summerland%2BLibel%2BSuit.

724 "Fiftieth Anniversary," *The Los Angeles Times*, April 5, 1898, 13, accessed August 21, 2019, https://www.newspapers.com/image/378343982/.

725 The People's Party (also known as the Populist Party or the Populists) was a left-wing agrarian late 19th century political party in the United States. The Populist Party emerged in the early 1890s as an important force in the Southern United States and the Western United States, but the party collapsed after it nominated Democrat William Jennings Bryan in the 1896 United States presidential election. *Wikipedia, The Free Encyclopedia*, https://en.wikipedia.org/w/index.php?title=Hot_air_engine&oldid=905264692 (accessed August 21, 2019).
"People's Party (United States)," Wikipedia, accessed August 15, 2019, https://en.wikipedia.org/wiki/People%27s_Party_(United_States).

726 "Populist Caucus," *The Los Angeles Times* (Los Angeles, California), August 16, 1898, accessed July 12, 2019, https://www.newspapers.com/image/378332636/?terms=W.%2BP.%2BAllen.

727 Email from Judith M. Johnson on August 22, 2019.

728 "United States Census, 1850," database with images, *FamilySearch*, (https://familysearch.org/ark:/61903/1:1:MXLK-DK3 : 12 April 2016), Frederick Allen in household of Ebenezer Allen, Galveston city, Galveston, Texas, United States; citing family 289, NARA microfilm publication M432 (Washington, D.C.: National Archives and Records Administration, n.d.).

729 "Maine Marriages, 1771-1907," database, *FamilySearch*, (https://familysearch.org/ark:/61903/1:1:F4XS-44N : 10 February 2018), Edward C. Allen and Lillian D. Ham, 07 May 1890; citing Civil, Portland, Cumberland, Maine, reference ; FHL microfilm 12,026.

730 "Maine Marriages, 1771-1907," database, *FamilySearch*, (https://*familysearch*.org/ark:/61903/1:1:F4F8-C9M : 10 February 2018), Edward C. Allen and Mary S. Bennett, 15 May 1858; citing Gray, Cumberland, Maine, reference ; FHL microfilm 10,932.

731 "United States Census, 1880." database with images, *FamilySearch*, https://FamilySearch.org : 14 June 2016. Citing NARA microfilm publication T9. Washington, D.C.: National Archives and Records Administration, n.d.

732 "Maine Patents," *Bangor Daily Whig and Courier* (Bangor, Maine), December 16, 1887, accessed September 5, 2019, https://www.newspapers.com/image/7189994/?terms=%22Edward%2BAllen%22.

733 "Maine Patents," *Bangor Daily Whig and Courier* (Bangor, Maine), June 16, 1888, accessed September 5, 2019, https://www.newspapers.com/image/18339966/?terms=%22Edward%2BAllen%22.

734 *Find A Grave*, database and images (https://www.findagrave.com : accessed 19 August 2019), memorial page for Edward C. Allen (2 Oct 1836–23 Mar 1925), Find A Grave Memorial no. 113514069, citing Mayberry Cemetery, Windham Center, Cumberland County, Maine, USA ; Maintained by Find A Grave (contributor 8).

735 "United States Census, 1850," database with images, *FamilySearch*, https://familysearch.org/ark:/61903/1:1:MXLK-DK3 : 12 April 2016), Frederick Allen in household of Ebenezer Allen, Galveston city, Galveston, Texas, United States; citing family 289, NARA microfilm publication M432 (Washington, D.C.: National Archives and Records Administration, n.d.) and "United States Census, 1860", database with images, *FamilySearch*, (https://familysearch.org/ark:/61903/1:1:MXFB-FNP : 12 December 2017), Fred Allen in entry for W Allen, 1860.

736 C. W. Marston, *Galveston City Directory, 1868-1869*, book, 1868; Galveston, Texas. (https://texashistory.unt.edu/ark:/67531/metapth636855/: accessed August 15, 2019), University of North Texas Libraries, The Portal to Texas History, https://texashistory.unt.edu; crediting Rosenberg Library.

737 Heller, John H. *Galveston City Directory, 1870*, book, 1870; Galveston, Texas. (https://texashistory.unt.edu/ark:/67531/metapth636853/: accessed August 16, 2019), University of North Texas Libraries, The Portal to Texas History, https://texashistory.unt.edu; crediting Rosenberg Library.

738 "United States Census, 1880," database with images, *FamilySearch*, (https://familysearch.org/ark:/61903/1:1:MFNZ-YZJ : 15 July 2017), Fred Allen, 1880; citing enumeration district ED 63, sheet 26C, NARA microfilm publication T9 (Washington D.C.: National Archives and Records Administration, n. d), roll 1305; FHL microfilm 1,255,305.

739 Morrison & Fourmy, *Morrison & Fourmy's General Directory of the City of Galveston: 1886-1887*, book,1886/1887; Houston, Texas. (https://texashistory.unt.edu/ark:/67531/metapth894033/: accessed August 12, 2019), University of North Texas Libraries, The Portal to Texas History, https://texashistory.unt.edu; crediting Rosenberg Library.

740 "Texas, County Tax Rolls, 1837-1910", database with images, *FamilySearch*, (https://familysearch.org/ark:/61903/1:1:QJ85-PXK3 : 19 July 2017), Fred Allen, 1886. "Texas, County Tax Rolls, 1837-1910", database with images, *FamilySearch*, (https://familysearch.org/ark:/61903/1:1:QJ85-5T9L : 19 July 2017), Fred Allen, 1894. "Texas, County Tax Rolls, 1837-1910", database with images, *FamilySearch*, (https://familysearch.org/ark:/61903/1:1:QJ85-5X3X : 19 July 2017), Fred Allen, 1891.

741 "Fred Allen & Co's." *The Galveston Daily News* (Galveston, Texas), Vol. 54, No. 259, Ed. 1 Sunday, December 8, 1895, newspaper, December 8, 1895; Galveston, Texas. (https://texashistory.unt.edu/ark:/67531/metapth465597/: accessed September 5, 2019),University of North Texas Libraries, The Portal to Texas History, https://texashistory.unt.edu; crediting Abilene Library Consortium.

742 "United States Census, 1900," database with images, *FamilySearch*, (https://familysearch.org/ark:/61903/1:1:M3GH-MVB : accessed 5 September 2019), Fred Allen, Galveston city Ward 1, Galveston, Texas, United States; citing enumeration district (ED) 114, sheet 7A, family 128, NARA microfilm publication T623 (Washington, D.C.: National Archives and Records Administration, 1972.); FHL microfilm 1,241,637.

743 Morrison & Fourmy, *Morrison & Fourmy's General Directory of the City of Galveston: 1901-1902*, book,1901/1902; Houston, Texas. (https://texashistory.unt.edu/ark:/67531/metapth894024/: accessed August 12, 2019), University of North Texas Libraries, The Portal to Texas History, https://texashistory.unt.edu; crediting Rosenberg Library.

744 Courtesy of the Rosenberg Library, 2310 Sealy Street, Galveston, Texas.

745 *Find A Grave*, database and images (https://www.findagrave.com : accessed 19 August 2019), memorial page for Frederick Allen (1849–9 May 1901), Find A Grave Memorial no. 128070640, citing Lakeview Cemetery, Galveston, Galveston County, Texas, USA ; Maintained by Find A Grave (contributor 8) .

746 Morrison & Fourmy, *Morrison & Fourmy's General Directory of the City of Galveston: 1901-1902*, book,1901/1902; Houston, Texas. (https://texashistory.unt.edu/ark:/67531/metapth894024/: accessed August 12, 2019), University of North Texas Libraries, The Portal to Texas History, https://texashistory.unt.edu; crediting Rosenberg Library.

747 W. A. Fayman & T. W. Reilly, *Galveston City Directory, 1875-1876*, book, 1875; (https://texashistory.unt.edu/ark:/67531/metapth636884/: accessed August 14, 2019), University of North Texas Libraries, The Portal to Texas History, https://texashistory.unt.edu; crediting Rosenberg Library.

748 John H. Heller, *Heller's Galveston Directory, 1876-1877*, book, 1876; Galveston, Texas. (https://texashistory.unt.edu/ark:/67531/metapth636850/: accessed August 19, 2019), University of North Texas Libraries, The Portal to Texas History, https://texashistory.unt.edu; crediting Rosenberg Library.

749 John H. Heller, *Heller's Galveston Directory, 1878-1879*, book, 1878; Galveston, Texas. (https://texashistory.unt.edu/ark:/67531/metapth636857/: accessed August 14, 2019), University of North Texas Libraries, The Portal to Texas History, https://texashistory.unt.edu; crediting Rosenberg Library.

750 John H. Heller, *Heller's Galveston Directory, 1880-1881*, book, 1880; Galveston, Texas. (https://texashistory.unt.edu/ark:/67531/metapth636851/: accessed August 19, 2019), University of North Texas Libraries, The Portal to Texas History, https://texashistory.unt.edu; crediting Rosenberg Library.
Morrison & Fourmy, *Morrison & Fourmy's General Directory of the City of Gal-*

veston: 1881-1882, book, 1881/1882; Houston, Texas. (https://texashistory.unt.edu/ark:/67531/metapth894032/: accessed August 19, 2019), University of North Texas Libraries, The Portal to Texas History, https://texashistory.unt.edu; crediting Rosenberg Library.

751 Morrison & Fourmy, *Morrison & Fourmy's General Directory of the City of Galveston: 1891-1892*, book, 1891/1892; Houston, Texas. (https://texashistory.unt.edu/ark:/67531/metapth894028/: accessed August 19, 2019), University of North Texas Libraries, The Portal to Texas History, https://texashistory.unt.edu; crediting Rosenberg Library.

752 Courtesy of Judith M. Johnson, Johnson-Morrow Family Tree, accessed May 20, 2016, Ancestry.com.

753 Morrison & Fourmy, *Morrison & Fourmy's General Directory of the City of Galveston: 1884-1885*, book, 1884/1885; Houston, Texas. (https://texashistory.unt.edu/ark:/67531/metapth894029/: accessed August 19, 2019), University of North Texas Libraries, The Portal to Texas History, https://texashistory.unt.edu; crediting Rosenberg Library.

754 Morrison & Fourmy, *Morrison & Fourmy's General Directory of the City of Galveston: 1898*, book, 1898; Houston, Texas. (https://texashistory.unt.edu/ark:/67531/metapth894031/: accessed August 19, 2019), University of North Texas Libraries, The Portal to Texas History, https://texashistory.unt.edu; crediting Rosenberg Library.
Morrison & Fourmy, *Morrison & Fourmy's General Directory of the City of Galveston: 1899-1900*, book, 1899/1900; Houston, Texas. (https://texashistory.unt.edu/ark:/67531/metapth894022/: accessed August 19, 2019), University of North Texas Libraries, The Portal to Texas History, https://texashistory.unt.edu; crediting Rosenberg Library.

755 "Flotsam and Jetsam," *The Galveston Daily News* (Galveston, Texas), May 17, 1888, accessed August 20, 2019, https://www.newspapers.com/image/22270672/?terms=Ebenezer%2BAllen.

756 "Justus Zahn, Galveston Photographer," Courtesy of the Rosenberg Library, 2310 Sealy Street, Galveston, Texas, http://rosenberg-library-museum.org/treasure-of-the-month/past-treasure-of-the-month/2013-03/.

757 Courtesy of Judith M. Johnson, Johnson-Morrow Family Tree, accessed May 20, 2016, Ancestry.com.

758 Courtesy of the Rosenberg Library, 2310 Sealy Street, Galveston, Texas.

759 Courtesy of Judith M. Johnson, Johnson-Morrow Family Tree, accessed May 20, 2016, Ancestry.com.

760 Morrison & Fourmy, *Morrison & Fourmy's General Directory of the City of Galveston: 1901-1902*, book,1901/1902; Houston, Texas. (https://texashistory.unt.edu/ark:/67531/metapth894024/: accessed August 12, 2019), University of North Texas Libraries, The Portal to Texas History, https://texashistory.unt.edu; crediting Rosenberg Library.

761 "Notice," *The Galveston Daily News* (Galveston, Texas), August 3, 1866, accessed August 16, 2019, Newspapers by Ancestry.

762 John H. Heller, *Heller's Galveston City Directory, 1872*, book, 1872; Galveston, Texas. (https://texashistory.unt.edu/ark:/67531/metapth636856/: accessed August 16, 2019), University of North Texas Libraries, The Portal to Texas History, https://texashistory.unt.edu; crediting Rosenberg Library.

763 "Supreme Court Decisions," *The Galveston Daily News* (Galveston, Texas), October 30, 1872, accessed August 16, 2019, Newspapers by Ancestry.

764 No. 824, *The Austin Weekly Statesman* (Austin, Texas), October 2, 1873, accessed August 16, 2019.

765 W. A. Fayman, & T. W. Reilly, *Galveston City Directory, 1875-1876*, book, 1875; (https://texashistory.unt.edu/ark:/67531/metapth636884/: accessed August 14, 2019), University of North Texas Libraries, The Portal to Texas History, https://texashistory.unt.edu; crediting Rosenberg Library.

766 John H. Heller, *Heller's Galveston Directory, 1876-1877*, book, 1876; Galveston, Texas. (https://texashistory.unt.edu/ark:/67531/metapth636850/: accessed August 14, 2019), University of North Texas Libraries, The Portal to Texas History, https://texashistory.unt.edu; crediting Rosenberg Library.

767 "Meyer vs. Anderson et al." *The Southwestern Reporter*, March 19-May 21, 1888, accessed August 19, 2019, vol. 7 814.

768 John H. Heller, *Heller's Galveston Directory, 1876-1877*, book, 1876; Galveston, Texas. (https://texashistory.unt.edu/ark:/67531/metapth636850/: accessed August 19, 2019), University of North Texas Libraries, The Portal to Texas History, https://texashistory.unt.edu; crediting Rosenberg Library.

John H. Heller, *Heller's Galveston Directory, 1878-1879*, book, 1878; Galveston, Texas. (https://texashistory.unt.edu/ark:/67531/metapth636857/: accessed August 19, 2019), University of North Texas Libraries, The Portal to Texas History, https://texashistory.unt.edu; crediting Rosenberg Library.

John H. Heller, *Heller's Galveston Directory, 1880-1881*, book, 1880; Galveston, Texas. (https://texashistory.unt.edu/ark:/67531/metapth636851/: accessed August 19, 2019), University of North Texas Libraries, The Portal to Texas History, https://texashistory.unt.edu; crediting Rosenberg Library.

Morrison & Fourmy, *Morrison & Fourmy's General Directory of the City of Galveston: 1881-1882*, book, 1881/1882; Houston, Texas. (https://texashistory.unt.edu/ark:/67531/metapth894032/: accessed August 19, 2019), University of North Texas Libraries, The Portal to Texas History, https://texashistory.unt.edu; crediting Rosenberg Library.

Morrison & Fourmy, *Morrison & Fourmy's General Directory of the City of Galveston: 1884-1885*, book, 1884/1885; Houston, Texas. (https://texashistory.unt.edu/ark:/67531/metapth894029/: accessed August 19, 2019), University of North Texas Libraries, The Portal to Texas History, https://texashistory.unt.edu; crediting Rosenberg Library.

Morrison & Fourmy, *Morrison & Fourmy's General Directory of the City of Galveston: 1886-1887*, book, 1886/1887; Houston, Texas. (https://texashistory.unt.edu/ark:/67531/metapth894033/: accessed August 19, 2019), University of North Texas Libraries, The Portal to Texas History, https://texashistory.unt.edu; crediting Rosenberg Library.

769 Morrison & Fourmy, *Morrison & Fourmy's General Directory of the City of Galveston: 1891-1892*, book, 1891/1892; Houston, Texas. (https://texashistory.unt.edu/ark:/67531/metapth894028/: accessed August 19, 2019), University of North Texas Libraries, The Portal to Texas History, https://texashistory.unt.edu; crediting Rosenberg Library.

770 Morrison & Fourmy, *Morrison & Fourmy's General Directory of the City of Galveston: 1893-1894*, book, 1893/1894; Houston, Texas. (https://texashistory.unt.edu/ark:/67531/metapth894023/: accessed August 19, 2019), University of North

Texas Libraries, The Portal to Texas History, https://texashistory.unt.edu; crediting Rosenberg Library.

Morrison & Fourmy, *Morrison & Fourmy's General Directory of the City of Galveston: 1895-1896*, book, 1895/1896; Houston, Texas. (https://texashistory.unt.edu/ark:/67531/metapth894034/: accessed August 19, 2019), University of North Texas Libraries, The Portal to Texas History, https://texashistory.unt.edu; crediting Rosenberg Library.

771 Morrison & Fourmy, *Morrison & Fourmy's General Directory of the City of Galveston: 1896-1897*, book, 1896/1897; Houston, Texas. (https://texashistory.unt.edu/ark:/67531/metapth894025/: accessed August 18, 2019), University of North Texas Libraries, The Portal to Texas History, https://texashistory.unt.edu; crediting Rosenberg Library.

772 *Find A Grave*, database and images (https://www.findagrave.com : accessed 19 August 2019), memorial page for Josephine S Allen (unknown–7 Sep 1897), Find A Grave Memorial no. 132948277, citing Lakeview Cemetery, Galveston, Galveston County, Texas, USA ; Maintained by Floyd Lanny Martin (contributor 47610184).

773 "Historical Marker Application for the City of Allen," Ebenezer Allen, Collin County History, accessed May 10, 2018, https://www.collincountyhistory.com/allen-ebenezer.html.

774 John Neely Bryan (1810-1877) was an Indian trader, farmer, lawyer, and founder of Dallas, Texas. Bryan made his first trip to the future site of Dallas, Texas, in 1839. He settled on the east bank of the Trinity River, not far from the present location of downtown Dallas. *Handbook of Texas Online*, Cecil Harper, Jr., "Bryan, John Neely," accessed January 16, 2019, http://www.tshaonline.org/handbook/online/articles/fbran.

775 Ken Byer, "Ebenezer Allen," *Allen American, Star Local Media*, September 24, 2015.

776 *Handbook of Texas Online*, George C. Werner, "Houston and Texas Central Railway," accessed January 17, 2017, http://www.tshaonline.org/handbook/online/articles/eqh09.

777 An easement is a right given to another person or entity to trespass upon or use land owned by somebody else. Easements are used for roads, for example or given to utility companies for the right to bury cables or access utility lines. The Balance, accessed August 13, 2019, https://www.thebalance.com/definition-of-easements-1798543.

778 Gwen Pettit and Lindy Fisher, *Between the Creeks* (Allen: Lindy Fisher, 2005), 402-407.

779 Plat refers to a plan, map, or chart of a piece of land with actual or proposed features (such as lots). Wikipedia contributors. (2019, August 13). Plat. In Wikipedia, The Free Encyclopedia. Retrieved 17:45, November 13, 2019, from https://en.wikipedia.org/w/index.php?title=Plat&oldid=910604444.

780 Lindy Fisher, *Between the Creeks*, July 2006; (texashistory.unt.edu/ark:/67531/metapth752794/: accessed February 27, 2019), University of North Texas Libraries, The Portal to Texas History, texashistory.unt.edu; 236.

781 Fisher, 169.

782 A cowcatcher is an inclined frame on the front of a railroad locomotive for throwing obstacles off the track. Meriam-Webster, accessed August 13, 2019, https://www.merriam-webster.com/dictionary/cowcatcher.

783 Ken Byler, "Is that Art on the Tracks?" *Allen American, Star Local Media*, September 24, 2015. Courtesy of Ken Byler.

APPENDIX – THE ANNEXATION PROCESS: 1836-1845

784 Annexation Process: 1836-1845 - A Summary Timeline, Texas State Library and Archives Commission, accessed March 21, 2017, https://www.tsl.texas.gov/ref/abouttx/annexation/timeline.html and "Timeline: 1844-1848," "A Continent Divided: The U.S. - Mexico War," Center for Greater Southwestern Studies, UT Arlington Library Special Collections, accessed March 21, 2017, https://library.uta.edu/usmexicowar/timeline.

APPENDIX – ORDINANCE OF ANNEXATION

785 *Journals of the Constitution Convention of Texas, 1845*, pub. in Austin by

Miner and Cruger, Printers to the Constitution, 1846 367-370. https://www.tsl.texas.gov/ref/abouttx/annexation/4july1845.html.

APPENDIX – JOINT RESOLUTION FOR ANNEXING TEXAS TO THE UNITED STATES

786 Richard Peters, ed., *The Public Statutes at Large of the United States of America* (Boston: Chas. C. Little and Jas. Brown, 1850), vol.5, 797-798. https://www.tsl.texas.gov/ref/abouttx/annexation/march1845.html.

APPENDIX – AN ACT TO ESTABLISH THE GALVESTON AND RED RIVER RAILROAD

787 Hans Peter Mareus Neilsen Gammel, *The Laws of Texas, 1822-1897 Volume 3*, 1898; Austin, Texas. (texashistory.unt.edu/ark:/67531/metapth6728/m1/961/: accessed April 5, 2018), University of North Texas Libraries, The Portal to Texas History, texashistory.unt.edu; 950-957.

APPENDIX – ALLEN'S BROADSIDE ON THE ACT RELATING TO LANDS IN PETERS' COLONY

788 Gammel, 950-957.

APPENDIX – AN ACT RELATING TO LANDS IN PETERS' COLONY

789 Papers. Headright Certificate Law and Legal Definition, USLegal.com, accessed August 15, 2018, https://definitions.uslegal.com/h/headright-certificate%20/.

790 "land scrip" is a certificate entitling the holder to obtain a certain portion of the public land either by entry or the payment of a portion of the price, accessed August 15, 2018, https://www.merriam-webster.com/dictionary/land%20scrip.

791 Bounty land served as both an incentive and reward for military service. It was issued to eligible veterans or their heirs by the Continental Congress and federal government through congressional acts passed between 1776 and 1856. "What is Bounty Land?" Fold3HQ, accessed August 15, 2018, https://blog.fold3.com/what-is-bounty-land/.

792 Gammel, 950-957.

APPENDIX – SPIRITUALISM IN THE ALLEN FAMILY

793 Ann Brenoff, "History of High Spirits," *Los Angeles Times*, June 17, 2007, accessed June 6, 2016, http://articles.latimes.com/2007/jun/17/realestate/re-guide17.

794 The cable-tool rig was the first method of drilling a hole. The cable refers to the manila hemp rope employed to suspend the wooden rods and the drilling tools in the earliest operations. The cable (manila rope or wire line) pulled the string of tools up and down using a spring pole or a walking beam at the surface. The heavy bit has a blunt chisel end which cracks, chips and smashes the rock by the repeated blows delivered in a measured or regular cadence. Samuel T. Pees, "Oil History," Petroleum History Institute, accessed February 22, 2018, http://www.petroleumhistory.org/OilHistory/pages/Cable/cable.html.

795 Oil sands are a mixture of sand, water, clay, and bitumen (the heaviest of hydrocarbon mixtures found in crude petroleum). The mixture is usually between 1% and 20% bitumen. "What is an oil sand?" Fuel Chemistry Division, accessed February 22, 2018, https://www.ems.psu.edu/~pisupati/ACSOutreach/Oil_Sands.html.

796 Wikipedia contributors, "Summerland, California," *Wikipedia, The Free Encyclopedia,* https://en.wikipedia.org/w/index.php?title=Summerland,_California&oldid=846316765 (accessed December 7, 2019).

797 Mark Mau and Henry Edmundson, Engineering and Technology History Wiki, accessed June 6, 2016, http://ethw.org/First_Steps_.

798 Emily Brooks, "The Spooky Story of Summerland," *The Horizon*, November 8, 2011, accessed June 6, 2016, http://blogs.westmont.edu/horizon/2011/11/08/the-spooky-story-of-summerland/.

799 Courtesy of Judith M. Johnson, Johnson-Morrow Family Tree, accessed May

23, 2016, Ancestry.com.

APPENDIX - THE ORDINANCE OF THE TEXAS CONVENTION

800 The Constitution of the State of Texas, as Amended in 1861, The Constitution of the Confederate States of America, The Ordinances of the Texas Convention, and An Address to the People of Texas. Austin: Printed by John Marshall, State Printer, 1861. pp. 18-19. https://www.tsl.texas.gov/ref/abouttx/secession/1feb1861.html.

APPENDIX - TEXAS DECLARATION OF CAUSES

801 The 3rd clause of the 2nd section of the 4th article of the Federal Constitution states: "No Person held to Service or Labour [sic] in one State, under the Laws thereof, escaping into another, shall, in Consequence of any Law or Regulation therein, be discharged from such Service or Labour [sic], But shall be delivered up on Claim of the Party to whom such Service or Labour [sic] may be due." U.S. Constitution - Article 4 - Section 2, assessed February 16, 2018, https://www.us-constitution.net/xconst_A4Sec2.html.

802 Ernest William Winkler, ed., *Journal of the Secession Convention of Texas 1861*, Edited from the original in the Department of State (Austin: Texas Library and Historical Commission, 1912), 61-65.

APPENDIX – ACT TO ADMIT TEXAS TO THE CONFEDERATE STATES OF AMERICA

803 James M. Matthews, ed., Statutes at Large of the Provisional Government of the Confederate States of America from the Institution of the Government, February 8, 1861, to Its Termination, February 18, 1862, Inclusive....Richmond: R. M. Smith, Printer to Congress, 1864, 44, https://www.tsl.texas.gov/ref/abouttx/secession/1march1861.html.

APPENDIX – ORDINANCE TO RATIFY THE CONFEDERATE CONSTITUTION

804 The Constitution of the State of Texas, as Amended in 1861, The Constitution of the Confederate States of America, The Ordinances of the Texas Convention, and An Address to the People of Texas. Austin: Printed by John Marshall, State Printer, 1861, pp. 24-25, https://www.tsl.texas.gov/ref/abouttx/secession/5march1861.html.

805 Appendix – Ebenezer Allen Will

806 An olographic testament is one "entirely written, dated, and signed in the handwriting of the testator," according to Louisiana Civil Code 1575. accessed February 19, 2018. info.legalzoom.com/handwritten-wills-legal-louisiana-not-notarized-4135.html.

807 Courtesy of Judith M. Johnson, Johnson-Morrow Family Tree, Ancestry.com

808 Courtesy of Judith M. Johnson, Johnson-Morrow Family Tree, Ancestry.com

APPENDIX – JOSEPHINE ALLEN VS. WILLIAM R. BAKER

809 A covin is a collusive agreement between two or more persons to the detriment of a third, fraud, trickery. accessed September 10, 2019, https://www.merriam-webster.com/dictionary/covin.

810 Sylvinia Josephine Allen.

811 The reference to Ebenezer Allen as "Union man and a fugitive from the state" is discussed in "Spy or Double Agent" in chapter Death.

812 "Case 220 - Josephine Allen v. W. R. Baker," Term of 1873, Texas. Supreme Court. Cases argued and decided in the Supreme Court of the State of Texas, during the latter part of the term beginning December 2, 1872, and closing November 28, 1873, and during the term beginning December 1, 1873, and until the change of judges made under the amendments to the Constitution adopted on December 2, 1873. Volume 39., book, 1882; St. Louis, Mo. (texashistory.unt.edu/ark:/67531/metapth28534/: accessed May 10, 2018), University of North Texas Libraries, The Portal to Texas History, texashistory.unt.edu; 199-205.

APPENDIX – EBENEZER ALLEN TIMELINE

813 "United States Census, 1870," database with images, *FamilySearch*, (https://familysearch.org/ark:/61903/1:1:M66M-C96: 17 October 2014), Sylvia Allen in household of Hannah B. Leavitt, Maine, United States; citing p. 43, family 385, NARA microfilm publication M593 (Washington D.C.: National Archives and Records Administration, n.d.); FHL microfilm 552,058.

CPSIA information can be obtained
at www.ICGtesting.com
Printed in the USA
JSHW031308121020
8659JS00001BB/1

9 781647 649203